XX

LABOR

IN AMERICA

THE GROWTH
OF AMERICA
SERIES

XXXXXXXXXXXXXXXXXXXXXXXXXXXXXXXXXXXXXXXXXX

xxxxxxxxxxxxxxxxxxxxxxxxxxxxxxxxxxxxxxxx
xxxxxxxxxxxxxxxxxxxxxxxxxxxxxxxxxxxxxxxx

LABOR
IN AMERICA

xxxxxxxxxxxxxxxxxxxxxxxxxxxxxxxxxxxxxx

A History

xxxxxxxxxxxxxxxxxxxxxxxxxxxxxxxxxxxxxx

FOSTER RHEA DULLES

xxxxxxxxxxxxxxxxxxxxxxxxxxxxxxxxxxxxxx

THOMAS Y. CROWELL COMPANY
NEW YORK

xxxxxxxxxxxxxxxxxxxxxxxxxxxxxxxxxxxxxxxx
xxxxxxxxxxxxxxxxxxxxxxxxxxxxxxxxxxxxxxxx
xxxxxxxxxxxxxxxxxxxxxxxxxxxxxxxxxxxxxxxx

XXX

PREFACE

XXXXXXXXXXXXXXXXXXXXXXXXXXXXXXXXXXXXXXXXXXX

ORGANIZED labor in America, today a force of some fifteen million wage earners, is bound to exercise a vital influence on the future economic and political development of the nation. The American people generally have come to accept the importance of free trade unions in helping to maintain our democratic way of life, but the growing power of the unions has at the same time created new and challenging problems in labor relations. In spite of its present position, however, the labor movement has only recently become so strong. The struggle of the unions for recognition and public support has been long, hard-fought and on occasion bloody. The present-day attitudes of labor can hardly be understood except against the background of this protracted struggle.

The purpose of this book is to give an account of the rise of American labor for the general reader, tracing it from vague colonial beginnings through the exciting days of the New Deal and the second World War. Emphasis has been placed upon national organization—the National Labor Union, the Knights of Labor, the A.F. of L. and the C.I.O. It is impossible to cover in a single book every phase of labor activity. The history of individual unions, the role of women and minority groups in labor organization, the growth of workers' education and of union social welfare activities, and the relation of the American labor movement to that in other countries have had to be subordinated to a more comprehensive record. In telling this story of labor against the background of our national development, it is hoped that despite such necessary limitations, the contemporary scene has been set in the perspective so necessary for any real understanding.

The author has relied heavily upon the many earlier studies of American labor to which reference may be found in the bibliographical notes, but has used primary sources wherever the material appeared to

Preface

demand further research. Several academic colleagues have read the manuscript in whole or in part, and the author would like to express his appreciation on this count to Professors Alma Herbst, Henry R. Spencer and Robert E. Mathews, and to David and Ruth S. Spitz. He is also indebted for suggestions and advice to Robert L. Crowell and Arthur B. Tourtellot, respectively publisher and editor of the series of which this book is a part. For typing and retyping an often almost indecipherable manuscript, he would most gratefully thank Edith Snare and Sally Dulles. As in every one of his books, a final expression of deep appreciation is due Marion Dulles for her keen, careful and constructive criticism of the manuscript at every stage of its development.

FOSTER RHEA DULLES

XXX

CONTENTS

XXXXXXXXXXXXXXXXXXXXXXXXXXXXXXXXXXXXXXXXXXX

XX

LABOR

IN AMERICA

XXXXXXXXXXXXXXXXXXXXXXXXXXXXXXXXXXXXXXXX

XXX

I: COLONIAL AMERICA

XXXXXXXXXXXXXXXXXXXXXXXXXXXXXXXXXXXXXXXXXXXXX

THE PRINCIPAL SOURCES of labor in colonial America were indentured servants and slaves. Free workers were a small minority in the seventeenth and eighteenth centuries. As the little towns scattered along the Atlantic seaboard gradually grew and prospered, however, mechanics and artisans who had either come directly from the Old World or risen out of the ranks of bound labor to build their own lives in freedom became of increasing importance. There were carpenters and masons; shipwrights and sailmakers; tanners, weavers, shoemakers and tailors, smiths, coopers, glaziers, printers.

The skilled craftsmen among these workers at first plied their trades independently, but as the centers of population grew, master workmen set up small retail shops and employed journeymen and apprentices to work for them for wages. By the close of the eighteenth century, these journeymen were beginning to form local trade societies—the genesis of the first unions and of what was to become in time the organized labor movement.

The simple economic pattern of those distant days provides no real basis for comparisons with the complex industrial scene of the twentieth century. The status of a small handful of independent artisans and mechanics does not have any valid relation to that of the huge mass of industrial workers in our modern society. The occasional and sporadic instances of labor protests in the colonial period could hardly be further removed from the nationwide strikes which in recent years have halted production in the coal mining, steel fabrication and automobile manufacture on which our closely knit economy is so wholly dependent. Nevertheless certain underlying conditions were operative in colonial days that were strongly to influence the whole course of American labor.

A constant scarcity of workers served to maintain wage rates well above European levels in the seventeenth and eighteenth centuries;

the opportunities for advancement in the New World nullified the hard and fast class lines that were the feudal heritage of the Old World, and the frontier generally fostered a spirit of sturdy individualism. While industrial revolution was to transform completely the old economic order, these basic factors in the American way of life, affecting not only labor but all the other elements in our society, were to endure. They served to bring the workers into the broad current of democratic advance that has characterized our history and played an important part in giving to the organized labor movement in America its distinctive and unique character.

The early settlers had no more than landed in Virginia and Massachusetts than they realized the imperative need for workers in the forest wilderness that was America. In both the first voyage to Jamestown and three succeeding expeditions, the Virginia Company had sent over to the New World a motley band of adventurers, soldiers and gentlemen. In growing despair of establishing a stable colony out of such unsatisfactory material, Captain John Smith finally entered a violent protest. "When you send again," he wrote home emphatically, "I entreat you rather send but thirty carpenters, husbandmen, gardeners, fishermen, masons, and diggers of trees' roots, well provided, than a thousand such as we have."

Plymouth fared better. Artisans, craftsmen and other laborers largely made up the little band of Pilgrims and the Bishop of London rudely characterized even their leaders as "guides fit for them, cobblers, tailors, feltmakers, and such-like trash." The Puritan settlers of Massachusetts Bay in 1630 also had a majority of artisans and tillers of the soil. But in spite of this advantage, the founders of New England soon felt, as had those of Virginia, the scarcity of persons content with performing the humble tasks of society. Governor Winthrop of Massachusetts wrote despairingly in 1640 of the difficulty of keeping wage earners on the job. They were constantly moving on to frontier communities where pay was higher or else taking up land to become independent farmers. Cotton Mather made it "an Article of special Supplication before the Lord, that he would send a good servant. . . ."

While tillers of the soil and "diggers of trees' roots" were a first and primary consideration in these early days of settlement, the demand for skilled workers rapidly mounted. The colonists were perforce compelled to become carpenters and masons, weavers and shoemakers, whatever their background, but both on southern plantations and in New England towns, trained artisans and mechanics were always needed.

The ways in which the labor problem was met varied greatly in different parts of America. The circumstances of early settlement and natural environment led New England to rely largely on free workers. The south was ultimately to fall back almost wholly on Negro slaves. In the majority of colonies during the seventeenth century, and continuing on through the eighteenth in the middle colonies, the bulk of the labor force was recruited from indentured servants. It has been estimated, indeed, that at least half, and probably more, of all the colonists who came to the New World arrived under some form of indenture and took their place as wholly free citizens only after working out their terms of contract.

There were three sources for such bound labor: men, women and children whose articles of indenture were signed before leaving the Old World; the redemptioners, or so-called free-willers, who agreed to reimburse their passage money by selling their labor after landing in the colonies, and convicts sentenced to transportation to America. Once in the colonies, these various groups coalesced into the general class of bound servants, working without wages and wholly under their masters' control for a set term of years.

So great was the demand for labor that a brisk trade developed in recruiting workers. Agents of the colonial planters and of British merchants scoured the countryside and towns of England, and somewhat later made their way to the continent, especially the war devastated areas of the Rhineland, to cry abroad the advantages of emigrating to America. They distributed handbills at country fairs extravagantly describing the wonders of this new land where food was said to drop into the mouths of the fortunate inhabitants and every man had the opportunity to own his own land. The promises held forth were often so glowing and enthusiastic that the ignorant and the credulous gladly signed articles of indenture with little realization of the possible hardships of the life upon which they were entering. The "crimps" who worked the English countryside, and so-called "newlanders" operating on the continent, did not hesitate at fraud and chicanery.

Thousands of persons were "spirited" out of England under these circumstances, and far from trying to prevent such practices the local authorities often encouraged them. The common belief that England was over-populated led them to approve heartily of the overseas transportation of paupers and vagabonds, the generally shiftless, who might otherwise become a burden upon the community. Indeed, magistrates sometimes had such persons rounded up and given the choice between emigration and imprisonment. It was also found to be an easy way to take care of orphans and other minors who had no means of support: the term "kidnaping" had its origin in this harsh mode of peopling the colonies.

In 1619 the Common Council of London "appointed one hundred Children out of the swarms that swarme in the place, to be sent to Virginia to be bound as apprentices for certain yeares." The Privy Council inquired into this matter, and after commending the authorities "for redeeminge so many poore Soules from misery and ruyne," authorized the Virginia Company to "imprison, punish and dispose of any of those children upon any disorder by them committed, as cause shall require; and so to Shipp them out for Virginia, with as much expedition as may stand for convenience."

Some forty years later, the Privy Council appears to have become aroused over the abuse of this practice by the Virginia Company. Two ships lying off Gravesend were discovered to have aboard both children and other servants "deceived and inticed away Cryinge and Mourning for Redemption from their Slavery." It was ordered that all those detained against their will—"a thinge so barbarous and inhumane, that Nature itself much more Christians cannot but abhor it"—should be at once released.

Under these circumstances the line between voluntary and involuntary transportation—especially when it involved the ignorant poor and young children—was very hard to draw. There were undoubtedly many bound servants in the colonies who might have echoed the pathetic lament of the young girl described in the "Sot-Weed Factor, or, a Voyage to Maryland," a tract published in London in 1708:

> In better Times e'er to this Land
> I was unhappily Trapann'd;
> Perchance as well I did appear,

As any Lord or Lady here,
Not then a slave for twice two Year
My clothes were fashionably new,
Nor were my Shifts of Linnen Blue;
But things are changed, now at the Hoe
I daily work, and Barefoot go,
In weeding Corn or feeding Swine,
I spend my melancholy Time.
Kidnap'd and Fool'd, I thither fled,
To shun a hated Nuptial Bed,
And to my cost already find
Worse plagues than those I left behind.

As time went on the prison and the gaol contributed an increasing number of emigrants who crossed the Atlantic as "His Majesty's Seven-Year Passengers." They were at first largely made up of "rogues, vagabonds and sturdy beggars" who had proved "incorrigible," but during the eighteenth century more serious offenses were added to the list for which transportation overseas was meted out. The pre-revolutionary roster of such immigrants in one Maryland county, adding up to 655 persons and including 111 women, embraced a wide range of crimes—murder, rape, highway robbery, horse-stealing and grand larceny. Among the women, there were many whom contemporary accounts succinctly described as "lewd."

The colonies came to resent bitterly this influx of the refuse from English prisons—"abundance of them do great Mischiefs. . . . and spoil servants, that were before very good"—and they found it increasingly difficult to control them. But in spite of their protests, the practice was continued, and in all some fifty thousand convicts are believed to have been transported, largely to the middle colonies. In Maryland, which seems to have been a favored dumping ground, they made up the bulk of indentured servants throughout the eighteenth century.

"Our Mother knows what is best for us," a contributor to the *Pennsylvania Gazette* ironically observed in 1751. "What is a little House-breaking, Shoplifting, or Highway-robbing; what is a son now and then corrupted and hanged, a Daughter debauched, or Pox'd, a wife stabbed, a Husband's throat cut, or a child's brains beat out with an Axe, compared with this 'Improvement and Well peopling of the Colonies?'" Benjamin Franklin bitterly declared that the policy of "emptying their jails into our settlements is an insult and contempt the cruellest, that ever one people offered another." Its consequences were reflected, from quite a different point of view, in Dr. Samuel Johnson's famous remark on Americans: "Sir, they are a race of convicts, and ought to be content with anything we allow them short of hanging."

Whether convicts, vagabonds, children "spirited" from the country-side, or redemptioners, both voluntary and involuntary emigrants to the New World experienced discomforts and suffering on their voyage across the Atlantic that paralleled the cruel hardships undergone by Negro slaves on the notorious Middle Passage. They were indiscriminately herded aboard the "white guineamen," often as many as three hundred passengers on little vessels of not more than two hundred tons burden—overcrowded, unsanitary, with insufficient provisions. Typhus and other diseases invariably took a terrible toll of lives. The mortality rate was sometimes as high as fifty per cent, and young children seldom survived the horrors of a voyage which might last anywhere from seven to twelve weeks.

"During the voyage," reads one account of the experiences of redemptioners recruited from the German Palatinate, "there is on board these ships terrible misery, stench, fumes, horror, vomiting, many kinds of seasickness, fever, dysentery, headache, heat, constipation, boils, scurvy, cancer, mouth rot, and the like, all of which come from old and sharply-salted food and meat, also from the very bad and foul water, so that many die miserable. . . . Add to this want of provisions, hunger, thirst, frost, heat, dampness, anxiety, want, afflictions, and lamentations, together with other trouble, as e. g., the lice abound so frightfully, especially on sick people, that they can be scraped off the body. The misery reaches a climax when a gale rages for two or three nights so that everyone believes that the ship will go to the bottom with all human beings on board. In such a visitation the people cry and pray most piteously."

Nor did the hardships of the immigrants necessarily end when port was finally reached. Those for whom contracts had already been arranged, were handed over to their unknown masters. If the redemptioners did not immediately find employment themselves, they were put up for sale by the ship captains or merchants to whom they owed their passage money. Families were often separated under these circumstances when wives and offspring were auctioned off to the highest bidder. The terms of servitude varied with age and might run from one to seven years. More generally, those over twenty without specific articles of indenture were bound out for four years "according to the custom of the country."

The colonial newspapers often carried notices of prospective sales. On March 28, 1771, the following announcement appeared in the *Virginia Gazette:*

> Just arrived at Leedstown, the Ship Justitia,
>   with about one Hundred Healthy Servants.
>
> Men, Women and Boys, among which are many
> Tradespeople—viz. Blacksmiths, Shoemakers,
> Tailors, House Carpenters and Joiners, a
> Cooper, several Silversmiths, Weavers,
> A Jeweler, and many others. The Sale will
> commence on Tuesday, the 2nd. of April, at
> Leeds Town on Rappahannock River. A
> reasonable Credit will be allowed, giving
> Bond with Approved Security to
>   Thomas Hodge

If the sales were not concluded at the port of entry, groups of the redemptioners were taken back country by "soul drivers" who herded them along the way "like cattle to a Smithfield market" and then put them up for auction at public fairs.

The importation of servants was highly profitable. A fifty acre headright was granted the planter in some of the colonies for each immigrant, and there was always the sale of the indenture. In the case of sturdy farm hands and particularly skilled artisans, prices might run to high figures. William Byrd reported to his agent in Rotterdam, in 1739, that he was in a good position to handle heavy shipments. "I know not how long the Palatines are sold for who do not pay passage to Philadelphia," he wrote, "but here they are sold for Four years and fetch from 6 to 9 pounds and perhaps good Tradesmen may go for Ten. If these prices would answer, I am pretty Confident I could dispose of two Shiploads every year. . . ."

The treatment accorded bound servants varied a great deal. In John Hammond's seventeenth century account, "Leah and Rachel, or, the Two Fruitfull Sisters Virginia and Mary-land," their labor was said to be "not so hard nor of such continuance as Husbandmen, nor Handecraftmen are kept at in England." The hours of work were reported as those between the rising and setting sun, but with five hours off in the heat of the day during the summer, Saturday half holidays and "the Sabbath spent in good exercises." George Alsop, himself an indentured servant, wrote home in 1659 almost glowing accounts of life in Maryland. "The servants of this province, which are stigmatiz'd for Slaves by the clappermouth jaws of the vulgar in England," he declared, "live more like Freemen than the most Mechanical Apprentices in London, wanting for nothing that is convenient and necessary."

Other accounts, however, give a harsher picture of general conditions. While colonial laws called upon masters to provide their servants with adequate food, lodging and clothing, there were many instances where the diet was as meager as the labor was exhausting. Moreover, the servants were rigidly confined to the immediate vicinity of the place where they were employed, tavern keepers were not allowed to entertain them or sell them liquor, their terms of service might be extended for a long list of minor offenses, and they were subject to whippings and other corporal punishment by their masters for disobedience or laziness. Servant girls could be held in longer bondage because of bastardy, and their masters were sometimes not above conspiring to this end. "Late experiments shew," read one report, "that some dissolute masters have gotten their maides with child, and yet claim the benefit of their services."

The indentured servants were recognized as fellow Christians and were entitled to their day in court—in these respects, at least, their status being quite different from that of Negro slaves. But their masters' quasi-proprietary rights naturally made it extremely difficult for them to secure redress for any injuries or indignities. While humane masters undoubtedly treated their servants well, it is not difficult to believe the report that they were often subjected to "as hard and servile labor as the basest Fellow that was brought out of Newgate."

Court records are concerned with instances of willful ill-treatment and are revealing if not typical. A certain Mistress Ward whipped her maidservant on the back so severely, with the added pleasantry of putting salt in the wounds, that the girl shortly died. On the finding of a jury that such action was "unreasonable and unchristianlike," Mistress Ward was fined 300 pounds of tobacco. In another case, Mistress Mourning Bray defiantly told the court that under no circumstances would she allow her servants to "go to play or be Idle" and the unlucky complainant was stripped and given thirty lashes. A third trial resulted more favorably for another maidservant. She was discharged from the further employ of a master who had climaxed frequent beatings by hitting her over the head with a three-legged stool when he found her reading a book on Sunday morning. "Youe disembling Jade," the court records report him as having shouted, "what doe youe doe with a booke in your hand?"

One sorely beset servant took his own revenge. According to his story, he had "an ill-tongued Mistriss; who would not only rail, swear and curse at me within doors, whenever I came into the house casting on me continually biting Taunts and bitter Flouts, but like a live Ghost would impertinently haunt me, when I was quiet in the Ground at work." Driven to distraction, he one day seized an axe and murdered not only his ill-tongued mistress but also his master and a maidservant.

Advertisements often appeared in the colonial newspapers for runaway servants. One such notice referred to an English servant-man who had "a pretty long visage of a lightish complexion, and thin-flaxen hair; his eye tooth sticks out over his lower teeth in a remarkable manner," and another to a shoemaker and fiddler who "loves to be at frolics and taverns and is apt to get in liquor and when so is subject to fits." Others offered special rewards for runaway bricklayers, tailors, carpenters, and even schoolmasters. Occasional descriptions of their clothes give a vivid glimpse of multi-colored vests and blue, green and yellow coats. One runaway was said to have been wearing "a double-breasted cape coat, with white metal buttons, and an old jacket of bluish color, good shoes, and large white buckles, and no stockings except he stole them."

A more cheerful notice appeared in the *Maryland Gazette* on September 6, 1745. John Powell was able to report that the man who had previously been advertised as a runaway had been found to have "only gone into the country a cyder-drinking." Since he had returned to his master, the notice continued, all gentlemen and others with watches or clocks needing repair could now have them done "in the best manner, and at reasonable rates."

For the servant who faithfully served out the term of his indenture there were substantial rewards. Grants of land were the exception rather than the rule, but in some cases at least the industrious were given "a competent estate" and there was universal provision for some form of "freedom's dues." In Massachusetts, for example, the law specifically stated that all servants that had served diligently and faithfully for seven years should not be sent away empty-handed. What this meant varied, of course, not only from colony to colony but in terms of individual articles of indenture. The freedom's dues generally included at least clothing, tools of some sort, and perhaps such livestock as would enable the servant to start farming on his own account. Typical indentures called for "a pigg to be pay'd at every years end" and "double apparell at the end of the term."

Throughout the seventeenth and eighteenth centuries indentured servants, both men and women, could thus look forward to establishing a life of their own. Once they had obtained their freedom, Hugh Jones wrote in 1724, they may "work Day-Labour, or else rent a small Plantation for a trifle almost; or turn overseers, if they are expert, industrious and careful, or follow their trade. . . . especially Smiths, Carpenters, Taylors, Sawyers, Coopers, Bricklayers, etc."

Many of them made the most of these opportunities, their earlier status forgotten as they became independent farmers or workingmen; others drifted off to the back country, shiftless and unenterprising, to create in the southern colonies an unhappy class of poor whites. But whatever their individual destiny as the country grew and expanded, indentured servants played a vital part in the building of colonial America.

Free labor in the colonies was made up of immigrant artisans and mechanics who had been able to pay their own passage money and of recruits from the ranks of bound servants who had served out their terms of indenture. The available supply of such workers nevertheless remained highly limited and the towns along the Atlantic seaboard continually suffered from an acute labor shortage. Even this early, high wages and relatively favorable working conditions could not stop the steady migration westward. The frontier with its cheap land constantly drained the seaboard.

"The genius of the People in a Country where every one can have Land to work upon," a colonial official reported to the Board of Trade in 1767, "leads them so naturally into Agriculture, that it prevails over every other occupation. There can be no stronger instance of this, than in the servants imported from Europe of different trades; as soon as the Time stipulated in their Indentures is expired, they immediately quit their Masters, and get a small tract of land, in settling which for the first three or four years they lead miserable lives, and in the most abject Poverty; but all this is patiently borne and submitted to with the greatest cheerfulness, the Satisfaction of being Land holders smooths over every difficulty, and makes them prefer this manner of living to that comfortable subsistence which they could procure for themselves and their families by working at the Trades in which they were brought up."

This situation bore most heavily upon New England, where relatively few indentured servants were available, and led to such high wage rates and such an independent attitude on the part of both skilled and unskilled workers that the colonial authorities felt compelled to act. The result was the first labor legislation in America affecting free workers. Maximum wages were established by law, changes in occupation prohibited, and various class distinctions in dress and deportment prescribed to keep the lower classes in a subordinate role.

As early as 1630 the General Court in Massachusetts undertook to enforce a wage ceiling of two shillings a day for carpenters, joiners, bricklayers, sawyers, thatchers and other artisans, and of eighteen pence for all day laborers, with the further provision that "all workmen shall worke the whole day, alloweing convenient tyme for food and rest." To combat what appears to have been a prevailing practice of supplementing such wages with allowances for liquor ("without which it is found, by too sad experience, many refuse to worke"), the Court further decreed that anyone who gave wine or strong liquors to any workmen, except in cases of necessity, would be fined twenty shillings for each offense.

Forty years later, another law reaffirmed these general wage rates, stating more specifically that the working day should be "10 houres in the daye besides repast," and extended its provisions to additional artisans. Carpenters, masons, stonelayers, coopers and tailors were to be paid two shillings a day, special piece rates were established for shoemakers, coopers and smiths, and, finally, the new statute declared "that whereas it appears that Glovers, Sadlers, Hatters, and Several other artifficers doe at present greatly exceed the rules of equitie in their prizes, they are all required to moderate the same according to the rules prescribed to others. . . ."

These maximum wages were in part compensated by price regulation of certain basic commodities to hold down the cost of living, but the clear intent of the General Court was both to help employers and to keep the workers in their place on grounds of public policy. "The excessive deerenes of labour by artifficers, Labourers, and Servants" was felt to have highly unfortunate consequences in the puritanic eyes of the New England fathers. "The produce thereof" they sternly declared, "is by many Spent to mayntayne such bravery in Apparell which is altogether unbecomeing their place and ranck, and in Idleness of life, and a great part spent viciously in Tavernes and alehouses and other Sinful practices much to the dishonor of God, Scandall of Religion, and great offence and griefe to Sober and Godly people amongst us."

Economics and morality walked hand in hand with our forebears. Their high-minded ideal of low wages and long hours as conducive to the workers' wellbeing had a pragmatic value that was not lost upon later generations. The nineteenth century—if not the twentieth—would find long working hours defended in this same puritanic spirit as necessary to combat idleness and to safeguard labor from the temptations to which it might otherwise be dangerously exposed. The "wholesome discipline" of factory life was in time to be sanctified by employers as an antidote to the lure of the saloons and beer parlors which replaced colonial taverns.

An even more direct restriction on what might be called conspicuous consumption by the workers was laid down in another law regulating just what they should wear. "We declare our utter detestation and dislike," this edict read, "that men and women of mean condition should take upon themselves the garb of gentlemen." The ban included "wearing gold or silver lace or buttons, or points at their knees, or to walk in boots, or women of the same rank to wear silk or tiffany scarfs, which though allowable to persons of greater estates, or more liberal education, yet we cannot but judge it intolerable in persons in such like conditions."

These laws could not be enforced. Although the authorities continued to link the demand for higher wages with intemperance, sabbathbreaking, gaming and mixed dancing as among "the Mischievous Evils the Nature of Man is prone unto," they could not control the situation. The General Court ultimately relegated the task to the local town governments, but even then the scarcity of labor proved to be a more decisive factor than arbitrary legislation in determining wage rates and social customs.

Although the bulk of settlers tilled their own land and provided through home manufactures most of their immediate needs, making their own clothing, household furniture and many of the tools and utensils essential for everyday life, craftsmen and artisans played an increasingly important economic role as the eighteenth century advanced. Many of them were itinerant workers, going from town to town to work at whatever job offered or making on order anything the farm families might need. One man sometimes plied several trades. A blacksmith would be also a toolmaker, a tanner a shoemaker, or a soap boiler serve as a tallow chandler. How far a craftsman might be prepared to extend his services is suggested by an advertisement in the *New York Gazette* in June, 1775. John Julius Sorge announced that he could make artificial fruit; do japan work; manufacture cleaning fluid, toilet water, soap, candles, insecticides, and wine, and remove hair from ladies' foreheads and arms.

With the further growth of colonial towns, the demand for artisans increased. There were more and more of the small retail shops in which a master workman employed a number of journeymen workers; that is, artisans or mechanics who worked for wages, and also trained boys as apprentices to whatever trade was being practiced. Printing shops, tailoring and shoemaking shops, hat shops, cabinet-making shops and bakeries were among such establishments. The work was generally done on order—so called "bespoke work"—and the shop might often be the master's home where the journeymen and apprentices could board as well as work. At the same time, the expansion of the building trades led master carpenters and master masons to employ journeymen and train apprentices.

In both New England and the middle colonies, there were also all manner of little mills needing both skilled and unskilled wage earners, and shipyards, ropewalks, distilleries, breweries, paper and gunpowder factories. On the large plantations of the south, home manufactures created a need for skilled labor. Robert Carter had a smithy, a fulling mill, a grain mill, salt works and both spinning and weaving establishments on his plantation where he employed free white workers as well as Negro slaves.

There was at least a beginning of manufacture on a larger scale. By the middle of the eighteenth century, ironworks had been established in Pennsylvania, Maryland, and New Jersey which employed a considerable number of men. One set up by Peter Hasenclever, the best known colonial ironmaster, included six blast furnaces, seven forges and a stamping mill, and he is said to have brought five hundred workers over from Germany for their operation. The glass works of Henry Steigel, at Mannheim, Pennsylvania, must have had a considerable labor force for they included a plant so large "that a coach and four could turn around within the brick dome of its melting house." Linen factories with as many as fourteen looms foreshadowed mounting employment in textile mills. In 1769 a "manufacturing house" in Boston had four hundred spinning wheels, and six years later the United Company of Philadelphia for Promoting American Manufacture employed four hundred women in the production of cotton goods. Some of these latter enterprises provided work for the indigent and for orphans—without wages—as a service to the community.

In addition to the workers in manufacturing establishments, moreover, other groups of wage earners were of growing importance. The most numerous were sailors and fishermen, and every town also had its quota of day laborers. Household servants were never available in sufficient numbers to meet the needs of the more wealthy members of the community. "Help is scarce and hard to gett, difficult to please, uncertaine . . ." remained a familiar complaint in colonial society.

With the approach of the Revolution, the increasing opportunities for wage earners and a diminishing labor supply as men were drafted for military service drove up wages. The earlier attempts to fix maximum rates and control prices were consequently renewed. The Articles of Association adopted by the Continental Congress stressed the importance of such regulations and several of the new state governments undertook to enforce them. At a convention held in Providence in 1776, attended by delegates from Massachusetts, New Hampshire, Rhode Island and Connecticut, agreement was reached on a general program of price and wage control. Farm labor was not to be paid more than three shillings and four pence a day (almost three times the rate a century earlier) and the wages of artisans and mechanics were to be so fixed as to maintain their normal relationship to farm wages at this new rate. The states concerned acted promptly on this resolution—an early example of an interstate compact—and when the matter was brought before the Continental Congress, it referred to the remaining states "the propriety of adopting similar Measures."

Other conventions, however, were not as successful as that held at Providence in reaching mutual agreement upon prices and wage scales. The south was already showing its reluctance to fall in line with standards set in the northern states and the experience of different sections was confused and conflicting. While further action was taken locally in some instances, the Continental Congress finally decided that the whole program was not only impractical "but likewise productive of very evil Consequences to the great Detriment of the public Service and grievous Oppression of Individuals." It advised the states to repeal existing laws and this first attempt at a controlled economy made no further headway.

Although conditions of colonial life made for a greater measure of social and economic equality in America than prevailed anywhere in the Old World, the workers still did not enjoy political liberty. The franchise was restricted to property owners and the skilled artisans and mechanics were as helpless in asserting their rights as day laborers. By the 1780's, however, there was a growing demand for broader privileges on the part of workers in seaboard towns. In supporting the movement that led to American independence, these workers were protesting not only against oppression by a distant England, but against the controls exercised by the ruling class at home.

The role of small tradesmen, artisans and mechanics in promoting the revolutionary cause was particularly important in Massachusetts. Again and again when the ardor of merchants and farmers appeared to be subsiding, the "rage of patriotism" was stimulated by the zeal of those whom the Tories derisively called the "Mobility" or the "Rabble." The popular party in Boston, so astutely led by Samuel Adams, was in large part made up of wharfingers, shipwrights, bricklayers, weavers and tanners who were equally opposed to rule by British officials or colonial aristocrats. The Sons of Liberty, and later the local Committees of Correspondence, were generally recruited from workers from the docks, shipyards and ropewalks. The famous "Loyall Nine," which was to instigate the mob action that led to the Boston Massacre and the Boston Tea Party, included two distillers, two braziers, a printer, a jeweler, a painter and a ship captain.

Such an alignment of forces was also true of other colonies. The Ancient and Honorable Mechanical Company of Baltimore, the Firemen's Association of Charleston, the Heart-and-Hand Fire Company of Philadelphia were the nuclei for the Sons of Liberty in those cities. In each instance their muster rolls show that their membership was primarily made up of small tradesmen and artisans.

This is not to say that other elements in colonial society did not play their full part in the revolutionary movement. The first protests against British taxation came largely from the merchant class and it provided the original leadership in organizing the Sons of Liberty. But the mechanics, artisans and small tradesmen voiced the more radical demands in support of colonial liberties and kept up their agitation when the merchants were willing to compromise. Their zealous activity, indeed, often aroused conservative fears that the revolutionary movement was getting wholly out of hand. "The heads of the mobility grow dangerous to the gentry," Gouverneur Morris wrote agitatedly on one occasion, "and how to keep them down is the question."

They could not be kept down. Their demonstrations, sometimes leading to riot and disorder, both reflected and intensified an increasing hostility toward the British authorities on the part of the common people. The Boston Massacre, for example, grew directly out of a dispute that had arisen between colonial workingmen and British troops. "A particular quarrel happened at a Rope-Walk with a few Soldiers of the 29th. Regiment," General Gage reported; "the Provocation was given by the Rope-Walkers, tho' it may be imagined in the course of it, that there were Faults on both Sides. This Quarrel it is supposed, excited the People to convert a general rising on the Night of the 5th. of March."

While the role of artisans and mechanics in the Revolution has long since been recognized, it is more difficult to determine their part in the adoption of the Constitution. As far as establishment of the new government reflected a conservative trend whittling away the democratic gains made during the struggle for independence, emphasizing the protection of property interests rather than individual liberties, the workingmen might be expected to oppose its acceptance. They had been neither directly nor indirectly represented at the Constitutional Convention, and little consideration was given in its deliberations to either their rights or those of the common people generally. Nevertheless there were workers' demonstrations in favor of ratification in some cities, and their support has been held partly responsible for the Federalists' victory in New York city.

Whatever their contribution to the movement for independence and the establishment of the United States, the workers did not win any substantial gains during these years. It is not necessary to quote the conservative views of such a strong advocate of government by the rich and the wellborn as Alexander Hamilton to demonstrate how far removed the United States was from a democratic society at the close of the eighteenth century. There were everywhere fears of the "levelling spirit" which had seemed so pronounced during the Revolution, and of the threat to national stability in any further concessions to the democratic masses.

Even Thomas Jefferson, stoutly declaring that "the influence over the government must be shared by all the people," had no idea of including the propertyless workers within the scope of those to be granted the franchise and allowed to hold public office. The democracy which he supported was a democracy of small freehold farmers and he gravely doubted whether artisans, mechanics, and laborers, without the stabilizing influence of being land owners, could ever develop the republican virtues which he felt essential for the functioning of a free society.

He strongly opposed the development of manufactures in the United States because he was afraid of the influence on our institutions of an increasing number of urban workers. He would have had our workshops remain in Europe rather than risk the creation of a wage-earning class whose principles and manners he held in suspect. "The mobs of great cities," Jefferson wrote in fearful contemplation of what he felt was happening in Europe, "add just so much to the support of pure government, as sores do to the strength of the human body."

In spite of the high promise of the Declaration of Independence, the political status of the wage-earning class in American society had thus not materially improved. Its standard of living remained high in comparison with conditions in Europe, but with advancing prices in the post-revolutionary period, workers in the little towns strung along the Atlantic seaboard seldom had very much of a margin over extreme poverty. While John Jay complained bitterly in 1784 of "the wages of mechanics and labourers, which are very extravagant," the pay for unskilled workers hardly ever exceeded fifteen shillings a week—less than the equivalent of $4.

"On such a pittance," John Bach McMaster has written, "it was only by the strictest economy that a mechanic kept his children from starvation and himself from jail. In the low and dingy rooms which he called his home were wanting many articles of adornment and of use now to be found in the dwellings of the poorest of his class. Sand sprinkled on the floor did duty as a carpet. There was no glass on his table, there was no china in his cupboard, there were no prints on his walls. What a stove was he did not know, coal he had never seen, matches he had never heard of. Over a fire of fragments of boxes and barrels, which he lit with the sparks struck from a flint, or with live coals brought from a neighbor's hearth, his wife cooked up a rude meal and served it in pewter dishes. He rarely tasted fresh meat as often as once in a week, and paid for it a much higher price than his posterity. . . . If the food of an artisan would now be thought coarse, his clothes would be thought abominable. A pair of yellow or buckskin or leather breeches, a checked shirt, a red flannel jacket, a rusty hat cocked up at the corners, shoes of neat's-skin set off with huge buckles of brass, and a leather apron, comprised his scanty wardrobe."

For all the hardships such a way of life implied—and it must be remembered that the wealthy also lacked many comforts that today would be considered essential—America was still a land of magnificent opportunity. Artisans and mechanics could confidently hope to improve their living conditions and the fluidity of classes meant that there were no barriers holding back the industrious and energetic from further advancement. In a society still based upon agriculture and handicraft industries, moreover, the craftsman had a recognized and respected status that served in part to compensate for meager economic resources. His way of life may have been simple, but he lived in a simple society untouched by industrialism.

Over the horizon were far-reaching changes that would vitally affect both the society in which he lived and his own status. They would in the name of progress open up the possibilities of a far higher standard of living than wage earners had ever before enjoyed in this or any other country. But these changes also demanded adjustments which were to prove highly difficult, and nineteenth century labor often felt itself cut off from the benefits that industrial progress appeared to promise. In the face of new barriers to the realization of their hopes and aspirations, the nation's workers were to find that only through organization could they secure the rights and privileges to which they felt entitled.

XXX

II: THE FIRST UNIONS

XXXXXXXXXXXXXXXXXXXXXXXXXXXXXXXXXXXXXXXXXXX

THE REAL BEGINNINGS of labor organization awaited the transformation in economic society brought about early in the nineteenth century by the rise of merchant capitalists who established business on a wholesale basis. The master workmen in the colonial period, bringing together journeymen and apprentices for work on common projects or joint enterprises, and paying them wages, had not created an employer-employe relationship in any modern sense. There was no real differentiation between the interests of the journeymen and those of the masters who labored side by side with them. The price lists set up for "bespoke work" determined wages, and to a very considerable extent the functions of merchant, master and journeymen were united in the same person.

Under such circumstances, masters and journeymen acted together to maintain the standards of their craft, uphold price lists and generally protect themselves from unfair competition. There were occasions when the journeymen protested against the controls exercised by the masters in their capacity as employers. In occupations that did not bring them together in close and natural association, disputes sometimes arose that led to sporadic strikes and incipient labor revolt. But generally speaking, the extremely simple economic organization of the seventeenth and eighteenth centuries precluded any significant concerted action on the part of workers. Before considering the changes effected by the rise of the merchant capitalists, however, such labor protests or strikes as did occur during the colonial period may well be considered for the light they may throw on the conditions that ultimately led to union organization.

The earliest record of what might be considered a labor disturbance goes back to 1636. A group of fishermen employed by one Robert Trelawney at Richmond Island, off the coast of Maine, were reported to have fallen "into a mutany" when their wages were withheld. Some forty years later the licensed cartmen of New York, ordered to remove the dirt from the streets for threepence a load, not only protested such a low rate of pay but "combined to refuse full compliance." Other comparable incidents occasionally were noted in the colonial press during the eighteenth century and in 1768 a "turn-out" of journeymen tailors in New York—perhaps the first really authentic strike against employers—has an almost modern ring. Some twenty workers struck because of a reduction in their wages and publicly advertised that in defiance of the masters they would take private work. They would be on call at the Sign of the Fox and Hound, their notice in the papers read, at the rate of three shillings and six pence per day, with diet.

The masters themselves sometimes joined forces to protect their interests as revealed in a somewhat earlier account of trouble among the Boston barbers appearing in the *New England Courant*. Thirty-two master barbers "assembled at the Golden Ball, with a Trumpeter attending them," and jointly agreed to raise their rates for shaving from 8s. to 10s. per quarter, and "to advance 5s. on the Price of making common Wiggs and 10s. on their Tye ones." It was also proposed that "no one of their Faculty should shave or dress Wiggs on Sunday morning," a resolution that led the *Courant* to observe censoriously that "it may be concluded, that in times past such a Practice had been too common among them."

The Revolutionary period, with its wartime inflation, stimulated further protests on the part of workers who found living costs rising much faster than wages. The New York printers were a case in point. In November, 1778 the journeymen demanded—and received—an increase in pay under circumstances which again have a very modern flavor except for the courtesy with which the printers voiced their demands.

"As the necessaries of life are raised to such an enormous price," read the journeymen's protest as it appeared in the *Royal Gazette,* "it cannot be expected that we should continue to work at the wages now given; and therefore request an addition of Three Dollars per week to our present small pittance; It may be objected that this requisition is founded upon the result of a combination to distress the Master Printers at this time, on account of the scarcity of hands; but this is far from being the case; it really being the high price of every article of life, added to the approaching dreary season. There is not one among us, we trust, that would take an ungenerous advantage of the times—we only wish barely to exist, which it is impossible to do with our present stipend."

To this letter James Rivington, the well known Tory printer and publisher of the *Gazette,* briefly replied: "I do consent to the above requisition."

There were other concerted protests or strikes in these and the immediately following years—on the part of seamen in Philadelphia in 1779, New York shoemakers in 1785, and journeymen printers in Philadelphia in 1786. "We will support such of our brethren," these printers declared, "as shall be thrown out of employment on account of their refusing to work for less than $6 per week." The employers at first refused to meet their demands but the turn-out was ultimately successful.

The members of the building trades were also restive and a long smoldering conflict broke out in 1791 between journeymen and master carpenters in Philadelphia. The former declared that their employers were trying to reduce wages "to a still lower ebb, by every means within the power of avarice to invent." They specifically demanded a shorter working day and additional pay for overtime. They bitterly complained that they had heretofore "been obliged to toil through the whole course of the longest summer's days, and that too, *in many instances,* without even the consolation of having our labour sweetened by the reviving hope of an immediate reward."

What settlement may have been reached in this dispute is not known. The masters blamed the conditions of trade for the low wages and declared that they "had in no instance, discovered a disposition to oppress or tyrannize."

These strikes and turn-outs did not in any case involve an organization that could be termed a labor union. The workers merely got together on some temporary basis to press their demands or to take joint action to protect their interests. Such trade societies as did exist, and there were a number of them in the latter part of the eighteenth century, had been formed not to promote economic aims but for philanthropic purposes. They were mutual aid societies, often including both journeymen and masters, which provided various sickness and death benefits for their members. Almost every important trade in such cities as New York, Philadelphia and Boston had such a society by the 1790's and in some instances there were organizations of broader scope—the General Society of Mechanics and Tradesmen in New York, the Association of Mechanics of the Commonwealth of Massachusetts, the Albany Mechanics' Society.

In supporting such members as might by accident or sickness be in need of assistance and aiding the widows and orphans of those who died in indigent circumstances, these societies sought to free both masters and journeymen from "the degrading reflection arising from the circumstances of being relieved . . . by private or public charity." The workers were self-respecting and proud. Thus early in our history they were prepared, as stated in the charter of one society, "to demand relief . . . as a *right.*"

Many mutual aid societies also had social features and provided meeting rooms and recreation. The house rules of the Friendly Society of Tradesmen House Carpenters, organized in Philadelphia in 1767, reveals both the scope of such activities and also the strict regulations governing the deportment of members. A fine of sixpence had to be paid into the common stock of the society by any member who "presumes to curse or swear, or cometh disguised in Liquor and breeds Disturbance . . . or promoteth Gaming at Club Hours."

While in general, economic activity fell wholly outside their scope, the charter of the New York Society of Journeymen Shipwrights stipulating automatic dissolution if the organization made any attempt to fix wages, it was inevitable that these societies should in time become concerned over employment problems. The line between mutual aid and bona fide trade associations thus becomes almost impossible to distinguish. The Federal Society of Journeymen Cordwainers, established in Philadelphia in 1794, has, however, been called the first "continuous organization" of wage earners in the United States and is perhaps entitled to be considered the original trade union. Its membership was solely made up of journeymen shoemakers, it conducted a strike and picketed the masters' shops in 1799, and remained in existence for twelve years.

A few months after the Philadelphia cordwainers organized, the journeymen printers in New York formed what was to be the first of a long line of unions in that trade, and two years later there was also established in New York a relatively long-lived society of Journeymen

Cabinet Makers. The latter organization published in the papers a complete price list—which in effect meant wage scales—with the further provision that the journeymen chairmakers would "work ten hours per day; employers to find candles."

These tentative beginnings of organization pointed the way toward the more general growth of trade societies—as the first unions were long called—that followed upon the rise of the merchant capitalists. It was not until the retail shop and custom-order work gave way to wholesale business and the old easy relationship between master and journeyman was broken down that the workers really felt compelled to combine against their employers. But with the beginning of the nineteenth century, the skilled artisans and mechanics in trade after trade followed the even earlier example of printers and shoemakers in forming societies whose avowed purpose was to guard their interests against "the artifices or intrigues" of employers and to secure adequate reward for their labor. These societies might still have mutual aid features but the major emphasis had shifted to economic action.

The merchant capitalists were interested both in importing goods from abroad and in setting up larger manufacturing establishments at home. They sought to develop broader markets and to introduce the cheap goods which would sell in such markets. With the capital at their command they could secure raw materials in bulk, provide the working places and eventually the tools for the artisans and mechanics they employed, warehouse the finished products, and then transport them to all parts of the country. The small retail shops with their emphasis upon quality and highly skilled craftsmanship could not meet the competitive conditions such large-scale operations fostered.

These trends were increasingly emphasized as the opening up of the country created ever more favorable opportunities for business expansion. The development of improved means of transportation—canals, turnpikes, and steamboats—widened the market which was accessible for the manufacturers and merchants of the Atlantic seaboard. The highways leading to the west were crowded with high-peaked, canvas covered wagons carrying to the new communities of western New York and the Ohio Valley the clothes, shoes, furniture, kitchenware, tools, and iron utensils turned out in eastern towns and cities. A national market was in the making which overshadowed the old local markets dependent upon retail trade and bespoke work, and it set the pace for economic progress. On a small scale, there was taking place the same sort of development that would result from mass production in the later stages of the industrial revolution. The eclipse of the retail shop by the wholesale establishment foreshadowed that of the local manufacturing plant by the industrial combinations and mergers of the 1880's and 1890's.

Under constant pressure to reduce costs in meeting the highly competitive conditions of this new world of business, employers sought to hold down wages, lengthen the working day of their employes, and tap new sources of cheap labor. They tried to break down the restrictions of the traditional apprenticeship system; they began to employ both women and children wherever possible; they introduced the sweat shop and the practice of letting out contracts to prison labor. For skilled craftsmen, whatever their trade, such moves were a threat not only of lower standards of living but of loss of status. They were at once aroused to combat such developments and realized that only through concerted action could they hope to protect their rights.

For a time the artisans and mechanics were able to meet their employers on relatively equal grounds. The scarcity of skilled labor that had been so characteristic of the colonial period was still a basic fact in American economy. "The objections to the pursuit of manufactures in the United States," Alexander Hamilton had stated in his famous *Report on Manufactures*, "represent an impracticability of success arising from three causes; scarcity of hands, dearness of labor, want of capital." Moreover, the expanding frontier still continued in this period to draw off many workers attracted by the easy availability of cheap land or the greater opportunity for plying a trade in the western settlements. The new towns springing up along the land and river highways in the Ohio Valley often offered even higher wages than the older communities in the east.

Newspapers of the period afford constant evidence of this demand for workers. There were frequent advertisements of jobs: "Wanted, two or three journeymen coopersmiths; liberal wages will be paid," "Wanted, six or eight carpenters; will be allowed the use of tools," and "Wanted, four or five journeymen bricklayers." The contractors building the City Hall in New York in 1803, were forced to advertise for stonecutters in the papers of Philadelphia, Baltimore and Charleston, promising high wages, repair of all tools, and assurances that although there was yellow fever in other parts of the city, the workingmen need have no fear of it.

Nevertheless the skilled workers soon found themselves fighting a defensive war against the mounting resources of the employers. Their wages did not keep up with the cost of living in the first decades of the nineteenth century, nor even maintain their relative level with the wages of unskilled workers. The general average about 1818 was probably not more than $1.25 a day except in a few special trades such as that of ship carpenters. New York typesetters, for example, were earning $8 a week and journeymen tailors in Baltimore $9. In comparison, the great demand for laborers on canals and turnpikes, in the construction of buildings and on other comparable projects, had driven up the wages of day laborers from about $4 a week at the close of the revolution to $7 a week and sometimes more. When they were fed and lodged, their actual pay might amount to more than artisans and mechanics could command. An advertisement for men to work on the road being built from the Genesee River to Buffalo, promised $12 a month, with food, lodging and whiskey every day. Although the skilled craftsmen could still live in relatively comfortable circumstances, especially in the eyes of foreign visitors who compared their status with that of workers in Europe, they realized that conditions were changing to their disadvantage and that it was going to grow harder rather than easier for them to maintain old standards.

The organizations that sought, under these circumstances, to safeguard the status of the skilled workers were most general among printers, cordwainers, tailors, carpenters, cabinetmakers, shipwrights, coopers and weavers. Especially important were the journeymen printers and cordwainers. It has already been noted that they were union pioneers, and succeeded in maintaining active societies throughout the first twenty years of the nineteenth century, not only in New York and Philadelphia, but also in Boston, Baltimore, Albany, Washington, Pittsburgh and New Orleans. The members of the building trades were also organized in almost every city, and among other societies were those of millwrights, stone-cutters, handloom weavers and hatters. Prior to 1820 there were no organizations among factory operatives—although some 100,000 persons were employed in cotton mills by that year—and there is no evidence of women taking part in the burgeoning labor movement.

These early trade societies were in effect closely restricted craft unions, wholly local in character and necessarily small in membership. The workers who belonged to them were bound to conform to strict rules and regulations: to keep union proceedings secret, agree under oath to abide by established wage scales, and always to assist fellow members to get employment in preference to any other workers. Initiation fees were about fifty cents with monthly dues amounting from six to ten cents. Attendance at regular meetings was required, with fines for unjustified absence. Moreover, rigid discipline was enforced and union members could be expelled for such lapses as frequent intoxication, gross immorality or "giving a brother member any abusive language in the society-room during the hours of meeting." The societies were deeply concerned with maintaining the standards of the crafts they represented and thereby providing assurance that their membership included all the best workmen in the community.

The basic objectives remained those which have ever since been of primary concern for organized workers—higher wages, shorter hours and improved working conditions. The attempts on the part of employers to lower standards by hiring untrained workers—foreigners and boys, eventually women—also led to vigorous efforts to enforce what today would be called a closed shop. The New York Typographical Society complained bitterly that the superabundance of learners, runaway apprentices and half-way journeymen undermined the wage rates of "full-fledged workers." In common with many other societies—probably with most of them—it maintained a strict rule that none of its members should work in any shop which employed workers who did not belong to the organization. There were many turn-outs in this and later periods against employers who tried to take on artisans or mechanics who were not union members in good standing, and the society regulations were rigidly upheld. The pressure being exerted against the craftsmen appears, in fact, to have led to a more concentrated effort to establish the principle of the closed shop than in any later period. The Journeymen Cordwainers of New York not only had a specific provision in their constitution against working in any non-union establishment, but were prepared to impose fines upon any journeyman coming to the city that did not join the society within a month.

In their dealings with employers, the societies introduced the principles of collective bargaining. In the case of the Philadelphia shoemakers, a deputation had "waited upon the employers with an offer of compromise" as early as 1799, and many instances might be cited of journeymen submitting a price list and coming to terms after protracted negotiations. When agreements had been reached between a society and the employers, a member of the former was often designated "to walk around" from shop to shop to see that it was being kept. In other instances, "tramping committees" were set up to supervise enforcement of the contract.

The strikes or turn-outs, as they were more frequently called—whereby the workers sought to uphold their interests when wage negotiations failed, employers refused to abide by the terms of an agreement, or non-members of the society were employed—were generally peaceful during this period. The employes simply quit their jobs and stayed at home until some sort of a settlement could be reached. The struggle appears often to have been fought out in the newspapers rather than in violent action. Workers and employers would put their respective cases before the public through notices in the press. Appeals and counter-appeals for popular support reflected a general acceptance of the important role of public opinion in determining a proper basis for labor relations.

There were, however, occasions when more forceful measures were taken by strikers. Six journeymen stayed on the job during a turn-out of Philadelphia shoemakers and were kept hidden in their employer's garret. The strikers kept up a sharp eye for them and when they briefly emerged one Sunday night to visit a near-by tavern, beat them up severely. On another occasion when a shop was boycotted because of refusal to accept the prescribed wage scales and the employer advertised for fifty new journeymen, the strikers established what was in effect a picket line and forcefully maintained it. There was deep resentment against non-union workers who would take the place of strikers and attacks were not unusual upon persons already being called "scabs."

Noisy demonstrations and sometimes violence marked the rather frequent turn-outs of sailors. During one strike in New York, in which the seamen demanded an increase in wages from $10 to $14 a week, so much disturbance was created that a parade of strikers had finally to be broken up by the constables. Another time the sailors tried to board and rifle a vessel whose owner had especially aroused their ire. Learning of the planned assault, a group of citizens took over the defense of the vessel and when the strikers moved in behind a drum and fife corps, with colors flying, "they were three times repulsed, with broken and bloody noses." The seamen were not organized and were an especially obstreperous lot. Artisans and mechanics did not approve of tactics that they felt unbecoming to skilled craftsmen.

The growth of journeymen societies and their militant activity were matters of mounting concern to employers. They in turn soon began to cooperate to block demands for higher wages and to combat the closed shop. While the journeymen had organized in self-defense as changing economic conditions undermined their former independent status, the masters also found themselves hard pressed to maintain their position in an increasingly competitive capitalist society. When they were unable to meet the challenge of organized employes on their own ground, they sought protection from the courts and attacked the journeymen societies as combinations or conspiracies in restraint of trade.

The first of such actions was the prosecution, in 1806, of the Journeymen Cordwainers of Philadelphia. The case grew out of one of the recurrent strikes for higher wages on the part of these aggressive shoemakers, and the trial judge proved to be a sympathetic supporter of the employers. In his charge to the jury he characterized the strike as "pregnant with public mischief and private injury" and left the twelve good men and true little choice as to the verdict he expected them to bring in.

"A combination of workmen to raise their wages," he declared, "may be considered in a two-fold point of view; one is to benefit themselves . . . the other is to injure those who do not join their society. The rule of law condemns both. . . ." The grounds for such a decision were found in the old common law principle that wherever two or more persons conspired to do something jointly, even though they were individually entitled to take such action, the public interest was en-

dangered. While its application to labor organizations seeking no more
than an increase in wages would appear to have raised some doubts even
in the judge's own mind, he quickly brushed them aside. "If the rule be
clear we are bound to conform to it," he stated, "even though we do not
comprehend the principle upon which it is founded. We are not here
to reject it because we do not see the reason for it."

Four years later the Journeymen Cordwainers of New York, and then
in 1815 another organization of Pittsburgh shoemakers, were indicted on
similar charges of criminal conspiracy. On both occasions the court
again found for the employers. The emphasis, however, had somewhat
shifted from outright condemnation of any combination for raising
wages. The New York judge did not wholly deny the right of workingmen to organize for such a purpose, but he declared that the means they
were employing "were of a nature too arbitrary and coercive, and went
to deprive their fellow citizens of rights as precious as any they contended for." In the Pittsburgh case a further point was stressed. A combination of workingmen attempting to enforce their demands by concerted action against an employer was said to be an illegal conspiracy
not only because of its injurious effect upon the employer, but because
it was prejudicial to the interests of the community. The judge in this
instance dismissed the question of whether the journeymen or the masters were the oppressors as irrelevant and condemned the former's society
because it tended "to create a monopoly or restrain the entire freedom
of trade."

These conspiracy cases aroused widespread resentment among the
workingmen. Were all other combinations, among merchants, among
politicians, among sportsmen, among "ladies and gentlemen for balls,
parties, and banquets" to be permitted, they asked, and only the poor
laborers combining against starvation to be indicted?

"The name of freedom is but a shadow," read one appeal to the public,
"if, for doing, what the laws of the country authorize, we are to have
taskmasters to measure out our pittance of subsistence—if we are to
be torn from our firesides for endeavouring to obtain a fair and just support for our families, and if we are to be treated as felons and murderers
only for asserting our right to take or refuse what we deem an adequate
reward for our labor."

The issue was injected into local policies. Federalists and Jeffersonian

Republicans were at the time engaged in a bitter controversy over the
general use of English common law in the United States, and the latter
considered the application of what they termed its undemocratic
principles to labor unions a challenge to the whole cause of liberty. The
right of association could not be divorced from other fundamental
rights, the Republicans declared, and they zealously took up the workingmen's cause.

". . . Would it be believed," an editorial in the *Philadelphia Aurora,*
the leading Jeffersonian paper, stated in 1806, "at the very time
when the state of the negro was about to be improved attempts were
being made to reduce the whites to slavery? Was there anything in the
Constitution of the United States or in the Constitution of Pennsylvania
which gave one man a right to say to another what should be the price
of labor? There was not. It was by the English common law that such
things became possible."

The controversy was to continue for many years to come but the
decisions against the workingmen stood. They did not stop the further
organization of labor societies nor wholly prevent the use of strikes and
boycotts. When the employers resorted to the courts, however, the
workingmen were hard pressed to defend themselves against conspiracy
charges.

If these cases were a first blow at the early movement for labor organization, the new unions were soon confronted by a much more serious
threat to their existence. In 1819 the country suffered a serious depression. As business activity was curtailed and the demand for labor automatically declined, even skilled workers found it increasingly difficult
to get jobs. They could no longer afford to hold out for higher wages or
seek to enforce a closed shop. They were driven to accept whatever
jobs were offered, regardless of wages or working conditions. Under
such circumstances, the young labor unions could not maintain their
membership and rapidly broke up. While some of them managed to
survive, the great majority fell by the wayside as economic distress
spread throughout the country.

This was to be a recurrent phenomenon during the nineteenth century.
Labor unions throve in periods of prosperity when the rising demand for

workers gave their members effective bargaining power. They dwindled away whenever depression and the scarcity of jobs forced every man to look out for his own interests no matter how it might affect those of workers generally. The first time that labor succeeded even partially in maintaining union strength during hard times was in the 1890's.

This was far in the future, however. The newly organized unions of the opening years of the century were so local in scope and so inexperienced, that they had no chance whatsoever of holding the line when employers aggressively took advantage of every opportunity to break down wage scales and undermine the closed shop. But in what was to become a familiar pattern, returning prosperity after 1822 led to a re-emergence of unionism. The few societies of artisans and mechanics that had somehow managed to survive depression took on a new lease of life as the bargaining position of their members was strengthened, and new organizations sprang up to replace those that had succumbed.

Not only were the societies of journeymen printers and cordwainers, tailors and carpenters, and other skilled workers revived, but for the first time there was a tentative beginning of organization among factory workers in the textile mills of New England. Moreover these new unions were especially active and did not hesitate to resort to strikes and boy-cotts to enforce their demands. Successful turn-outs for both higher wages and shorter working hours were reported in contemporary news-papers on the part of tailors in Buffalo, ship carpenters in Philadelphia, cabinet makers in Baltimore and journeymen painters, tailors, stone-cutters and even common laborers in New York. The organization of mill hands also led to a first strike on the part of female workers when the weavers at Pawtucket, Rhode Island turned out in 1824. The meeting at which the women agreed on this action was reported in the *National Gazette:* "It was conducted, however strange it may appear, without noise, or scarcely a single speech."

Even more significant than the revival and militancy of these local labor societies was a further step in the organization of labor, going beyond limited craft lines. In 1827 there was established in Philadelphia a Mechanics' Union of Trade Associations. In the terminology of today, this meant rather an association of unions, or a city central. It was the first labor organization in the country which brought together the workers of more than a single craft, and it was to make possible concerted action on the part of the workers in Philadelphia on a citywide basis.

This new association grew out of a strike of carpenters who were demanding a ten-hour day and had obtained the support of such other members of the building trades as the bricklayers, painters, and glaziers. The strike failed, but the experience in working together led to a call for more permanent organization. All existing labor societies were asked to join the association and those trades that had no unions were requested to organize at once and send delegates.

The Mechanics' Union was not primarily concerned with such limited goals as higher wages and shorter hours even though it had grown out of a strike for the ten-hour day. A new note was introduced into the activity of labor societies by raising the broad issue of equality for producers generally. The changes effected by the new economic order had aroused among the workers increasing concern over their social as well as economic status. The Philadelphia labor leaders sought some means to maintain the position of workers in the face of what appeared to be newly developing class lines. They did not think of themselves as wage earners arrayed against employers, but rather as members of "the productive and mechanical classes" whose goal was to promote the prosperity and welfare of the entire community.

"If the mass of people were enabled by their labour to procure for themselves and families a full and abundant supply of the comforts and conveniences of life," the preamble of the new organization's constitution stated, "the consumption of articles, particularly of dwellings, furniture and clothing, would amount to at least twice the quantity it does at present, and of course the demand, by which employers are enabled either to subsist or accumulate, would likewise be increased in an equal proportion. . . . The real object, therefore, of this association, is to avert, if possible, the desolating evils which must inevitably arise from a depreciation of the intrinsic value of human labour . . . and to assist, in conjunction with such other institutions of this nature as shall hereafter be formed throughout the union, in establishing a just balance of power, both mental, moral, political and scientific, between all the various classes and individuals which constitute society at large."

Such aims, already suggesting the purchasing power theory as an argument for higher wages, had definite political implications. The Mechanics' Union of Trade Associations, indeed, never engaged in direct trade union activity but turned at once to politics. It appealed to the artisans and mechanics of Philadelphia to "throw off the trammels of party spirit, and unite under the banner of equal rights." It called for the nomination of candidates for local office who would represent the interests of the working classes.

XX

III: THE WORKINGMEN'S PARTIES

XXXXXXXXXXXXXXXXXXXXXXXXXXXXXXXXXXXXXXXXXXXX

IN URGING ITS MEMBERS to nominate candidates for public office, the Mechanics' Union of Trade Associations in Philadelphia broke fresh ground for labor and inaugurated what was to become a widespread political movement of workingmen's parties. It soon spread to other towns in Pennsylvania; to New York where wide popular support developed not only for local parties in New York city itself but in many upstate localities, and into Massachusetts and other parts of New England. Ultimately workingmen's parties were established in at least a dozen states. As far west as Ohio, as well as along the Atlantic seaboard, local groups of farmers, artisans and mechanics named their own political candidates and in some instances elected them. For a brief time they were highly important, and sometimes held an actual balance of power between the major parties in local elections.

An equally widespread growth of labor newspapers took place in the early 1830's, with no less than sixty-eight such journals upholding the workingmen's cause and agitating for labor reforms. Their enthusiasm and assurance knew no bounds. "From Maine to Georgia, within a few months past," commented the *Newark Village Chronicle* in May, 1830, "we discern symptoms of a revolution, which will be second to none save that of '76." "Throughout the vast republic," the *Albany Working Men's Advocate* stated shortly afterwards, "the farmers, mechanics and workingmen are assembling . . . to impart to its laws and administration those principles of liberty and equality unfolded in the Declaration of Independence."

These developments were both a first expression of the awakening forces of Jacksonian democracy, with which the workingmen's political activity was gradually to merge, and a further demonstration of that demand for equal citizenship first voiced in Philadelphia. The country was rapidly expanding in these years. The opening up of new western territory, the building of turnpikes and canals, the steady growth of manufactures, and the rise of cities everywhere created a spirit of buoyant confidence. What the workers of the country basically sought was the right to share fully in the benefits of national growth and development, and they felt that under conditions as they had developed in the 1820's they were being shut off from opportunities to which they were entitled. Having newly obtained political power through the removal of voting property qualifications, they were ready to enter the lists in support of their own interests.

There was little question that the general status of labor was continuing to deteriorate as a result of the changes wrought in our economy by the rise of merchant capitalism. The ordinary divisions within society were deepening. Contemporary critics saw on the one hand the producing masses, made up of the laboring poor, and on the other a wealthy non-productive aristocracy bulwarked by special privilege. Banking and other monopolies accentuated this cleavage, and the great majority of the country's workers saw little improvement in the conditions under which they labored even though trade and commerce expanded and the nation as a whole grew more prosperous.

Wages rose but not in proportion to the rise in the cost of living. Twelve and fifteen hours remained the usual day's work. During the summer, artisans and mechanics were on the job as early as four in the morning, took an hour off for lunch at ten and another for dinner at three, and then quit work only with sunset. They were often paid in depreciated currency whose value was constantly fluctuating. Should their employer fail and be unable to pay them, they had no redress and yet when they could not meet their own obligations, they were liable to imprisonment for debt.

Moreover the workingmen felt that government was wholly on the side of the aristocracy and that its policies were helping to perpetuate the conditions which were depressing the position of all labor. They had no faith in either major party, whatever its professions of goodwill, because the men chosen for public office were invariably representatives of the class that they had come to believe was oppressing them. Heretofore they had been politically helpless to do anything about redressing a balance of power they saw swinging steadily against them. Armed with the vote, they declared themselves unwilling any longer to accept passively policies which in government, finance or business sought to reserve special privilege for the favored few at the expense of the great majority.

In forming their own parties, the workers tried to secure participation in government by members of their own class—the producers—and they were convinced that in doing so, they were serving the best interests of the people as a whole. Their party platforms vigorously attacked every instance of special privilege, and particularly banking monopoly, but indicative of their general objective of establishing equal citizenship, their foremost demand was invariably free public education. Seeking to secure representation for "the plain people" in every governmental process, they recognized that education for the masses was a first step toward an effective democracy. On more specific grounds, the workingmen also demanded abolition of imprisonment for debt and mechanics' lien laws; the revision of a militia system that bore heavily upon the poor; the direct election of all public officials; greater equality in taxation, and the complete separation of church and state.

The political agitation of the workers and the formation of their local parties thus reflected a spirit of liberal reform that was actually much broader than any labor movement. The revolt of the workers in eastern cities was to become more and more closely linked with that among farmers in the new western settlements in the great upsurge of democracy that on the national stage led to the election of Andrew Jackson as spokesman for the interests of the common man. While the workers may not have universally supported the Democrats in 1828, there can be no question but that they swung heavily behind Jackson as he demonstrated his mounting concern in the issues they put forward. In championing the cause of "the humble members of society," he pointedly included mechanics and laborers as well as farmers. Jacksonian democracy had a broader basis than Jeffersonian democracy, and was compounded both of the individualistic spirit of the frontier and the equalitarianism of eastern workingmen.

The local parties formed by the workers were to become inextricably involved in the complex and shifting political patterns of the 1830's.

Whatever their ultimate fate, however, their influence in quickening the demand for reform and promoting progressive principles was important. Commenting on the course of one workingmen's party in Massachusetts, a Whig newspaper sourly charged that there was no distinction between "Working-Menism and Jacksonism." If this was not always true, it was sufficiently close to the mark to suggest that the victories won by the advance of Jacksonian democracy were in many instances victories that owed a great deal to the workers' support.

The significance of the growing political power of the workingmen was demonstrated in other ways. In opposition to Jackson's espousal of the cause of the common man, the newly organized Whigs for a time sought to uphold Federalist traditions favoring government by the rich and the well-born. They especially attacked the proposition of "throwing open the polls to every man that walks." But when they found themselves unable to stem the growing political power of small farmers and urban workers, they began to shift their ground. Attacking Jackson for emphasizing class distinctions—as later day conservatives were to attack Franklin D. Roosevelt—they maintained that there was no warrant for setting off aristocracy and democracy as opposing forces in our national life. "These phrases, *higher and lower orders*," one Whig editor declared, "are of European origin and have no place in our Yankee dialect." However conservative their ideas might still be, it was no longer politically feasible for them to uphold aristocratic principles and they were compelled to recognize the right of all classes in society to share in government.

By the close of the Jacksonian period, the original workingmen's parties had long since fallen by the wayside, but the producing masses of the nation had won the political recognition that had been their first objective. Both major parties were continually angling for labor support. When in 1836 the editor of the *Ohio People's Press,* to cite a single example, shifted his political allegiance from Jackson to Harrison, he called for support of the latter on exactly the same grounds on which he had originally backed the former. The program advocated by Harrison, he maintained, would "restore to the farmer, the mechanic and the working-man their proper station and influence in the Republic." The extension of the franchise and growing political awareness of the workers had made labor for the first time a political power.

Among the various local workingmen's parties, the experience of the one organized in New York is at once most revealing of the influence they were temporarily able to exert and of the complicated factors that brought about their collapse. This party grew out of a meeting of "mechanics and others" that had been summoned on April 23, 1829, to protest against any lengthening in the prevailing ten-hour day already won in that city by the early trade unions. Deciding to broaden the scope of their activity, the delegates sent out a call for a larger meeting. It was attended by some 6,000 persons and a set of resolutions was adopted dealing with the broad principles of workingmen's rights. Consideration of ways and means for implementing this program was then delegated to a Committee of Fifty, and on October 19 it brought in a report, of which 20,000 copies were subsequently circulated, that vigorously attacked the existing social order and called for a convention to nominate for the New York assembly political candidates from among those "who live by their own labour *And None Other*." Four days later this convention was held. After all non-workers "such as bankers, brokers, rich men etc." had been expressly warned to leave the hall, the workingmen agreed upon an assembly slate which included a printer, two machinists, two carpenters, a painter and a grocer.

From the very first, however, rivalry and intrigue over the leadership of the new workingmen's party threatened to split its ranks. It was to be dominated by several highly individualistic reformers whose philosophy and ideas went far beyond the practical demands in which the workers themselves were primarily interested. Four such persons stand out especially for their influence on the labor party in New York, and on the course of the workingmen's general political activity.

In its earliest stages, the party was largely under the control of Thomas Skidmore, a machinist by trade, who had been instrumental in persuading the workers to broaden their program as a means of "coercing their aristocratic oppressors" into maintaining the ten-hour day. Wholly self-educated, he was a violent, fanatical devotee of the workers' cause and had developed an agrarian philosophy that questioned the entire basis for existing property rights. He believed that in giving up his original and natural right to land to become a smith, a weaver, a builder or other laborer, every man was entitled to a guaranty from society "that reasonable toil shall enable him to live as comfortably as others." Any system that failed to provide such social security was inherently wrong in his opinion, and he hoped to lead a workingmen's revolt in favor of basic political reforms.

His views were shortly to be set forth in a formidable treatise which he comprehensively entitled *"The Rights of Man to Property; Being a Proposition to Make it Equal among the Adults of the Present Generation; and to Provide for its Equal Transmission to Every Individual of Each Succeeding Generation, on Arriving at the Age of Maturity."* Skidmore specifically proposed that all debts and property claims should be at once canceled, and the assets of society as a whole sold at public auction with every citizen having equal purchasing power. After such a communistic division of property, the maintenance of equality would be assured by doing away with all inheritance.

Without fully understanding all the implications of this radical program, the members of the New York Workingmen's Party allowed Skidmore to draw up their original platform. It was based upon the forthright premise that "all human society, our own included as well as every other, is constructed radically wrong," and condemned both the private ownership of land and the inheritance of wealth. Its more specific provisions, however, set forth the objectives which were fundamental to the workingmen's movement everywhere. The platform demanded communal education, abolition of imprisonment for debt, mechanics' lien laws and the elimination of licensed monopolies.

A second leader, who accepted at least in part the Skidmore program but was to be far more influential in the workingmen's movement in these and later years, was George Henry Evans. A printer by trade, he founded the *Working Man's Advocate,* perhaps the most important labor journal of these years, as the organ for the New York party, and turned out a continuous stream of articles and editorials promoting the workers' interests. Reflecting the influence of Skidmore, his paper first carried the slogan: "All children are entitled to equal education; all adults to equal property; and all mankind, to equal privileges." But his views were to be later modified although he remained throughout his life a strong advocate of basic agrarian reforms.

As if such leadership were not enough to condemn the Workingmen's Party in the eyes of all conservatives, it was further damned by the participation in its activities of another brace of radical reformers:

Robert Dale Owen and Frances Wright. Having but recently moved to
New York from the cooperative community at New Harmony, Indiana,
where the former's father, the English reformer Robert Owen, had attempted to put into practice his socialistic program for replacing the
factory system, these two naturally seized upon the workingmen's movement as a medium for promoting their own particular brand of reform.
They had founded a paper, the *Free Enquirer*, to publicize their ideas
and it was soon campaigning vigorously in support of the new party.

Robert Dale Owen was twenty-eight at this time, a short, blue-eyed,
sandy-haired young man whose idealism and earnest sincerity gave
him a very real influence. In spite of a rasping voice and clumsy gestures,
he was a forceful speaker at workingmen's meetings and he was also a
prolific and able writer. He believed strongly in a more equitable distribution of wealth, was opposed to organized religion, and advocated
more liberal divorce laws, but his primary interest was in free, public
education. He single-mindedly felt that it was the only effective means
for regenerating society and had developed an elaborate educational
program which called for a system of "state guardianship."

All children, whether of the rich or of the poor, according to this
scheme, were to be removed from their homes and placed in national
schools where they would receive the same food, be dressed in the
same simple clothing, and taught the same subjects in order to promote
the general cause of democracy. "Thus may luxury, may pride, may
ignorance be banished from among us," read one report on state
guardianship; "and we may become what fellow citizens ought to be,
a nation of brothers." While the workers were not wholly to approve
this particular program, Owen contributed a great deal to their educational ideas.

Frances Wright was at once the most zealous, the most colorful and
in the eyes of contemporaries, the most dangerous of these reformers
associated with the Workingmen's Party. Although a free thinker, and
so outspoken an advocate of women's rights and easy divorce that she
was generally accused of advocating free love, she did not look the part
of a radical agitator. Tall, slender, with wavy chestnut hair, she completely dazzled the workingmen's audiences she was constantly addressing. Conservatives were as much shocked by the daring effrontery of
a female in appearing on the lecture platform as by her unorthodox

views, but few of those who actually heard her speak were wholly immune to her charms. "She has always been to me one of the sweetest of sweet memories," Walt Whitman, taken to one of her meetings by his carpenter father, was to write in later years: "we all loved her; fell down before her: her very appearance seemed to enthrall us . . . graceful, deerlike . . . she was beautiful in bodily shape and gifts of soul."

Fanny Wright was born in Scotland and falling early under the influence of Jeremy Bentham became even as a young woman the militant champion of reform that she was to remain throughout her life. On first coming to this country, she had taken up the cause of the enslaved Negro and established at Nashoba, Tennessee, a colony where she tried to prepare groups of slaves, purchased at her own expense, for freedom and eventual colonization outside of the United States. When this project failed, she joined the community at New Harmony and then accompanied Robert Dale Owen to New York to cooperate with him in editing the *Free Enquirer*.

Undaunted by her disappointments at Nashoba and New Harmony, with her zeal for reform in no way abated, she enthusiastically adopted the workingmen's movement. She saw in it not only a protest against social inequality but a basic revolt on the part of the oppressed for which history offered no parallel. "What distinguishes the present from every other struggle in which the human race has been engaged," she wrote in the *Free Enquirer*, "is, that the present is, evidently, openly and acknowledgedly, a war of class . . . it is the ridden people of the earth who are struggling to throw from their backs the 'booted and spurred' riders whose legitimate title to starve as well as work them to death will no longer pass current; it is labour rising up against idleness, industry against money; justice against law and against privilege."

The newspapers railed against Fanny Wright. They attempted to dismiss her as "an exotic of some notoriety"; they called her "the great Red Harlot of Infidelity." But no matter what abuse they flung at her, she shamelessly went on expressing her "alarming principles" on public platforms and in the press.

When the Workingmen's Party took the field under such sponsorship in the New York elections of 1829, with its slate of tradesmen and artisans, the conservatives were nonplussed. They at first attempted to dismiss any possible threat to their own interests, but as the vote of the laboring classes appeared to be swinging heavily behind the new party, they became thoroughly aroused. "We understand with astonishment and alarm," the *Courier and Enquirer* protested, "that the 'Infidel Ticket,' miscalled the 'Workingmen's Ticket,' is far ahead of every other Assembly ticket in the city. What a state of things we have reached! A ticket got up openly and avowedly in opposition to social order, in opposition to the rights of property, running ahead of every other!" Even more shrill were the outcries of the *New York Commercial Advertiser:* "Lost to society, to earth and heaven, godless and hopeless, clothed and fed by stealing and blasphemy . . . such are the apostles who are trying to induce a number of able-bodied men in this city to follow in their course. . . ."

In the result, such fears proved to be exaggerated. The Workingmen's Party did not sweep the city. Nevertheless, it polled some 6,000 votes, out of a total of 21,000 cast in the election, and sent one of its candidates, a carpenter, to the assembly. "The sun of liberty has not pursued his steady and unchanging course for half a century in vain," George Henry Evans started a rhapsodic editorial in the *Working Man's Advocate,* and then, abruptly dropping his metaphor, observed more moderately that the result has proved "beyond our most sanguine expectations, favorable to our cause—the cause of the people."

Nevertheless a growing divergence in the views of the party's self-constituted leaders, and a revolt on the part of the rank-and-file membership against the extreme radicalism of Thomas Skidmore, soon led to internal dissension and factional fights. At a meeting in December, 1829, a resolution was adopted in which the workingmen explicitly stated that they had "no desire or intention of disturbing the right of property in individuals, or the public." As Robert Dale Owen then moved in to try to take over Skidmore's repudiated leadership, opposition also arose to his program of state guardianship. The workingmen were ready to make education their foremost party plank, but they would not support "any attempt to palm upon any man, or set of men, the peculiar doctrines of infidelity, agrarianism, or sectarian principles." They declared that the school system should be based "upon a plan that shall leave to the father and the affectionate mother the enjoyment of the society of their offspring."

The consequences of these inner conflicts, in part promoted by politicians seeking the workingmen's support for their own purposes, was a three-way split in the original organization. Skidmore and the few followers he could hold in line established a straight-out Agrarian Workingmen's Party. Another faction, whose interests were promoted by George Henry Evans in the *Working Man's Advocate* and which was still supported by the Owenites and Fanny Wright, struggled to maintain the original party. A third group broke away under new leadership, with the support of the *Evening Journal,* another labor news sheet, and became known as the North American Party after the name of the hotel where its meetings were held.

Between the last two groups especially there was embittered and continuing strife. They were soon endorsing rival politicians, putting rival tickets in the field, flinging verbal brickbats at each other through the pages of their respective organs, breaking up each other's meetings. The original Workingmen's Party, finding itself under attack because of the radical views of Owen and Fanny Wright, frantically denied the implications of these charges. "The cries of Infidelity and Agrarianism are mere political scarecrows," it asserted, "such as were formerly set up to terrify the democrats of 1801." The North American Party was accused of selling out to local politicians and the workingmen were called upon to avoid "the political trimmer, the pettifogger, the office hunter." Unity was essential if they were to make their influence felt—"Yoke not, therefore, the noble war horse with the ignoble ass."

While the intra-party contest raged in New York, local parties sprang up in such cities as Albany, Troy, Schenectady, Rochester, Syracuse and Auburn. Plans were made to hold a state convention of workingmen and to nominate candidates for governor and lieutenant governor. It was finally summoned, with seventy-eight delegates from thirteen counties, but the split in New York city proved disastrous when rival delegations attended the convention. The professional politicians took over and succeeded in winning the workingmen's vote in support of a Democratic office seeker. "The Working Men Betrayed," shrieked the *Advocate,* and declared its adherents would nominate their own slate.

In the resulting confusion, the election of 1830 found three factions of workingmen each putting forward its own nominees in the city elections and endorsing rival candidates for the governorship. Without cohesion or unity, an easy prey to professional political influences and the blandishments of Tammany Hall, the Workingmen's Party as originally constituted broke up. The Democrats won both the state and local elections and there was an end to any further effective organization among the forces of labor in New York. The *Working Man's Advocate* insisted that nothing could so effectually prevent the final accomplishment of labor's objectives as a coalition with any other party for the temporary purpose of electing particular men. The workers' votes, however, had already swung over to Tammany.

If the experience of the New York artisans and mechanics in trying to set up an independent political organization was short-lived, very much the same story might be told of the activities of other workingmen's parties. In many instances, particularly in Pennsylvania and Massachusetts, they succeeded for a time in aligning the labor vote behind their own candidates and exercising an important and occasionally decisive influence in local politics. But just as in New York, internal friction and external pressures led to factionalism and gradual disintegration. Self-constituted leaders sought to promote their own individual panaceas of reform, which as in the case of the programs promoted by Skidmore, Evans, Owen and Fanny Wright, were often at variance with the real interests of the workers. And when reformers were ousted, politicians were quick to move in to take over control and try to swing the workingmen's votes for one or another of the major parties.

In Massachusetts an attempt to bring about a broader political organization of workers was made in 1832 with the formation of the New England Association of Farmers, Mechanics and Workingmen. The successes won by this group in local elections inspired the nomination of a governor, but the association was soon deeply involved in the major political struggles of the day with its own gubernatorial candidate urging the working class to rally in support of the Democrats.

In spite of the failure of the workingmen's parties themselves, wide acceptance of many of the principles for which they stood marked the final stages of their merger with the larger forces of Jacksonian democracy. Both major parties were greatly influenced, as we have seen, by the new political power of the workers. However, it was the Democrats rather than the Whigs that most directly supported labor's aims. When

Jackson launched his war against the United States Bank, vigorously attacking monopoly and special privilege on a score of fronts, artisans, mechanics and laborers naturally rallied behind him. If the labor vote was not wholly cast in favor of a single party—as, indeed, it never has been—the workers generally hurrahed for Jackson in 1832 as the foe of monopoly and the friend of the people.

The conservatives gave warning in terms that were to be repeated a century later in another period that found marked class divisions in a presidential election. "Elect Jackson," one factory owner told his employes, "and the grass will grow in your streets, owls will build nests in the mills, and foxes burrow in the highways." But the workers turned out nevertheless to help return him to office. In New York they marched to the polls singing:

> Mechanics, cartmen, laborers
> Must form a close connection,
> And show the rich aristocrats,
> Their powers at this election. . . .
>
> Yankee Doodle, smoke 'em out
> The proud, the banking faction
> None but such as Hartford Feds
> Oppose the poor and Jackson.

The twists and turns of politics in the 1830's are one thing, however, and another is the steady growth of progressive principles and the practical achievement of the reforms the workers sought. As the popular support for the original aims of the workingmen's parties gathered increasing force, and the liberal elements in the community as a whole took them up, steady progress was made in meeting the demands that first flared forth on the mastheads of the labor press.

A first case in point was education reform. At the head of the editorial column in almost every workingmen's newspaper, there had been placed the demand figuring so prominently in the campaign of the New York party—Equal Universal Education. At this time, only the vaguest consideration was being given to the needs of children whose parents were unable to afford private institutions. New England was ahead of the rest of the country in having tax supported schools, but even in such populous and wealthy states as New York, New Jersey, Pennsylvania and Delaware (to say nothing of the new states in the west or the backward states of the south), the only provision for the children of workingmen and other poor families was the charity school—inadequate, inefficient and socially degrading. The Public School Society reported, in 1829, that there were over 24,000 children between the ages of five and fifteen in New York who had no schooling whatsoever, or almost the same number as that enrolled in all charity and private schools. Some years later, a more extensive report in Pennsylvania declared that 250,-000 out of the 400,000 children in that state did not attend school. For the country as a whole, over-all estimates placed the total at over a million, with a corresponding measure of complete illiteracy.

The workingmen resented equally the lack of opportunity for an education as reflected in these figures, and the odium attached to such public schools as there were because they were charitable institutions. Without going so far as to accept all the doctrines of Robert Dale Owen and Frances Wright, they universally agreed with them in insisting upon the importance of free, republican education which would be available on terms of complete equality for the children of both rich and poor. The workingmen based their position on the philosophy of equal rights inherent in the Declaration of Independence, and bulwarked it with the unassailable argument that as future citizens, it was imperative that all children have the education that would enable them to vote intelligently. Never have a people had greater faith in education—"the greatest blessing bestowed upon mankind"—than this generation of Americans. The workers could not have been more determined in demanding it for their children as a right to which they were morally entitled.

"It appears, therefore to the committees," read a typical report of a workingmen's group in Philadelphia, "that there can be no liberty without a wide diffusion of real intelligence; that the members of a republic, should all be alike instructed in the nature and character of their equal rights and duties, as human beings, and as citizens. . . ." It was also argued in this report that only an effective system of public schools could prevent children from being exposed too early to the pernicious

influences of society and thereby "yield an abundant harvest for mag-
dalens and penitentiaries" or fall victim to intemperance—"that assas-
sinator of private peace and public virtue." The major emphasis was
invariably placed, however, on the importance of education as the
very foundation of the democratic forms of government which America
exemplified. "A system that shall unite under the same roof the children
of the poor man and the rich, the widow's charge and the orphan," was
the demand put forward by the reorganized Workingmen's Party of
New York in 1829, "where the road to distinction shall be superior
industry, virtue and acquirement, without reference to descent."

Opinions differed as to the type of education which should be provided, but stress was in most instances laid upon the importance of
practical training as well as the liberal arts. Public institutions, it was
urged in another report of the Philadelphia workingmen, should be
"so located as to command health, exercise at the various mechanic
arts, or agriculture, at the same time [that] a knowledge of the natural
sciences, and other useful literature is taught."

The educational campaign had of course other than working class
support. It was taken up by many reformers and awoke progressively
wider attention. At the same time, it was long opposed by conservatives
who felt that the advantages of schooling should be closely restricted
and that it was wholly unwarranted to tax the rich for the education
of the poor. "*Universal, Equal* Education," the *National Gazette* declared, "is impossible, if the trades, manufactories and manual labor
are to be successfully prosecuted,—unless the standard of education be
greatly lowered and narrowed."

Nevertheless this campaign waged so vigorously for Equal Republican, Scientific, Practical Education began to bear fruit. State legislatures
took the issue under more serious consideration than they ever had
before, and new laws were gradually adopted, first authorizing and then
requiring local communities to levy taxes for public education. The
turn perhaps came when Pennsylvania, where the workingmen had
been so active, finally adopted a free, tax-supported system in 1834. The
bill embodying this program narrowly missed defeat. In response to
a protesting petition with 32,000 signatures, the senate tried to substitute a provision "for the education of the poor gratis." But the principle
of a public school system free to all on terms of equality triumphed.

Other states fell in line and the victory for which the workingmen had so long contested was ultimately won.

Another issue for which labor battled valiantly and successfully during this period was abolition of imprisonment for debt. The antiquated practice of throwing a man into jail when he could not meet his financial obligations was still in almost universal effect in the 1820's. The Boston Prison Discipline Society estimated, at the close of the decade, that some 75,000 persons were being imprisoned annually for debts, and that in at least half of the cases, the sums involved were less than $25. In one instance, a woman was taken from her home and the care of her two children for a debt of $3.60, and in another a man was thrown into jail for a $5 debt owing his grocer, even though it had been contracted while the debtor was ill. Thirty-two persons were found in one prison for debts which in every case were less than $1.

Obviously this system bore most heavily on the poor and its injustice rankled deeply. "A law that makes poverty a crime," one workingman political candidate declared, "and a poor man a felon, after these very laws have made poverty inevitable, is not only cruel and oppressive, but absurd and revolting." Adding to the miseries of the situation, the debtors' jails were shockingly overcrowded and insanitary, and there was often no provision for feeding the prisoners, who remained wholly dependent upon private charity. In New Jersey, according to one report, there were "food, bedding and fuel" for criminals, but for the debtors only "walls, bars and bolts."

Reform was long overdue yet it still awoke opposition from the business community. Even John Quincy Adams felt obliged to point out what he considered would be the dangerous effects of doing away with debt imprisonment upon the security of property and the sanctity of contracts. These considerations were felt by merchants and lawyers to be more important than what President Jackson declared to be the injustice of exerting such a "grinding power over misfortune and poverty."

The workingmen's drive first led to the passage of laws whereby the poor debtor could win release by taking a bankruptcy oath, and then to limitations upon the amounts for which he could be imprisoned. But soon the states were one by one forced to accept the inescapable logic of abolishing the system altogether. Ohio took this step in 1828 and the next decade saw its example followed by New York, New Jersey, Connecticut, Virginia and other states. The practice still lingered on in some parts of the country, but its complete disappearance was clearly foreshadowed by the end of the 1830's.

The attack upon the militia system, largely promoted by the workingmen's parties, was also successful. In most states, attendance at annual drills and parades, generally lasting three days, was compulsory for every citizen. The militiamen had to pay all their own expenses and provide their own equipment, while failure to attend was punished by fines or imprisonment. For the workingmen such regulations meant not only a loss in wages while attending the drill, but what were for them heavy expenses. The rich, on the other hand, could easily afford to escape their obligations by paying the same fines without difficulty. After 1830, compulsory service was either modified or completely abolished. President Jackson called attention to the issue in his annual message in 1832, urging that wherever the old system still prevailed—as in New York— its inequalities should be carefully examined.

Other instances of economic or social advance owed much to the workers. Their demand for mechanics' lien laws, at once taken up by Tammany Hall in New York, led to widespread adoption of such legislation. Their opposition to the existing auction system, to general incorporation laws, to the issuance by local banks of small currency notes, and to other economic abuses was an important factor in the passage of remedial laws.

The rise of the workingmen's parties did not at all represent a class movement and it was not completely a labor movement. The workingmen were confused and baffled by the changes that were taking place in their social status, and they sought somehow to establish greater equality between producers and those who lived on the fruits of the producers' toil.

As their movement fell into the hands of doctrinaire reformers or professional politicians, they began to feel that their entry into politics was wholly futile. The broad and distant goal of equality seemed to be a glittering mirage. They gradually returned to more practical aims—

higher wages, shorter hours—which had been neglected in their new absorption in politics. Economic action to attain these immediate objectives now appeared to the rank and file of trade union members to hold far greater possibilities for enabling them to maintain their standard of living. "The Trades' Unions never will be political," the *National Laborer*, of Philadelphia, declared in characteristic expression of this new attitude, "because its members have learned from experience that the introduction of Politics into their Societies has thwarted every effort to ameliorate their Conditions."

The social gains inspired by the original workingmen's parties were at least a partial denial of this emphatic statement. Nevertheless, labor was unable throughout the nineteenth century to organize with political effectiveness in party battles. When later attempts were made to establish a national party, they completely failed. The experience of the 1830's was a first demonstration that labor had no real basis for setting up a distinctive party. Its aims were broadly liberal, and taken over by the major parties whenever the workers were able, directly or indirectly, to exercise sufficient pressure. The flirtation of the New York Workingmen's Party with the radical agrarianism of its original leaders was brief. The workers themselves were basically conservative in their views, and the equality they sought was within the framework of the existing political and economic structure of the country. They wanted to share in the benefits of emerging capitalism rather than to overthrow it. Fanny Wright might declaim upon a war of classes. Such sentiments did not echo the views of the workingmen themselves.

There was no single unifying principle to hold the workers together. Unlike their contemporaries in Europe, they were not inspired to common political action to obtain the franchise, because they had already won the vote as part of the nationwide triumph of democratic principles in the 1820's. Nor were they drawn to the support of socialism, as were workers in England and on the continent. The interests of American wage earners were too closely allied with the interests of the people generally to provide a basis for a distinctive class solidarity that would find political expression in a third party. The opportunities afforded by an expanding economy, the continued fluidity of class lines, and the individualism of the frontier carved out the channels along which the

American labor movement was to develop in sharp contrast to the situation in Europe.

If for a time the workingmen's parties of the 1830's seemed to foreshadow the possible creation of a labor party, their absorption in the general advance of Jacksonian democracy marked the sharp reversal of any such trend.

IV: LABOR STRENGTH
IN THE 1830'S

THE ORIGINAL WORKINGMEN'S PARTIES rose and fell within a very brief span of time. Whatever may be claimed for their political influence, their existence as distinctive political organizations was too ephemeral to bulk very large in the history of the labor movement. The return of the trade societies to economic action was in many ways a far more significant development. During these years in which such marked progress was being made in social reform in the country as a whole, and particularly during Jackson's second administration from 1833 to 1837, union activity was more widespread and more militant than it would be again for several decades.

The workingmen continued to feel, as their excursion into politics had already demonstrated, a sense of degradation in their changing social position. The revived trade unions were to be primarily concerned with wages and hours, but they also reflected the desire of their members to regain status in the community. As the old society they had known appeared to be dissolving, with onetime independent craftsmen sinking to the level of wage earners, artisans and mechanics more than ever hoped through union membership to reaffirm the dignity of labor and to win greater public recognition of its social as well as economic values.

"As the line of distinction between employer and employed *widened*," wrote one labor leader in 1834, "the condition of the latter inevitably verges toward a state of vassalage . . . hostile to the best interests of the community, as well as the spirit and genius of our government." The trade societies sought to combat this trend by creating a solidarity among the workers that would safeguard them from any such complete and helpless subordination to the employing class.

Conditions within the country in the early 1830's encouraged the growth of unions. On the one hand mounting prosperity strengthened the bargaining power of the workers, and on the other determined

efforts on the part of employers to hold down wages in the face of
rising prices forced them to organize in self-defense. Not only did trade
societies among almost all classes of workers multiply rapidly, but
further attempts were made to link these local unions in citywide federations which would promote labor unity. A beginning was even to be
made in still broader organization that foreshadowed establishment of
a truly national labor movement. Moreover the aggressive attitude of
the members of these unions led to a wave of strikes that provided a
dramatic chapter in the long struggle of the workers to establish their
rights.

So general did this activity become that no trade appeared to be im-
mune to its contagious militancy. "The barbers have struck," the *New
York Times* exclaimed in April, 1836, "and now all that remains for
Editors is to strike, too."

Never before in time of peace had there been such a rapid increase in
the cost of living as resulted from the wild-cat boom of the early 1830's
with all its speculation and extravagant inflation. The easing of bank
credit and the profligate issue of paper money, which were the immediate consequences of President Jackson's successful attack upon the
United States Bank, forced prices up all along the line. In New York,
flour went from $5 a barrel in 1834 to $8 in April, 1835 and then to $12
a year later. Other foodstuffs followed the same upward spiral, clothing
and household goods rose phenomenally, and the advance in rents
was from twenty-five to forty per cent. It was generally estimated
that the cost of living increased some sixty-six per cent between 1834
and 1836.

Wages invariably lagged behind in this upward march, and the
further measures taken by employers to hold down their own costs
constituted an even greater threat to the workers' living standards. With
the virtual collapse of the apprenticeship system in many trades, young,
half-trained boys were taken on at lower wages than the prevailing rate
for journeymen. Women were brought in, again at lower pay, to replace
male workers. They were most widely employed as tailoresses, seamstresses and shoe binders (contemporary estimates stating that 12,000
of the 20,000 engaged in such work earned no more than $1.25 a week),

but they also offered new competition to printers, cigar makers and other workers. The report of a Philadelphia committee, in 1836, declared that "of fifty-eight societies, twenty-four are seriously affected by female labour, to the impoverishment of whole families, and the benefit of none but the employers." Finally, there was widespread resort to convict labor. Mechanics and artisans complained bitterly that through this developing practice of letting out contracts to prisons, whatever the benefits for the convicts themselves, articles were manufactured at prices "from 40 to 60 per cent below what the honest mechanic, who supports himself and family, can afford."

Under such circumstances, there was hardly an urban community in which the workingmen were not driven to act together in mutual defense of their interests. In Philadelphia, the cordwainers reorganized, the handloom weavers formed a new society, and bricklayers, plumbers, blacksmiths, cigar makers, comb makers and saddlers, among other trades, were unionized. The older societies in New York were revived, with the printers, cordwainers and tailors once again in the lead, and cabinet makers, hat finishers, basket makers, locksmiths, pianoforte makers, and silk hatters joining the union ranks. The organizations in Baltimore included bootmakers, stonecutters, coopers, carpet weavers and coach makers. The same story could be told of every other city on the Atlantic seaboard, and also of upstate New York, Washington, Pittsburgh, Louisville and other manufacturing centers in the west.

The further organization among workers other than the traditional mechanics and artisans was making at least some headway. By this time there was a rapidly developing textile industry in Massachusetts and Rhode Island, factories in Connecticut were turning out clocks and watches, and iron foundries in Pennsylvania presaged the further growth of large-scale industry. In addition to the employes in such establishments, other new groups of wage earners included machinists and engineers, freight handlers, firemen on steamboats, stage drivers, gatekeepers on turnpikes and canal bridges. While these workers still remained largely unorganized, pioneering unions among the cotton factory operatives, tinplate and sheet iron workers and many other groups won increasing support.

Women were also brought into the labor movement with their own trade societies. Baltimore had a United Seamstresses Society; New York its Ladies' Shoebinders and Female Bookbinders, as well as a Female Union Association, and in Philadelphia there was a Female Improvement Society. As an early sign of organized activity among the women employes of the New England textile mills, there was formed, in 1833, the Female Society of Lynn and Vicinity for the Protection and Promotion of Female Industry, and, a year later, the Factory Girls' Association.

A picturesque view of the trade societies as they existed in New York about this time is found in the description of a spectacular demonstration in that city celebrating the triumph of the French revolution in 1830. Although Tammany Hall took over control of the affair, the unions dominated it. Their delegations were the most prominent feature in a parade whose line of march was some three miles long and which was joyfully watched by crowds estimated at thirty thousand persons.

The elaborate floats, as described in the *Working Man's Advocate,* were the sensation of the day. The printers had two elegant presses ("tastefully gilded and ornamented") which they had borrowed from the manufactories of Messrs. Rust and Hoe and set up on two separate cars drawn by four horses. The butchers, in dress described as characteristic of their profession and mounted on prancing white horses, were also on hand. On one of their floats the skin of an ox had been so stuffed as to take on a life-like appearance and had been gaily decorated with ribbons and cockades. On another a butcher's stall had been erected where "sausages were manufactured to the great amusement of the people."

The cordwainers had made extensive and elegant preparations for the demonstration and on one of their floats two young ladies were busily engaged in binding shoes. The manufacturers of steam engines exhibited a perfect steam engine ("the smoke from the pipes ascended, the water wheels revolved"), and the cabinet makers had such splendid specimens of furniture that the *Advocate's* reporter found himself unable to describe them. The carvers and gilders were in the line with portraits of Jefferson and Lafayette in superb gilt frames; the tobacconists won the applause of the admiring crowd by distributing small plugs of tobacco; the saddlers and harness makers had mounts furnished with the most shining examples of their ware; the bookbinders boasted a float in the form of a mammoth book hauled by four sturdy horses;

and the chair makers graciously built on route a "Grecian Post Maple Chair."

The shouts and huzzas, the waving pennants, tricolored cockades and "star spangled banners," made for a great occasion. Only a small part of the throng could be accommodated about the reviewing stand where the venerable ex-President Monroe had the place of honor until the "chilly state of the atmosphere" compelled him to leave. There were fervid speeches and an ode written by Samuel Woodworth, printer, was sung to the tune of the *Marseillaise* with the accompaniment of the orchestra from the Park Theatre:

> Then swell the choral strain,
> To Hail the blest decree.
> Rejoice, rejoice, the Press shall reign
> And all the world be Free.

That night the various societies held commemorative banquets (a dinner was sent in to the inmates of the debtor's prison by the sympathetic delegates of the ninth ward), and a great concourse of workingmen foregathered at the Masonic Hall. After a sumptuous entertainment had served as prelude "for the enjoyment of the mental repast," a glowing panegyric was delivered on the success of the French revolutionary movement and the part played in it by workingmen.

"Move on then, mechanics and working men," the speaker of the evening declared in his eloquent peroration, "in your glorious career of mental independence, with republican education for your polar star, union and firmness your sheet anchor, and the day is not distant which shall crown your noble effort with victory, and your country shall stand redeemed from the poison of fashion and the canker worm of party— and in their place shall spring up the tree of pure republicanism, yielding the choice fruits of real equality of rights; then man shall be judged by his actions and not by his professions; by his usefulness to society as an industrious citizen and not by the texture of the garb which covers him."

The address was followed by toasts—fourteen formal toasts and thirty-one volunteer toasts—happily "interspersed with appropriate songs, odes and recitations." The enthusiastic diners toasted the workingmen of Paris, and the workingmen of New York; they drank to the memory of Jefferson and Lafayette, to Bolivar, to true democrats, universal education, free enquiry; they toasted "the Original Working Men—May they not oblique to the right or the left," and the "Simon Pures—May they not be frightened by the cries of Fanny Wrightism, Agrarianism or any other *ism*, but stick to true republicanism."

Forty-five toasts, as the bottles circulated and the workingmen cheered. "The greatest hilarity and unanimity," concludes the account of the *Working Man's Advocate* "characterized the proceedings of the evening, and the company separated at an early hour, much gratified with the manner in which they had been entertained."

The rapid growth and development of the trade societies led naturally to the movement for closer association in promoting their common aims. A precedent for such cooperation had been established by the Mechanics' Union of Trade Associations in Philadelphia, but as we have seen, this group had almost immediately become absorbed in politics. What the workingmen now sought in forming "trades' unions"—that is, unions of local trade societies that represented in modern terminology central trades councils—was a basis for joint economic activity.[1] The trades' union, in the words of the constitution of one of these new organizations, was a "compact, formed of Societies and Associations of Mechanics and Working Men, which, having discovered that they were unable to combat the numerous powers arrayed against them, united together for mutual protection."

The General Trades' Union of New York was the most important of

[1] The terminology of labor organization in this period is admittedly confusing. The "trade societies," as suggested in the text, were the equivalent of modern "trade unions," and the new "trades' unions" corresponded more nearly to today's "central trades councils" established in the cities by the A.F. of L. and the C.I.O. At this very time, however, the "trade societies" were beginning to be called "trade unions" although "trades' unions" were the association of the local societies.

One of the earliest examples of the use of union in the modern sense of the term, in a pamphlet published in 1836 which was called *Dialogue Between Strike and Steady*, had this interesting comment: "My objection to your Union is, that you wish to use the very compulsion, you will not yourselves endure."

these new central trades councils, and there were comparable organizations in Philadelphia, Boston, Baltimore, Washington, Cincinnati, Pittsburgh, Louisville and other manufacturing cities. Their number had grown to thirteen by 1836, with fifty-two associated societies in New York, fifty-three in Philadelphia, twenty-three in Baltimore, and sixteen in Boston.

The final coordinating step in this activity was taken in 1834 when the summons went out to establish a national organization embracing all trades. Representatives of local societies in New York, Brooklyn, Boston, Philadelphia, Poughkeepsie and Newark met in the first named city and formed the National Trades' Union. Its purposes were to advance the welfare of the laboring classes, promote the establishment of trades' unions in every part of the country, and publish such information as would be useful to mechanics and workingmen. In the light of the failure of the workingmen's parties, its leaders were determined that the new organization should not be drawn off into political activities. The workingmen "belonged to no party," one Massachusetts labor leader declared; "they were neither disciples of Jacksonism nor Clayism, Van Burenism nor Websterism, not any other ism but workeyism."

National organization of the workers was not to be really effective at this time. It was to wait upon the nationalizing of business in the years following the Civil War. But the attempt to form such a federation attests the strength and vitality of the labor movement of the 1830's. As the result of the zeal of local societies, city trades councils and the National Trades' Union, there were in the country as a whole an estimated 300,000 unionized workers. On a relative basis, so large a number of wage earners would not again be enrolled in union ranks for half a century. In New York, some two-thirds of all the city's workers were said to be members of one or another of its fifty-odd labor unions.

In increasingly active defense of their rights, trade union members did not hesitate either to threaten or actually go out on strike when their employers refused to meet what they felt were their legitimate demands. When the latter tried to hold down wages or bring in untrained workers at lower pay, there were turn-outs in almost every trade and in every city. Printers and weavers, tailors and coachmakers, masons and bookbinders walked out. The carpenters in New York earning $1.50 a day struck for $1.75 and having won it, promptly struck again for $2.

The girls working in New England cotton mills again went on strike. "One of the leaders mounted a pump," the *Boston Transcript* reported, "and made a flaming . . . speech on the rights of women and the iniquities of 'monied aristocracy' which produced a powerful effect upon her auditors, and they determined to have their own way, if they died for it." As in the first waves of strikes instigated by the original trade societies, such turn-outs were almost always peaceful, but they became so general that the business community became increasingly alarmed. Between 1833 and 1837 no less than 168 were recorded in contemporary newspapers.

As in later periods, the employers sought to attribute these disturbances not to labor's legitimate grievances, but to the activity of radical and subversive agitators, generally supposed to be foreigners. "I fear the elements of disorder are at work," a conservative New Yorker, Philip Hone, onetime mayor, noted in his diary; "the bands of Irish and other foreigners instigated by the mischievous councils of the trades union and other combinations of discontented men, are acquiring strength and importance which will ere long be difficult to quell." Whatever the workers' complaints (and Hone noted himself the tremendous increase in the cost of living), he felt that any strike, however orderly, was an "unlawful proceeding."

The demand of workers throughout the east for a ten-hour day came to a head during this exciting period in a concerted outbreak of strikes. There had been earlier agitation for such a reduction in the hours of work. It had been the background for the formation of the Mechanics' Union of Trade Associations in Philadelphia in 1827, and of the Workingmen's Party in New York two years later. But the workers were now ready to use their strongest weapon as a means of coercing employers to grant their demands.

"All men have a just right, derived from their creator," stated a resolution of the journeymen carpenters in Philadelphia, "to have sufficient time each day for the cultivation of their mind and for self-improvement; Therefore, resolved, that we think ten hours industriously imployed are sufficient for a day's labor."

On this same note demands were also made by New England workingmen for a shorter day and surprisingly enough found support from such a conservative paper as the *Boston Transcript*. "Let the mechanic's labor be over," it urged, "when he has wrought ten or twelve hours in the long days of summer, and he will be able to return to his family in season, and with sufficient vigour, to pass some hours in the instruction of his children, or in the improvement of his own mind."

In other periods of labor's long struggle for shorter hours, stress would be laid upon the ill effects of prolonged, exacting toil on the workers' health and well being, or upon the importance of spreading work to combat the danger of unemployment. In the 1830's, however, the emphasis upon time for self-education, which was considered so essential to enable the newly enfranchised laboring classes to fulfill their obligations as citizens, was a great deal more than merely a facile argument to bolster their cause. There is every evidence that the workers were deeply interested in education for themselves as well as for their children. The crowded workingmen audiences at the popular lyceum lectures of these years, the growing vogue for circulating libraries, and the insistent demand for free, public schools all attest a deep concern born of the idealistic belief that education alone could provide the basis for a successful democracy.

"We have been too long subjected," a circular of striking workingmen in Boston in 1835 stated, "to the odious, cruel, unjust and tyrannical system which compels the operative Mechanic to exhaust his physical and mental powers. . . . We have rights, and we have duties to perform as American citizens and members of society, which forbid us to dispose of more than Ten Hours for a day's work."

Such arguments did not, however, carry much weight with employers. The proposal for a ten-hour day, one newspaper declared, "strikes the very nerve of industry and good morals by dictating the hours of labour. . . . To be idle several of the most useful hours of the morning and evening will surely lead to intemperance and ruin." A statement published in the *Boston Courier* by a group of merchants and shipowners further emphasized the serious loss to the community in any reduction of the working day and deplored the "habits likely to be generated by the indulgence of idleness." However deeply grounded the real objection to shorter hours in its effect upon business profits, it was, indeed, this professed fear that leisure would undermine the workers' morals and foster intemperance, already noted in the attitude of employers in colonial New England, that became the chief stock in trade of the conservative opposition to any change in the traditional sun-up to sunset system.

The organized workingmen in city after city refused, however, to be persuaded by such arguments and stood their ground. Their universal demand was for a working day from six in the morning until six in the evening, with an hour off for breakfast and another for dinner. In Baltimore, the members of seventeen trades joined forces in a strike for this reform in 1833, and two years later the carpenters of Boston, with the support of masons, stonecutters and other workers in the building trades, walked-out with similar demands. Both of these movements failed. In Philadelphia, on the other hand, an even more widely organized and popularly supported strike was to win a resounding victory in 1835 that had wide reverberations.

It was initiated by the coal heavers and other common laborers but they were soon joined by cordwainers, handloom weavers, cigar makers, saddlers, printers and members of the building trades. A circular relating the experiences of the Boston workers had an electric effect in unifying those of Philadelphia, and strengthened their determination not to give in. A popular demonstration was staged in which workers of all trades paraded through the streets, with fife and drum, and banners inscribed "from 6 to 6."

"We marched to the public works," wrote their leader, John Ferral, a handloom weaver and fiery labor agitator, "and the workmen joined in with us. . . . Employment ceased, business was at a standstill, shirt sleeves were rolled up, aprons on, working tools in hand were the order of the day. Had the cannon of an invading enemy belched forth its challenge on our soil, the freemen of Philadelphia could not have shown a greater ardor for the contest; the blood-sucking aristocracy, they alone stood aghast; terror stricken, they thought the day of retribution was come, but no vengeance was sought or inflicted by the people for the wrongs they had suffered from their enemies."

The common council of the city was the first to give in, establishing a ten-hour day for all public servants. The master carpenters and master cordwainers followed, and other employers then quickly fell in line until the ten-hour day prevailed throughout the city. "The mechanics of

Philadelphia stood firm and true," Ferral wrote; "they conquered, because they were united and resolute in their actions. The presses which could not retard the progress of public opinion, nor divert it from its just objects, viz. the adoption of the ten-hour system . . . now proclaim the triumph of our bloodless revolution. . . ."

The movement spread to other parts of the country and in many instances won a corresponding success. Soon the ten-hour day had widely replaced, for artisans and mechanics, the former sun-up to sunset. In the factories that were being established for the New England textile industry, and in many other manufacturing industries, the work day was long to remain twelve hours and more. In some trades the gains of the 1830's were to be lost. But a very real victory had been won for the workers by their concerted stand in the strikes of Philadelphia and other cities. Moreover the Federal Government was soon to be induced to establish a ten-hour day for all public works. Congress had refused to take any notice of the frequent memorials addressed to it on the subject, but when striking shipwrights directly appealed to President Jackson in 1836, the system was installed at the Philadelphia navy yard. Four years later, Van Buren even more directly admitted his debt to the workingmen for their political support by an executive order which established ten hours as the work day on all government projects.

The employers held out as long as they could in combatting the workers' demands both for higher wages and a shorter working day. They continued whenever possible to undermine their employes' bargaining power by drawing upon cheaper sources of labor. But where skilled artisans and mechanics were concerned, they found it increasingly difficult to maintain their position. The craft unions succeeded in enforcing a closed shop which tied the employers' hands. Through public cards listing as "unfair" any journeyman who did not join a union and designating as "foul" any establishment where an "unfair man" was given work, they largely controlled the labor market. This was not of course always true, but the records of the time reveal an unexpected power on the part of the organized workers in the skilled trades.

Under these circumstances the employers turned more and more to mutual protective associations which were prepared to act together in opposing "every injurious combination" of the workingmen. In New York a group of Employers, Curriers and Leather Dealers took up arms against the General Trades' Union and mutually agreed that they would not employ "any man who is known to be a member of that or any other society which has for its object the direction of terms or prices for which workmen shall engage themselves." In Philadelphia the master carpenters took the lead in calling for formation of an Anti-Trades' Union Association. A set of resolutions was adopted declaring the trades' union to be arbitrary, unjust, mischievous and a powerful engine of the leveling system that would reduce masters to the status of journeymen. Employers had every right, it was maintained, to make whatever contract with their employes they chose without the interference of any workingmen's society.

When the employer associations were again unable to hold out against the labor societies, court action was once more in order. The drive to break up unions as conspiracies in restraint of trade was vigorously renewed, and as in the opening years of the century, the employers found willing allies among conservative members of the bench.

The case of the *People* v. *Fisher,* decided in the New York Supreme Court in 1835, was a first important demonstration in this period that the opposition of the courts to labor unions had not changed. A society of journeymen cordwainers in Geneva, New York, was prosecuted for conspiring to raise wages and thereby, as claimed by the plaintiffs, committing an act injurious to trade and commerce and a misdemeanor under existing laws. The presiding judge ruled in the employers' favor. On the theory that the interests of society were best served when the price of labor was left to regulate itself, he declared that in combining to raise wages the cordwainers were working a public injury because "a conspiracy for such an object is against the spirit of the common law."

"Competition is the life of trade," the decision concluded. "If the defendants cannot make coarse boots for less than one dollar per pair, let them refuse to do so; but let them not directly or indirectly undertake to say that others shall not do the work for a less price. . . . The interference of the defendants was unlawful; its tendency is not only to individual oppression, but to public inconvenience and embarrassment."

The effect of this decision was to encourage other employers to seek to suppress the trade societies even though they did not engage in strikes, and when the courts continued to follow a flagrantly anti-labor policy, a storm of protest arose among workingmen and their sympathizers. It came to a head in New York after a further case in 1836 where the presiding judge strongly charged the jury to find a society of journeymen tailors guilty of conspiracy in restraint of trade.

"They were condemned," William Cullen Bryant wrote in vehement defense of the tailors in the *New York Evening Post*, "because they had determined not to work for the wages offered them! Can any thing be imagined more abhorrent. . . . If this is not Slavery, we have forgotten its definition. Strike the right of associating for the sale of labor from the privileges of a freeman, and you may as well at once bind him to a master or ascribe him to the soil. . . ."

The outraged labor leaders of New York distributed throughout the city circulars, inscribed with a coffin, that called upon all workingmen to attend court on the day set for sentencing the convicted tailors.

"On Monday, June 6, 1836," the circulars read, "these Freemen are to receive their sentence, to gratify the hellish appetites of the Aristocracy. On Monday, the Liberty of the Workingmen will be interred! Judge Edwards is to chant the requiem! Go! Go! every Freeman, every Workingman, and hear the melancholy sound of the earth on the Coffin of Equality! Let the court-room, the City Hall—yea, the whole Park, be filled with Mourners!" The crowd which actually turned out does not appear to have reached the hoped-for proportions and it was entirely peaceful. A week later, however, after the tailors had been duly sentenced, another mass meeting was held which drew some 27,000 persons and the offending judge was dramatically burned in effigy.

The reaction against these trials was in fact so strong that juries could not fail to be influenced by it, and in two other conspiracy cases the same summer verdicts of not guilty were returned. Finally, in 1842, Chief Justice Shaw of the Massachusetts Supreme Court rendered an important decision in the case of *Commonwealth* v. *Hunt*, which appeared to provide a firm basis for the legality of unions.

The case was that of the Journeymen Bootmakers' Society of Boston, whose members had agreed not to work for any person employing a journeyman who did not belong to their organization. Chief Justice Shaw stated that the manifest purpose of the society was to induce all those engaged in the same occupation to become members, and that this could not be considered unlawful. Nor could he see that in attempting to accomplish it by refusing to work for any employer who engaged a journeyman not a member, the bootmakers were employing criminal means. He cited as a possible parallel a society whose members might undertake to promote the highly laudable cause of temperance by agreeing not to work for anyone who employed a user of ardent spirits. In other words, agreement for common action to achieve a lawful object was not necessarily a criminal conspiracy. "The legality of such an association," the decision concluded, "will . . . depend upon the means to be used for its accomplishment. . . ."

So far as the labor societies might still have to prove that the means they adopted to attain their ends were in every case lawful, this decision was not a complete victory for labor. It had, indeed, turned upon certain technicalities in the indictment. But both union organization and even the principle of the closed shop had nevertheless received substantial support. It would not be until a much later period that labor again found itself on the legal defensive, fighting renewed conspiracy charges under the anti-trust laws and the arbitrary use of injunctions against strikes and boycotts.

In the ten-hour movement, the revolt against the conspiracy laws, and in their strikes, the workingmen of the 1830's had the full and active backing of their general trades' unions. These organizations were ready to render whatever assistance they could, both in supporting the local societies in their demands and in extending financial assistance when workers went out on strike. In New York, Philadelphia, Boston—wherever general trades' unions had been formed—there was close cooperation among the workers as a result of this leadership. Monthly dues were paid in to the central organization, making possible the creation of a strike fund, and in many instances, additional union appropriations were made to aid the members of other societies out on strike. Occasionally such aid was extended from one city to another. When a delegation of Philadelphia bookbinders appealed to New York's General Trades' Union for aid in February, 1836, a resolution favoring such action was at once adopted. It called upon all members to support "their fellow mechanics who are at this inclement season driven to a stand for their rights against aristocratical tyranny." Varying sums of money were sent to the book-binders not only by unions in New York but also by those of Washington, Baltimore, Albany and Newark.

The National Trades' Union, which had met first in 1834 and held conventions in the next two succeeding years, did not have the close organization of the general trades' unions. It remained little more than an annual conference which debated labor issues and occasionally addressed memorials to Congress—on the ten-hour day, prison labor or public lands. It also went on record, although refusing to enter upon direct political action, in support of many of the reforms being promoted by the Jackson Democrats. It attacked "this American banking system, this rag-money system, this sysem of legalized monopolies which makes the rich richer and the poor poorer." It was in no sense a class conscious movement, however. "Our object in the formation of the Trades' Union," declared its organ, *The Union*, on April 21, 1836, ". . . was not to create a feeling of enmity against the non-producers; . . . [but] to raise in the estimation of themselves and others, those who are the producers of the necessaries and luxuries of life."

Perhaps the greatest contribution of the National Trades' Union to the cause of labor was that of bringing together the workingmen's leaders from various parts of the country. It gave them a sense of common purpose and of support for their activities which encouraged them, as in the case of the ten-hour movement, to keep up their local struggles for labor's rights.

John Ferral, the aggressive handloom weaver who led the successful ten-hour strike in Philadelphia, was a prominent figure at union conventions. No one more strongly urged direct economic action by the labor societies or warned more often of the danger of their being diverted from their main purposes by political blandishments. "The office holders and office seekers of all parties have tried to lure us into the meshes of their nets," he wrote, "but experience came to our aid, and, coy as the young deer, we shied off from their advances; we felt grateful for their proffered aid, but told them 'we knew our own rights, and knowing dared maintain them.'" His initiative and energy were perhaps the most important factors in the organization of the Philadelphia General Trades' Union. He served as chairman of one of its original organizing committees, was constantly involved in its activities, and references to his "spirited addresses" run through all the proceedings of the union.

Another Philadelphia delegate was William English, for a time secretary of the General Trades' Union. He was a journeyman shoemaker, and both a radical and highly erratic champion of the workers' cause. His critics declared he did not have an idea that he had not borrowed or stolen from someone else, but his impassioned addresses always held popular attention.

The principal representative of the New England workingmen was Charles Douglas, one of the founders of the New England Association of Farmers, Mechanics and Other Workingmen, and editor of the *New England Artisan*. His opposition to political activity, although the New England Association had become directly involved in state campaigns in Massachusetts, was no less pronounced than that of John Ferral. His special interest was the status of the factory operatives in the textile mills, and he was one of the first spokesmen for this class of workers.

Attending at least one National Trades' Union meetings was his co-worker in this cause, Seth Luther, the so-called "Traveling Agent" of the *Artisan* and a prototype of many later labor agitators. He was one of the most picturesque of the leaders of this period, a tall, lanky, tobacco-chewing Yankee, habitually wearing a bright green jacket, who toured through the factory towns calling upon the workers to defend their rights. "You cannot raise one part of the community above another unless you stand on the bodies of the poor," he repeatedly declared, and in support of this thesis, he issued a stream of pamphlets depicting the harsh life of the women and children working in the cotton mills under the lash of factory managers. His style was grim, sardonic, highly colored. "While music floats from quivering strings through the perfumed and adorned apartments . . . of the rich," Luther wrote, "the nerves of the poor woman and child, in the cotton mills, are quivering with almost *dying agony*, from *excessive labor* to support this splendor."

The first president of the National Trades' Union was Ely Moore. Originally a student of medicine, he had abandoned the profession to become a journeyman printer, and then entered actively into the labor movement. He suffered from ill health, which was eventually to force his retirement from the political scene, but not before he had proved himself both an able organizer and effective administrator in union activities. Tall, handsome, with curly black hair brushed back over a broad forehead, invariably well dressed and habitually carrying an ivory-headed cane, he was possessed, according to contemporaries, with a thrilling power of eloquence. He headed the General Trades' Union in New York before taking over his post in the National Trades' Union, and in the former capacity had sounded the keynote of the developing labor movement in addressing the workingmen as Pioneers in the Great Cause.

"To you, then, gentlemen, as the *actual* representatives of the Mechanic interests throughout the country," Moore declared, "the eyes of thousands and thousands are turned; for should the experiment succeed here, and the expectations of the friends of the 'Union' be realized, other Unions of a kindred character will be formed, in every section. . . ." But should they fail, he then went on to warn his audience, "the haughty aristocrats of the land will hail the event with exulting hearts and hellish satisfaction."

Moore soon made his position in labor circles the springboard for entry into active politics, and with the support of the unions and Tammany Hall, he was sent to Congress the same year that saw him chosen head of the National Trades' Union. There he won national prominence as a spokesman for the interests of labor and played a notable part in introducing the various memorials addressed to Congress by the union. Whenever he spoke he seems to have commanded rapt attention for his pleas in behalf of workingmen's rights and his vehement attacks upon "the heartless cupidity of the privileged few."

During the aftermath of the popular excitement aroused in New York by the conspiracy trial of the journeymen tailors, he rose on one occasion in April, 1836, to defend labor under unusually dramatic circumstances. A representative from South Carolina had warned of a possible workingmen's insurrection. Although he was so ill that he had to steady himself by leaning on his cane, Moore addressed his audience in a ringing voice that reached to every corner of the House. How could the interests and safety of the state be plotted against, he asked peremptorily, by a group composing three-fourths of the state? "Sir," he declared, glaring at the Speaker as his audience listened intently and one southern congressman was heard to murmur that the high priest of revolution was singing his swan song, "there is much greater danger that capital will unjustly appropriate to itself the avails of labor, than that labor will unlawfully seize upon capital."

"My eye was fixed upon him," wrote a reporter describing the scene for the *Democratic Review;* "I saw him grow paler than ever; till a deadly hue swept over his face; his hands were arrested in the air—he grasped at emptiness—a corpse seemed to stand with outstretched hands before the agitated crowd—his eyes were closed—he tottered, and amid the rush and exclamations of the whole house, fell back insensible into the arms of one of his friends."

Moore recovered from this attack of illness but he would not again address the House. His friends felt that he was in too poor health to undergo the strain that public speaking imposed upon one of his excitable, nervous temperament. But his oration went rapidly through four editions and played its part in arresting the drive to outlaw unions by court action. Public opinion was more and more swinging to their support. "What but a general revolt of all the laboring classes is to be gained," William Cullen Bryant asked in the *New York Evening Post,* "by these wanton and unprovoked attacks upon their rights?"

The labor movement of these years cannot be compared with that of a century later. It grew out of conditions in American society that still had only a remote parallel with those of a period in which the great mass of workingmen are wage earners in mass production industries. The members of the early labor societies were, as we have seen, largely mechanics and artisans, relatively independent, who did not like to think of themselves as belonging to a permanent and distinct wage earning class.

In considering contemporary divisions in American society, the lines they saw were those between aristocracy and democracy, between the rich and the poor, rather than between employers and employes. They were greatly aroused, as stated in an address of the New England Association, by "the low estimation in which useful labour is held by many whose station in society enable them to give the tone to public opinion." They resented the trend whereby all those who could, sought to find some means of living without hard work and condemned the more use-

ful and industrious portion of the community to a life of constant toil—
"stripped of the better share of their earnings, holding a subordinate, if
not degraded situation in society, and frequently despised by the very
men, and women and children who live at ease upon the fruits of their
labour." The dignity of labor, and the respect due workingmen, were as
much the concern of the labor unions of the 1830's as improvement in
actual working conditions.

Whatever may be said of the high purpose of the labor unions of the
1830's, and whatever progress they made in achieving both their broader
and more immediate aims, their days were numbered. In 1837 the
prosperity that had provided the background for their growth and ac-
complishments came to a sudden end. The bubble of speculation was
rudely punctured. As prices plunged precipitately downward, hard
times again swept over the entire nation. Trade and commerce dried up,
manufacturing sharply declined, and business stagnated in the formerly
prosperous towns and cities of both the Atlantic seaboard and the west.

The workingmen again faced what depression has always meant for
labor—declining wages and unemployment. When the alternative to
work was starvation for themselves and their families, they deserted the
unions as they had in 1819 for fear of employer retaliation, and did not
dare strike to protect the gains they had won when things were going
well. With few exceptions, the journeymen societies that had seemed so
powerful completely folded up. They were crushed by economic circumstance, and in their collapse their newspapers and their federations
also disappeared almost overnight. The depression of 1837 brought the
emerging labor movement to a halt, as that eighteen years earlier had
broken up the original trade societies. Unionism would not regain a
comparable measure of strength and vitality for another half century.

Had organized labor survived this financial and economic panic, its
subsequent history might have followed a quite different course. For
strong unions would perhaps have been able to cope with the new needs
and new problems confronting labor when the full impact of the industrial revolution made itself felt in American society. Its long shadow
was falling over the land in the 1830's and the new class of factory operatives was constantly growing. The skilled workers already organized
were prepared to cooperate with these weaker wage earners, and they
could have helped to promote at this early stage of industrialization the

establishment of effective unions among the unskilled. But this was not to be. As the steady expansion of manufactures tended to depress the wage-earning class, labor failed to develop for the workers as a whole any program that could successfully uphold their interests.

V: THE IMPACT OF
INDUSTRIALISM

IN THE COURSE of his American tour in 1842, Charles Dickens visited Lowell, Massachusetts where the new textile manufacturers of New England had established one of the country's first factory towns. The young women and girls who made up most of the working force appeared to him as paragons of virtue—happy, contented and exemplary in their conduct. With their neat and serviceable bonnets, warm cloaks and shawls, "they were all well dressed, but not to my thinking above their station; . . . from all the crowd I saw in the different factories that day, I cannot recall or separate one face that gave me a painful impression."

The English traveler also admired the well-ordered rooms in the factories, some of them with plants growing in the windows, and the fresh air, cleanliness and comfort; he was impressed with the boarding houses where the young women lived under careful chaperonage, and he was particularly struck with what he reported as three startling facts: there were joint-stock pianos in many of the houses, nearly all of the young ladies subscribed to circulating libraries, and a magazine was published—the *Lowell Offering*—that was entirely made up of stories and articles by the factory operatives. Gazing happily upon this industrial paradise, Dickens compared it with the manufacturing centers of England and earnestly begged his countrymen "to pause and reflect upon the difference between this town and those great haunts of misery."

Although it could also have been pointed out, even in 1842, that the factory girls worked incredibly long hours, were badly overcrowded in their boarding houses, and found their lives wholly ordered and controlled by the paternalistic factory owners, the picture that the enthusiastic Dickens drew of Lowell was not wholly out of keeping with the facts. Other visitors confirmed his general impressions. They too wrote

73

of the pleasant atmosphere, of the cultural opportunities of circulating libraries and lecture rooms, and of the gay appearance of the young ladies, not only with neat bonnets over the carefully curled ringlets of their hair, but wearing silk stockings and carrying parasols. Lowell may not have been amusing as the French traveler, Michael Chevalier, wrote, but it was "clean, decent, peaceful and sober."

In these early stages of the industrial revolution, at least some parts of the United States seemed to have escaped the more unlovely aspects of its advent in Europe. The Massachusetts capitalists who established the first textile mills, wanted to prevent the oppression of the workers that had so notoriously resulted from the development of the factory system abroad. They intended to draw their labor supply from the New England farming population, to a very great extent young women and girls, and attractive conditions helped them to secure the type of workers they wanted. In the Rhode Island mills, where whole families were induced to move to town with husband, wife and children all playing their part in tending the looms and spindles, the situation was quite different. Factory hands were callously exploited. The idea behind Lowell, however, was virtually that of a female boarding school, except that the young women worked in the mills rather than at their studies.

Everything possible was done to safeguard their health, and even more particularly, their morals. They had to live in the boarding houses, where they were under strict supervision and the doors were closed at 10 P. M. They were expected to attend church. Not only was discharge an immediate consequence of immodesty, profanity or dancing, to say nothing of more serious lapses from morality, but insofar as male workers were concerned, the Lowell Manufacturing Company stated that it would not "continue to employ any person who shall be wanting in proper respect to the females employed by the company, or who shall smoke within the company's premises, or be guilty of inebriety."

The long hours of work were long but not as oppressive as they might appear. Tending the looms was not so arduous as other types of factory work were to become, and the young ladies had frequent opportunities to rest, to read, to talk among themselves, and to water the plants on the window sills. After paying for their board and lodging, they seldom had more than $2 a week left out of their wages, but for members of farm families for whom any cash income was almost unknown, even this small sum seemed like riches. It generally went into the bank and there was a time when the deposits of the Lowell girls were said to average as much as $500.

The most important distinction between conditions in this early period and later years, however, was that the workers still did not in any sense consider themselves permanently employed. Most of the young women came in from the country to work at Lowell for only the few years necessary to save up money to get married, or enough to go out to Ohio and other parts of the new west as schoolteachers. Moreover, if they did not like the work, or should be laid off in slack times, they could easily return to their farm homes. They were neither firmly attached to the mills nor wholly dependent upon them.

The relatively happy circumstances of this life did not last, however, for very long. Far-reaching changes were already well underway at the time of Dickens' visit to Lowell. As competition increased in the textile industry, the benevolent paternalism of the millowners gave way to stricter controls which had nothing to do with the well-being of the workers. Wages were reduced, the hours of work lengthened, and the equivalent of the speed-up was introduced into factory processes. For a work day from 11½ to 13 hours, making up an average week of 75 hours, the women operatives were generally earning less than $1.50 a week (exclusive of board) by the late 1840's, and they were being compelled to tend four looms whereas in the 1830's they had only taken care of two. When the manager of one mill at Holyoke, Massachusetts, found his hands "languorous" because they had breakfasted, he ordered them to come before breakfast. "I regard my work-people," an agent at another factory said, "just as I regard my machinery. So long as they can do my work for what I choose to pay them, I keep them, getting out of them all I can."

Embittered complaints began to take the place of earlier satisfaction as these conditions grew steadily worse. "These ladies have been imposed upon egregiously by the aristocratic and offensive employers, assuming to be their lords and masters," wrote the *Lynn Record*. Orestes Brownson, radical friend of labor, declared that "the great mass wear out their health, spirits and morals without becoming one whit better off." In the *Voice of Industry*, a new labor newspaper devoted to the cause of mill workers, there were frequent attacks upon the policies that the employers were following.

"Your factory system is worse by far than that of Europe," stated an open letter in this journal addressed to Abbott Lawrence. "You furnish your operatives with no more healthy sleeping-apartments than the cellars and garrets of the English poor. . . . The keepers are compelled to allow . . . but one room for six persons and generally crowd twelve and sometimes sixteen females into the same hot, ill-ventilated attic. . . . You shut up the operatives two or three hours longer a day in your factory prisons than is done in Europe. . . . You allow them but half an hour to eat their meals. . . . You compel them to stand so long at the machinery . . . that varicose veins, dropsical swelling of the feet and limbs, and prolapsus uter, diseases that end only with life, are not rare but common occurrences."

The factory girls themselves more and more resented "the yoke which has been prepared for us," and tried to combat the reductions in wages and increase in work. Even in the 1830's, as we have seen, they had experimented with strikes, and now a decade later they pledged themselves not to accept additional looms without wage increases and called for shorter working hours. But they could make no headway, and as a consequence began to return to their farm homes. The so-called "slavers"—long, low black wagons which cruised about the countryside as far afield as Vermont and New Hampshire—could no longer recruit mill hands with promises of easy work and high wages that were known to be false. The New England farm girls were quitting the mills.

Their place was taken by a new class of workers even less able to protect their interests. A rising tide of immigration had by mid-century made available a great reservoir of Irish and German girls, and some French-Canadians, who had no other alternative than to accept work in the mills no matter what the wages or hours. Conditions grew worse rather than better under these circumstances. The infusion of cheap immigrant labor, as a committee of the Massachusetts legislature noted in 1850, was causing "an entire modification and depression of the state of society in and about manufacturing places."

While the textile trade provides a striking example of what happened to working conditions with increasing industrialization, the same thing was taking place in other trades. The Lynn shoemakers had enjoyed a high degree of independence in the 1830's with their own work shops and the opportunity to fall back on farming or fishing should trade fall off. "When the spring opened," read one perhaps too idyllic account of a worker's life, "the horizon of his hopes expanded. Less clothing and fuel were needed. The clam banks discounted more readily; haddock could be got at Swampscott so cheap that the price wasn't worth quoting. The boys could dig dandelions. . . . Then if the poor man had his little 'spring pig' that he had kept through the winter, 'pork and dandelions' were no small item in the bill of fare while 'greens' lasted." But the masters steadily tightened their control over manufacturing and wages were reduced and paid in store orders rather than cash. The shoemakers gradually found themselves forced from their own work shops, from their fishing and farming in off hours, into the new factories with whose machine processes they could no longer compete.

In the pages of *The Awl*, a journeymen shoemakers' paper, resentment was repeatedly expressed against manufacturers who pretended to pay the workers a living wage but "did by other means reduce them to degradation and the loss of that self-respect which had made the mechanics and laborers the pride of the world." The protesting shoemakers of Lynn called upon their fellow artisans in the larger cities to take concerted action to demonstrate "that we are not menials or the humble subjects of a foreign despot, but free, American citizens." Nothing came of this agitation. A way of life was inevitably passing, and the shoemakers as well as the textile workers were inextricably caught in the toils of the factory system.

The printers' trade was also being revolutionized by the invention of new presses and the use of steam power. These developments not only tended to throw men out of work and to depress wages, but encouraged the transfer of control over their trade from the printers themselves to outside management. A highly independent profession was transformed through the widened gulf between employer and employe. Their long record of organization helped the printers, and they were to continue to enforce union rules governing apprentices and working conditions with considerable success, but they were facing new forces that made it increasingly difficult to maintain either their wages or their general status.

Among other trades, the introduction of power looms worsened conditions for the hand-loom weavers whose weekly wages, never very

high, were virtually halved by the mid-forties; the relatively well paid
journeymen hatters suffered a decline in their pay, between 1835 and
1845, from about $12 to $8 a week, and the cabinetmakers found themselves compelled to work longer and longer hours to earn as much as $5
a week in the face of competition from the wholesale production of
German immigrants who were said to "work rapidly, badly and for almost nothing."

The greater supply of cheap labor, indeed, was as important as the
introduction of machinery in cutting wages, not only in the New England
cotton mills but throughout industry. In the first half century of our
national history, approximately one million immigrants entered the
country, but in the single decade from 1846 to 1855, the total was almost
three million. Famine in Ireland and suppression of the revolutionary
uprisings on the continent accounted for a swelling stream of workers
crossing the Atlantic, and there was an increasing proportion of mechanics and laborers, as contrasted with farmers, among these new-
comers. They tended to settle in the east, drawn to the rapidly growing
cities and manufacturing centers, and were available for all kinds of
work, more often unskilled than skilled, at wages greatly reduced from
anything which native artisans and mechanics considered essential for
decent living conditions. Immigration, that is, was perhaps for the first
time providing a labor surplus which counteracted the effect of cheap
land and the frontier in drawing workers off from the eastern states. A
pattern that was to become even clearer in the 1880's and 1890's, when
the trend of immigration showed still greater gains and a further shift
toward the ignorant, unskilled and poverty-stricken peasants of southeastern Europe, was already outlined in the 1850's.

The general conditions among workers in the seaboard cities graphically revealed the effect of such immigration. Two separate estimates
of a workingman's family budget in the early 1850's, the one in the *New
York Times* and the other in the *New York Tribune,* gave a minimum for essential expenditures, for rent, food, fuel and clothing, that
amounted to approximately $11 a week. "Have I made the working-
man's comforts too high?" asked Horace Greeley in commenting on this
budget. "Where is the money to pay for amusements, for ice-creams,
his puddings, his trips on Sunday up or down the river in order to get
some fresh air?" But except for those in the building trades, whose rela-

tively high wages just about met this budget, there were few urban workers who even approached it—not the factory operatives, not the workers, men and women, employed in the clothing trades, and most assuredly not the common laborers. Shortly before publishing his budget, Greeley had actually estimated that "the average earnings of those who lived by simple labor in our city—embracing at least two thirds of our population—scarcely, if at all, exceed one dollar per week for each person subsisting thereon."

Contemporary descriptions afford ample evidence of the part that inadequate wages played in creating the slum areas of such cities as New York, Philadelphia and Boston. Over-crowding, lack of sanitary conveniences, dirt, filth and disease already stood in stark and glaring contrast to the comfortable, spacious, well-furnished homes of the wealthy. There was in New York a cellar population, estimated to total over 18,000, crowded into damp, unlighted, ill-ventilated dens with anywhere from six to twenty persons—men, women and children—living in a single room. In the notorious Five Points, hundreds of families were squeezed into ramshackle buildings, their only sanitary conveniences outside privies. Boston had equally depressing and unhealthful slums. "This whole district," a Committee on Internal Health reported in 1849, "is a perfect hive of human beings without comforts and mostly without common necessaries: in many cases huddled together like brutes without regard to sex, age or a sense of decency, grown men and women sleeping together in the same apartment, and sometimes wife, husband, brothers and sisters in the same bed."

The situation that Thomas Jefferson had foreseen when he spoke of the mobs of great cities adding just as much to pure government "as sores do to the strength of the human body," appeared to have developed. The workers themselves began to protest against immigration as creating "a numerous poor and dependent population." The abject condition they had known in their own countries, the *Voice of Industry* declared, made such immigrants all the more helpless victims of exploitation in the United States, satisfied to work "fourteen and sixteen hours per day for what capital sees fit to give them."

The harsh effect of industrialism and the mounting tide of immigration served in large measure to prevent any reconsolidation of the ranks of labor. The workingmen did not resume on a comparable scale either the political or trade union activity that had had such dynamic drive before the panic of 1837. Baffled by the new forces let loose by industrialism, they seemed to be frantically seeking means of escape. Organization was almost forgotten. Instead, the workers became involved in the more general reform movements of the day that reflected a middle-class, humanitarian revolt against the changes being wrought in American society by machines and factories. The 1840's were pre-eminently a period of vague, idealistic, utopian reforms, each one of which was held forth by its zealous advocates as a complete panacea for all the evils of the day. Communism and land reform, abolition and feminism, temperance and vegetarianism . . . there was no end to the agitation and propaganda which marked the ferment of social change.

The reformers themselves were forever seeking to win the support of workingmen for their various causes. They descended in droves upon every meeting or convention that might be summoned to consider labor issues, and sometimes succeeded in wholly dominating it. The first formal meeting of the New England Workingmen's Association in 1844, called to inaugurate a revived ten-hour movement, had only a scattering of delegates from labor societies in comparison with the brilliant array of reformers. George Ripley, of Brook Farm; Horace Greeley and Albert Brisbane; Wendell Phillips and William Lloyd Garrison; Charles A. Dana, William H. Channing, and Robert Owen were all on hand, eagerly seeking to win new disciples. The meeting was thrown open in sweeping enthusiasm "to all those interested in the elevation of the producing classes and Industrial Reform and the extinction of slavery and servitude in all their forms." However generous the impulses behind such activity, they could not have been more vague and diffusive.

The imagination of some of the workers during this period was caught by the glowing promises of the "Associationists." Through the formation of independent, socialistic communities, all of whose members were working toward a common end, the Associationists promised an escape from the consequences of the industrial revolution and actually hoped to recreate the simpler society of an earlier day. This idea was primarily derived from the utopian socialism of Charles Fourier, with its elaborate system of phalanxes, designed both to dignify labor and increase production, which had been introduced to America by Albert Brisbane. In 1840 Brisbane published "The Social Destiny of Man," a detailed exposition of Fourier's program, but far more important in spreading the gospel of Association were his writings in the column which Horace Greeley placed at his disposal in the *New York Tribune.*

Greeley was, indeed, to do everything possible to promote this tempered form of socialism as one phase of his general support for the interests of workingmen. An idealistic Yankee, who had come to New York as a farm boy to enter the printing trade, he was a familiar figure at labor gatherings and his round moon face, with its fringe of whiskers, was known to thousands of workers. "Why should those by whose toil ALL commodities and luxuries are produced or made available," he asked, "enjoy so scanty a share of them?" He realized perhaps more than any of his contemporaries among public men the effects of the exploitation of the workingmen resulting from the industrial revolution, and he felt that any lasting betterment for society depended upon their organization. He not only opened the columns of the *Tribune* to Albert Brisbane but ran a weekly letter dealing with socialism from a European correspondent—Karl Marx.

Fourierism, in any event, won many converts through the *Tribune* and even before Brisbane laid out his own plan for a North American phalanx, a group of workingmen launched the Sylvania phalanx in western Pennsylvania. Other communities quickly followed on the heels of this experiment and even the idealistic founders of Brook Farm, whose colony represented an intellectual revolt against the spirit of the times, were persuaded to adopt the form and organization of a Fourierite community. In all, some forty phalanxes, with perhaps 8,000 members, were established during the 1840's.

They were not a success. One by one they fell by the wayside, the North American phalanx itself ceasing operations in 1854. Community living and community production did not prove practical. Nor did they in any way meet the needs of labor. In spite of the enthusiastic propaganda, the answer to industrialization did not lie in an attempt to escape from it. The hopeful dreams of the Associationists foundered on the rock of economic and social forces that could not be so easily withstood or diverted.

As the phalanxes collapsed, some attempt was made to provide a partial substitute in the interests of the workingmen by establishing both consumers' and producers' cooperatives. "The direction and profits of industry," the proponents of cooperation declared, "must be kept in the hands of the producers." In Massachusetts, in New York and in other parts of the country, protective unions were organized which undertook to set up self-employing workshops whose products were to be sold at wholesale prices for the benefit of the union's members. There were other instances of cooperatives such as the Journeymen Molders' Union Foundry, which established a plant near Cincinnati, the Boston Tailors' Associative Union, and a Shirt Sewers' Cooperative Union Depot in New York. But whether consumers' or producers' cooperatives, these early ventures were no more successful than the phalanxes. Various factors accounted for their failure, but basically the conditions of American life, perhaps the American temperament, did not provide a fertile soil for the growth of cooperation. They lent themselves rather to competition and individualistic striving to make the most of the opportunities a young and growing country afforded. Cooperation was to be revived again and again in the future and to have some limited success, but neither in the 1840's nor later could it provide any real solution to the problems confronting the laboring classes.

Another and more significant reform which won widespread labor support was a new agrarianism. The original workingmen's parties had been in part wrecked by the internal friction and external attacks resulting from their flirtation with the radical agrarian ideas of Thomas Skidmore, but the new revelation did not involve the assault upon all property which Skidmore had launched so vigorously in "The Rights of Man to Property." The agrarianism of the 1840's and 1850's was far more moderate. Its thesis was that the people as a whole had a natural right to the existing public lands, and that they should be equally distributed in farm lots of 160 acres which would be both inalienable and exempt from seizure for debt. Through such a program, it was maintained, the workingmen would be assured of his just share in the national wealth and be freed from his complete dependence on the masters of capital.

The high priest of this reform was George Henry Evans. After the dissolution of the Workingmen's Party in New York, he had retired in 1836 because of ill-health to a farm in New Jersey, and only emerged with his new message in 1844. Re-establishing the *Working Man's Advocate*, his old paper, he dedicated himself to agrarianism and in season

and out demanded action by Congress to promote his program. "This is
the first measure to be accomplished," he wrote in the *Advocate*, "and
it is as idle to attempt any great reforms without that as it is to go to work
without tools. Place the surplus mechanics on their own land in the west
in Rural Townships with their large Public Square and Public Hall in
the center of each, leaving full employment to those who remain in the
cities. . . ." There was hardly a labor meeting at which he did not
appear to present this plan, wholly disregarding the practical question
of whether the workers, even if they could, would want suddenly to
pull up stakes and take up farming in the distant West.

The climax of his activities was the establishment of the National
Reform Association in 1845. His earlier experience had led him to distrust third party political action, and the purpose of the new organization was to demand support for his program from all candidates for
public office as the condition for securing the workingmen's votes. The
strategy was that which the American Federation of Labor was to adopt
almost half a century later: reward your friends, punish your enemies.
Evans hoped to make it effective by demonstrating that the agrarians
meant business. "We, whose names are annexed, desirous of restoring
to man his Natural Right to Land," the membership pledge of the National Reform Association stated, "do solemnly agree that we will not
vote for any man, for any legislative office, who will not pledge himself,
in writing, to use all the influence of his station, if elected, to prevent
all further traffic in the Public Lands of the states and of the United
States, and to cause them to be laid out in Farms and Lots for the free
and exclusive use of actual settlers."

Although support for this program was by no means limited to the
workingmen, their close ties with the National Reform Association were
clearly revealed in the membership of the original central committee.
It included four printers, two cordwainers, a chair maker, a carpenter,
a blacksmith, a bookbinder, a machinist, a picture frame maker, and a
clothier. Associated with Evans, moreover, were such trade union leaders of the 1830's as John Commerford, who had been president of the
General Trades' Union in New York, and John Ferral, leader of the
Philadelphia Trades' Union. The new labor journals, re-emerging after
the panic of 1837, almost universally made land reform one of their
basic demands.

The movement was strongly opposed by capitalists and employers in the eastern states. "By your policy you strike down our great manufacturing interests," one of their spokesmen declared in Congress, ". . . You turn thousands of our manufacturers and labourers out of employment. . . . You depreciate the value of real estate. You make a bid for our population, by holding out inducements for our productive labourers to leave their old homes, under the seductive promise of land for nothing, and railroads without taxes, thereby decreasing our population and consequently increasing the burden of those that remain in the old states." But farmers and other settlers in the West joined forces with the eastern workingmen in supporting the movement. With its alluring slogan of "Vote Yourself a Farm," the National Reform Association appeared to be making substantial headway.

The workingmen of the 1840's were not to profit from its program and its relevancy to their relief from industrial oppression may also be questioned. The movement instituted by Evans, however, was to lead directly to passage of the Homestead Act in 1862. While it did not provide for either inalienability or exemption from seizure for debt, it granted free land to all bona fide settlers.

Land reform was closer to the interests of the workingmen than many of the mid-century humanitarian movements, but the most immediately practical undertaking was the renewed drive for the ten-hour day. While it had been widely won for artisans and mechanics in the 1830's, factory employes, as we have seen, were not generally affected. The new movement was primarily for the relief of this new group of wage earners. Unlike the earlier drive it did not take the form of trade union activity—the factory operatives were unorganized—but of political pressure upon state legislatures to establish a ceiling on hours in private industry. The National Reform Association even unbent sufficiently to make the demand for a ten-hour day one of its subsidiary planks, and it was taken up by many other workingmen's associations formed for this specific purpose.

The most protracted struggle took place in Massachusetts where the development of the textile industry created both the greatest need for reform and the strongest opposition to it. A call for concerted action on the part of the workers, seeking to bring together various local associations, was first issued in 1844 and was responsible for formation of the

New England Working Men's Association. Both Fourierites and land reformers tried to take over control of this organization, and for a time appeared to have succeeded in diverting attention from the ten-hour issue, but the agitation in favor of the latter reform nevertheless gained increasing headway. Almost swamped with petitions (one from Lowell being 130 feet long with some 4,500 signatures), the Massachusetts General Court felt compelled to make an official investigation.

Its committee reported that the average working day in the textile factories ranged from 11 hours and 24 minutes to 13 hours and 31 minutes, according to the season, and that there was no question but that shorter hours and more time for meals would benefit the workers. It also asserted the right and duty of the legislature to regulate hours whenever public morals or the well-being of society were menaced. In spite of such premises, however, it concluded, largely on the grounds that industry would be driven from the state, that no action should be taken. "The remedy is not with us," the committee stated, casually brushing aside legislative responsibility. "We look for it in the progressive improvement of art and science, in a higher appreciation of man's destiny, in a less love for money, and a more ardent love for social happiness and intellectual superiority."

The factory operatives attacked the report as clearly reflecting "a cringing servility to corporate monopolies" and renewed a struggle which now crossed state lines and aroused the workers throughout the country. New arguments and counter-arguments were advanced. Labor did not emphasize, as it had in the 1830's, the need for more time for self-education and fulfillment of the duties of citizenship. It stressed instead the improvement in the quality of work that should result from shorter hours. The employers, however, were more concerned over production costs. In combatting the workingmen's views they stated that shorter hours would have to mean a lower day's wage. At the same time they reasserted a paternalistic attitude toward the workers' welfare. "The morals of the operatives will necessarily suffer," one of them stated, "if longer absent from the wholesome discipline of factory life, and leaving them thus to their will and liberty, without a warrant that this time will be well employed."

While the debate still raged over conditions in Massachusetts, the reformers succeeded in winning at least partial victories in a number of other states. New Hampshire passed the first state ten-hour law in the nation's history in 1847; Pennsylvania adopted a bill the next year providing that no person should work more than a ten-hour day or sixty-hour week "in cotton, woolen, silk, paper, bagging and flax factories," and during the 1850's, Maine, Connecticut, Rhode Island, Ohio, California and Georgia also fell in line with some sort of ten-hour laws. There was a catch, however, in almost every case. The ten-hour provision could be circumvented by "special contracts." The employer could virtually disregard the law, that is, by refusing to hire anyone unless he were willing to accept a longer working day, and through combining with other employers he could effectively blacklist any worker who attempted to stand up for his legal rights.

The inclusion of the special contract clause was defended by employers as necessary to protect the right of a citizen to sell his services as he himself saw fit. It was an argument to be advanced even more aggressively in later years when the Fourteenth Amendment was interpreted as specifically safeguarding individual freedom of contract from any infringement by state laws. Its speciousness, although he had originally opposed hour legislation, was exposed by Horace Greeley.

"To talk of the Freedom of Labor, the policy of leaving it to make its own bargains, etc.," he wrote in the *Tribune* on September 18, 1847, "when the fact is that a man who has a family to support and a house hired for the year is told, 'If you will work thirteen hours per day, or as many as we think fit, you can stay; if not you can have your walking papers: and well you know no one else hereabout will hire you'—is it not most egregious flummery?"

The workers in Massachusetts undoubtedly thought so, and in continuing their struggle through a series of Ten-Hour Conventions, they insistently demanded effective legislation that would not mean simply a standardization of the working day but a real—and enforceable—abridgment of the hours of labor. ". . . We do declare, explicitly and frankly," it was stated in 1852, "that our purpose, and our whole purpose, is, the enactment of a law which shall prohibit, in stringent and unmistakeable terms, and under adequate penalties, the corporations, chartered by the laws of the State, from employing any person in laboring more than ten hours in any one day. This is just the law—and all the law—we want on this subject."

This straightforward demand was not realized in Massachusetts— nor in any other state. The inclusion of the special contract clause rendered such laws as were passed unenforceable, and factory workers remained subject to whatever conditions their employers chose to impose upon them. "The ten-hour law will not reduce the hours of labor," one newspaper emphatically stated in regard to the New Hampshire bill. ". . . Its authors did not intend any such result. It will also fail, we think, to humbug the working-men—the only object had in view by the demagogues who originated it."

A final effort to keep the ten-hour movement alive was undertaken through a series of industrial congresses, a further outgrowth of such organizations as the National Reform Association and the New England Working Men's Association. They were first set up on a national basis, and then in the form of state or other local conventions. Instead of furthering practical labor aims, however, they proved to be somewhat vague and ambiguous assemblages, once again attracting reformers rather than trade union delegates. They tried to influence legislation in favor of free land and cooperation as well as the ten-hour day by promising political support to those who would advocate these reforms, but no real progress was made. Moreover while it was again hoped to "eschew partyism of every description," as George Henry Evans had advocated for the National Reform Association, the politicians were soon successfully taking over. The Industrial Congress in New York, for example, originally sought to limit membership to delegates of labor organizations, but Tammany Hall was before long in almost complete control.

The old story of the workingmen's inexperience in politics and the intriguing guile of the professional politicians was being repeated. James Gordon Bennett predicted the fate of the New York Industrial Congress in 1850. "It will fall into the hands of a few wire-pullers, who will turn it to their own advantage and sell the trades to the highest bidder," he wrote prophetically in the *New York Herald*. "Then will be acted over again the farces already played in this city, in which the trades have been made the ladder of needy or ambitious politicians, who kicked them away the moment they gained the summit of their aspirations."

It was not until well into the 1850's that labor began to free itself from its absorption in the hazy garrulity of reform associations and conventions and return to straight-forward trade union activity. An improvement in economic conditions, although interrupted by another brief depression in 1857, promoted this shift from the ineffectual pursuit of vaguely humanitarian panaceas. Once again the bargaining position of the workers was strengthened and the way opened to effective action through the practical weapon of strikes. The unions of this period, however, were to reveal in one important respect a somewhat different philosophy from that held by the earlier societies of the 1830's. They were much less concerned over the solidarity of labor, and fastened their attention far more narrowly on the needs of their own individual membership. Little effort was to be made to form city centrals or any other labor federations comparable to the general trades' unions.

The unions of both periods were primarily made up of artisans and mechanics; that is, skilled craftsmen, and they were largely concentrated in the old established trades. But whereas those in the earlier period were wholly sympathetic toward the organization of unskilled workers and factory operatives, and prepared to cooperate with such societies as they might form, there was little interest in these groups of workers on the part of the trade unions of the 1850's. New lines were being drawn between skilled and unskilled workers and the former were already reluctant to link their activity in any way with the latter.

The more limited scope of the labor movement during these years resulted from a growing realization of the almost insuperable difficulties in trying to organize the mass of workers who were being drawn into factories and mills. Such hopes as there had once been that this could be done appeared to be quenched by two basic considerations. In the first place, many of these factory workers at the time were women and children who were willing and able to work at much lower wages than male employes; and in the second, the ranks of male workers were being constantly swelled by the immigrants who accepted jobs regardless of the working conditions involved. The idea of the solidarity of all labor was not entirely forgotten, and was to be revived after the Civil War. The attitude of the unions in the 1850's, however, seemed to foreshadow that of the American Federation of Labor when it placed its organizational emphasis on the development of strong unions among the skilled workers rather than the more nebulous goal of unity for all labor.

While the revived unions of the 1850's consequently stressed the maintenance of apprenticeship rules, the closed shop and higher wages and shorter hours for their own members, they did not promote with any vigor the labor movement as a whole. They lacked the dynamic drive of their predecessors. In accepting the impracticability of trying to establish by political pressure or reform the equality that had been so much the concern of the workers in the 1830's, they were perhaps realistic. They recognized, as a resolution of one society frankly stated, that under existing conditions "there exists a perpetual antagonism between Labor and Capital . . . one striving to sell their labor for as much, and the other striving to buy it for as little, as they can." But their efforts to combat capital on these grounds were not to be very successful.

The most interesting development of the time was the first real attempt to form national trade unions. The National Typographical Union, the National Molders' Union and the Machinists' and Blacksmiths' National Union were organized, and a National Protective Association was founded by railway engineers with delegates representing fourteen states and fifty-five railways. Other embryonic national unions were also started by cordwainers, upholsterers, plumbers, stone cutters and cotton mule spinners. None of these organizations was too successful but they helped pave the way for more effective activity in later years.

In other respects, the general organization of labor conformed to familiar patterns. The local unions still retained various benefit features, collected dues from their members and sought to maintain strike funds, engaged in collective bargaining with employers, and were prepared to call strikes when their legitimate demands were not met. At times strikes were widely prevalent. "Each spring," the *New York Tribune* declared on April 20, 1854, "witnesses a new struggle for enhanced wages in some if not most of the trades of this and other cities." Public opinion recognized that there was real reason for the restlessness of the workers in the already customary failure of wages to keep pace with advancing living costs, and the unions' demands often received sympathetic support in the press. "Men should always have a fair compensation for their labor," the *Trenton Daily State Gazette* stated on April 24, 1857 in commenting on an agreement newly reached among master and journeymen carpenters in that city, "and we believe it is seldom that they demand more."

One strike toward the close of the period, breaking out early in February, 1860, awoke widespread concern and was to prove the most extensive yet recorded in American history. It was called by the shoemakers of Natick and Lynn, Massachusetts, and spread throughout New England. With the formation of mechanics' associations in some twenty-five towns, close to 20,000 workers were ultimately reported to have turned out. In making the demand for higher wages responsible for this strike, the shoemakers declared that they were acting in the interests of the manufacturers as well as in their own interest "inasmuch as the wealth of the masses improves the value of real estate, increases the demand for manufactured goods, and promotes the moral wealth and intellectual growth of society." Their emphasis upon the purchasing power of wages did not, however, convince their employers of the desirability of meeting their demands.

The strike was described in newspaper headlines as "Revolution in the North," "Rebellion Among the Workmen of New England," and "Beginning of Conflict between Capital and Labor." For almost the first time, the police and militia were called out in a labor disturbance. But there was no violence and in many towns the workers had the sympathy and support of their fellow citizens. Many female employes took part in the strike and in their demonstrations and parades, they proved to be zealous advocates of the cause. "They assail the bosses," a reporter for the *New York Herald* wrote from Marblehead, "in a style which reminds one of the amiable females who participated in the first French Revolution."

Before the end of the second week the employers began to come to terms with the strikers. While refusing in most cases to recognize their unions or to sign written agreements with them, they granted wage increases substantially meeting the workers' demands. The strike had proved successful.

As the 1850's drew to a close, the slavery issue began to impinge on the labor movement as it did on every phase of economic or political activity throughout the country. Among northern workingmen, the same divisions of opinion were evident as among other elements of the population. In New England there was strong abolitionist sentiment, especially among operatives in the cotton mills, but in other parts of the country there was little disposition to allow sympathy for the Negro to be carried so far as to favor a war to effect his freedom. It was felt in the growing industrial centers that the slavery of the white wage earner was often quite as degrading as the slavery of the Negro and that reform might better begin at home. Even after Lincoln's election in 1860, many unions vigorously supported the various compromise proposals that were being put forward to reconcile northern and southern differences.

Thirty-four leading trade unionists, indeed, banded together for action early in 1861 and with the slogan "Concession not Secession," summoned a National Workingmen's Convention to protest against the government's course. "Under the leadership of political demagogues and traitors," they vehemently stated in the *Mechanics' Own,* ". . . the country is going to the devil as fast as it can, and unless the masses rise up in their might, and teach their representatives what to do, the good old ship will go to pieces." Their meeting was held in Philadelphia on February 22 with parades, speech-making and resolutions upholding the Crittenden Compromise. It was not a very impressive affair, however, and it could not in any event exercise any appreciable influence on the forces that were so soon to plunge the country into war.

Once hostilities were declared, the workers enlisted in great numbers in response to President Lincoln's call for troops, and many of those who had been most strongly opposed to war were among the early volunteers. In a number of cases, the members of unions entered the service as a group. "It having been resolved to enlist with Uncle Sam for the war," read a typical resolution by one such organization, "this union stands adjourned until either the Union is safe or we are whipped."

The war was to bear heavily upon labor. The workers were subject to the draft, while the wealthy could escape service by paying bounties, and they suffered severely from an inflation that for manufacturers and tradesmen meant rising profits. There were rumblings of discontent as the issuance of greenbacks whirled the cost of living ever higher. "What would it profit us as a nation," the workers asked, "were we to preserve our institutions, save our constitution, and sink the masses into hopeless poverty and crime?" They were prepared to play their full part in the war effort, but their resentment flared against profiteers and speculators.

By 1863 the situation in New York shockingly reflected what a good thing war could be for those in a position to make money out of it. The hotels, theaters, jewelry establishments and other luxury stores were doing a phenomenal business. The "shoddy," as the profiteers were called, were spending fortunes with reckless, shameless extravagance. "The men button their waistcoats with diamonds of the first water," said *Harper's* "and the women powder their faces with gold and silver dust." The hard-hit workingmen earned no such profits and strikes soon spread as they demanded that wages be kept in some reasonable relation to rising prices.

The bricklayers in Chicago insisted on a rise; conductors and horse-car drivers walked out in New York; the union printers in St. Louis struck for higher wages; carpenters, painters and plumbers were everywhere threatening to throw down their tools unless their demands were met; the iron molders sought a fifteen per cent advance; shipwrights and longshoremen went on strike, and the locomotive engineers called out their members.

In occasional instances, martial law was proclaimed to combat such disturbances with troops acting as strikebreakers. But labor had a friend in the White House. While Lincoln may not have fully understood the implications of an organized labor movement, his sympathies were with the workers. With one possible exception, he would not support strike intervention by the government. "Thank God we have a system of labor where there can be a strike," he had declared prior to the war, and he steadfastly maintained his faith in labor and respect for labor's rights throughout the national emergency. The democracy which he affirmed was predicated on his belief that "working-men are the basis of all government." In his first annual message to Congress he had declared that labor was prior to, and independent of, capital which could never have been created without labor's first existing. Meeting a delegation from the New York Workingmen's Democratic Republican Association in 1864, he reiterated these views: "Labor is the superior of capital, and deserves much the higher consideration."

Under these circumstances, the strength of labor increased during the Civil War and the trade unions took a fresh lease on life. Between 1863 and 1864, the number rose from 79 to 270, and it was estimated that the total of organized workers was over 200,000—still fewer than thirty years earlier but more than at any time in the 1840's or 1850's. Moreover there were among these unions 32 organized on a national basis which showed far greater stability than those of the 1850's. The most prominent among them was the reorganized Iron Molders' International Union,[1] but the Machinists and Blacksmiths, the Locomotive Engineers, the American Miners' Association and the Sons of Vulcan (iron puddlers) were other strong organizations which also revealed the changing character of the labor movement.

The wartime revival of unionism was accompanied by the re-emergence of an influential labor press that began to put forward organized labor's views and advocate labor reform. *Fincher's Trades' Review,* the organ of the Machinists and Blacksmiths, was the most important of these papers and with representation on its editorial board from other unions, it became a national spokesman for the whole labor movement. Its editor, Jonathan Fincher, was an able and indefatigable reporter, and a forthright commentator on labor issues. Other labor journals were a new *Workingman's Advocate,* published in Chicago; the New York *Trades' Advocate* and the *Weekly Miner.*

A further advance was the establishment of new trades' assemblies, corresponding to the old general trades' unions. The local unions of Rochester, New York, first revived this form of organization and within a short time almost every city had a trades' assembly. They became a source of very real strength and introduced a new labor weapon, the boycott, as a means of coercing employer compliance with union demands. "All the trades unite for this purpose," read a contemporary report of the boycott, "and when a case of oppression is made known a committee from the Trades' Assembly calls upon the offender and demands redress. If the demand is not complied with every trade is notified, and the members all cease trading at the obnoxious establishment." The trades'

---

[1] The international union, introduced by the Molders, was so-called because of the inclusion of Canadian locals.

assemblies also sponsored picnics, balls and other social activities, and in some instances maintained libraries and reading rooms.

Labor emerged from the Civil War on the offensive. It was prepared to move into fields of even broader national organization, seeking to bring the new unions together in a unified movement that could meet more effectively the consolidated forces of capital. But it still had a weary road to travel.

VI: TOWARD NATIONAL ORGANIZATION

BETWEEN THE CIVIL WAR and the close of the nineteenth century, the United States underwent phenomenal industrial expansion. The railroads flung out new networks of rails to span the continent and knit the country into an economic whole. The burning stacks of steel mills lighting the skies over Pittsburgh symbolized the growth of a gigantic industry made possible by the discovery of the incalculable iron resources of the Mesabi range. Oil gushed from the wells being driven in western Pennsylvania and Ohio. In the great slaughterhouses of Chicago and St. Louis, thousands of cattle and hogs were butchered daily. The textile mills of New England hummed with activity and a ready-made clothing industry grew up out of the sweatshops of New York and other eastern cities. Everywhere new factories and mills reflected the triumphs of the machine and the growth of mass production. As cities and manufacturing towns mushroomed along the Atlantic seaboard and in the Middle West, the face of America was transformed.

The basic factors behind these developments were the nation's illimitable resources, its great labor reserves and an insatiable demand for the products of the new industries, but the immediate driving force of industrial expansion was provided by a group of visionary, ambitious and ruthless business leaders and financiers. Jay Gould, E. H. Harriman and James J. Hill fashioned an empire of railroads, Carnegie an empire of steel, Rockefeller an empire of oil. The corporation became the accepted form of business organization and under the leadership of such men, mercilessly crushing their competitors, mergers and consolidations were effecting the further nationalizing of business. Gigantic trusts sprang up in scores of industries—in oil and steel, sugar, linseed oil, stoves, fertilizers. Monopoly was the goal of the industrialist and a complacent government and complacent courts, wedded to the economic doctrines of laissez faire, gave free rein to policies that rapidly created a concentration of economic wealth and power that the country had never before known.

The laboring forces were swept along on this tide of expansion. Although such development would have been wholly impossible without them, they had no voice in determining the course of economic growth. The workingmen became almost helpless pawns in the hands of corporate employers. As the onetime independent craftsmen were drawn into the factories, mills and foundries where their special skills had little value, and where they were called upon to perform only single, automatic steps in the complicated processes of mass production, they lost the bargaining powers they had previously enjoyed. Industry looked upon labor as a commodity, to be bought as cheaply as possible. Little more sense of responsibility was felt toward the workers than toward the raw materials of manufacture.

"Before this concentration began, while as yet commerce and industry were conducted by innumerable petty concerns with small capital, instead of a small number of great concerns with vast capital," Edward Bellamy was to write in *Looking Backward*, his famous Utopian romance, "the individual workman was relatively important and independent in his relations to the employer. Moreover, when a little capital or a new idea was enough to start a man in business for himself, workingmen were constantly becoming employers and there was no hard and fast line between the two classes. Labor unions were needless then and general strikes out of the question. But when the era of small concerns with small capital was succeeded by that of the great aggregations of capital, all this was changed. The individual laborer, who had been relatively important to the small employer, was reduced to insignificance and powerlessness over against the great corporation, while at the same time the way upward to the grade of employer was closed to him. Self-defense drove him to union with his fellows."

With the laws of supply and demand so completely determining wages, everything possible was done by industry to make certain that the supply of labor would be plentiful. During the Civil War the business interests of the country had taken a first step in enlisting the support of Congress to make assurance doubly sure on this point. There was passed, in 1864, a contract labor law which permitted the advance of passage money to prospective immigrants in return for a lien upon their wages. With such encouragement the American Emigrant Company, capitalized at $1,000,000 and backed by such prominent figures as Chief Justice Chase, Secretary of the Navy Welles, Senator Sumner and Henry Ward Beecher, undertook to meet the requirements of an expanding economy by building up the resources of available workers. Its announced program was "to import laborers, especially skilled laborers, from Great Britain, Belgium, France, Switzerland, Norway and Sweden, for the manufacturers, rail-road companies, and other employers of labor in America." Its advertisements declared it was prepared to provide, at short notice and on reasonable terms, miners, puddlers, machinists, blacksmiths, molders and mechanics of every kind.

The agents of the American Emigrant Company, together with those of the railroads, the steamship companies, and many industrial corporations, were soon drumming up trade in this new form of contract labor almost as had the "newlanders" two centuries before in their continental quest for indentured servants. "These men, when they arrive," stated an alarmed report to a labor convention, "as a general rule, have but little money; consequently they are compelled to work at starvation prices. . . . We stand no chance of competing with these men. . . ."

In California and in the construction of the first trans-continental railway, labor needs were met by importing Chinese coolies and the West Coast was to have its own peculiar problems. The abortive experiment was even made, although on a very small scale, of employing them for the shoe industry in Massachusetts. "They are with us!" exclaimed the *Boston Commonwealth* in June, 1870, "the 'Celestials'—with almond eyes, pigtails, rare industry, quick adaptation, high morality, and all—seventy-five of them—hard at work in the town of North Adams, making shoes."

As time went on the number of European immigrants mounted steadily—almost half a million entered the country in 1880 and in the following decade over five million, or nearly twice the total for the previous ten years. Moreover there was a gradual shift in the source of supply. The great bulk of the new immigration no longer came from northwestern but from southeastern Europe. The steerage of the trans-Atlantic steamships was crowded with Italians, Poles, Czechs, Slovaks,

Hungarians, Greeks and Russians—ignorant, unskilled, penniless peasants. They provided an apparently inexhaustible reserve of cheap labor for mines, mills and factories.

Immigration had always impinged upon the efforts of American labor to raise living standards, but by the close of the century its influence in holding down wages was more pronounced than ever before. For not only was the supply of unskilled workers constantly augmented by importation from Europe, but the gradual disappearance of available free land in the West was shutting off the escape valve that the frontier had traditionally represented in times of unemployment and economic depression. However indirect the effect of the western movement may actually have been in relieving the pressure in earlier years, the closing of the frontier meant that an entirely new epoch had begun in American history. There was still opportunity but it was to be far more limited than in the expansive days of western settlement.

In the 1840's and 1850's the workers had already felt that the conditions under which they lived were deteriorating, but the skilled artisans and mechanics could still maintain standards that deeply impressed all foreign visitors. As more and more wage earners were now drawn in their search for work into factories, mills and shops, they wholly lost their former independence and were also paid relatively lower wages. Crowded together in cities and towns growing far too rapidly to absorb them, they labored under the constant shadow of pay cuts and unemployment. For the occasional few there was still opportunity to climb the economic ladder—many of industry's leaders were to rise from the ranks of labor—but the great bulk of industrial workers, alien or native, could no longer expect to escape from the wage-earning class and by becoming employers, join the aristocracy of wealth. "The hope that the workingmen may enter this circle," the *Workingman's Advocate*, of Chicago, declared as early as 1866, "is a glittering delusion held up before him to distract his attention from the real object of his interests."

The cruel paradox of "progress and poverty," which Henry George noted in the 1870's, was not even then anything new and it became increasingly apparent as the years went by. Economic growth and expansion were undeniable facts, and so were the rise in the national income and the improvement in living standards for the country as a whole. Yet at the same time many millions lived in abject poverty in the densely packed slums. They were all too often without the most simple comforts and conveniences which their own labor made possible for others. They struggled merely to maintain their families above the level of actual hunger and want. While circumstances were better for those who still retained special skills, the great majority worked such long hours for such little pay that their status was a tragic anomaly in the light of the prosperity so generally enjoyed by business and industry.

As the introduction of machinery caused an increasing division of labor, permitting more and more of the work of manufacture to be done by the semi-skilled or unskilled, employers were able to use "green hands" rather than the artisans and mechanics of an earlier day. Migratory workers threatened the jobs of local workers, and periodic unemployment undermined the onetime security of established craftsmen. As business became nationwide, moreover, the competition of different manufacturing areas meant that prices and wages were no longer determined by local conditions. They fluctuated as a consequence of economic changes wholly beyond the control of the employers or workers immediately concerned.

In this new national market, for example, the makers of stoves in Troy and Pittsburgh, Philadelphia or Detroit, had to meet the competition of manufacturers in Chicago and St. Louis. Wage scales in the East were linked with those in the West. If the iron molders in Troy or St. Louis wished to protect themselves from wage cuts in time of business recession, they had to look beyond merely local conditions and search out means to uphold the wages of comparable workers in other parts of the country.

It became increasingly clear under these new conditions that labor had to meet the challenge of nationwide industry by itself organizing on a nationwide basis. This meant in the first instance, an attempt to build up national unions which would enable the workers in any trade to safeguard their wage scales against competition from whatever quarter, and in the second, an effort to confront the community of interests growing up among all employers by a like community of interests among all workers. There was to be much talk of the solidarity of labor as a new group of leaders sought to bring the national unions, political labor parties, cooperatives and other labor reform associations into what might be termed a united front to combat the rising power of organized capitalism.

In seeking to effect this broader national organization in the years immediately following the Civil War, labor was nevertheless still so confused by the new forces of industrialism as to be wholly uncertain as to what course it should follow. It was drawn into various political movements, beguiled by new promises of reform, and caught up in controversy over socialist theory and radical concepts of class struggle. There was continued debate over the relative benefits of political as against economic action, and the advantages of craft unions as opposed to more all-inclusive unions.

On many occasions, the workers took matters in their own hands regardless of the fine-spun theories being discussed at labor conferences. Feeling themselves ground down more and more heavily under the heel of capitalist exploitation, they ignored a leadership that appeared to be out of touch with the actualities of economic circumstance and rose in spontaneous revolt to protect their rights. Before the Civil War, strikes had been local, short-lived and generally peaceful, but in the latter half of the century their character was drastically to change. The country was to experience widespread and violent industrial strife.

The initial step toward a national organization of labor was taken in 1866. A group of union leaders, wholly forgetful of similar moves in the 1830's, summoned what they called "the first National Labor Congress ever convened in the United States." It was held in Baltimore and attended by some seventy-seven delegates from various local unions, trades' assemblies and national unions. The avowed purpose of the conference was to create a new unity within the ranks of labor as a whole. In organizing what was to become the National Labor Union, provision was made for the membership not only of the skilled workers enrolled in existing trade unions, but of unskilled workers and also farmers. At last all those who toiled were "to rise in the majesty of their strength" and challenge the employing class to acknowledge their rights and privileges.

From the outset the National Labor Union was reformist and politically minded. It was the first broad attempt to bring all labor together on a common program, but it still reflected the utopianism of pre-Civil War days and the feeling then so current that the producers could make over society in their own image in spite of the gathering forces of industrialism. The independence and individualism of a frontier society made it almost impossible for the nineteenth century American workingman, for all the evidence to the contrary, to accept the permanence of a wage-earning class.

The leaders of the National Labor Union were not greatly interested in such practical objectives as concerted trade union pressure for the immediate improvement of working conditions. They declared that the labor movement was dependent on trade unions and urged every workingman to join one. Meeting at Baltimore, however, they upheld political action as the most effective means of promoting the workers' interests and they strongly deprecated resort to strikes. The advocates of economic rather than political action were able to defeat a motion for the immediate formation of a straight-out political labor party, but the conference nevertheless agreed that one should be set up "as soon as possible."

The general aims of the National Labor Union were set forth in an "Address to the Workingmen of the United States." It primarily emphasized, as "the first and grand desideratum of the hour," a demand for the adoption of laws establishing eight hours as a legal day's work in every state in the union. As we shall see, this represented a reform with deeper implications than the earlier drive for a ten-hour day and for a time it appeared to dominate labor activity. The National Labor Union, however, also sought to promote both consumers' and producers' cooperatives, reviving the old movement of the 1840's, and partly as a means to make capital more readily available for such enterprises, it was to become more and more absorbed in currency and banking reform. The abolition of convict labor; the restriction of immigration, particularly of Chinese coolies on the West Coast, in order to safeguard the living standards of native workers; the disposal of public lands only to actual settlers, and the establishment by the national government of a Department of Labor, were further objectives set forth in 1866.

These largely political goals were supplemented by appeals for the broader organization of working people. The interests of women in industry were recognized, the new union pledging individual and undivided support to "the sewing women, factory operatives, and daughters of toil," and the head of the Troy Laundry Workers, a union of female workers, was made one of the association's assistant secretaries. The organization of Negroes was also encouraged, but in this first recognition of their possible role in the labor movement, they were urged to form their own unions rather than invited to join the National Labor Union.

The formation of this new organization was for the first time to create a national labor leadership and among the men figuring most prominently in its activities—chosen its president in 1868—was William H. Sylvis. Commenting on the gathering of labor leaders that attended the convention that chose him president, the *New York Sun* bore witness to the prominence he had won throughout the country by declaring that his "name is familiar as a household word."

Sylvis was at this time a man of forty, medium-sized and strongly built, with a florid complexion, light beard and mustache, and "a face and eyes beaming with intelligence." Few labor leaders have been more devoted to the cause, more willing to sacrifice every personal consideration in working for labor's interests, or commanded more loyalty and affection on the part of his fellow workers. He was very literally to wear himself out in their behalf. "I love this Union cause," he declared on one occasion. "I hold it more dear than I do my family or my life. I am willing to devote to it all that I am or have or hope for in this world."

His views on the policies labor should promote underwent marked shifts and changes. He was erratic and highly inconsistent in his thinking. But whatever his position at a particular moment, he defended it aggressively. He once assailed his critics as a "two-faced, snarling crew, who act the part of puerile wiffets." His most telling shafts were always reserved, however, for the new capitalist class that he so strongly felt was seeking only to exploit the workers—"a monied aristocracy—proud, imperious, and dishonest . . . blasting and withering everything it comes in contact with."

Sylvis was born, the son of a wagon maker, in Annoph, Pennsylvania, in 1828 and as a boy worked in the local iron foundry. It was some time in the 1840's that he graduated from his apprenticeship and was duly invested with the "freedom suit" that marked his new status as a journeyman molder—a fine broadcloth coat, white shirt, woolen hose, calfskin boots and high silk hat. Continuing to work at his trade in and about Philadelphia, he joined the local Stove and Hollow-Ware Molders' Union and at once became an active labor organizer. He was inspired with the idea of bringing all molders together in a single organization and it was largely through his efforts that a convention was held in Philadelphia, in 1859, at which forty-six delegates from eighteen locals established the National Molders' Union.

It collapsed with the outbreak of the Civil War and Sylvis himself enlisted for a short period of army service. In 1863, however, he was again back at his chosen work and was elected president of the revived Iron Molders' International Union. His only interest was in building up this organization and through his unflagging zeal, he introduced new methods and techniques in labor organization. Traveling back and forth across the country, often begging a ride in the engineer's cab because he had no money for railway fare, he met with groups of local molders in city after city, helped them organize locals and admitted them to membership in the national union. Returning for the annual convention in 1864, he was able to boast that "from a mere pigmy, our union has in one short year grown to be a giant." With fifty-three locals and a total membership of 7,000 (soon to rise to 8,500), the Iron Molders' International Union had by 1865 become the strongest and most closely knit labor organization in the country.

Sylvis was to look back upon this period when he traveled so widely and came in such intimate contact with so many workingmen in New England, the seaboard states, the Midwest and Canada as the happiest in his life. But he exhausted the slight capital at his disposal and was wholly dependent upon small funds given him by the molders. "He wore clothes until they became quite threadbare and he could wear them no longer," his brother wrote of these days. ". . . The shawl he wore to the day of his death . . . was filled with little holes burned there by the splashing of molten iron from the ladles of molders in strange cities, whom he was beseeching to organize."

Sylvis also proved himself to be as capable in administration as he was in organization. Control was effectively centralized in the national union, a per capita tax on all union members provided a revenue which built up a substantial strike fund, and the issuance of union cards and publication in the labor press of a "scab album" made possible general enforcement of a closed shop. Sylvis believed strongly in collective bargaining and did not encourage strikes, but when they proved to be the workers' only resource, he was ready to back them up to the hilt—"the results will depend on who can pound the hardest."

Until the winter of 1867–1868, the policies pursued by the Molders' Union were uniformly successful but during that difficult season the National Stove Manufacturers' and Iron Founders' Association launched an all-out counter-attack. Wages were cut and members of the union laid off. When the workers went out on strike, the employers were then in a strong enough position to lock them out. The embattled molders fought back for months as best they could but their strike funds became exhausted, internal dissensions eventually broke their united front, and they began to straggle back to work on the employers' terms. Sylvis was able to save the union from complete extinction, but with the failure of the strike it largely lost the strength and influence it had once exerted.

He was so discouraged by this experience that he increasingly shifted his attention from trade unionists to more general labor reform and thus found in the new National Labor Union broader scope for his activities. He was ready to support, as vigorously as he had formerly supported union organization, the drive for the eight-hour day by legislative enactment, the formation of cooperatives and currency reform. Reversing his earlier views, he threw all his influence behind the trend within the National Labor Union to promote these reforms by political action. "Let our cry be REFORM," he demanded in his first circular as its president. ". . . Down with a monied aristocracy and up with the people."

Meetings of the National Labor Union clearly revealed the growing absorption with political reform. Among the delegates at the convention in 1868 (whose "philosophic and statesmanlike views of the great industrial questions" were warmly commended by the *New York Herald*) were representatives of eight-hour leagues, land reform associations, anti-monopoly societies and many other political causes. Conspicuous among them were two advocates of woman suffrage, Elizabeth Cady Stanton and Susan B. Anthony. Their presence created something of a furor for while Sylvis and other leaders supported woman suffrage, the delegates as a whole were not prepared to go this far. They agreed to seat the suffrage leaders only after making it plain that in so doing they were not endorsing their "peculiar ideas." The *Herald* nevertheless noted that Miss Anthony was "delightfully insinuating and made no mean impression on the bearded delegates."

The National Labor Union took a step at this same convention which clearly foreshadowed its own transformation into a third party. It encouraged the formation of labor reform parties in the several states and urged them to undertake direct political action. The trade unionists found their interests increasingly subordinated to the promotion of causes that concerned them only indirectly, if at all. The old story of the labor congresses of pre-Civil War days was being repeated. The only difference in the experience of the National Labor Union was that it was not so much captured by the reformers (in spite of the "delightfully insinuating" Miss Anthony) as controlled by labor leaders who had themselves turned reformers. Sylvis was the outstanding example of this trend, but other onetime trade unionists were by the close of the 1860's no less zealous partisans of reform and political activity.

The impetus given to the National Labor Union by the election of Sylvis as its president was to prove short lived. On the eve of its annual convention in 1869, he was suddenly overtaken by death. The blow was a harsh one for the labor movement and "cast a veil of despondency upon the whole working class." There was scarcely a union that did not adopt laudatory resolutions, and the labor press published innumerable editorials upon the irreparable loss of a great leader in the zenith of his fame. "Sylvis! The National Calamity," one paper headed its comment upon his death; the *Working Man's Advocate* appeared with black borders.

From Europe came further condolences from the leaders of the International Workingmen's Association—the First International—with which Sylvis had sought to establish an alliance in the "war between poverty and wealth." A letter signed among others by Karl Marx declared that the world could ill afford the loss of "such tried champions in the bloom of life as him whose loss we mourn in common."

The contributions that Sylvis had made to the labor cause were the example and inspiration of his organizing zeal in building up the Molders' International Union, and his stalwart support of the rights of the workers on the national stage. He had made himself a true spokesman for labor and his words commanded attention and respect. Short as his life was, he stands out as the first really national labor leader the country had known.

Whether the history of the National Labor Union would have been much different had he lived is problematical. It had already gone off on a somewhat dubious political tangent, and Sylvis had encouraged rather than sought to restrain the diversion of its energies to reform. In any event its days were numbered. Richard F. Trevellick, a coworker with Sylvis and head of the International Union of Ship Carpenters and Caulkers, succeeded him as president. He too had moved away from an early interest in trade unionism to mounting concern with politics. Under his presidency the National Labor Union made the final plunge and at the annual convention in 1872 transformed itself into the National Labor Reform Party. A program primarily emphasizing currency reform was adopted and Judge David Davis of Illinois was nominated for the presidency. When Davis withdrew his name, the political movement largely collapsed and with that collapse, the National Labor Union ended its days.

Although the National Labor Union was both so short lived and so unsuccessful, certain of the issues with which it was concerned demand further consideration. The first of these was that campaign for a legislative eight-hour day that in 1866 was declared to be "the question of all others, which at present engrosses the attention of the American workman." It was based upon theories that went much deeper than the old arguments that upheld a shorter working day in order to promote the health, the moral well-being or the educational opportunity of workers. The eight-hour day, according to its advocates, was to transform the existing organization of society by raising both the wages and status of the workers, thereby gradually narrowing the gap between employer and employe "until the capitalist and laborer are one."

The high priest of the eight-hour movement was Ira Steward, a Boston machinist and loyal union member, who was so deeply convinced that his ideas were the solution for all labor's problems that he could not be swerved from his self-appointed task of promulgating them at all times and in all places. "Meet him any day as he steams along the street," wrote a contributor to the *American Workman*, ". . . and, al-

though he will apologize and excuse himself if you talk to him of other
affairs . . . if you only introduce the topic of 'hours of labor,' and show
a willingness to listen, he will stop and plead with you till night-fall."

He addressed innumerable workingmen's audiences on the eight-
hour day, testified before the Massachusetts legislature, wrote pamphlets and articles for the labor press, and organized first the Labor
Reform Association and then the Grand Eight Hour League of Massachusetts. His ideas seized upon the imagination of the workers. Eight-
hour leagues sprang up all over the country and in making their program its own, the National Labor Union was reflecting a nationwide
interest in this proposed reduction of labor's working day.

Steward's basic theory clearly pointed to ideas and practices that in the
twentieth century were to be even more widely accepted. In favoring
the reduction of the working day to eight hours, he assumed that it
would not mean any loss of wages. The workers would demand pay at
least equal to what they had been receiving for ten and twelve hours
work, and since such a demand would be universal, the employers
would have no valid ground for refusing it. Any resistance "would
amount to the folly of a 'strike' by employers themselves, against the
strongest power in the world, viz., the habits, customs and opinions of
the masses." With their increased leisure, the workers would then be in
a position to enjoy, and consequently would want to purchase, more of
the products of industry. Maintaining that it was a "mechanical fact,
that the cost of making an article depends almost entirely upon the
number manufactured," Steward then asserted that the manufacturers
would immediately profit from an expansion of their markets because
onetime luxuries could be widely sold to the working population.

The major point stressed by Steward was that the reduction of working hours could be effected without any cut in wages, and this idea was
popularized by a jingle attributed to his wife:

> Whether you work by the piece or work by the day
> Decreasing the hours increases the pay.

It was at least problematical whether employers would actually pay
their old wages for a legislative eight-hour day in the hope of building

up purchasing power for their goods. The eight-hour leagues were highly successful, however, in promoting this optimistic view of a complete regeneration of capitalistic society. Both the national government and a number of states, moreover, were induced to take action to meet the workers' demands. The former established an eight-hour day for all its employes in 1868, and six states also made eight hours "a legal day's work."

As in the case of the earlier legislative drive for a ten-hour day, however, the action taken by the states was to prove illusory. The new laws were again subject to the reservation "where there is no special contract or agreement to the contrary," and there appeared to be no way to circumvent such limitations. A contemporary report to the National Labor Union was wholly discouraging. "Your committee wishes also further to state," it read, "that Eight Hour laws have been passed by six states, but for all practical purposes they might as well have never been placed on the statute books, and can only be described as frauds on the laboring class."

Faced with these actualities, the movement lost the support it had temporarily commanded. Maximum-hour laws were to remain an objective of social reformers. They were eventually to be adopted by the states without qualifying clauses, and in the 1930's Congress approved comparable legislation for all employes engaged in interstate trade. But during the last quarter of the nineteenth century, labor gave up the attempt to secure a shorter working day by political action and returned to economic pressure. The eight-hour movement of the 1880's and 1890's found the unions making demands directly upon employers, as had the original trade societies, and seeking to enforce compliance through strikes.

As the maximum-hour drives of the 1860's subsided, a new enthusiasm for cooperation as the solution of labor's problems took its place and was in turn whole-heartedly supported by the National Labor Union. Again more was involved than in comparable agitation in the 1840's. The sponsors of cooperation envisaged the complete renovation of society as had the proponents of the eight-hour day. Through the establishment of producers' cooperatives in every trade, the workingmen were to set up a system of self-employment which would ultimately do away with the wage system, provide practical means for an equitable distribution of the profits of industry, and wholly free labor from its bondage to capital.

Sylvis had himself taken the lead in this movement with the establishment of cooperatives by the iron molders. Not only had their local unions set up foundries at Troy, Rochester, Chicago, Cleveland, Louisville and other cities, but after its disastrous strike experiences, the national union itself went directly into cooperation in 1868. Impulsively changing its name to the Iron Molders' International Cooperative and Protective Union, it embarked on an ambitious project, at a cost of $15,000, for a large foundry at Pittsburgh. So enthusiastic was Sylvis over this program that at one time in 1868 he appeared to be ready to give up everything else to promote it. "The time has come," he stated, "when we should abandon the whole system of strikes and make co-operation the foundation of our organization and the prime object of all our efforts."

Other unions followed the molders' example. The machinists set up a number of shops on a joint stock basis; the shoemakers established both producers' and consumers' cooperatives; the coopers organized some eight shops in Minneapolis, and comparable projects were started by bakers, printers, hatters, carpenters and shipwrights.

For a time some of these cooperatives appeared to be successful but one by one they gradually failed. There was strong opposition to them on the part of the business community, which attacked such "Frenchy theories of communism," and they faced cut-throat competition. But the real trouble was in their own business operation. The union officials lacked managerial skill and the cooperatives were run inefficiently, sometimes even dishonestly, with the result that they got into increasing difficulties. Moreover, there was a basic handicap, in a day when large capital outlays had already become necessary for any productive enterprise, in the unions' lack of available funds and the virtual impossibility of their obtaining credit.

The latter consideration, indeed, caused the National Labor Union to turn its attention to currency reform as a basic factor in any move by labor to help itself. On the surface there was nothing more to this agitation, growing out of the proposed retirement of the greenbacks issued during the Civil War, than a demand for an inflationary policy to combat falling prices. It seemed to be a strange shift of emphasis from the days when the workers had favored hard money. The theories underlying Greenbackism, however, went deeper than any mere change in the price level. Labor aligned itself with the farmers on this issue because it promised radical reform of the whole financial, economic system. Like the eight-hour day and cooperation, currency reform also looked toward the creation of a producers' commonwealth to replace capitalism.

Taking their ideas in large part from the proposals for a new monetary system that had been advanced as early as 1848 by Edward Kellogg, the currency reformers urged the transformation of the public debt into bonds bearing three per cent interest, and interconvertible at will with a legal tender currency based not upon gold but upon the physical wealth of the country. Such a program, it was believed, would break down the monopoly of "irresponsible banking associations," abolish the "robbery of interest rates," and free the economic system from that dependence upon gold whereby "the very heart's blood of the workingman was mortgaged from the cradle to the grave."

Here was a final panacea for assuring labor its natural rights. "It would effect," the National Labor Union declared in already familiar phrases, "the equitable distribution of the products of labor between non-producing capital and labor, giving to laborers a fair compensation for their products, and to capital a just reward for its uses, remove the necessity for excessive toil and afford the industrial classes the time and means necessary for social and intellectual culture."

Once again Sylvis, who had been swept along in turn by trade unionism, the eight-hour movement, and cooperation, eloquently preached this newest reform. Everything else was forgotten. "There are about three thousand trades' unions in the United States," he wrote. ". . . We must show them that when a just monetary system has been established, there will no longer exist any necessity for trade unions."

It was through adopting this program and allying itself with the political Greenback movement, however, that the National Labor Union lost the support of trade unionists and then collapsed after trying to run a political campaign in 1872. Still, currency revision had its impassioned devotees among both farmers and workers, and local Greenback-Labor parties were formed throughout the country in succeeding years to press the demand for legal tender currency and interconvertible bonds. Eventually such parties coalesced to set up a national Greenback-

Labor Party, and in the mid-term elections of 1878 succeeded in polling over a million votes and sending fourteen representatives to Congress.

The pressure this party exerted helped to bring to a halt the further retirement of greenbacks, but the basic measures for which the currency reformers agitated were passed by. The outstanding notes were made redeemable in gold in the resumption act of 1878. With the adoption of this measure the Greenback-Labor Party, which appeared to have temporarily aligned labor and agriculture on a common program, soon disappeared. Greenbackism had won the support of reformist-minded labor leaders, but it may well be doubted whether it had ever evoked very much enthusiasm among the rank-and-file workers. They could hardly be expected to understand its implications, and so far as they supported it, they did so largely as an expression of their discontent with existing conditions and willingness to accept any program which promised them relief.

After the collapse of the National Labor Union in 1872, various efforts were made to set up some new organization that would eschew politics and get labor back on the straightforward path of trade unionism and economic action. A series of industrial congresses were held between 1873 and 1875 whose delegates declared that "the great desideratum of the hour" was no longer the eight-hour day, currency revision or any other reform but "the organization, consolidation, and cooperative effort of the producing masses." Two secret societies were also formed—the Industrial Brotherhood and the Sovereigns of Industry—with the same general aims. These efforts, however, represented moves on the part of a few leaders to impose some sort of control over labor from the top down, and they did not have any really substantial backing. They provided little more than forums for discussion and debate.

Moreover economic conditions at this time had once again cut the ground out from under the labor movement and created seemingly insuperable barriers to any effective activity. In 1873 the country was swept by a panic that ushered in an even more prolonged and severe depression than that of the 1830's. There was a repetition of the old story of falling prices, business stagnation, curtailed production, wage cuts and unemployment. As mines, mills and factories reduced operations or actually closed up, some three million persons were thrown out of work. Hard times not only brought an abrupt end to such nebulous strivings for labor unity as the National Labor Union and the industrial congresses, but again they almost completely shattered the existing national unions. They could no more survive the harsh impact of wage cuts and mounting unemployment than the promising unions forty years earlier had been able to survive the disrupting consequences of the panic of 1837.

There were some thirty national unions when the crisis developed. The *Labor Standard* listed only nine in 1877 and the total strength of unionized labor was reported to have declined from 300,000 to perhaps 50,000. Union after union had the same experience. The Knights of St. Crispin was a remarkable organization of shoemakers which had been established on industrial lines, rapidly built up a membership of 50,000, and proved itself to be amazingly effective in enforcing the closed shop through a series of successful strikes. But it collapsed as quickly as it had risen and by 1878 had completely disappeared. The Machinists and Blacksmiths lost two-thirds of their members and the Coopers almost three-fourths. Even the more stable National Typographical Union suffered a loss of half its members, while the newly organized Cigar Makers' National Union fell from almost 6,000 to little more than 1,000. Trade unionism was not entirely crushed, but with employers taking every advantage of hard times to combat it, and the workers unable to protect themselves, it was virtually forced underground.

In the decade since the Civil War, labor had failed to adjust itself to the new conditions of an industrialized society and had not yet attained the underlying strength to withstand depression. Its leaders advanced innumerable ideas and programs, but their shifting, changing attitude toward trade union activity, reform and politics did not command the popular support of the great mass of workers or inspire any real feeling of cohesion. For all the wordy talk at labor conventions, and the articles and appeals of the labor press, there appeared to be an increasingly wide gap between the handful of active participants in the labor movement and their nominal followers.

As far as there had been any definite philosophy behind the activities promoted by the National Labor Union, it was based upon the reform thesis that the producers could somehow take over and direct the economic system. There was as yet no general realization that the machine, mass production and large scale capital investment made it impossible for the workers to control the means of production by such simple expedients as producers' cooperatives. The reformers were looking backward instead of forward. A permanent wage earning class was an actuality which the leaders of labor were still highly reluctant to accept. The eight-hour movement, Greenbackism and cooperation sprang from middle class concepts of how society might be regenerated rather than from any real understanding of the immediate needs of the workers in a capitalistic order.

XXX

VII: AN ERA OF UPHEAVAL

XXXXXXXXXXXXXXXXXXXXXXXXXXXXXXXXXXXXXXXXXXX

THE DEPRESSION of the 1870's ushered in one of the most confused periods in American labor history. Against the somber background of hard times, the workers rose to protest violently what they considered their ruthless exploitation by employers. Demonstrations by the jobless were held in city after city, often calling out forceful intervention by the police; strikes among miners led to bloodshed and killing, and in 1877 a spontaneous uprising on the part of railway workers caused such widespread rioting that the country seemed to be facing a general labor insurrection.

Even after these disturbances subsided, the unrest and dissatisfaction of the workers continued to simmer dangerously below the surface and when in the 1880's the country again experienced depression, with the usual cycle of wage cuts and unemployment, so many strikes broke out that the period has been called that of "the Great Upheaval." As never before the nation came to realize the explosive force inherent in the great mass of industrial workers that were the product of its changing economy.

It was not surprising that the public, as well as conservative business interests, felt the country endangered as these disturbances flared up. Among the hordes of immigrants entering the country, there were foreign radicals who sought to fasten upon American labor the socialistic and even anarchistic ideas widely prevalent in Europe in these years, advocating direct action rather than the slow processes of reform. Fear of their influence colored many reports of unemployment demonstrations and of strikes, and came to a head in the tragic Haymarket Square riot of 1886. The opprobrium of radicalism and violence was cast over the entire labor movement.

In their outcries against communism and anarchism, however, the conservatives were greatly exaggerating the radicalism of American

114

labor. In spite of its left-wing elements, it remained basically conservative. The improvement of existing conditions rather than the overthrow of capitalism was still labor's goal. In holding foreign radicals responsible for the disturbed labor scene of the 1870's and 1880's, the newspapers of that era, as those of many later periods, tended to disregard the underlying factors of low wages and unemployment that were basically responsible for the workingmen's discontent.

The violence that marked such a dramatic revolt as the great railway strike of 1877 must be set against the background of a long depression unrelieved by any public consideration of the plight of those whose wages were cut or who were unable to earn any wages whatsoever, the unfeeling attitude of such great employers as the railroads which were controlled by bankers and financiers interested only in profits, and the lack of any organization among the workers to direct their protests against injustice in effective form. The smoldering discontent among the railway workers did not need the spark of radical agitation to burst into open revolt. It flared up naturally as wage cut added to wage cut drove the frustrated workers to strike out blindly in a gesture of embittered defiance.

These years of labor strife were also to witness the slow growth of the Knights of Labor and of those national unions which in mounting rivalry with the Knights were later to band together in the American Federation of Labor. But these basically more important developments were for a time overshadowed by the unorganized violence and radical agitation which reflected labor's growing pains in a capitalistic society where the human factor in industrial relations was still so largely ignored.

As the effects of the panic of 1873 deepened and widened, there were scenes of disorder in cities throughout the country. In New York, Chicago, Boston, Cincinnati and Omaha, crowds of unemployed workers gathered in huge meetings to protest against the intolerable circumstances in which they found themselves with factories and workshops closed down. Unemployment in an industrialized society was far more serious than it had ever been in the less complex agrarian society of the first half of the nineteenth century. Homeless, hungry and despairing, the workers refused to disperse when the police sought to break up their gatherings. They fought back in defense of what they considered their right of free assembly and challenged society to meet their demands.

The most noted of these outbursts was the Tompkins Square riot in New York on January 13, 1874. A meeting of the unemployed had been called to impress upon the city authorities the need for relief and it was at first approved, the mayor himself promising to speak. Evidence that radical agitators were prepared to address the proposed gathering, members of the American section of the International Workingmen's Association having participated in the arrangements, then caused a last minute cancellation of the police permit. At the scheduled hour, Tompkins Square was nevertheless densely packed with working people who knew nothing about the change in the official attitude toward the meeting. Suddenly a squadron of mounted police appeared on the scene. Without warning, they charged into the crowd, indiscriminately swinging their clubs and hitting out at everyone within reach. Men, women and children were ridden down as they fled in panic and scores of innocent bystanders were severely injured in trying to escape the police charge.

The *New York Times* reported the next day that the police applied their clubs with "reasonable but not excessive severity" and that "the scrambles of the mob as the officers advanced were not unamusing." Ignoring the underlying causes for the workingmen's discontent, and whatever rights they had in seeking unemployment relief, it took the attitude that the demonstration was wholly the work of alien radicals. "The persons arrested yesterday," it editorialized, "seem all to have been foreigners—chiefly Germans or Irishmen. Communism is not a weed of native growth."

There was one young laboring man who took very much to heart the lesson that the Tompkins Square riot appeared to teach of the risks trade unions ran in accepting radical leadership. The youthful Samuel Gompers was on hand when the mounted police charged the crowd, barely saving his own head from being cracked open by jumping down a cellarway.

"I saw how professions of radicalism and sensationalism," he wrote years later in his autobiography, "concentrated all the forces of society against a labor movement and nullified in advance normal, necessary activity. I saw that leadership in the labor movement could be safely entrusted only to those into whose hearts and minds had been woven the experience of earning their bread by daily labor. I saw that betterment for workingmen must come primarily through workingmen. . . ."

In the wake of such disturbances as the Tompkins Square riot and unemployment demonstrations in other cities, outbreaks of violence in the anthracite coal fields of eastern Pennsylvania next awoke public attention. The workers in this industry, following the lead of the soft coal miners who had established the Miners' National Association, had formed a union of their own in the Miners' and Mine Laborers' Benevolent Association. It succeeded in reaching a trade agreement with the Anthracite Board of Trade but in December, 1874, the operators independently cut wages below the agreed upon minimum. The miners at once walked out of the pits and in what became known as "the long strike," they tried to compel the operators to restore the wage cuts. As hunger and want began to exact their toll among the workers and compelled many of them to return to the pits, something like open war developed between the remaining strikers and the coal-and-iron police sent into the area by the operators to protect strikebreakers.

Into this troubled situation there was then projected another element whose exact role in the long strike it is still impossible to determine. At the time, however, sensational reports appeared in the press of the operations of a secret organization among the miners, the Ancient Order of Hibernians, more popularly known as the Molly Maguires, which was said to be terrorizing the coal fields and preventing those miners who wished to return to work from doing so. The members of this society were also charged with attempting to intimidate the coal operators, as they had once sought to intimidate Irish landlords under the leadership of the redoubtable widow named Molly Maguire from whom they took their name, by violent threats against foremen and superintendents, sabotage and destruction of mine property, outright murder and assassination. It has subsequently been revealed that the operators themselves instigated some of these attacks on the mines in order to provide an excuse for moving in, not only to crush the Molly Maguires but also all union organization. This interpretation of the wave of violence that swept over eastern Pennsylvania would appear to be substantiated at least in part by the steps taken to suppress the disorders.[1]

[1] *The New York Times* announced, on December 7, 1947, that the Reading

The bitterly anti-labor head of the Philadelphia and Reading Railroad, which controlled many of the mines, took the initiative in this
campaign. He hired a Pinkerton detective, one James McParlan, to get
proof of the criminal activity of the Molly Maguires at any cost. Posing
as a fugitive from justice, McParlan won his way into their confidence,
conspired with them in their plots and apparently originated some of
them to make sure his charges would hold, and finally succeeded in
turning up evidence in the fall of 1875 that led the authorities to make
a series of arrests. His testimony on the stand and that of other witnesses
turning state's evidence was in many instances suspect, but the trials
resulted in the wholesale conviction of twenty-four of the Molly
Maguires. Ten of them were hanged for murder and the others sentenced
to jail for terms from two to seven years.

Peace and order were restored in the coal fields. Whatever the power
and influence of the secret society had really been, it was shattered by
this attack. But the operators had also succeeded in breaking the Miners'
Benevolent Association and forcing the strikers back to work on their
own terms. The long strike ended in complete failure for the workers
and the virtual collapse of their union.

Unemployment riots and violence in the anthracite coal fields were
but a prelude to the railroad strikes of 1877 which led to disorders and
rioting that called for the intervention of federal troops before they
could be suppressed. The workers at first commanded public sympathy.
Their wages had been arbitrarily cut while high dividends were still
being paid on watered stock, and the railways were in any event highly
unpopular in the 1870's. "It is folly to blink at the fact," the *New York
Tribune* reported, "that the manifestations of Public Opinion are almost
everywhere in sympathy with the insurrection." But as the violence continued uncontrolled, the choice appeared to become one between civil
law or chaos. Although not everyone agreed with the *Nation's* blunt
statement that the strikers should have been confronted by "trained
bodies of men sufficient to overawe or crush them at the first onset," it

----

Company had just released thousands of secret documents bearing on the history
of the Molly Maguires which tended to bolster this view that the coal operators had
at least in part instigated their activities.

was recognized that the government could not evade its responsibility to restore public order.

The strikes, breaking out early in July, 1877, in protest against the wage cuts, were spontaneous. The first one was on the Baltimore and Ohio and it was at once followed by similar moves on the part of railway workers on the Pennsylvania, the New York Central and the Erie. Within a brief time all lines east of the Mississippi were affected, and the movement then spread to the Missouri Pacific, the St. Louis, Kansas and Northern, and other western lines. Railroad traffic throughout the country was interrupted and in sections completely paralyzed. As rioting flared up dangerously in Baltimore and Pittsburgh, Chicago and St. Louis, and even San Francisco, the country was confronted with its first industrial outbreak on a national scale. "It is wrong to call this a strike," the *St. Louis Republican* exclaimed, "it is labor revolution."

The strikers on the Baltimore and Ohio were the first to clash with authority at Martinsburg, West Virginia and order was restored at that point only after two hundred federal troops had been sent to the scene. Rioting on a much larger scale occurred in Baltimore. There the strikers stopped all trains, refused to allow them to move, and began to seize railroad property. When the militia, called out by the governor of Maryland, marched from their armory to the railway station, a gathering crowd of workers and their sympathizers attacked them with brickbats. stones and clubs. The troops opened fire and broke for the station, but the rioters had had a taste of blood. They kept up the assault and set fire to the station. When police and firemen arrived, the mob for a time tried to prevent them from putting out the blaze but finally gave way. Disturbances continued through a wild and riotous night, and only the arrival of federal troops the next morning brought any real return of order. By then the toll of victims had mounted to nine persons killed, and more than a score (of whom three later died) gravely injured.

In the meantime a still more serious outbreak took place in Pittsburgh, where the strikers also stopped the trains and took possession of railway property. Here popular sympathy was wholly with the railway workers because of a deep seated resentment against the policies of the Pennsylvania. The local militia, openly fraternizing with the strikers, refused to take any action against them. The arrival of a force of 650 soldiers dispatched from Philadelphia to protect railway property, consequently precipitated a pitched battle in which the troops opened fire and after killing some twenty-five persons, and wounding many more, took over possession of the roundhouse and machine shops.

The infuriated strikers, their ranks swelled by miners, mill hands and factory workers, returned to the attack with arms seized from near-by gun shops and laid siege to the troops. As night fell, freight cars were set afire and pushed into the roundhouse until it too was blazing. The troops, surrounded by flames and nearly suffocated with smoke, fought their way out amid a hail of bullets and retreated across the Allegheny River.

The field was now left clear to what had become a mob of four or five thousand persons, swelled by hoodlums and tramps. Railway tracks were torn up, freight and passenger cars broken open, and what could not otherwise be destroyed, set afire. Some two thousand cars, the machine shops, a grain elevator and two roundhouses with one hundred and twenty-five locomotives went up in flames. The Union Depot itself was burned down. As the rioting continued unchecked, the more unruly and criminal elements broke into the liquor stores and began to pillage at will without regard to whose property they were robbing. They carried off furniture, clothing, provisions.

"Here a brawny woman could be seen hurrying away with pairs of white kid slippers under her arms," read one contemporary description; "another carrying an infant, would be rolling a barrel of flour along the sidewalk, using her feet as the propelling power; here a man pushing a wheelbarrow loaded with white lead. Boys hurried through the crowd with large-sized family Bibles as their share of the plunder, while scores of females utilized aprons and dresses to carry flours, eggs, dry goods, etc. Bundles of umbrellas, fancy parasols, hams, bacons, leaf lard, calico, blankets, laces and flour were mixed together in the arms of robust men, or carried on hastily constructed hand barrows."

It was not until after a weekend of drunken pillaging, in which the damage was estimated at from five to ten million dollars, that the police, reinforced by bands of armed citizens, began to restore some semblance of order. In the meantime, the entire state militia had been called out and following an emergency cabinet meeting, President Hayes ordered all federal troops in the Atlantic Department made available to cope with the emergency. Only when the regulars arrived in Pittsburgh, was full protection finally accorded railway property.

Headlines and editorials declared that communism was at the bottom of the strike and responsible for its violence in Baltimore, Pittsburgh and other parts of the country. It was described as "an insurrection, a revolution, an attempt of communists and vagabonds to coerce society, an endeavour to undermine American institutions." *The New York Tribune* stated only force could subdue this "ignorant rabble with hungry mouths"; the *Times* characterized the strikers as "hoodlums, rabble, bummers, looters, blacklegs, thieves, tramps, ruffians, incendiaries, enemies of society, brigands, rapscallions, riffraff, felons and idiots," and the *Herald* declared that the mob was "a wild beast and needs to be shot down." Reading such headlines as "Pittsburgh Sacked—The City Completely in the Power of a Howling Mob," and "Chicago in the Possession of Communists," an alarmed public was swept by hysterical fears.

As the federal troops reached the scene in city after city, however, the rioting subsided as quickly as it had flared up. The strikers not only made no further attempts to interfere with the railroads' operations, but gradually went back to work. They knew when they were beaten; they knew they had no chance with government upholding the railroads. By the end of July, the trains were generally running again and the strikes were over.

The outbreaks of violence and mob action had demanded vigorous enforcement of law and order, but in the suppression of the strikes, the original grievances of the railway workers appeared to have been completely overlooked. The *New York Tribune*, which had at first admitted that public opinion was largely with the workers, took the position that they should have been willing to practice greater self-denial and economy until conditions had settled down. It was not impossible to sustain life on two dollars or even one dollar a day, it editorialized, and if the railway employes were unwilling to work for such wages, they had no right to prevent others from taking jobs they spurned. In adopting such an attitude, "they deserve no sympathy, but only punishment."

This attitude reflected a view widely held during these years as to the need for workingmen to submit to whatever conditions prevailed in industry. "God intended the great to be great and the little to be little," the noted preacher, Henry Ward Beecher, once wrote. ". . . I do not say that a dollar a day is enough to support a working man. But it is enough to support a man! Not enough to support a man and five children if a man insists on smoking and drinking beer. . . . But the man who cannot live on bread and water is not fit to live."

The month of July, 1877 had, in any event, been one of the most turbulent in American history and the long-term consequences of its disorder and rioting were to be highly important. The business community was aroused as never before to the potential power of industrial workers and embarked on an aggressive program to suppress all labor activity, reviving the old conspiracy laws, seeking to intimidate the workers from joining unions, imposing the "iron clad" oath, and enlisting strikebreakers whenever trouble threatened. The lesson driven home for labor was the need for organization and authority that would prevent strikes from developing into uncontrolled mob action which inevitably invited suppression by state or federal troops. Capitalism had won this first round of industrial strife, but was fearful of the future. Labor had lost, but it had a new realization of its latent strength.

The violence that marked both unemployment demonstrations and railway revolt in the 1870's had its counterpart in another round of strikes during the next decade, but the Haymarket Square riot in 1886 served more than any other outbreak of these years to arouse and alarm the public. The anarchists were held responsible for this tragic affair, and while only a tiny segment among the workers in Chicago were at all influenced by their violent "propaganda by the deed," the repercussions of the riot affected the entire labor movement. The foes of unionism made the most of this dramatic incident in trying to discredit organized labor and fasten upon it the stigma of being radical, revolutionary, and un-American.

The left-wing groups within the labor movement were in this as in other periods constantly shifting their alignments and organizing new parties which reflected the vagaries of the revolutionary European factions from which they largely sprang. The American section of the International Workingmen's Association had been dissolved in 1876 as a result of a split within the parent body abroad, and the socialist forces in the United States had formed a new Working Men's Party. It was not important, its small membership largely drawn from among German and other European-born immigrants, but it had been active during the railway strike in 1877, instigating violence and trying to foment a general strike.

Its ranks were soon split by further internal quarrels. There was embittered rivalry between the Marxian socialists, who sought to promote trade unionism as a base for the revolutionary activity that was eventually to overthrow the capitalist state, and the Lassalleans, who urged direct political activity as a far more effective means of achieving the same end. In addition to these two groups, a third flirted with the far more radical doctrines of anarchism which were being preached in this country by Johann Most, a big, black-bearded German immigrant who had formerly been a socialist but arriving in the United States in 1882 had become a fiery exponent of revolutionary violence. The radicals who espoused his brand of anarchism established an International Working People's Association, to become known as the Black International, which succeeded in winning control of the Central Labor Union in Chicago. It had some 2,000 members drawn from German and Polish metal workers, cabinet makers and packing-house employes, and through the pages of its organ, *The Alarm,* openly called for immediate revolution.

Nothing could have been less representative of American labor than this little coterie of foreign-born revolutionaries, and there was even less chance than in the case of the communists of their views winning support among the rank and file of the workers. But there was always the risk of the anarchists' precipitating some form of violence, and the Chicago newspapers were constantly stressing a danger which they were quick to discover in every demonstration of labor militancy. "The Nihilistic character of the procession," read one report of a labor parade in which members of the Central Labor Union apparently participated, "was shown by the red badges and red flags which were thickly displayed throughout it."

When in 1886 a movement spread across the country for general strikes in favor of the eight-hour day, the Chicago anarchists were ready to take advantage of every opportunity to preach their own doctrines

of revolutionary violence. The day set for the strike itself—May 1—
passed off very quietly, but two days later a clash between strikers and
strikebreakers at the McCormick Harvester plant in Chicago led to
police intervention and the death of four men. Here was the sort of
situation for which members of the Black International were waiting.
That night leaflets were circulated through the city calling upon the
workers to avenge their slaughtered comrades.

"The masters sent out their bloodhounds—the police," this incendiary
appeal read; "they killed six of your brothers at McCormick's this afternoon. They killed the poor wretches because they, like you, had the
courage to disobey the supreme will of your bosses. . . . To arms we
call you, to arms!"

A protest meeting was summoned for Haymarket Square the next
evening, May 4, and some three thousand persons gathered to hear
impassioned and inflammatory speeches by the anarchist leaders. But it
was an entirely peaceful meeting for all these alarms (the mayor himself
attended it and left upon finding everything so quiet), and when a cold
wind began to blow gusts of rain through the square, the crowd gradually
melted away. The meeting had, in fact, virtually broken up when a police
detachment of two hundred men arrived and their captain peremptorily
ordered such workers as remained to disperse. Suddenly there was a
sharp explosion. Some one had hurled a bomb into the ranks of the
police, killing one outright. They at once opened fire and there were
answering shots from the workers. During the affray seven police in
all were either killed or fatally wounded, and some sixty-seven injured;
four workers were killed and fifty or more injured.

Not only Chicago but the entire country was outraged by the bomb
throwing. The anarchists were at once blamed and there was universal
demand that they be hunted down and brought to trial. The police
combed the city for suspects, and finally eight known anarchist leaders
were arrested and charged with murder. In a frenzied atmosphere compounded equally of fear and the desire for revenge, they were thereupon
promptly found guilty—seven of them sentenced to death and the
eighth to fifteen years' imprisonment. There was no evidence whatsoever connecting them with the bombing. They were condemned out
of hand for their revolutionary views and the incitements to violence
which had supposedly caused the bombing. "Convict these men, make

examples of them, hang them," urged the state's attorney, "and you save our institutions. . . ."

Two of the convicted men pleaded for executive clemency and were given life imprisonment. Six years later Governor John Peter Altgeld pardoned them, together with the eighth man who had been sentenced to fifteen years' imprisonment, on the ground that they had not been granted a fair trial. So violent was the feeling against the anarchists even at this late date, that Altgeld was assailed throughout the country for what has since been universally recognized as an act of simple justice.

Organized labor was in no way associated with the Haymarket Square bombing and had at once denied any sympathy whatsoever for the accused anarchists. The Knights of Labor were as violent in condemning them as the most conservative newspapers. "Let it be understood by all the world," their Chicago organ declared, "that the Knights of Labor have no affiliation, association, sympathy or respect for the band of cowardly murderers, cut-throats and robbers, known as anarchists. . . ." Wholly disregarding the complete failure of the prosecution to connect the accused men with the actual crime with which they were charged, the Knights clamored for their conviction. "Better that seven times seven men hang," it was declared, "than to have the millstone of odium around the standard of this Order in affiliating in any way with this element of destruction."

The reason for such an outburst was obvious. The capitalistic enemies of labor were seeking to hang upon the labor movement this "millstone of odium" by charging that the Knights of Labor and the unions generally were permeated by the spirit of anarchism and communism. An hysterical public appeared ready to believe it. The whole labor movement was blackened by the bomb tossed by some unknown hand into the police squad at Haymarket Square. It did not matter that its responsible leaders and the overwhelming mass of the workers were as opposed to both anarchism and communism as any other group in society. All labor was thrown on the defensive.

This whole episode was to have an important influence on the developing trend of trade unionism, but it has taken us beyond our account of the growth of the labor movement as a whole. As already noted, the rise of the Knights of Labor during the 1880's was far more significant than the activities of the radical fringe that was always present in the labor movement, but never deeply affected its native philosophy.

XXXXXXXXXXXXXXXXXXXXXXXXXXXXXXXXXXXXXXXXXX
VIII: RISE AND DECLINE OF
THE KNIGHTS OF LABOR
XXXXXXXXXXXXXXXXXXXXXXXXXXXXXXXXXXXXXXXXXX

IT WAS SEVENTEEN YEARS before the Haymarket Square riot and eight years before the great railway strike that the first step had been taken in the organization of what was to become the Noble and Holy Order of the Knights of Labor. Nevertheless it was the years of labor unrest and industrial strife that intervened between these two events which saw its rise to an unprecedented pinnacle of power. Even though there was at the same time a slow revival of national unionism, and Samuel Gompers was stubbornly promoting the policies that were to come to fruition with the formation of the A.F. of L., the future of American labor in the mid-1880's appeared to lie with the Knights of Labor. For the first time a labor association seemed strong enough to challenge industry on its own grounds. "It is an organization," one contemporary writer stated emphatically, "in whose hands now rests the destinies of the Republic. . . . It has demonstrated the overmastering power of a national combination among workingmen."

The Knights were to be accused in the feverish atmosphere of these days of promoting the radical ideas being preached by foreign agitators, and the repercussions of the Haymarket Square riot contributed to a decline in their strength almost as rapid as had been their rise to power. But the Noble and Holy Order was in reality quite in the American tradition and its underlying philosophy did not differ very much from that of the National Labor Union. Its leaders looked toward the ultimate creation of some sort of industrial commonwealth, whose outlines were always somewhat hazy, but the emphasis was invariably placed upon the need for a long process of education and agitation to attain this goal rather than direct action. And in the meantime the Knights were prepared to work within the existing economic system, originally going even so far as to oppose all strikes.

More significantly they sought to promote a unionism that would embrace all workers, the skilled and the unskilled, in a single labor organization. They recognized the vital importance of the role of industrial workers in our emerging capitalist system, and were convinced that trade unionism as it had been known had to give way to labor organization on a much broader basis. Their attitude in some measure foreshadowed the industrial unionism of a later day, but rather than a federation or congress of individual unions, the Knights continually emphasized the solidarity of labor and looked toward a centralized association which would include the workers in all industries and occupations. Their ideal of a pervasive unity among workingmen everywhere—"an injury to one is an injury to all"—was a high-minded concept, but had it been attained, it would have been fraught with grave risks both for labor and for society as a whole. The concentration of power resulting from a single, unified labor organization would have gravely endangered democratic institutions.

Regardless of such possible considerations, the Knights of Labor did not succeed in realizing their aims. Their efforts to bring the unskilled workers within the fold of organized labor won only temporary success. However right in theory they may have been as to the importance of the organization of the unskilled, they were ahead of the times. The great mass of such workers, largely drawn from the ranks of the newly arrived immigrants, were separated by almost insuperable barriers of race, language and religion. Employers were quick to take advantage of every opportunity to stir up the friction and animosities that blocked any real cooperation. Moreover as the workers' ranks were constantly swelled by new arrivals, a tremendous reservoir of potential strikebreakers was always at hand to furnish cheap replacements for those who dared to take part in any union activity. The unskilled, industrial workers did not have in the 1880's either the cohesiveness or the bargaining power to make their inclusion in the organized labor movement practicable. In the face of unrelenting employer opposition it was not, indeed, until after the restriction of immigration in the 1920's and government support for labor organization in the 1930's that industrial unionism—with some few notable exceptions such as in coal mining—was successfully promoted.

The members of the traditional trade unions—the counterpart of the mechanics and artisans of an earlier day—realized this in the 1880's, and became increasingly unwilling to link their fortunes with such weak allies as the unskilled workers proved to be. They felt driven to sacrifice the solidarity of labor as preached by the Knights in order to protect their own interests by organizing more exclusively along craft lines. The national unions vigorously combated the Knights of Labor and the A.F. of L. became the embodiment of a "new unionism" concerned only with the immediate needs of its own membership.

Nine inconspicuous tailors, meeting in the hall of the American Hose Company, in Philadelphia, founded the Knights of Labor on December 9, 1869. Members of a local Garment Cutters' Association which had been forced to dissolve because of lack of funds to maintain its benefit program, they decided to form a new association which originally differed little from any other craft union except that it was a secret society and its activities were centered about an elaborate ritual. But one of the group had a far broader vision of labor organization and his fellow members were soon caught up by his idealistic enthusiasms. This was the concept of a new labor solidarity that would make it possible to include in a single unified order, without regard to nationality, sex, creed or color, all the nation's workers.

There was no idea of class struggle in the thinking of the founders of the Knights of Labor. They did not plan any attack upon the citadels of industry—"no conflict with legitimate enterprise, no antagonism to necessary capital." While they looked forward ultimately to "the complete emancipation of the wealth producers from the thralldom and loss of wage slavery," this was to be gradually brought about by mitigating the evils of the existing economic system and establishing producers' cooperatives. In time a new industrial commonwealth would then be created in which moral worth rather than material wealth would be accepted as the true standard of individual and national greatness.

The leader of the nine tailors who met in Philadelphia and the principal exponent of these ideas was Uriah S. Stephens. He was born in Cape May, New Jersey, in 1821 and educated for the Baptist ministry. Forced to abandon his studies after the panic of 1837, he became apprenticed to a tailor and the 1840's found him working at his trade in Philadelphia.

Some time later he traveled extensively—to the West Indies, Mexico and California—but on the eve of the Civil War he was back again in Philadelphia. He attended the workers' anti-war convention in 1861 and the next year helped to organize the Garment Cutters' Association. Never a trade unionist in any strict meaning of the term, believing unions to be too narrow in their outlook and circumscribed in their operations, Stephens drew from his religious background that vision of the universality of labor which was symbolized in the mysticism of the Knights of Labor's secret ritual.

"Cultivate friendship among the great brotherhood of toil," he was to advise his followers; "learn to respect industry in the person of every intelligent worker; unmake the shams of life by deference to the humble but useful craftsman; beget concert of action by conciliation. . . . The work to which this fraternity addresses itself is one of the greatest magnitude ever attempted in the history of the world. . . . It builds upon the immutable basis of the Fatherhood of God, and the logical principle of the Brotherhood of Man. . . ."

This was the strain that ran through all his writing and addresses. In pursuing the ultimate goal of consolidating "all branches of labor into a compact whole," he dismissed the idea of organizing separate trades or callings and would have done away with both boycotts and strikes whose benefits he felt were "partial and evanescent." His vision embraced all mankind. "Creed, party and nationality," he wrote, "are but outward garments and present no obstacle to the fusion of the hearts of worshippers of God, the Universal Father, and the workers for man, the universal brother."

Stephens' role in the foundation of the Knights of Labor was all important, and he became the first Grand Master Workman when it was nationally organized. Nevertheless he did not stay with it for very long. He turned to politics, as had so many labor leaders of the mid-century period; and, becoming interested in currency reform, he ran unsuccessfully for Congress on the Greenback ticket in 1878. Resigning his post in the Knights, he then drifted away from the labor movement altogether and died in 1882 without witnessing the Order's unexampled rise to prominence. Yet his influence lived on. "All through our rituals and laws," the *Journal of United Labor*, organ of the Knights, wrote upon announcement of his death, "will be found the impress of his brain, and inspiration of his keen insight into the great problems of the present hour."

In the meantime, the original Philadelphia assembly of the Knights of Labor grew very slowly. The secrecy which had been adopted to enhance the mystical appeal of ritual and ceremony, as well as to protect members from possible employer retaliation, was rigidly maintained. A prospective new member would be invited to attend a meeting of the group without being told what it was, and only after having given satisfactory answers to various questions as to his opinion upon "the elevation of labor" would he be considered eligible for initiation. The ritual was passed on by word of mouth and outsiders had no way of knowing the existence of the Order, let alone its purposes. In all public documents or notices, the name was designated by five asterisks.

Provision was made for expansion through the admission of "sojourners," workers in other crafts than that of tailoring, on the payment of an initiation fee of $1. When their number became sufficient they could "swarm" and form an assembly of their own. But it was not until 1872 that a second assembly, made up of ship carpenters, was actually established. The pace of growth then speeded up. In the next two years some eighty locals were formed in and about Philadelphia, and in 1874 the first assembly outside this immediate area was established in New York. These groups were all composed of workers in distinct crafts— garment cutters, ship carpenters, shawl weavers, masons, machinists and blacksmiths, house carpenters, tin plate and iron workers, stone cutters and gold beaters.

The next step in the evolution of the Knights—pointing toward the ultimate goal of labor unity—was the formation of district assemblies made up of delegates from the local assemblies. The first of these units was established in Philadelphia in 1873, and the next year one was set up in Camden, New Jersey, and another in Pittsburgh, a first step toward invasion of the West. Soon there were district assemblies in Ohio, West Virginia, Indiana and Illinois as well as Pennsylvania, New York and New Jersey, with a membership that included unskilled and semi-skilled workers in addition to craft workers.

As time went on, many local assemblies were established as mixed assemblies made up of workers in different trades. Miners, railway workers and steel workers joined the Knights in increasing numbers, and wherever there were not enough members of a single trade to form a trade assembly, especially in small towns and rural areas, the mixed assembly became a general catchall. Eventually the mixed assemblies outnumbered the trade assemblies and with their inclusion of unskilled workers gave the Knights their distinctive character. In all, some fourteen district assemblies, with a total membership of about nine thousand, had been formed when the leaders of the movement decided that the time had come to send out a call for a general convention to form a national body.

This meeting was held in Reading, Pennsylvania, in January, 1878 with thirty-three delegates. After long discussion a constitution was adopted setting up a General Assembly as the supreme authority of the Knights with control over both the district and the local assemblies. In theory the new organization was highly centralized, but the district assemblies had authority within their own jurisdictions and were never subject to as rigid control as the constitution theoretically contemplated. The Order became, however, a truly national organization in a sense never attained by its predecessors, and it further differed from them in that the membership remained on an individual basis rather than through affiliated unions. The workingman anxious to join simply applied for membership in a local assembly, was duly initiated, paid chapter dues, attended meetings and so became an accredited Knight of Labor.

Membership was open to all wage earners and to all former wage earners (although the latter could not exceed one-fourth of the membership in any local assembly) with the exception of lawyers, doctors, bankers and those who sold or made their living through selling liquor—to which excluded group were later added stockbrokers and professional gamblers. "It gathers into one fold," stated a later provision in the constitution, "all branches of honorable toil."

The preamble to the constitution, taking over the general principles that had been put forward by the earlier Industrial Brotherhood, called attention to "the recent alarming development and aggression of aggregated wealth" and stated that unless it were checked, it would inevitably lead "to the pauperization and hopeless degradation of the toiling masses." Only through unification could labor be assured of the fruits of its toil, the Knights declared, and to bring this about, "we have formed * * * * * with a view of securing the organization and direction, by cooperative effort, of the power of the industrial classes. . . ."

The constitution itself set forth many of the traditional demands of organized labor and also outlined certain new goals. It called for the establishment of cooperatives, the reservation of public lands for actual settlers, the eight-hour day, and a fiat currency in very much the same terms as had the National Labor Union. It demanded abolition of the contract system for prison labor, the prohibition of child labor, equal pay for the sexes, establishment of bureaus of labor statistics, and, by later amendment, government ownership of the railways and telegraphs, and adoption of a graduated income tax.

These provisions were largely reformist or political. In so far as industrial action was concerned, the Knights of Labor supported boycotts, which were to become increasingly important, but they strongly favored arbitration rather than resort to strikes which they at first wholly opposed. While a resistance fund was eventually set up for use in certain carefully defined contingencies, it was provided that only thirty per cent of the money collected could be directly used for strikes, with sixty per cent set aside for cooperatives and ten per cent for education. The Knights had had to recognize that strikes might sometimes be necessary, but they were unwilling to support them except when definitely approved by their Executive Board. "Strikes at best afford only temporary relief," the revised constitution of 1884 was to state, "and members should be educated to depend upon thorough education, cooperation and political action, and through these the abolition of the wage system."

This cautious attitude was in part due to the experience of the workers during the railway strikes of 1877. The lawlessness to which these strikes had led, with consequent intervention by federal troops, seemed to make such direct action a very dubious expedient in the minds of the leaders of the Knights of Labor. But they had no solution to the problem of how arbitration was to be enforced should employers refuse to deal with their representatives. The Knights consequently became involved in strikes in spite of themselves, and when the local assemblies were threatened by retaliatory measures on the part of industry, the Executive Board felt bound to come to their aid.

The ambiguities of its position on the strike issue might also seem to mark the stand of the Noble and Holy Order on political questions. The contemplated reforms went in some respects even beyond those put forward by the National Labor Union, and yet the Knights sought to remain primarily an industrial rather than a political organization. While they engaged in lobbying activities and in time entered even more directly into politics, they made no attempt to set up a labor party. "Politics must be subordinated to industry," the General Assembly declared in 1884, and made it clear that "this Order is in no way bound by the political expression of its individual members."

The basic policies of the Knights of Labor, in short, remained somewhat vaguely idealistic and humanitarian, in the pattern originally set forth by Uriah Stephens, and they sometimes appeared to be highly contradictory. The Knights sought to emphasize their industrial character, and yet agitated an all-inclusive program of social reform; they discouraged strikes and yet became deeply involved in them; they called for political action and denied that they had any direct concern with politics. Moreover while the Order was theoretically highly centralized, leading to charges that its policies were dictatorially determined by a handful of leaders, its membership actually took things very much in their own hands and went their own way.

The first General Assembly set the stage for further expansion. A membership of 9,287 rose to 28,136 a year later, and then declined to 19,422 in 1881. The secrecy that had at first provided a protective screen safeguarding members from employer attack began to react upon the Order as a whole. It became associated in the public mind with such other secret societies as the Molly Maguires, and aroused such suspicion and hostility on the part of the Catholic Church that Catholics were forbidden to join it. Measures were consequently taken to make the name of the Order public, remove the oath from the initiation proceedings, and eliminate all scriptural passages from the ritual. Through the intercession of Cardinal Gibbons, who was persuaded that there was nothing about the revised ritual offensive to religious doctrine, the Pope was then induced to withdraw his condemnation and uphold the propriety of Church approval. The membership rapidly recovered its losses after these moves to do away with secrecy. It had doubled in 1882, to a total of over 42,000, and within the next three years rose to more than 100,000.

Upon Stephen's retirement in 1879, only a year after formation of the General Assembly, Terence V. Powderly was chosen as his successor in the exalted post of Grand Master Workman. This young labor agitator, for he was only thirty at the time, had been born at Carbondale, Pennsylvania, in 1849. The son of Irish Catholic parents who had emigrated to this country in the 1820's, he worked while a young boy as a switch tender in the local railway yards but soon decided that he wanted to become a machinist. When seventeen, he was apprenticed to this trade, and three years later got a journeyman's job in the shops of the Delaware and Western Railroad in Scranton.

In the next few years he successively joined the International Union of Machinists and Blacksmiths, became the Pennsylvania organizer for the Industrial Brotherhood, and, in 1874, was initiated into the Knights of Labor. After a brief period of "sojourning," he organized and became Master Workman of Assembly No. 222 and corresponding secretary for District Assembly No. 5. His mounting interest in labor politics also led to participation in the activities of the Greenback-Labor party and in 1878 he was elected on its ticket as the labor mayor of Scranton.

Powderly was to continue to hold this latter post until 1884, even though he had in the meantime been elected Grand Master Workman of the Knights. He always had many and varied interests. He studied law and later practiced at the bar, served as a county health officer, was part owner and manager of a grocery store, became vice president of the Irish Land League. At one time he applied, unsuccessfully, for the post of head of the Bureau of Labor Statistics in Washington, established largely through the efforts of the Knights, and after he finally lost the presidency of the Order in 1893, he obtained a government post in the Bureau of Immigration. He was at first Commissioner General and then chief of the Division of Information, living until 1924 when his stormy career as a labor leader was almost forgotten by a generation far removed from the turbulent industrial strife of the 1880's.

Powderly did not look like a labor leader. Slender and under average height, he had wavy light brown hair; a blond drooping mustache, and mild bespectacled blue eyes. He dressed conventionally and well, his usual costume a double-breasted broadcloth coat, stand-up collar, plain tie, dark trousers and small, narrow shoes. His manners were formal and polite, giving every appearance of a man of breeding and refinement. "English novelists take men of Powderly's look," commented John Swinton, a labor journalist, "for their poets, gondola scullers, philosophers and heroes crossed in love but no one ever drew such a looking man as the leader of a million of the horny-fisted sons of toil."

He was strait-laced, almost puritanical in his point of view. A convinced total abstainer, he warred incessantly against the saloon and had little toleration for those who liked to drink. While he inspired both affection and loyalty among his followers, he was never an easy mixer or really at home in labor gatherings. He had his own sense of humor, as shown in his autobiographical writings, but there was no natural give and take about the man.

On assuming his post as Grand Master Workman, he did yeoman work in building up the Knights of Labor's membership. He was an eloquent and persuasive speaker and an indefatigable letter writer. Yet even in these early days of enthusiasm, he never dedicated himself to the labor movement with the wholehearted devotion of such a leader as William Sylvis. He continually protested that his other interests did not allow him to give full time to his job as Grand Master Workman, and on occasion petulantly complained that his health (which, it is true, was never very good) was not equal to the heavy demands being made upon it. He not only resented the incessant requests for him to speak, but with a sense of his own importance that time would not diminish, he insisted that when he did speak, it should be under circumstances suitable to his high office in the Order.

"I will talk at no picnics," he once wrote exasperatedly in the *Journal of United Labor*. "When I speak on the labor question I want the individual attention of my hearers and I want that attention for at least two hours and in that two hours I can only epitomize. At a picnic where . . . the girls as well as the boys swill beer I cannot talk at all. . . . If it comes to my ears that I am advertised to speak at picnics. . . . I will prefer charges against the offenders for holding the executive head of the Order up to ridicule. . . ."

For all his prima donna attitude, or perhaps because of it, there was no gainsaying his skill as an organizer, while his able handling of the dispute with the Catholic Church was largely responsible for Cardinal Gibbons' intercession with the Pope in the Knights' behalf. He was also a past master at labor politics and built up a personal machine that enabled him to keep close control over the General Assembly during these years of growth and expansion. There were times when he declared that there was nothing he wanted more than to hand over his post to someone else, but this did not prevent him from vigorously combatting any opposition to his policies, sharply assailing his opponents, and clinging firmly to office.

Powderly's ideas and theories were closely in accord with the underlying aims of the Knights of Labor as expressed in their original First Principles—and they had the same idealistic, broadly humanitarian and often contradictory scope. He believed in education rather than direct economic action, but it was not always clear for what he was agitating. He was given to uttering vague generalities, clothed in the most grandiloquent phrases.

"The Knights of Labor is higher and grander than party," he declared on one occasion. "There is a nobler future before it than that which clings to its existence amidst partisan rancor and strife. . . . We seek and intend to enlist the services of men of every society, of every party, every religion, and every nation in the crusade which we have inaugurated against these twin monsters, tyranny and monopoly; and in that crusade we have burned the bridges behind us; we have stricken from our vocabulary that word fail; we aim at establishing the complete rights of man throughout the world. . . ."

Cooperation was the means whereby he apparently hoped to achieve these idealistic aims. At times he seemed to be ready to place major emphasis on some other reform "In my opinion," he told the General Assembly in 1882, "the main, all absorbing question of the hour is the land question. . . . Give me the land, and you may frame as many eight-hour laws as you please yet I can baffle them all and render them null and void." His zeal for temperance also led him to emphasize this campaign. "Sometimes I think it is the main issue," he wrote while engaged in one of his periodic attacks on the "rum seller" and the "rum drinker." But sooner or later he would return to cooperation as the ultimate solution for labor's problems.

The Knights of Labor became very active in various ventures along these lines. Many of the district assemblies set up both consumers' and producers' cooperatives, some 135 in all, and the national organization itself purchased and for a time operated a coal mine at Cannelburg, Indiana. These undertakings, whether in mining, cooperage, shoe manufacturing, printing or other industries generally failed, however, for the same reasons as had most previous experiments along these lines. The Knights of Labor were no more successful than the National Labor Union in meeting the competition of private enterprise, securing the capital funds necessary for the expansion of their undertakings, or in providing them with efficient management.

Their funds were to be greatly dissipated in these ventures and their failure played an important part in the Order's ultimate collapse. Powderly nevertheless clung to his conviction that cooperatives represented the only way in which labor could establish the self-employment that was its ultimate salvation.

"It is to cooperation . . ." he told the General Assembly in 1880, "that the eyes of the workingmen and working women of the world should be directed, upon cooperation their hopes should be centered. . . . There is no good reason why labor cannot, through cooperation, own and operate mines, factories, and railroads. . . . By cooperation alone can a system of colonization be established in which men may band together for the purpose of securing the greatest good to the greatest number, and place the man who is willing to toil upon his own homestead." He likened the movement to the Revolution and long after it had been abandoned by the Knights, he continued to assert his faith in the ultimate creation of a cooperative commonwealth. "My belief that cooperation shall one day take the place of the wage system," he wrote years later in his autobiographical *The Path I Trod*, "remains unshaken."

Although these long-term aims were his real concern, as head of the Order he had to deal with such immediate and practical issues as shorter hours and higher wages—objectives in which the Knights themselves were far more interested. This raised the question of strikes. As an idealistic man of peace, Powderly opposed them. "The tendency of the times is to do away with strikes," he wrote in 1883; "that remedy has been proved by experience to be a very costly one for employer and employe." He was later to boast that "not once did I, during my fourteen years' incumbency of the office of General Master Workman, order a strike." But in his attitude on this vital issue of the 1880's, lay perhaps his greatest weakness. As the Knights of Labor repeatedly became involved in strikes, both with and without the approval of their governing body, the Grand Master Workman had a responsibility in supporting them which he could not avoid. There were times when Powderly did so courageously in spite of his own inner conviction that they were futile, but in other instances he seemed to be so timid as to be ready to conclude any sort of settlement with employers. His vacillating attitude often led to confusion, and broke down the united labor front that under more forthright leadership might have carried the strikes through to real success.

Powderly was at heart a humanitarian, thinking in terms of the general elevation of the producing class to a higher level in contemporary society. "If I had the right to give myself a name," he later wrote in his autobiography, "I would call it equalizer." Nothing could have more clearly portrayed his impatience with the immediate, short-run objectives that most interested the great majority of workers in their growing acceptance of their status as wage earners.

"Just think of it!" he once wrote in self-pitying explanation of his position. "Opposing strikes and always striking. . . . Battling with my pen in the leading journals and magazines of the day for the great things we are educating the people on and fighting with might and main for the little things. Our Order has held me in my present position because of the reputation I have won in the nation at large by taking high ground on important national questions, yet the trade element in our Order has always kept me busy at the base of the breastworks throwing up earth which they trample down."

It was when hard times again hit the country in the 1880's, leading to widespread wage cuts and unemployment in the traditional pattern of the economic cycle, that the Knights of Labor became involved in the strikes that were first to promote their spectacular growth and then precipitate their gradual decline. Powderly was to be tried and found wanting. But both the rise of the Noble and Holy Order and its ultimate collapse were in reality due to economic and social forces far beyond his control.

As restive workers sought to combat the exactions of employers trying to reduce operating costs, there were walkouts in 1883-1884 by glass workers' unions, telegraph operators, cotton spinners in Fall River, Philadelphia shoemakers and carpet weavers, miners in both Pennsylvania and the Hocking Valley in Ohio, Troy iron molders and shopmen on the Union Pacific. Knights of Labor participated in each of these strikes and in four of them, played a major role. What was most significant was that while the other strikes were crushed by the employers, those in which the Knights engaged most actively resulted, with a single exception, in victories for the workers. The most important of these strikes was that of the railway shopmen, which succeeded in forcing the Union Pacific to restore wage cuts all along the line.

The victory of the workers in this strike was in large part due to the aggressive leadership of Joseph R. Buchanan, a militant labor agitator who had joined the Knights in 1882. A onetime prospector in Colorado, he typified the new west—a large, rough, domineering type of man. His success in leading the shopmen's strike was primarily due to the creation of a feeling of unity among the workers through organization of the Union Pacific Employes' Protective Association and the subsequent establishment of local assemblies of the Knights of Labor.

A year after the Union Pacific affair another strike of railway shopmen broke out on the lines making up the so-called Southwest System—the Missouri Pacific; the Missouri, Kansas and Texas; and the Wabash. It had no sooner got underway through spontaneous work stoppages than Buchanan hurried to the scene, as a representative of the Knights of Labor assemblies on the western railroads, and repeated his earlier success on the Union Pacific by organizing the disaffected workers of the Southwest System into local assemblies. With the support of the trainmen, the striking shop workers were able to put up such a strong front that again they won their demands.

These victories, so surprising in the light of the disastrous experience of the railway strikes in 1877, redounded to the credit of the Knights of Labor and their prestige began to soar even though so far only local assemblies had been involved in the strikes. But an even more sensational success was won a little later in 1885 when the Noble and Holy Order clashed directly, as a result of further disputes on the Wabash, with Jay Gould, the powerful, astute and unscrupulous financier who controlled the entire Southwest System. The Wabash had begun in April and May to lay off shopmen who were members of the Knights of

Labor in what appeared to be a determined effort to break the local unions. The district assembly that had been organized the previous year in Moberley, Missouri at once called a strike and appealed to national headquarters for help. The executive board was still seeking to maintain a general anti-strike policy but it was forced to recognize that the very existence of the Order was at stake in this challenge to the organization of railway workers. When the Wabash bluntly refused to halt its lay-offs, the board consequently felt driven to take action. All Knights of Labor still working on the Wabash were ordered out, and those on other railways in the Southwest System and on the Union Pacific were instructed not to handle any Wabash rolling stock. The workers responded enthusiastically. Trains were stopped and the cars uncoupled, engines were "killed," and widespread sabotage, in some cases leading to disorder and violence, spread throughout the Southwest.

The threat to his entire transportation system, which the Knights appeared to be strong enough to tie up completely, forced Gould to consider coming to terms. A series of conferences was held in New York and the country was treated to the amazing spectacle of the management of one of the nation's greatest railway systems negotiating with the executive board of a nationwide labor organization. Nothing like it had ever before happened. Moreover the result was an understanding. Gould agreed to end all discrimination against Knights of Labor on the lines he controlled, reputedly saying that he had come to believe in labor unions and wished that all his railroad employes were organized. Powderly called off the strike and promised that no further work stoppages would be authorized until conferences had been held with the railway officials.

"The Wabash victory is with the Knights," exclaimed the *St. Louis Chronicle* in astonishment. "No such victory has ever before been secured in this or any other country."

For the nation's workers generally, Gould's apparent capitulation was the signal for an overwhelming rush to join an organization which had proved itself to be so powerful. During the next few months, more local assemblies of the Knights of Labor were formed than in the previous sixteen years. The new membership came largely from the unskilled or semi-skilled workers on the railroads, in mines and in the mass production industries, strengthening particularly the so-called mixed assemblies. But all trades and occupations were represented including many persons who were not wage earners at all—farmers, shopkeepers and small employers—while thousands of women and Negroes also joined the Order. Between July 1, 1885 and June 30, 1886, the number of local assemblies rose from 1,610 to 5,892 and total membership shot up from around 100,000 to over 700,000. "Never in all history," exulted the editor of one labor paper, "has there been such a spectacle as the march of the Order of the Knights of Labor at the present time."

So great was the influx that harassed organizers found themselves initiating new members so rapidly that they wholly lost control of the situation and were for a time compelled to suspend the formation of new assemblies. There was no question that the Order was expanding much too rapidly. Powderly was later to state that "at least four hundred thousand came in from curiosity and caused more damage than good." Nevertheless in the spring of 1886, the Knights of Labor appeared to have taken over control of the entire labor movement and to be virtually all-powerful.

Wild rumors magnified even the astounding growth that had actually taken place. The membership was said to be almost 2,500,000 with a war chest of $12,000,000. The conservative press conjured up the frightening prospect of the Order wholly dominating the country. It was prophesied that it would name the next president, or even more fearfully that it would overthrow the whole social system.

"Five men in this country," an article in the *New York Sun* stated, "control the chief interests of five hundred thousand workingmen, and can at any moment take the means of livelihood from two and a half million souls. These men compose the executive board of the noble order of the Knights of Labor of America . . . They can stay the nimble touch of almost every telegraph operator; can shut up most of the mills and factories, and can disable the railroads. They can issue an edict against any manufactured goods so as to make their subjects cease buying them, and the tradesmen stop selling them. They can array labor against capital, putting labor on the offensive or the defensive, for quiet and stubborn self-protection, or for angry, organized assault as they will."

As the head of this powerful organization, Powderly was said to have become an absolute czar of labor, ruling his followers with "despotism and secrecy." Actually he was overwhelmed by the uncontrolled expansion of the Order and the tremendous responsibility suddenly thrust upon him. "The position I hold," he ruefully commented, "is too big for any ten men. It is certainly too big for me. . . ."

But the public saw in the Knights of Labor a closely controlled and disciplined organization that could apparently win any contest against employers to which it gave its aggressive support. The Knights of Labor were at the peak of their astounding prestige.

Everywhere workers were singing:

> Toiling millions now are waking—
> See them marching on;
> All the tyrants now are shaking,
> Ere their power's gone.
>
> *Chorus:*
> Storm the fort, ye Knights of Labor,
> Battle for your cause;
> Equal rights for every neighbor—
> Down with Tyrant laws!

The very scope of early victories, however, held the seeds of dissolution. Success had gone to the Knights' head. Although the *Journal of United Labor* warned of the danger that "in the excess of joy, our members may imagine themselves invincible," and the executive board plaintively declared that far too many strikes were taking place at the same time, the rank-and-file workers were not to be restrained. The huge, unwieldly membership of the Order recognized no disciplinary control and had no sense of responsibility. Making the most of what were thought to be the weak points of industry, the workers continued to press their demands upon employers and to count upon the Order in supporting them. Out of this situation were to come a succession of defeats, as discouraging for the Knights as their original triumphs had been stimulating.

A first setback resulted from another strike on the part of the railway

workers on the Southwest System. The employes of the Missouri Pacific
and the Missouri, Kansas and Texas were still discontented. They had
been ready to strike in support of the shopmen on the Wabash in 1885,
and with highly exaggerated ideas of the strength of the Knights of
Labor were seeking a pretext the following spring to walk out in demand
for higher pay. When a Knights of Labor foreman on the Texas and
Pacific Railway was fired, the Master Workman of District Assembly
No. 1, a local leader named Martin Irons, promptly called a strike without awaiting any official authorization. It quickly spread from the Texas
and Pacific to workers on the other lines.

"Tell the world that men of the Gould Southwest system are on strike,"
read one grandiloquent appeal. "We strike for justice to ourselves and
our fellowmen everywhere. Fourteen thousand men are out. . . . Bring
in all your grievances in one bundle at once, and come out to a man,
and stay out until they are all settled to your entire satisfaction. Let
us demand our rights and compel the exploiters to accede to our demands. . . ."

Such extravagant demands were all that Gould, and the officials of
the railways he controlled, needed in order to convince them that the
Knights of Labor should be crushed. There is no reason to believe that
Gould ever really favored unionization in the slightest. He retreated in
1885 only to gather force for a counter-attack in 1886. Powderly, indeed,
was later to charge that the management of the Texas and Pacific had
instigated the new strike, actually coercing Irons into calling out the
men against his will. However that may be, the southwest railroads now
fought the strikers with all the weapons at their command. When the
workers again uncoupled cars and killed engines, management hired
strikebreakers and Pinkerton guards, and appealed to the state governors for military protection. This time there were to be no concessions
and no compromises.

Powderly felt himself to be in an impossible situation. He did not
approve the strike and had nothing to do with calling it, but he found
himself accused by the railways of violating the pledge he had made not
to authorize any work stoppage without previous conferences. He sought
out Gould and tried to find a basis for settlement the strikers could
accept. But the railway magnate now had no idea of negotiating with
the Knights and the conversations were entirely fruitless.

In the meantime, things were going badly for the workers. Only some 3,000 out of 48,000 employes on the Gould system were reported to have actually turned out, and in their battles with the scabs, they were being worsted. Public opinion was also against them. "They are, in fact," the *Nation* declared, "trying to introduce into modern society a new right—that is, the right to be employed by people who do not want you and who cannot afford to pay what you ask." There was general condemnation for "the forcible resistance of the strikers, to the conduct of the business by anybody but themselves."

Finally, with the railroads refusing all concessions, a congressional committee investigating the strike, and public opinion becoming more and more outraged at the interruption to railway service, Powderly in effect washed his hands of the whole affair. He recognized the importance of the controversy for the prestige of the Noble and Holy Order and was unwilling to capitulate to Gould, but he saw no way in which the strike could be carried through successfully. Left with the responsibility the Grand Master Workman evaded, the executive council then gave way and ordered the men back to work. The Knights of Labor had suffered their first serious reverse and their organization among the workers on the Gould system collapsed.

There were to be further defeats as other employers, following Gould's lead, marshaled their forces to crush every workers' uprising and permanently break the power of the Knights. During the latter half of 1886, some 100,000 wage earners were involved in labor disputes, and in the great majority of these strikes and lockouts, they were wholly unsuccessful.

The Knights suffered most severely from a strike in the Chicago stockyards. The eight-hour day was the issue at stake and the associated meat packers not only refused to meet this demand but declared that they would no longer employ any members of the Order. The strike, nevertheless, tied up the packing houses completely and there seemed to be some chance of a compromise agreement when suddenly and without warning, Powderly ordered the men back to work with the threat of taking away their charters if they refused. He was to be accused both of selling out to the employers and of being unduly influenced by the intercession of a Catholic priest in this maneuver. His own account of the episode states that the strikers were bound to be defeated and that he took such action as he did to prevent further suffering and possible bloodshed. In any event, the Knights lost control of the situation as a result of their leader's erratic attitude. With the collapse of the strike, their prestige suffered another irremediable blow.

It was clear that the tide had turned. The aggressive counter-attack of industry, quick to take advantage of every opportunity, rolled back labor's earlier gains. As early as July, 1886, John Swinton had declared that while at the opening of the year the Golden Age appeared to be on hand, it already looked as if the workers "had been deceived by the will-o'-the-wisp." Now he was wholly convinced of it—"the money power had swept all before it and established its supremacy beyond challenge."

"Jay Gould, the enemy's generalissimo," Swinton continued, "had squelched the railroad strikes of the Southwest and this was followed by the failure of hundreds of other strikes. . . . The union men had been blacklisted right and left and a vast conspiracy against the Knights of Labor has shown itself in many localities. The laws had been distorted against boycotting. Pinkerton thugs had been consolidated into petty armies for the hire of capital. . . . The constitutional rights of citizens had been invaded, labor meetings broken up and labor papers threatened or suppressed."

The onslaughts of industry and consequent loss of strikes were not the only developments that now served to undermine the strength of the Knights of Labor. Its leadership seemed to become more and more bungling. Powderly sought to minimize industrial strife and direct attention toward cooperatives, and increasingly lost the confidence of the workers themselves. They felt that he no longer understood their real interests and was unwilling to support their legitimate demands upon their employers.

An example of what was considered his pusillanimous attitude was the policy he adopted when the reviving national unions, already associated in the Federation of Organized Trades and Labor Unions, predecessor to the American Federation of Labor, sought in 1886 to promote the general strike for an eight-hour day that provided the background for the Haymarket Square riot. Although the Knights of Labor strongly favored an eight-hour day, Powderly would not associate the Order with the strike call. "No assembly," he stated in a secret circular, "must strike for the eight-hour system on May 1st. under the impression they are obeying orders from headquarters, for such an order was not, and will not be given. . . ." Instead of such direct action, he suggested that the local assemblies have their members write short essays on the eight-hour day for simultaneous publication in the press on Washington's Birthday! Many of the district assemblies nevertheless adopted resolutions to support the general strike in spite of Powderly's attempt to dissuade them, and when May 1 arrived, thousands of Knights took part in this first mass demonstration on the part of the nation's workers to impress their demands upon industry.

It was not a success. Some 340,000 workers were estimated to have participated in the eight-hour movement and over half of this total actually went out on strike on May 1. But while 200,000 were said to have secured employer recognition of the eight-hour day, their gains proved to be short-lived. It was reported by the close of the year that employers had retracted for all but some 15,000 workers such concessions as they had temporarily felt compelled to grant. The anti-labor reaction that followed the Haymarket Square affair was perhaps largely responsible for this debacle, but the failure of the Knights of Labor to support the movement in the first instance was felt to be an important contributing factor.

When the Knights of Labor met for their convention in the fall of 1886, appearances still belied the inner weaknesses that were leading to dissolution. The National Assembly at Richmond was the most impressive labor gathering that the country had ever witnessed and the seven hundred delegates were formally welcomed by the governor of Virginia. But this strong showing was little more than a bright façade and there was something empty in the impassioned eloquence of the assembly speakers who attacked "the lash of gold" that was falling upon "the backs of millions." The failure of so many strikes, the collapse of the eight-hour movement, the unhappy consequences of most of the cooperative ventures, and the after-effects of the Haymarket Square riot, together with the widening breach between leaders and members, had started the Knights of Labor on a decline from which it would never recover. Many of the local assemblies simply dissolved and others made up of skilled craftsmen threw their support behind the movement that was leading to formation of the American Federation of Labor. For the Knights were already deeply involved in that decisive struggle with the emerging forces of the new unionism that was to complete their downfall. A membership of 700,000 dropped to 200,000 within two years. In 1893, it had further fallen to 75,000. The conservative press rejoiced at the disintegration of an organization which had once been thought to hold the destinies of the republic in its power. "The only wonder," one editor commented with relief, "is that the madness lasted so long."

For a time the leaders of the Knights of Labor sought to combat this trend by turning toward political as opposed to industrial activity. Powderly urged the workingmen to protect their interests by making their concerted pressure felt "upon that day which of all days is important to the American citizen—ELECTION DAY." The support of the Order was thrown behind local labor candidates for political office in a dozen cities in the fall of 1886, and the Grand Master Workman himself campaigned energetically for Henry George and his single tax program in the mayoralty election in New York. For while Powderly still did not believe in a third party movement, his feeling of frustration over the failure of economic action led him more and more to politics as a last resort. In 1889 he was urging the Knights "to throw strikes, boycotts, lockouts and such nuisances to the winds and unite in one strike through the legislative weapon in such a way as to humble the power of the corporations who rule the United States today."

In the final stages of decline, the agrarian elements within the Knights of Labor, which had always been present with the admission of farmers to membership, began to overshadow the influence of industrial workers. Powderly was ousted in 1893 and his post of Master Workman taken over by James R. Sovereign, of Iowa, who was exclusively interested in reform politics.

"It is not founded on the question of adjusting wages," Sovereign stated in 1894 in describing the functions of the Order, "but on the question of abolishing the wage system and the establishment of a cooperative industrial system. When its real mission is accomplished, poverty will be reduced to a minimum and the land dotted with peaceful happy homes.'"

The words had a familiar ring—Sylvis, Stephens, Powderly himself might have uttered them—but Sovereign had forgotten that mitigation of the wage system was to be a step toward its ultimate abolition, and that the workers themselves had flocked to join the Order not because of its vague and idealistic ultimate goals, but because of the support they thought it was prepared to give for immediate wage and hour demands. And the strength of the Knights of Labor had been in its militant membership. Now that assembly after assembly had drifted away, the Order reverted to something like the status of the old labor congresses. A handful of political-minded leaders occasionally met to urge measures which they were wholly unable to carry through.

In spite of its sorry end, the Noble and Holy Order had given a tremendous impetus to the organization of labor and both its successes and its failures were to be of continuing significance for the growth of the labor movement as a whole. For the Knights had, indeed, created a solidarity among the workers that had been but dimly felt before their advent, and they offered a challenge to the power of industry that revealed as never before the inherent strength of organization. After all, the growth within less than twenty years from a little secret society of seven journeymen tailors to a nationwide organization of seven hundred thousand workers was in itself an almost incredible achievement.

Failure was due to the interrelated effects of irresponsibility on the part of the membership and fumbling leadership; participation in poorly organized and consequently unsuccessful strikes; the dissipation of energy and funds in cooperative ventures doomed to collapse, and above all to the impracticality of trying to draw the unskilled, industrial workers into a single, unified labor organization and the consequent withdrawal of support by the national trade unions.

Powderly well realized before his final retirement that the Order was in the throes of final dissolution, and he felt that whatever the faults or virtues of its leadership, internal contradictions made its impending fate inevitable.

"Teacher of important and much-needed reforms," he wrote in 1893, "she had been obliged to practice differently from her teachings. Advocating arbitration and conciliation as first steps in labor disputes she had been forced to take upon her shoulders the responsibilities of the aggressor first and, when hope of arbitrating and conciliation failed, to beg of the opposing side to do what we should have applied for in the first instance. Advising against strikes, we have been in the midst of them. Urging important reforms we have been forced to yield our time and attention to petty disputes until we were placed in a position where we have frequently been misunderstood by the employee as well as the employer. While not a political party we have been forced into the attitude of taking political action. . . ."

The Knights of Labor had failed. Yet it was also true, as Powderly went on to state, that the Order had stamped deep its impression on the country and even in collapse could point "to its splendid achievements in forcing to the front the cause of misunderstood and downtrodden humanity."

XX

IX: THE AMERICAN FEDERATION OF LABOR

XXXXXXXXXXXXXXXXXXXXXXXXXXXXXXXXXXXXXXXXXX

QUESTION: You are seeking to improve home matters first?

ANSWER: Yes, Sir, I look first to the trade I represent . . . the interest of the men who employ me to represent their interests.

CHAIRMAN: I was only asking you in regard to your ultimate ends.

WITNESS: We have no ultimate ends. We are going on from day to day. We fight only for immediate objects—objects that can be realized in a few years.

IN THIS OFTEN QUOTED TESTIMONY given by Adolph Strasser, president of the International Cigar Makers' Union before the Senate Committee on Education and Labor in 1885, we find the core of the philosophy that underlay the revival of trade unionism and was to inspire the formation of the American Federation of Labor. The new leaders of organized labor were not interested in the reformation of society through creation of a cooperative commonwealth. While they did not wholly abandon the humanitarian, idealistic goals of their predecessors, they prided themselves above all else on being "practical men." They were primarily concerned with the improvement of wages, hours and working conditions for their own trade union followers within the framework of the existing industrial system.

While the old national trade unions had been almost wholly broken up during the somber days of depression in the 1870's, the very years that witnessed the dramatic rise of the Knights of Labor found them slowly coming back to life. In some instances they were associated with the Knights, joining the Order as national trade assemblies; in other cases they held wholly aloof and maintained a complete independence. Their role in the labor movement appeared in either event to be largely overshadowed by that of the Knights throughout the greater part of the 1880's. A public impressed with the apparent unity and strength of the Noble and Holy Order little realized that the future was to lie with the trade unions rather than with the inchoate masses of skilled and unskilled workers who were believed to be so completely at the beck and call of Terence V. Powderly.

The history of the national unions during these years conforms to no set pattern. Their revival after the 1870's was marked by rivalry and conflict, and all the intricate maneuvering of labor politics. But the "new unionism" which Strasser had in mind with his emphasis upon immediate and practical goals, gradually took shape and form as events demonstrated that the program of the Knights of Labor was failing.

This practical approach to labor problems was not of course entirely new. The original trade societies half a century earlier had stressed organization on a strictly craft basis, job protection and such forthright objectives as higher wages and shorter hours. The national unions of the late 1860's and early 1870's had these same ends in view, and an immediate progenitor of the new program could be found in the Molders' International Union in the days before William Sylvis was converted from trade unionism to reform. Nevertheless there was to be in many respects a fresh approach to the basic problem of the organization of labor born of the unhappy experience of the national unions during earlier periods of depression.

Among such unions one which had narrowly escaped complete extinction was the International Cigar Makers' Union. Its membership had dwindled to little more than a handful when its reorganization was undertaken by three militant leaders—Adolph Strasser, Ferdinand Laurrell and, most conspicuously, Samuel Gompers—who undertook to put it back on its feet with the adoption of sound, efficient practices. A New York local was established in 1875, Gompers taking over the presidency, and in 1877 Strasser was elected president of the international. A strike among the New York cigar makers in protest against the sweat-

shop system failed disastrously this latter year, but defeat merely
strengthened the determination of the new union officials to carry their
program through and give the cigar makers an organization that could
effectively protect their interests. "Trade unionism," as Gompers wrote,
"had to be put upon a business basis in order to develop power adequate
to secure better working conditions."

Initiation fees and high dues, together with a system of sickness and
death benefits, were adopted to ensure the stability and permanence of
the new union. The principle of equalization of funds, whereby a local
in a strong financial position could be ordered to transfer some part of
its reserves to any local in distress, was borrowed from the practice of
British trade unions. A highly centralized control gave the international
officers virtually complete authority over all local unions and guaranteed
both strict discipline in the promotion of strikes and adequate support
when they were officially authorized. The Cigar Makers laid paramount
stress on responsibility and efficiency. While they were prepared to use
the strike as the most effective weapon in enforcing a demand for trade
agreements, it was to be employed only when the union commanded the
resources to make it successful.

"With the administration of Strasser," Gompers wrote of these days
in his autobiography, "there began a new era for the Cigar Makers and
for all trade unions—for the influence of our work was to extend far.
There was the beginning of a period of growth, financial success, and
sound development for the International Cigar Makers' Union of
America, a period during which uniform regulations, high dues, union
benefits, union label, better wages, and the shorter work-day were
established."

Other unions adopted these procedures, notably the Brotherhood of
Carpenters and Joiners under the able leadership of Peter J. McGuire,
but the cigar makers were the real pioneers and they carried their reorganization through so successfully that they became the model for
the new unionism. Their experience graphically illustrated what could
be done on a firm foundation of financial stability and centralized authority. There was no nonsense about producers' self-employment, a cooperative commonwealth or any other utopian goal. "Necessity has
forced the labor movement to adopt the most practical methods," it was
stated emphatically. "They are struggling for higher wages and shorter

hours. . . . No financial scheme or plan of taxation will shorten the hours of labor."

This pragmatic approach was a revolt against both the middle class concepts of reform which had in the past appeared to lead labor down so many unproductive byways, and also against socialists theories which the leaders of the new unionism considered equally harmful. Both Strasser and McGuire had been socialists; Gompers was at one time under their influence. But the first two had become disgusted with socialist rivalry and dissension, and we have seen how his own experience turned Gompers against all radicalism. Convinced of the futility of seeking the salvation of labor from any such source, these leaders fell back strongly on "pure and simple" trade unionism. Their philosophy was based upon wage consciousness rather than class consciousness. They had no idea of trying to change the economic system, let alone seeking to overthrow it.

This is not to say that there were no radicals in the reorganized labor movement. The revolutionary element which had had a part in the rioting and disorder of the 1870's and 1880's was not entirely eliminated. The adherents of both Marxian and Lassallean socialism continued "to bore from within" in their attempts to swing labor into their respective camps and they were to win their converts among members of unions affiliated with the American Federation of Labor. But the responsible leaders of the new unionism strongly and successfully opposed all such influences, and were to become more and more conservative in their approach to economic and social issues.

If the driving force behind the new unionism came largely from the International Cigar Makers, it was Samuel Gompers above all others who was its most able spokesman and the principal architect of the national organization that was to promote its basic principles. He was not only to become the first president of the American Federation of Labor, but with the exception of a single year, he held that post until his death in 1924. The reorientation of the labor movement upon the decline of the Knights of Labor, and the success of the A.F. of L. in surviving the depression of the 1890's, were in large part the work of this stocky, matter-of-fact, stubborn labor leader whose character and philosophy were in such glaring contrast to the character and philosophy of Powderly.

Gompers was born in London's East End in 1850. His father, of Dutch-Jewish stock, was a cigar maker and at the age of ten the young Samuel was apprenticed to this trade. When the family emigrated to America in 1863, he first helped his father in making cigars in their tenement home in New York's East Side, but soon branched out to get a job of his own and as early as 1864 joined a local union.

The cigar making shops at this time were schools of political and social philosophy as well as manufactories, and there was no more avid student than the young immigrant from London already steeped in the background of British trade unionism. As he sat at his bench in the dark and dusty loft, dexterously fashioning cigars, he listened with eager attention to the talk of socialism and labor reform among his fellow workers. Most of them were European-born and many of them members of the International Workingmen's Association. They had the custom of having one of their number read the labor periodicals and other magazines aloud to them (chipping in to make up the pay he would otherwise have lost) and Gompers was often given this assignment.

As already suggested, his thorough exposure to Marxist philosophy did not, however, have the effect of making the young cigar maker a theorist. On the contrary it appears to have confirmed his hard-headed, practical approach to the problems of labor. He was perhaps greatly influenced in maintaining this point of view by Ferdinand Laurrell, who was a tough-minded Swedish immigrant experienced in all phases of radicalism. Laurrell advised him to read Marx and Engels, but to be constantly on guard against being carried away by their theorizing. He warned him not to join the Socialist Party. "Study your union card, Sam," he told Gompers, "and if the idea does not square with that, it ain't true."

It was with such a background that Gompers plunged into the task, in cooperation with Strasser and Laurrell, of rebuilding the Cigar Makers' Union. Looking back upon the experiences of those days, Gompers was always to think of them as responsible not only for his own career but for the future course of American labor. "From this little group," he wrote of the men with whom he had thrashed out his ideas in endless discussion, "came the purpose and initiative that finally resulted in the present American labor movement. . . . We did not create the American trade union—that is the product of forces and conditions. But we did create the technique and formulate the fundamentals that guided trade unions to constructive policies and achievements."

Gompers was twenty-nine when the International Cigar Makers' Union was reorganized and from this early period he followed an undeviating path. Unlike both Sylvis and Powderly, he stuck closely to his last and never admitted any other interests. He was neither a reformer nor an intellectual, and he scorned their pretensions to show labor the course it should pursue. In his complete distrust of such theorists, whom he considered "industrially impossible," he never tried himself to elaborate any philosophy of labor. He liked to talk about moral influence and intuition, but his approach to every question was wholly pragmatic.

His ideas tended to be narrow and limited, and his program was invariably one of immediate opportunism. While he once spoke vaguely of favoring abolition of the wage system, he did not actually look beyond the bounds of higher wages and shorter hours for the skilled workers of the craft unions. In breaking completely with such panaceas as currency reform, land settlement and cooperation, which had so intrigued the leaders of the National Labor Union and the Knights of Labor, he also abandoned their goal of labor solidarity. Gompers' realistic attitude was to place the labor movement, at least as far as the skilled workers were concerned, on a firmer and more stable basis than it had ever before attained, but his lack of breadth and vision was greatly to limit the role of the American Federation of Labor in advancing the cause of labor as a whole. He at one and the same time saved the trade union movement from possible complete breakdown, and threw away the opportunity for developing it along those broader lines which had been the highly idealistic dream of his predecessors.

In promoting the interests of his own union and then of the American Federation of Labor, his zeal was reenforced by an apparently inexhaustible fund of energy. There were never to be any complaints of being unable to meet the demands made upon his time. As an organizer and administrator, Gompers was tireless, traveling all over the country to address labor meetings and conventions. Once known as "Stuttering Sam," he outgrew any hesitations in his speech and eloquently boomed forth the exhortatory platitudes that were so much his stock in trade. His speeches, it is true, were sometimes rather vague and confused, for he had no real gift for oral expression. His manner was often solemn and pontifical. But with a flair for the dramatic that would also distinguish an even more theatrical labor leader of later days, he knew well how to hold the center of the stage.

Off the platform and outside the conference room, Gompers was friendly, easy-going and very much one of the boys. His nature was warm and open-hearted. He liked beer parlors, the theater, music halls, show girls and the Atlantic City boardwalk. He completely shed his official character when he foregathered with a group of friends for the evening, comfortably relaxed in the congenial atmosphere of the back room of a saloon, a big black cigar gripped in his teeth and a foaming stein of beer on the table. His conviviality shocked his strait-laced, puritanical rival in the Knights of Labor. "The General Executive Board," stated a pamphlet issued by the Knights in the midst of their struggle with the American Federation of Labor, "has never had the pleasure of seeing Mr. Gompers sober." It was an unfair comment by an ardent temperance advocate, but there was no question that Gompers hugely enjoyed his beer.

In appearance, Gompers looked far more like a labor leader than the somewhat effete Powderly. His short, thick-set, sturdily built body —he was only five feet, four inches tall—seemed to justify his boast that "the Gompers are built of oak," and the strong jaw beneath a broad forehead revealed both the force and stubbornness of his character. In the early 1880's he had dark, unruly hair and wore a drooping walrus mustache with a little tuft of hair on his chin. In later years, he was to be clean shaven with a glittering pince-nez shielding his dark, snapping eyes. He dressed well, was quite accustomed to a silk hat and Prince Albert on important occasions, and his manners were gracious. Business leaders somewhat patronizingly spoke of his being "very much of a gentleman."

For all his later hobnobbing with the great—captains of industry, Wall St. bankers, senators and presidents—he never lost touch with the workers themselves and liked to refer to himself as "one who had not grown up from the ranks but still is proud to be in the ranks." He was intensely loyal and always ready to sacrifice his personal well-being and comfort for the cause for which he worked. Impeccably honest, he was to die a poor man and in later years his widow had to accept work from the W.P.A.

None of this is to say that Gompers was not ambitious. He felt himself born to leadership and clung tenaciously to the presidency of the American Federation of Labor. He built up both a powerful political machine and a closely knit labor bureaucracy. He was something of a dictator in pushing his policies and never one to give way before younger, more progressive leadership as time went on and he grew older. But his ambition for power and a public career did not lead him to seek either riches or political preferment. He was to remain wholly content with "serving his class" by making trade unionism and the A.F. of L. his life work.

"I look back over the years of work for my trade," he wrote in his autobiography, "and I rejoice in the conviction that the bona fide trade union movement is the one great agency of the toiling masses to secure for them a better and higher standard of life and work."

The first move leading toward the alliance of national and international unions that eventuated in the American Federation of Labor was made at a Pittsburgh meeting of labor leaders in 1881. Attended by delegates from both the trade unions and the Knights of Labor, the original purpose of the conference was to set up an association that might embrace all labor. "We have numberless trade unions, trades' assemblies or councils, Knights of Labor and other various local, national and international unions," the call for the meeting stated. "But great as has been the work done by these bodies, there is vastly more that can be done by a combination of all these organizations into a federation of trades." The growing rivalry between adherents of the new unionism and the leaders of the Knights of Labor, however, was to make achievement of such a goal impossible, and the Federation of Organized Trades and Labor Unions that grew out of the Pittsburgh meeting was to be short-lived.

Although some of the national unions, as we have seen, were affiliated with the Knights as trade assemblies, they were becoming increasingly opposed to the doctrines of the Noble and Holy Order. More and more of them were breaking away altogether, and they naturally resented any attempted interference in their affairs or infringement on territory they felt to be within their jurisdiction. Their attitude was frankly expressed by McGuire of the Carpenters. "While there is a national or international union of a trade," he stated, "the men of that trade should organize under it and . . . the Knights of Labor should not interfere."

The Knights nevertheless did interfere. Recognizing the importance of the skilled workers belonging to the trade unions, and their strategic position in the labor world, the Order was anxious to hold their allegiance. Powderly, for example, promised the newly organized Amalgamated Association of Iron, Tin and Steel Workers, a craft union, that if it would join the Knights it could retain its separate identity and maintain its own system of government. But the skilled workers in this and other organizations saw themselves pulled down to the level of unskilled workers in submission to the Knights' control. They declared that they would maintain their autonomy against all outside pressure "to protect the skilled trades of America from being reduced to beggary."

Gompers attended the Pittsburgh meeting in 1881 as a delegate of the Cigar Makers and was chosen chairman of the committee on organization. Although he was actually a member of the Knights of Labor, having joined the Order in the 1870's, his opposition to its basic principles led him to make every effort to keep the proposed new federation a strictly trade union affair. His proposals were defeated after vigorous debate. "There seems to be something singular about the manner in which we are changing base," one delegate stated on the floor. "This Congress was widely advertised as a labor congress and now we are talking about trades. Why not make the Knights of Labor the basis for the federation?" While this was not done, the new organization did not draw any line between skilled and unskilled workers, and was theoretically to include all labor without distinction of creed, color or nationality.

The Federation of Organized Trades and Labor Unions was in many ways a transitional stage in labor's swing toward the restricted program of the new unionism. While the ideal of solidarity was upheld, the Federation was primarily concerned with such immediate gains as the wage earners might be able to win rather than fundamental reforms in the economic system. Its legislative program, for whose support it asked all trade bodies to seek representation in the legislature, called for the legal incorporation of trade unions, the abolition of child labor, enforcement of the statutory eight-hour day, prohibition of contract labor, uniform apprentice laws and repeal of the conspiracy laws.

The Federation did not, however, win any active support. The representatives of the Knights withdrew almost at once, and most of those of the national unions soon followed them. There were only nineteen delegates at the second annual convention and twenty-six at the third. Gompers was elected president in the latter year—1883—but he did not even attend the next meeting. Out of touch with the workers themselves, the new organization soon became, like the old National Labor Union, little more than an annual conference. Its only significant action was its promotion of the eight-hour strike on May 1, 1886, but as we have seen, it was unable to carry this movement through successfully without the support of the Knights of Labor.

The Federation was, indeed, about to give up the ghost entirely in 1886. The leaders of the national unions had become convinced that it did not hold out any hope of meeting their problems. In the face of the continued attacks being made on their form of organization by the Knights of Labor, who in the flush of victory were now stating that there was no place in the labor movement for independent trade unions, they decided to take a more forthright stand in their own defense. Another meeting of national unions was consequently called for May 18, 1886, in Philadelphia with the express purpose of seeking means "to protect our respective organizations from the malicious work of an element who openly boast that 'trades unions must be destroyed.'"

The ire of the trade unionists had been especially aroused by the interference of the Knights in the affairs of the Cigar Makers' International Union itself. As a result of internal dissensions in the New York local, involving the related issues of admitting unskilled workers and promoting socialism, a dissident faction had withdrawn from the parent body to form the Progressive Cigar Makers' Union. Strasser strongly condemned this move, refused to recognize the rebels in any way, and caustically described them as "tenement house scum." In the face of this situation, District Assembly 49 of the Knights of Labor jumped into the fray, aggressively supported the rebel union, and campaigned for its admission into the Order.

When the Philadelphia conference met, one more effort was made, at least in theory, to discover a common ground of understanding that might persuade the Knights to cease their hostility toward national unions. A "treaty" was proposed to reconcile the divergent aims of the two groups within the labor movement and bring their feuding to an end. The Knights were to agree that they would not initiate into the Order any trade unionist member without the permission of his union, or any other wage earner who worked for less than the prescribed wage scale of his craft, and they were also called upon to revoke the charter of any local assembly organized by workers in a trade where there was already a national union.

Was this actually a treaty? Its one-sided terms appeared rather a demand for the Knights' complete capitulation to the national unions. Some of the delegates at Philadelphia may have considered it the statement of a position from which they would be willing to retreat if the Order proved to be conciliatory. There can be little question, however, that in the minds of the adherents of the new unionism, it was a declaration of war. Their real aim was to swing the support of the national unions behind still another federation which would break away from the Knights of Labor altogether and concentrate wholly upon protecting the interests of the skilled craft workers. Gompers had wished to do this five years earlier, but the time had not been ripe. Now the increasing hostility between the Knights and the national unions, emphasized by the struggle over dual unionism among the Cigar Makers, provided the opportunity for decisive action.

The Noble and Holy Order played right into the hands of those favoring a complete break. In spite of some professions of willingness to explore means of reconciling the issues in dispute with the national unions, no official action whatsoever was taken in regard to the proposed treaty. Even though the failure of their strikes and the repercussions of the Haymarket Square affair were already weakening their position, the Knights were determined to adhere to their own program and saw no need to make any concessions. Powderly did not even submit the treaty for consideration at the Richmond assembly in October. The national unions were defied by the establishment of new national trade districts; the Progressive Cigar Makers were formally admitted to the Order, and no gesture whatsoever was made toward settling other jurisdictional quarrels.

The answer of the national unions was to meet again, at Columbus, Ohio, on December 8, 1886, and at this conference they were joined by the handful of delegates still representing the almost defunct Federation of Organized Trades and Labor Unions. Altogether there were present some forty-two representatives of twenty-five labor groups. Among the national unions participating were the Iron Molders, Miners and Mine Laborers, Typographers, Journeymen Tailors, Journeymen Bakers, Furniture Workers, Metal Workers, Granite Cutters, Carpenters and Cigar Makers. Their total membership approximated 150,000. The sole concern of the delegates had now become the promotion of the interests of the crafts which they respectively represented, and after due deliberation they formed a new organization for this purpose and elected Samuel Gompers as its first president. Here at last was the American Federation of Labor. Its date of origin was subsequently to be pushed back to 1881, the year in which the Federation of Organized Trades and Labor Unions was established, but although the A.F. of L. took over the treasury and records of its predecessor, the two groups were quite distinct and the history of the American Federation of Labor really begins in 1886.

A first principle of the new organization, growing out of the circumstances of its birth, was "strict recognition of the autonomy of each trade." The executive council set up to handle affairs on a national level was given no power whatsoever to interfere in those that fell within the jurisdiction of member unions. The unity of labor was to be promoted through education and moral suasion rather than through the centralized controls inherent in the structure of the Knights of Labor. Nevertheless the executive council had important functions. It issued the charters for constituent unions, and as a means for stamping out the dual unionism that was felt to be so threatening to the labor movement as a whole, was authorized to settle all jurisdictional disputes. A per capita tax was imposed on all member unions in order to build up the financial reserves that would enable the A.F. of L. to extend practical assistance in strikes and lock-outs, and a legislative program drawn up in the approved fashion of all labor organizations. Finally, there were to be formed under the general authority of the executive council, both city centrals and state federations further to influence the passage of labor legislation.

Major emphasis was definitely placed upon economic or industrial action. The A.F. of L. was to support the national and international unions in winning recognition from employers, entering into collective bargaining agreements, and maintaining a position which would enable them to strike effectively when other measures failed. The legislative program, which included most of the objectives that had been sought by the old Federation of Organized Trades and Labor Unions, was subordinated to this basic line of attack in frank recognition of the inadequacy of the policy of its predecessor. Moreover from the very first, the A.F. of L. was determined to refrain from direct participation in politics or support for any single party. It was to act upon the principle of rewarding labor's friends and punishing its enemies without regard to political affiliations.

In its early years, the American Federation of Labor was almost entirely Samuel Gompers. He had loyal associates but it was he who gave the new organization life and direction. "There was much work, little pay, and very little honor," he was later to write of these days, but such considerations did not daunt him. Setting up his headquarters in an eight-by-ten-foot office made available by the Cigar Makers, with little furniture other than a kitchen table, some crates for chairs, and a filing case made out of tomato boxes, he set about breathing vitality into the new organization with a zeal, devotion and tireless energy that largely accounted for its survival. He wrote innumerable letters, always in his own hand, to labor leaders throughout the country; for a time edited the *Trade Union Advocate* as a means of publicizing his campaign; issued union charters, collected dues, handled all routine business; managed conventions and went on speaking and organization tours, and slowly but persistently transformed the American Federation of Labor from a purely paper organization into a militant and powerful champion of labor's rights. He felt himself to be engaged in a holy cause and from the day the A.F. of L. came into being until his death thirty-eight years later, it was his entire life.

While the long-term struggle of the Federation was to be with the forces of industry, its early years were also marked by the continuing feud with the Knights of Labor. Further efforts were made in the late 1880's and early 1890's to draw the two organizations together, but these proved to be completely unsuccessful. The situation was not unlike that which would develop almost half a century later when the American Federation of Labor found itself in turn challenged by the dissident unions that were to form the Congress of Industrial Organizations. There were principles at stake but they were often overshadowed by the political rivalries and ambitions of contesting leaders.

Powderly moved steadily toward complete scorn of national unions. "I will tell you frankly," he wrote an associate in 1889, "I don't care how quick the National Trade Assemblies go out. They hinder others from coming to us and I am strongly tempted to advise them all to go it alone on the outside and see how it will go to turn back the wheels of the organization for the benefit of a few men who want to be at the head of something." Gompers grew no less caustic in his opinion of the Knights of Labor, their aims and aspirations. "Talk of harmony with the Knights of Labor," he was to say in 1894, "is bosh. They are just as great enemies of trade unions as any employer can be, only more vindictive. It is no use trying to placate them or even to be friendly."

Under such circumstances the possibility of labor unity faded away and the gradually dwindling strength of the Knights was counteracted by the slow growth of the American Federation of Labor. The latter was anything but spectacular. The original membership of 150,000 had increased to only 250,000 six years later. The violent counter-attack of industry upon all unions during these years, the generally repressive attitude of the government and the courts, and finally the trying times of the depression that developed in 1893 made it highly difficult to hold any labor organization together, let alone promote its growth and expansion. But Gompers stuck grimly to his task. He refused to allow the Federation to be drawn away from its immediate, practical aims and at the annual convention in 1893, he was able to look with pride upon what had already been accomplished.

"It is noteworthy," he told the assembled delegates, "that while in every previous industrial crisis the trade unions were literally mowed down and swept out of existence, the unions now in existence have manifested, not only the powers of resistance, but of stability and permanency."

The importance of the A.F. of L. in promoting the practical concepts of the new unionism should not obscure the fact that the national unions were the real basis for the revived labor movement—both at the close of the nineteenth century and in later years. They could exist without the A.F. of L., but the A.F. of L. had no meaning without them. Their autonomy was complete, and it was they who controlled the local unions that made up the membership of the labor movement. Their functions were to direct the activities of the locals, extend union organization through the trade or industry over which they had jurisdiction, provide such assistance as they could in collective bargaining and strikes (for which per capita taxes were levied for a general defense fund), and participate in the more general program of the A.F. of L.

With time the original craft unions were greatly to extend their jurisdiction and their names often reflect the history of this expansion. Many examples might be given, but one often cited as illustrating this trend is the International Association of Marble, Slate and Stone Polishers, Rubbers and Sawyers, Tile and Marble Setters Helpers and Terrazo Helpers. The introduction of new techniques and other economic changes, were to make the settlement of jurisdictional problems one of the major concerns of the A.F. of L. from the days of its foundation.

One important group of unions that did not affiliate with the A.F. of L. was the railway brotherhoods. The organization of railroad employes has followed its own course, and while based on craft lines has for reasons peculiar to itself differed considerably in other respects from that of other workers. The Locomotive Engineers organized as early as 1863, the Railway Conductors five years later, the Trainmen in 1873, and a decade later the Firemen. Although involved in the railway strikes of 1877, the four brotherhoods became increasingly conservative in subsequent years, and because of the hazardous nature of their members' work, the insurance and benefit features of their union programs have always been of primary importance. The permanent organization of other railway employes was to develop more slowly. After an attempt by Eugene V. Debs to form an all-inclusive American Railway Union in the 1890's, to which we shall return, separate unions of Shop Workers, Switchmen, Yardmasters, Signalmen, Telegraphers, and Railway and

Steamship Clerks were formed as affiliates of the A.F. of L. despite the continuing independence of the four brotherhoods.

The fact that the international unions survived the depression of the 1890's did not mean that labor was beginning to have its own way or that even the most strongly organized unions were able to meet employers on anything like equal terms. Wages remained low and hours long for the skilled workers in the 1890's, while the great mass of unskilled existed on the barest subsistence level. Labor was still considered a commodity to be bought at the cheapest rate possible, and its right to organize and bargain collectively had by no means been accepted. As industry sought to break the power of the unions with blacklisting, iron-clad oaths, strikebreakers and Pinkerton detectives, and in combatting strikes was able to call upon state militia and federal troops in the name of law and order, the workers found themselves struggling against what were still overwhelming odds.

The vitality of the American Federation of Labor held out hope for the future. In spite of Gompers' optimism, however, the continuing depression of the 1890's was to bear down heavily on the nation's wage earners and in the industrial warfare of these years, they were to suffer some of their most decisive defeats.

X: HOMESTEAD AND PULLMAN

WHILE THE LASTING SIGNIFICANCE of the 1890's in labor history is found in the final triumph of the American Federation of Labor over the Knights of Labor and the demonstrated strength of the new unionism, the decade was more dramatically marked by its great strikes. Never before had labor and capital been engaged in such organized private warfare as would develop at Homestead in 1892, nor had the public ever become more alarmed over the dangers of industrial strife than during the great Pullman strike two years later. These two outbreaks differed from the uprising of railway workers in 1877 primarily because they were strikes by powerful unions rather than spontaneous expressions of revolt, but they were marked by almost comparable violence and bloodshed. The gravity of the labor problem as it existed in the 1890's could hardly have been more heavily underscored.

Moreover the general discontent among industrial workers which was reflected in these strikes had its political repercussions as the depression of the 1890's deepened and urban unrest was linked with agrarian revolt in the rise of Populism. The alliance between midwestern farmers and eastern workingmen was not to be firmly cemented, in part because of the continued reluctance of the A.F. of L. to engage in direct political activity, but there was widespread fear in 1896 among conservatives that an election victory for the radical doctrines advanced by the Populists would undermine the capitalist system.

In the early morning of July 6, 1892, two barges were being towed slowly up the Monongahela River toward Homestead, Pennsylvania. There had been trouble at the local plant of the Carnegie Steel Company. The skilled workers at Homestead, members of the Amalgamated Association of Iron, Steel and Tin Workers, had refused to accept new wage cuts and were supported in their stand by the rest of the labor force. The company's general manager, tough-minded, stubbornly anti-labor Henry Clay Frick, thereupon peremptorily shut down the entire plant and refused any further negotiations with the union. Special deputy sheriffs had been sworn in to guard company property, which was enclosed by a high board fence topped with barbed wire, but the locked-out workers had run them out of town in the conviction that these preparations foreshadowed the use of strikebreakers. It was a challenge to his authority that Frick was only too glad to accept. Here was his chance to crush the Amalgamated once and for all. Aboard the two barges being towed up the Monongahela were three hundred Pinkerton detectives, armed with Winchester rifles.

As the steel company's private army drew alongside the Homestead mills and prepared to land, there was a sudden exchange of shots between the barges and the shore. The workers had entrenched themselves behind a barricade of steel billets and as the Pinkertons tried to take possession of the plant, they were beaten back in a raging battle that swirled along the river front. All that day, from four in the morning until five in the afternoon, the fusillade of shots continued. The strikers set up a small brass cannon behind a breastwork of railroad ties and opened a direct fire on the barges. Failing to sink them, they poured barrels of oil into the river and set the oil afire. With three men already dead and many more wounded, the Pinkertons were trapped. Deserted by the tug which had towed them upstream, helplessly crowded into the barge which lay farthest from the shore, they finally ran up a white flag and agreed to surrender. In return for a guarantee of safe conduct out of the community, they gave up their arms and ammunition.

But feelings were running too high at Homestead, where the casualties had included seven killed, for any easy re-establishment of order. When the Pinkertons came ashore, they were again attacked and had to run the gantlet of an infuriated mob of men and women, armed with stones and clubs, before they were safely entrained for Pittsburgh. An uneasy calm then settled over the little town as the Homestead workers, victorious in this first round, awaited the next moves by the company.

It was not until six days later that there was any further development. Then on July 12 the state militia, mobilized eight thousand strong by the governor of Pennsylvania upon Frick's appeal for aid, marched in quietly to take over control of Homestead under martial law. With such protection the Carnegie Company began bringing in scabs—the "black-sheep" whom the locked-out workers knew were being hired to take their jobs—and proceeded to file charges of rioting and murder against the strike leaders for the attack on the Pinkertons. The plant was then reopened with militia protection and non-union men given the Amalgamated members' jobs. When the strike was officially called off in November, two thousand strikebreakers had been brought in and only some eight hundred of the original Homestead working force of nearly four thousand were reinstated.

In the aftermath of the original battle another act of violence had occurred. On July 23, a Russian-born anarchist, Alexander Berkman, who had no connection whatsoever with the strikers but had been aroused by the Carnegie Company's employment of Pinkerton operatives, forced his way into Frick's office in Pittsburgh and tried to assassinate him. Although shot and stabbed, the steel executive was not fatally injured and his assailant was captured. The assault had been planned by Berkman and his woman companion, Emma Goldman, a no less ardent advocate of "propaganda by deed," and only lack of funds to make the trip to Pittsburgh, as she later revealed in her autobiography, had prevented her from accompanying Berkman on his mission. He was sentenced to twenty-one years in prison for assault with intent to kill. Released after thirteen years of his term, he was later deported, together with Emma Goldman, to Soviet Russia.

These shocking events aroused the country in some ways even more than had the Great Upheaval of the 1880's or the railway strikes a decade earlier. For the Homestead affair was not a spontaneous uprising on the part of unorganized workers. It was war between one of the most powerful of the great modern corporations and what was then one of the strongest unions in the country. Each party to the dispute had taken the law into its own hands. The *Chicago Tribune* gave over its entire front page on July 7 to a vivid account of what was described as "a battle which for bloodthirstiness and boldness was not excelled in actual warfare."

Until the Homestead strike, relations between the Carnegie Company and the union had been uniformly friendly and working conditions had been governed by a three-year contract for the skilled workers that provided for a sliding wage scale based on the price of steel billets.

Carnegie had professed himself to be wholly in favor of unions, stating in an article in the *Forum* some years earlier that the right of working-men to combine was no less sacred than that of manufacturers. More-over he had expressed real sympathy for workers threatened by the loss of jobs through the use of strikebreakers. "To expect that one de-pendent upon his daily wage for the necessaries of life," he had written, "will stand by peacefully and see a new man employed in his stead is to expect too much." But when the old union contract at Homestead expired in 1892, Carnegie himself was in England and negotiations were wholly in Frick's hands.

Had Carnegie been on the ground, the course of events might have been quite different, and yet the fact remains that he had given Frick a free hand and he could hardly have been unaware of his general manager's anti-labor attitude. Indeed, he told a reporter in the course of the strike that "the handling of the case on the part of the company had my full approval," and in a letter to Gladstone, the British states-man, he declared that his firm had offered the workers generous terms and "they went as far as I could have wished." Yet he also stated in this same letter that in seeking to enforce his terms by operating the Home-stead plant with new men, Frick had made a false step. "The pain I suffer," he told Gladstone, "increases daily. The Works are not worth one drop of human blood. I wish they had been sunk."

Frick, however, was in control and his intention in bringing in strike-breakers and Pinkerton guards, for which arrangements had been made even before the failure of wage negotiations, was clearly to smash the union. And he succeeded. It collapsed completely at Homestead and was greatly weakened in other steel mills in the Pittsburgh area where sympathetic strikes led to sharp reprisals. The Amalgamated was to make some further effort to organize the steel workers, but in the face of continued opposition by the Carnegie Company and its successor, the United States Steel Corporation, it steadily lost ground. An effective steel union would not be established until some forty years later when the Steel Workers' Organizing Committee was formed with the revival of industrial unionism in the 1930's.

The Amalgamated was affiliated with the American Federation of Labor and Gompers strongly expressed his sympathy for the strikers and aided in raising funds for the defense of those charged with responsi-bility for the attack on the Pinkertons. But the Federation was not in a position to offer any effective assistance and Gompers' grandiloquent phrases must have been cold comfort for the strikers.

"You Homestead steel workers," he was quoted as saying in the *Pittsburgh Leader;* "if there is a rose bush blooming it is your work; if there is anything under the sun which shines upon you, which makes Homestead valuable, it is your work. You refused to bow down to this wonderful autocrat, and the first answer he gave you was to send that band of hirelings into this peaceful community to force you to bow down to him, and ultimately drive you from your peaceful homes. I know not who fired the first shot on that memorable morning of the 6th. of July, but I do know the hearts of the American people beat in unison and sympathy with the brave men of Homestead. I am a man of peace and I love peace, but I am like that great man, Patrick Henry, I stand as an American citizen and, 'give me liberty or give me death.' "

Homestead was to take its place in the annals of labor history as one of the great battles for workers' rights, and its immediate repercussions were nationwide. There was agitated discussion in Congress over what such industrial warfare meant for the nation. Senator Palmer of Illinois declared that the Pinkerton army had become as distinctly recognized as the regular army—"the commander in chief of this army, like the barons of the Middle Ages, has a force to be increased at pleasure for the service of those who would pay him or them"—and he maintained that the workers had the right to resist its attack in defense of their jobs and homes. "The owners of these properties," he further stated in reference to such corporations as the Carnegie Company, "must hereafter be regarded as holding their property subject to the correlative rights of those without whose services the property would be utterly valueless."

Outside the ranks of labor itself, however, such progressive ideas found little support. Politics governed many expressions of opinion. Democratic newspapers opposed to a protective tariff seized the opportunity to show that for all the claims made for high duties as safeguarding the wages of the American workingmen, the steel industry was nevertheless reducing wages and exploiting its employes. They condemned the use of Pinkerton mercenaries and expressed sympathy for the locked-out workers. Some Republican papers, resenting the injection of the tariff issue, urged the Carnegie Company to follow a

more conciliatory course to refute Democratic charges. But more generally the press took the stand that even though the Homestead employes
did not want to work for the wages offered them, there was no justification for their seeking to prevent others from accepting such terms. "Men
talk like anarchists or lunatics," the *Independent* stated, "when they
insist that the workmen at Homestead have done right." The steel company was upheld in asserting its power to provide protection for whomever it chose to employ.

"If civilization and government are worth anything," the *Cleveland
Leader* declared, "the right of every man to work for whom he pleases
must and will be maintained." In an article in the *North American Review,* George Ticknor Curtis further developed this theory. "The first
duty of the legislative power," he stated, "is to emancipate the individual workman from the tyranny of his class. The individual workman
should not be permitted to commit moral suicide by surrendering his
liberty to the control of his fellow-workmen." To protect an illusory
right to decide the terms on which he could individually sell his services,
the workingman's right to associate with others in collective bargaining
was denied. The anti-union attitude of conservative employers could
not have been more clearly expressed.

There were a number of other violent strikes during these dark days
when the forces of the new industrialism were riding roughshod over
the right of workers to organize and protect their interests. Metal miners
at Coeur d'Alene, Idaho; switchmen in Buffalo, New York; and coal
miners in Tennessee walked out in defiance of their employers, and in
each instance their strikes were forcibly broken through the intervention of state militia. As depression settled ominously over the land and
the army of unemployed swelled to some three million, labor disputes
reached a peak involving even more workers—some 750,000—than the
strikes in 1886. Of all these conflicts, however, the Pullman strike of
1894 stood out most vividly.

The employes of the Pullman Palace Car Company were in one respect in a quite different situation from the great mass of industrial
workers. They had the privilege of living in a model town. The head of
the company, George M. Pullman, had established a community for his

employes with neat brick houses grouped about a little square where bright flower beds alternated with green stretches of lawn. The whole was "shaded with trees, dotted with parks, and pretty water vistas and glimpses here and there of artistic sweeps of landscape gardening." In the exuberant enthusiasm of the company press agent, Pullman was "a town, in a word, where all that is ugly and discordant and demoralizing is eliminated and all that which inspires self-respect is generously provided."

But were these happy attributes of life in Pullman actually so "generously provided?" The employes had no choice but to live within this feudal domain, renting their homes or apartments from the company, buying their water and gas from the company, paying the company for such other services as garbage removal and the daily watering of streets, buying supplies from the company store, subscribing to the company rental library. And rents for apartments in the model town, which in most instances had no bathtubs and one water faucet for every five families, were some twenty-five per cent higher than in near-by communities. A high premium was also charged for public utility services. "Oh, Hell!" the forthright Mark Hanna was quoted as commenting on his brother industrialist's baronial domain. "Model—. Go and live in Pullman and find out how much Pullman gets sellin' city water and gas ten per cent higher to those poor fools!"

With the depression of 1893, the Pullman Company was for a time hard hit and after laying off more than 3,000 of its 5,800 employes, it cut the wages of those kept on from twenty-five to forty per cent without any corresponding reduction in rents for the company houses. The consequences were disastrous. A worker seldom earned as much as six dollars a week after the company had made its deductions. In one instance, an employe found that after payment for rent was taken out, his pay check came to two cents. "He never cashed it," the Reverend W. H. Carwardine, of the Pullman Methodist Episcopal Church reported. "He has it framed." And yet at the same time such things were happening, the Pullman Company kept on paying dividends. Even after business began to improve, enabling the company to take back some 2,000 of its employes, no steps were taken to restore the wage cuts or to reduce rents.

Finally in May, 1894, a committee of employes asked for some consideration of their grievances. Pullman flatly refused to consider any wage adjustments on the ground that the company was still losing money, and he would take no action in regard to rents. There was no relationship whatsoever, he lightly declared, between the company's dual functions as employer and landlord. Almost immediately after the interview, in spite of definite assurances that there would be no discrimination against the grievance committee, three of its members were summarily discharged.

During this year of hardship and suffering, the Pullman workers had been extensively organized in locals of the American Railway Union. This new association, independent of all other labor federations, had been formed only the year before by Eugene V. Debs as an industrial union open to all white employes of the railroads. Upon the dismissal of the three members of the grievance committee, who were also members of the American Railway Union, the Pullman locals called a strike. When the company countered by laying off all workers and closing the plant, an appeal was made to the national convention for assistance. Attempts were made to submit the issues in dispute to arbitration, but when Pullman met these overtures with the uncompromising statement: "there is nothing to arbitrate," the American Railway Union prepared for action. On June 21 it adopted a resolution that if arbitration was not accepted within five days, its members would be ordered not to handle any Pullman cars.

When this boycott went into effect, involving not only the Pullman Company but railroads using its cars, the challenge of the union was promptly taken up by the General Managers' Association, a group made up of executives of twenty-four railways entering Chicago which altogether controlled some forty thousand miles of track. It ordered the discharge of any worker "cutting out" a Pullman car from any train. But the membership of the American Railway Union was not so easily frightened. Every time a man was fired for refusing to handle a Pullman car, the entire train crew would quit. By the end of July, the strike had become so general that nearly every railroad in the middle west was affected and the nation's entire transportation system seriously threatened.

"The struggle," Debs declared in a ringing appeal to the railway workers, ". . . has developed into a contest between the producing classes and the money power of the country. We stand upon the ground that the workingmen are entitled to a just proportion of the proceeds of their labor. . . ." But while there was sympathy for the strikers in some quarters, Mark Hanna again privately expressing his scorn for Pullman's refusal to arbitrate, the conservative press solidly supported the General Managers' Association. "The necessity is on the railroads to defeat the strike," the *Chicago Herald* declared, while the *New York World* stated that it was "war against the government and against society."

As leader of the railway workers' revolt, Eugene V. Debs sprang overnight into nationwide fame. The American Railway Union was only a year old and yet under his shrewd and capable leadership, it had already gained a membership—some 150,000—which was greater than that of the four railway brotherhoods and rivaled both the declining Knights of Labor and the slowly emerging American Federation of Labor. Both management and the trade unions feared that should he carry it to success in this contest with the railroads, the principle of industrial unionism which it embodied might win a victory that would set the pattern for future labor organization.

Debs was the son of French-Alsatian immigrants who had settled in Terre Haute, Indiana where his father kept a grocery store. Born in 1855, he had gone to work in the railway yards at the age of fourteen and become an engineer at sixteen. For a time he left the yards to work as a grocery clerk and play about with politics, but in 1878 he turned to the labor movement and two years later, at the age of twenty-five, was elected both national secretary-treasurer of the Brotherhood of Locomotive Firemen and editor of the *Locomotive Firemen's Magazine*. It was largely through his efforts that this union was built up during the next dozen years into a flourishing and financially sound organization.

However, Debs grew increasingly concerned over the exclusive attitude maintained by the brotherhood and the complete lack of cooperation between its members and other railway employes. He became convinced that only through the union of all workers on the nation's railroads in a single association could the interests of this important branch of labor be successfully promoted. In 1892 he suddenly resigned his well-paid post in the Brotherhood of Locomotive Firemen and undertook almost single-handedly to form the American Railway Union.

Debs was an able organizer, shrewd and practical; he was an eloquent and forceful speaker, and he was also an idealist prepared to make any sacrifice for a cause in which he believed. Throughout his life, he commanded an amazing measure of respect and loyalty. He was to be villified and abused as few men have been during the Pullman strike, attacked as a labor dictator, a criminal, an anarchist, a lunatic, a madman, but with time even those who continued to denounce the things for which he stood, could not help honoring the man. There could be no doubting his unflinching honesty and sincerity, whether in the 1890's as an aggressive labor leader or in later years as the spokesman of American socialism. No one ever identified himself more closely with the struggling masses in our national life or was a more passionate defender of the underprivileged.

"While there is a lower class I am in it," Debs once said in a much-quoted statement. "While there is a criminal element I am of it; while there is a soul in prison I am not free."

Tall and gaunt, nearly bald even at the time of the Pullman strike when he was thirty-nine, with high forehead and candid eyes, his manner was quiet and modest. Something about him not only awoke confidence but inspired affection. "There may have lived some time, somewhere," Clarence Darrow was to write, "a kindlier, gentler, more generous man than Eugene Debs, but I have not known him."

Debs had not desired the strike that was forced upon the American Railway Union by the appeal of the Pullman workers. Even though it had already won a surprising strike victory on the Great Northern Railway, he knew that his young organization was not yet strong enough for such a formidable encounter with the united railway corporations. But when Pullman refused to arbitrate, he felt that the union could not stand aside without betraying the Pullman employes. Forced to back them up, Debs consistently counseled moderation and restraint. He ordered the strikers to remain wholly passive and in no way to injure railroad property, and during the first phase of the strike these orders were rigidly obeyed.

The General Managers' Association, however, could not afford a peaceful strike. It was soon importing strikebreakers from Canada, secretly instructing them to attach mail cars to Pullman cars so that when the strikers cut out the latter, they could be accused of interfering with the mails. Conjuring up a still non-existent danger of violence, it induced Attorney General Olney, avowed friend of the railroads, to have 3,400 men, who were actually hired by the railroads and paid by the railroads, sworn in as special deputies to help keep the trains running. These tactics were successful. There were clashes between strikers and deputies; rioting broke out and railway property was destroyed. Promptly asserting that such violence had already become uncontrollable, the Managers' Association thereupon appealed to President Cleveland to send federal troops to restore order, safeguard the mails and protect interstate commerce. Four companies of the Fifteenth Infantry were sent to Chicago.

Governor Altgeld of Illinois immediately protested this move. The situation was not out of hand, he wired the President, and local officials were entirely capable of handling it. "The Federal Government," he stated, "has been applied to by men who had political and selfish motives for wanting to ignore the State government. . . . At present some of our railroads are paralyzed, not by reason of obstruction, but because they cannot get men to operate their trains . . . as Governor of the State of Illinois, I ask the immediate withdrawal of Federal troops from active duty in this State." But Altgeld's protest went unheeded. He had recently pardoned the anarchists involved in the Haymarket Square affair and the newspapers fiercely attacked him as the "friend and champion of disorder." Even though Cleveland had in an earlier message to Congress called for the investigation and arbitration of wage disputes, he looked no further on this occasion than maintenance of order. He stoutly maintained the position he had assumed and justified the use of federal troops, in spite of charges of usurping the functions of the state, on the ground that it was his constitutional duty to keep the mail trains operating.

"If it takes every dollar in the Treasury and every soldier in the United States to deliver a postal card in Chicago," he was reported as saying, "that postal card should be delivered."

Still the ranks of the strikers held firm and in spite of strikebreakers, special deputies and the army, three-fourths of the railroads running into Chicago were almost at a standstill. Moreover the strike was spreading. Sympathetic walkouts by engineers, firemen, repairmen, signalmen, yardmasters and other workers occurred on many lines in both the east and far west. At the same time violence was also increasing. As the struggle became intensified, the strikers could no longer be held in check by Debs' peaceful persuasions. When trains began to move under the protection of the troops, angry mobs sought to stop them. Tramps and hoodlums were soon taking advantage of the situation, as they had in the railroad strikes in 1877, and railway stores were looted, freight and passenger cars burned, and damage inflicted on other property.

As disorder spread, newspapers and magazines rang all the changes on the danger to society in what the *New York Tribune* declared to be "the greatest battle between labor and capital that has ever been inaugurated in the United States." It was almost universally insisted that "this rebellion must be put down" regardless of every other consideration. The attempt was made to draw a line between the railway workers and strike agitators. The former were said to be "the victims of selfish, cruel and insolent leaders" and all honest workingmen were called upon to free themselves from such "insufferable tyranny." The *New York Times* attacked Debs as "a lawbreaker at large, an enemy of the human race" and the *Chicago Herald* asserted that "short work should be made of this reckless, ranting, contumacious, impudent braggadocio . . ."

News stories carried alarming accounts of mob action and battles with the police and troops. With such a newspaper as the *Washington Post* screaming in its headlines that "Chicago Is at the Mercy of the Incendiary's Torch," the general impression given was that the entire city was in the throes of revolution and anarchy. However a correspondent for the *New York Herald,* somehow keeping his balance amid such exaggerated fears and alarms, reported to his paper on July 9 that business was going on as usual, the stores were crowded with shoppers, and "there is no sign of mob or riot or strike, even, about the main part of the city."

But the railroads had already played their trump card. They had persuaded Attorney General Olney to intervene directly and on July 2 a blanket injunction was obtained from Judge Peter J. Grosscup, of the federal district court, forbidding any person from interfering with the operation of the mails or other railroad transportation in interstate commerce, and from seeking to induce any employes of the railroads to refuse to perform their normal services. With the whole force of government and the courts thrown against him, Debs was desperate. For a

time he hoped to win labor support for a general strike, only to be re-
buffed by the American Federation of Labor. Gompers felt constrained
to call a labor conference to consider the issue but he was entirely opposed to a strike. It was, indeed, hardly surprising that an organization
that had been founded in opposition to industrial unionism should be
unwilling to throw its support behind the American Railway Union.

"We declare it to be the sense of this conference," a statement issued
by Gompers on July 13 read, "that a general strike at this time is inex-
pedient, unwise and contrary to the best interests of the working people.
We further recommend that all connected with the American Federation of Labor now out on sympathetic strikes return to work, and those
who contemplate going out on sympathetic strike are advised to remain
at their usual vocations."

Without help from any quarter, Debs then offered to call off the strike
and boycott if the Pullman Company would agree to reinstate all workers without discrimination. With the courts swinging into action, the
railroads had no further cause for concern. They bluntly rejected Debs'
peaceful overtures: there would be "no recognition of anarchism."

Judge Grosscup now summoned a special jury to hear charges that
the strike leaders were guilty of conspiracy in obstructing the mails, that
and under instructions from the court Debs and three of his aids were
promptly indicted. Arrested on this count, they were released on bail,
but within a week were rearrested for contempt of court in disobeying
the original injunction. This time they went to jail. Other injunctions
were enforced against individual strikers and nearly 200 were arrested
on federal charges in addition to the several hundred jailed by local
police. Deprived of all leadership and direction, completely demoralized, the railroad workers gave up what had become a wholly futile
struggle and gradually drifted back to work. The troops were withdrawn on July 20. Government by injunction had won its first victory
by completely crushing the Pullman strike.

After some delay the contempt charges brought against Debs were
sustained in the circuit court on the ground that under the terms of the
recently enacted Sherman Anti-Trust Act, the strike leaders had engaged in a conspiracy to restrain interstate commerce. The following
spring the Supreme Court, while not expressly ruling on the applicability
of the Sherman Act, upheld the lower court. The federal government

was declared to have inherent authority to intervene to protect any obstruction to interstate commerce or the transportation of the mails.

Debs went to jail in Woodstock, Illinois, for six months. The action of the courts had made him a martyr and on returning to Chicago after expiration of his sentence he was wildly acclaimed by a crowd of over 100,000 sympathizers. At a gigantic mass meeting he was hailed by Henry Demarest Lloyd as "the most popular man among the real people today . . . the victim of judicial lynch law." Debs had become convinced while in jail that the cause of labor was hopeless under capitalism. He became a socialist and was to dedicate his life from this time forward to struggle against a system that enabled employers, as he repeatedly declared, to call upon government in enforcing their dictate, "work for what we want to give you, or starve." Until his death in 1926, he campaigned ceaselessly for labor's rights under the socialist banner and was five times candidate of his party for the presidency.

Labor and its sympathizers bitterly denounced the intervention of federal troops and use of the injunction in the Pullman strike, but the policy of the government was vigorously upheld in other quarters. Both the Senate and the House adopted resolutions supporting President Cleveland, there were innumerable statements from public leaders praising his handling of the situation, and the conservative press hailed him as a national hero for so vigorously suppressing what was universally called the "Debs Rebellion." The power of government had been asserted in no doubtful fashion. "To Cleveland and to Olney," the historian James Ford Rhodes wrote, "we in this country of reverence for just decisions, owe a precedent of incalculable value."

Perhaps the most important consequence of the Pullman strike was its revelation of the power that the injunction placed in the hands of industry in combatting the demands of labor. What chance had wage earners when their employers could so easily go into court and obtain injunctions against both strikes and boycotts; when government was ready to throw all its force against labor regardless of right or wrong in the issues under dispute? The workers' hands appeared to be completely tied. The campaign for abolition of government by injunction that at once got underway, taken up by the American Federation of Labor in spite of its reluctance to run any risks in supporting the American Railway Union, became from that day on one of labor's primary concerns. It was still to be a vital issue in the 1940's as it had been in the 1890's.

The forceful suppression of such strikes as those at Homestead and Pullman fanned the mounting discontent of the workers, but unemployment created even greater discouragement and despair. Throughout the country "industrial armies" took to the road and began to march on Washington to demand relief. The most famous of them was Coxey's Army, which actually reached the capital only to be dispersed after its leader was arrested for trespassing on the White House lawn. But there were other groups of ragged, down-at-heel workers on the march. Throughout the country local authorities were called upon to break up these demonstrations and maintain law and order in the face of a constant danger of mob action.

In the meantime, the growing unrest among the nation's farmers, who also found themselves increasingly hard-pressed in a period of falling prices that cut the value of agricultural products almost in half, was fanning the sparks of agrarian revolt. Populism swept through the prairies and while it was to remain primarily an uprising of midwestern and southern farmers, eastern workingmen who felt that the hand of government was everywhere against them could not fail to be attracted by its tenets. For Populism challenged the whole concept of government by organized wealth. In very much the same pattern as Jacksonian Democracy, it strove to recover for the common people the political power that was felt to have been usurped by the business community.

The Populist Party, formally organized in 1892, accepted as its basic premise the idea that wealth belonged to those who produced it, and called for a union of all the laboring elements in the nation to uphold their rights. Every effort was made to win the adherence of industrial workers. While the demand for the free and unlimited coinage of silver was a reflection of agrarian discontent, other demands put forward were wholly industrial in character.

"The urban workmen," the Populist platform stated, "are denied the right to organize for self-protection, imported pauperized labor beats down their wages, a hireling standing army, unrecognized by our laws, is established to shoot them down, and they are rapidly degenerating into European conditions." To combat this situation, the Populists supplemented their program for currency and other general reforms by taking over many of the demands traditionally pressed by the National Labor Union, the Knights of Labor and even the A.F. of L. They called for restrictions on immigration, enforcement of the anti-contract labor law and of the eight-hour day on government projects, an end to the use of injunctions in labor disputes, and the outlawing of the "army of mercenaries known as the Pinkerton system."

The Knights of Labor were ready to throw their enfeebled strength behind the Populists, eighty-two delegates attending the convention in 1892. The workingmen groups which supported Henry George in his campaign for the single tax, and Edward Bellamy in the formation of Nationalist clubs dedicated to socialist reform, formally allied themselves with the People's Party. Eugene V. Debs, fresh from his conversion to socialism while brooding over the failure of the Pullman strike, wholeheartedly backed a program which he believed provided ground for the common people to unite against the money power. Only the American Federation of Labor, once again reflecting the influence of Samuel Gompers, officially held aloof.

A determined effort on the part of socialists within the Federation to swing it in favor of a labor third party on a platform demanding "collective ownership by the people of all means of production and distribution" had been defeated only a short time before. Gompers won out, but in the process had been defeated in 1894 for the presidency. John McBride, of the United Mine Workers, was elected to this post and the headquarters of the Federation removed to Indianapolis. Gompers' eclipse, however, was only temporary. At the next convention he was not only restored to the presidency, but the stand he had taken against socialism was emphatically reaffirmed. When the demand was voiced for the A.F. of L. to take a partisan position in support of Populism, its re-elected president was all the more determined to steer clear of any direct participation in politics. The American Federation of Labor was not prepared to endorse the party of free silver. "These Middle Class issues," Gompers declared in re-emphasizing the importance for wage earners of concentrating all their energies upon the problems of unionism, "simply divert attention from their own interest."

When the Democrats took over the Populist program in 1896, challenging not only the Republicans but the conservatives within their own party, they nevertheless commanded widespread support among industrial workers. Both parties fully recognized the importance of the labor vote. William Jennings Bryan went so far as to state in one speech that if elected president, he was prepared to make Gompers a member of his cabinet—a gesture that nonetheless failed to move the A.F. of L. chieftain. The Republican high command, with Mark Hanna astutely managing William McKinley's campaign from the wings, tried a different tack. The workers were warned by notices in their pay envelopes that a Democratic victory would mean the further closing of factories and the loss of jobs. Every effort was made to keep them in line by the most dire prophesies of economic disaster should "the socialistic and revolutionary forces" led by Bryan, Altgeld and Debs win the election.

In the event, the organized forces of capitalism, represented by the Republican Party, hurled back this onslaught of farmers and workers campaigning under Democratic banners. McKinley was elected. The alliance had not been powerful enough, or strongly enough welded, to create a farmer-labor party that could carry through successfully a program of economic and social reform. Samuel Gompers had kept his organization out of politics and perhaps saved it from going the way of earlier labor associations that had been wrecked on the shoals of partisanship, but the election victory in 1896 went to the conservative defenders of a social order that supported strikebreaking, the Pinkerton system and government by injunction.

As the excitement of the campaign of 1896 subsided, labor had reason for discouragement in taking stock of the situation in which it found itself. The gains that had been made in wages prior to the depression had been largely wiped out. The average annual earnings for manufacturing employes were estimated at no more than $406. Except in a few of the highly skilled trades, working time was far longer than the eight-hour day for which labor had been so long struggling. It generally ranged between fifty-four and sixty-three hours a week—and even more in steel mills, textile factories, and the tenement house sweatshops where women and children in the garment industry toiled endless hours for a mere pittance. Nowhere was there any real economic security for the industrial worker.

While there was a beginning of labor legislation, little progress had really been made in attaining the goals first put forward in the late 1860's by the National Labor Union. A Bureau of Labor Statistics had been set up by the federal government, and comparable bureaus by some thirty-two states; an Alien Contract Labor Law had been enacted; the Chinese Exclusion Acts were on the statute books, and in 1898 President McKinley was to recommend the creation of an Industrial Commission. There were also various state laws regulating certain phases of industrial activity and looking toward the improvement of working conditions in mines and factories. But over against such moderate gains was the weakened position of the unions in general. The old conspiracy laws had, in effect, been revived through the application to unions of the Sherman Act's ban on combinations in restraint of trade and the use of the injunction in suppressing strikes and boycotts.

Moreover the number of organized workers had declined from the peak figures of the 1880's. A total of approximately a million had fallen to little more than a third of this figure. Even though Gompers had been able to boast in 1893 that the national unions had for the first time withstood depression, the American Federation of Labor had only some 250,000 members in 1897, and there were perhaps another 100,000 workers in the Railway Brotherhoods and other unaffiliated unions. This was a more compact and effectively organized nucleus than in earlier years, but in total union strength it was not very much greater than organized labor had claimed in either the early 1830's or the late 1860's.

The great mass of unskilled industrial workers remained unorganized. With their employers able to draw upon limitless replacements from the continuing stream of immigrant labor and obtain support for strike-breaking from the government and the courts, they were wholly defenseless against long hours, low wages and arbitrary dismissal. The crushing defeat of both the Homestead and Pullman strikes had been a bitter lesson in the overwhelming power that could be mustered to smash the efforts of industrial employes to organize in protection of their rights. The only prospect of any promise for labor as a whole appeared to be the further strengthening of the old-line trade unions brought together within the protective fold of the A.F. of L.

XI: THE PROGRESSIVE ERA

THE PROGRESSIVE ERA, extending from Theodore Roosevelt's accession to the presidency in 1901 to our entry into the first World War sixteen years later, saw a quickening of the liberal spirit throughout the United States. The popular discontent with business domination which had boiled over in the campaign of 1896 had not subsided with the defeat of Bryan. It found new expression in a more general and less radical movement that hammered away at political and social reforms through the agency of both major parties. In a determined quest for a larger measure of social justice, the nation demanded an end to "invisible government" and special privilege in whatever form. If liberal aims were not to be wholly realized, there was effective advance in many sectors and "a bracing of the moral sense of the country" that gave the progressive era a distinctive character in sharp contrast to the climate of public opinion in either the 1890's or the 1920's.

On the national stage, strenuous efforts were made to control the trusts, regulate the railroads, reform the monetary system and reduce tariffs, while at the same time the states embarked on individual programs of economic and social reform seeking to mitigate the evils of the slum, safeguard the health of women and children in industry, and generally improve factory conditions. Nineteenth-century concepts of a laissez-faire economy gave way to an awakened sense of social responsibility that accepted the need for action by government to meet the mounting problems of industrialization and urban growth. Moreover these gains were made against a background of peace and prosperity that led to a substantial rise in living standards. Popular faith and confidence in democratic capitalism, dealt such severe blows in the mid-1890's, were once again renewed in a spirit of buoyant optimism.

Labor participated in these general gains and eventually was to benefit materially from the remedial legislation of both Congress and the states. Yet the status of the great bulk of workingmen did not improve during these years of the progressive era in terms commensurate with the national advance as a whole. The real wages of industrial workers; that is, wages in terms of purchasing power, actually declined. Moreover the increasing introduction of labor-saving machinery on the one hand, and the rising tide of immigration on the other, inter-acted to maintain a constant surplus of labor. Not only did this situation hold down wages, but it heightened the feeling of insecurity among workers over whom always hung the dread shadow of unemployment.

And in spite of the new legislation, actual working conditions for the great majority of wage earners were slow in showing any real change. The factory codes were still inadequate and all too often ineffectively enforced. In the coal mines, steel mills, packing houses; in the textile factories still callously exploiting women and children, and in the sweat-shops of the urban clothing industry, the harsh circumstances of life were a sad commentary on the prosperity enjoyed by the country as a whole.

As far as labor organization itself was concerned, the gains of these years were uneven and somewhat equivocal. For a time a new era of industrial relations appeared to have opened with bright promise of labor peace, but as the unions grew in strength, industrial counter-attack soon led to further strife and sharp setbacks for labor in the courts and on the picket line. Only toward the close of the period was this early advance renewed with substantial gains in union membership and enhanced bargaining power.

The organized labor movement was almost wholly dominated by the American Federation of Labor—to the radical eruption of the I.W.W. we shall return—and its concern was still the well-being and status of its affiliated unions whose membership was principally made up of skilled or semi-skilled workers. This was to remain a basically important consideration in forthcoming years. While the A.F. of L. unions in coal mining, the garment industry, and textiles were industrial in character, and others included some unskilled workers, the overwhelming number of employes in the great mass production industries—largely foreign-born, ignorant, unassimilated in the American culture—remained outside union ranks. As we follow the course of organized labor during the progressive period, it should be remembered that less than ten per cent of the nation's wage earners were directly involved.

At the close of what Secretary of State John Hay called our "splendid little war" with Spain, the favorable turn in relations between national unions and employers was so pronounced that the years from 1898 to 1904 have been called "the honeymoon period of capital and labor." Strikes occasionally disrupted such harmony, but at least in comparison with the turbulent industrial strife of the 1890's, there was great improvement. In many industries employers and wage earners alike seemed determined to seek out peaceful solutions to their problems. Responsible labor leaders had become convinced of the certainty of failure in such struggles as those epitomized by the Pullman strike, and many industrialists had come to realize the dangerous economic and political implications of strikes even when they were successfully suppressed. The country generally, sobered by past experience, increasingly demanded some way of dealing with industrial disputes that would safeguard the public interest.

This new approach to labor problems was best represented by the National Civic Federation. It had been first set up in Chicago in 1896, but with the turn of the century was operating on a nationwide basis with the avowed object of bringing capital, labor and the public together in a joint campaign to maintain industrial peace. In sharp contrast to the prevailing attitude in the 1890's that tended to identify all labor agitation with anarchy, it was founded on the premise that "organized labor cannot be destroyed without debasement of the masses." Anti-union employers were declared to be as great foes to national stability as radical or socialistic labor leaders. The National Civic Federation accepted unionization and trade agreements as basic principles, and was prepared to offer its services "in establishing right relations between employers and workers" whenever both parties were willing to submit their disputes to its arbitration.

The leaders in this movement were Mark Hanna and Samuel Gompers, and associated with them in the National Civic Federation were a group of outstanding public figures. Grover Cleveland, President Eliot of Harvard, Archbishop Ireland were among the representatives of the public; John D. Rockefeller, Jr., Charles M. Schwab and August Belmont were included in the employer group, and John Mitchell of the United Mine Workers, James O'Connell of the Machinists, and James Duncan of the Granite Cutters were among the spokesmen for labor. The membership list was an impressive one and for a time the influence exercised by the National Civic Federation appeared to be a highly hopeful augury for labor-capital cooperation.[1]

Several important employer groups came to terms with the unions on the basis of mutually acceptable trade agreements. Pacts were concluded between the National Founders' Association and the International Association of Machinists. The Newspaper Publishers' Association and the International Typographical Union entered upon a series of agreements. Railroad operators recognized and negotiated with the railway brotherhoods. There were of course exceptions to this apparent progress toward industrial peace and the acceptance of collective bargaining. A final attempt on the part of the Amalgamated Iron and Steel Workers to organize the steel industry, for example, failed completely when the United States Steel Corporation, whose board of directors had secretly adopted a resolution stating its unalterable opposition to any extension of union labor, crushed a hard-fought strike in 1901. This was an important and highly significant defeat, but the growing number of trade agreements that were the fruit of the A.F. of L.'s program and policies seemed to indicate a change in general employer attitudes that greatly encouraged labor. "It was the harvest," Gompers happily declared, "of the years of organization which were beginning to bear fruit."

The unions flourished under these circumstances and in many parts of the country attained a new position of importance. They were strongest, and showed the greatest gains, in those trades that had the longest history of labor activity. The Miners, the Printers, the Cigar Makers, the Carpenters, the Molders, the Longshoremen, the Brewers, and the Machinists stood in the forefront of international unions affiliated with

[1] At a meeting in 1902 Charles Francis Adams read an interesting paper in the light of present-day labor laws, on "Investigation and Publicity as Opposed to 'Compulsory Arbitration'" in which he proposed legislation to set up a commission to investigate and report to Congress whenever a labor dispute threatened to disrupt interstate commerce. It was to be without coercive powers.

the American Federation of Labor, and in each instance they showed substantial gains in membership.

The exposures of the muckrakers, delving during these years into every phase of our industrial life, aroused a certain measure of popular sympathy for labor's efforts to improve its bargaining position. "Capital must make up its mind to get along with organized labor," the *Springfield Republican* declared in 1902. "Such labor is here to stay, and the law is more likely to compel the unionization of labor than it is to outlaw the labor union. The sooner this fact is recognized, the sooner will the country be placed on the way toward attaining a permanent industrial peace." Several years later as spokesman of the new progressivism, Herbert Croly was equally emphatic in upholding labor organization. "Labor unions," he was to write in *The Promise of American Life*, "deserve to be favored because they are the most effective machinery which has yet been forged for the economic and social amelioration of the laboring classes."

Indicative also of changing popular attitudes was the role that government assumed in the most important strike of these years. For when the anthracite coal miners became locked in a bitter struggle with the operators in 1902, President Roosevelt exercised his influence not to crush the strikers, as had President Cleveland when he sent federal troops to Chicago in 1894, but to enforce arbitration. While his primary concern was to avert a possible coal famine, it did not blind him to the legitimate grievances of labor.

Since the 1870's, the turbulent days of the Long Strike and the Molly Maguires, there had been periodic outbreaks in the coal fields as the miners struggled to improve working conditions. But not until the organization of the United Mine Workers in 1890 were they able to present a solid front against the combined strength of the operators. This new union succeeded, however, in organizing the workers in the bituminous mines of Pennsylvania, Ohio, Indiana and Michigan, and won full recognition from the operators in an agreement governing both wages and hours. Fresh from this victory, it then moved in at the close of the 1890's upon the anthracite area of eastern Pennsylvania.

Its task here was more difficult. The operators were organized in a virtual trust under railroad domination and could hardly have been more opposed to union recognition, while there was such a large element of Poles, Hungarians, Slovaks, Italians and other newly arrived immigrants among the workers that they lacked all cohesive unity. Moreover the operators made the most of this lack of homogeneity, doing everything possible to stir up mutual animosities and frictions.

The United Mine Workers made slow progress in the face of such handicaps but while their membership in the anthracite area was still less than 10,000, ten times this number responded to a first strike call in 1900. The operators were ready to meet this attack but Mark Hanna intervened and persuaded them to avert a prolonged conflict. His motive was wholly political. The Republicans were campaigning in 1900 on a platform of prosperity symbolized by the full dinner pail, and a coal strike would have sounded an unfortunate note of discord in the theme song of party orators. The operators reluctantly concluded an unwritten understanding with the miners which did not mean recognition of their union but partially met their immediate demands through a ten per cent wage increase.

This was a truce, however, and not a settlement. The strikers had not won their real objectives and the operators regretted even the slight concessions they had been forced to make. With no real improvement in conditions, the United Mine Workers consequently put forward further demands in 1902 and this time the operators, resolved not to let any further political pressure postpone a showdown, bluntly refused to consider the miners' new proposals or to deal in any way with the union. Another strike call was issued and 150,000 workers now walked out of the mines.

Their grievances were very real. The pay was low by any standard, the ten hours of work a day were hard and dangerous, and a lack of steady employment through frequent lay-offs cut down average earnings to less than $300 a year. Accidents were common, with a death toll of 441 in 1901, and the mine owners did nothing whatsoever either to ensure greater safety or to compensate their employes for injuries. But even more galling to the workers than low wages and poor working conditions, was the rigid feudal system maintained by the operators through their control over the company towns. The workers, Samuel Gompers was later to write, "were brought into the world by the company doctor,

lived in a company house or hut, were nurtured by the company store
. . . laid away in the company graveyard."

With the outbreak of the strike on May 9, 1902, the operators at once
threw 3,000 coal and iron police into the area, together with 1,000 other
special deputies, and began moving in strikebreakers. They trumped-up
charges of violence, sabotage and rioting against the workers and demanded the further protection of state militia. The strike was to be
fought as another anarchistic, revolutionary uprising against property
rights and public order.

In spite of such provocation, there was relatively little resort to
violence. It was on the whole a more orderly strike than the coal fields
had perhaps ever experienced. The workers simply stayed away from
the pits and maintained a completely passive attitude. Their ranks held
firm for all the suffering and hardship which the strike entailed for their
families. If it was to be a fight to the finish, they were ready for it; they
would not mine coal until their demands were met.

This solidarity and order were in large part due to the able conduct
of the strike, and the strong hold exercised over the men, by the president of the United Mine Workers. Since 1898 this post had been held by
John Mitchell. He had started work in the mines as a boy of twelve,
thrown in his lot with the union during its darkest days, and risen to
leadership while still only twenty-eight in large part through his skill
in organizing the many nationalities working in the mines. Slight and
wiry, with his brown eyes and swarthy face giving him somewhat the
appearance of an Italian, he had a modest—almost diffident—manner.
His strength was in his patience, his conciliatory attitude both in union
politics and in employer relations, and his willingness to compromise
on anything but what he thought were major issues.

No labor leader of the period was more conservative in his social and
political attitudes, more willing to accept arbitration, or more disap-
proving of radicalism and violence. He had originally opposed the strike
in 1902, consistently refused to call out the bituminous miners in support of those in the anthracite fields because the former had signed a
contract with the operators, and was ready at any time to submit the
issues in dispute to settlement by any impartial body. He suggested a
committee of five to be appointed by the National Civic Federation,

or one composed of Archbishop Ireland, Bishop Potter and any third person they might choose.

"If they decide that the average annual wages received by the anthracite miners," he stated, "are sufficient to enable them to live, maintain and educate their families in a manner conformable to established American standards and consistent with American citizenship, we agree to withdraw our claims for higher wages and more equitable conditions of employment, providing that the anthracite mine operators agree to comply with any recommendations the above committee may make affecting the earnings and conditions of labor of their employees."

In contrast to the moderation displayed by Mitchell was the truculent attitude of George F. Baer, the tough, hard-boiled spokesman of the operators. His reply to Mitchell's proposals was that "anthracite mining is a business and not a religious, sentimental or academic proposition." He was out to break the union at whatever cost. There was to be no submission of the dispute, as he never hesitated to make clear, to any outside group, let alone direct negotiations with the union. He believed whole-heartedly in the paternalistic controls maintained by the operators. Answering an appeal that he should seek to bring the strike to an end as his Christian duty, he stated his position in terms that seemed even to the *New York Times* to "verge very close upon unconscious blasphemy."

"I beg you not to be discouraged," Baer wrote his correspondent. "The rights and interests of the laboring man will be protected and cared for—not by the labor agitators, but by the Christian men to whom God in His infinite wisdom has given the control of the property interests of this country. . . ."

As the strike dragged on, a growing scarcity of coal, reflected in steadily rising prices, began to create mounting public concern and a popular demand for settlement. Whereas popular sympathy had originally been with the miners, the conservative press now felt free to blame them for the continued halt in production, and whenever any disorders were reported in the coal fields, it made the most of them. The *Journal of Commerce* declared in a familiar vein that what was taking place was "insurrection, not a strike," and the *New York Evening Post* called for "stern measures of suppression."

With the continued failure of the operators to make a single conciliatory gesture, however, public support soon began to swing back in the miners' favor. Editorials and cartoons singled out Baer for strong condemnation after his assertion of "divine right" with rising criticism in many quarters for his stubborn obduracy. But the primary interest of the country was not in either the workers or the operators. It simply wanted coal. Perhaps public opinion was more aptly reflected in a cartoon in the *New York Herald* depicting the public stretched on a wrack with the operators pulling at one end, the miners at the other. Its caption read: "The victim is not particular which quits first."

President Roosevelt felt the force of this demand for peace in the coal fields. His own position on labor issues was somewhat equivocal but his concern now was in getting the mines open. He felt compelled to act to protect the public interest and, as his correspondence reveals, because he feared the political repercussions of a coal famine. His program was not to crush the strike, although the operators were demanding an injunction against the United Mine Workers as a conspiracy in restraint of trade under the Sherman Act, but to compel arbitration. To that end, he summoned a conference of both operators and strike leaders which was held at the White House on October 3.

While Mitchell declared himself willing to accept the findings of any commission appointed by the President, Baer once again bluntly refused to have anything to do with arbitration. His intransigeant stand, as contrasted with the conciliatory attitude of the miners' leader, infuriated Roosevelt. Baer not only attacked the strikers but angrily rebuked the President for seeking to negotiate "with the fomenters of . . . anarchy and insolent defiance of the law." The conference was stormy. "If it wasn't for the high office I hold," Roosevelt is reputed to have said of Baer, "I would have taken him by the seat of the breeches and the nape of the neck and chucked him out of that window."

Still, almost no coal was being mined. Although 10,000 state troops were thrown into the territory to protect the strikebreakers, the men would not go back to work. The public grew more and more restive. Even conservative newspapers now stated that the operators had forfeited their claim to popular support and should settle the strike on the basis of negotiations with the United Mine Workers. "And the public," the *Chicago Evening Post* declared, "will not wait very long either. . . ."

Roosevelt decided to intervene even more directly. He secretly drew up a plan to put the army in the field with orders to its commanding general to dispossess the operators and run the mines as a receiver, and dispatched Secretary of War Root to inform J. P. Morgan, as the real power behind the operators, that this was his alternative if arbitration was still refused. Under such direct governmental pressure, the mine owners were finally induced to capitulate. They requested the President to set up an arbitration commission. Even at this point, however, they still balked at going the whole way and declared that they would not accept a labor member on the commission. Negotiations again hung in the balance until Roosevelt overcame this last obstacle by the appointment of the Grand Chief of the Railway Conductors, not as a labor representative but as "an eminent sociologist"! On October 23, after more than five months in which their lines had held almost without a break, the miners went back to work.

The award of the President's commission, announced in March, 1903, granted a ten per cent wage increase, reduced the working day to eight and nine hours for different classes of workers, and set up a special board to settle disputes arising during the three years in which the award was to remain in force. The miners had not won recognition of their union. They had failed to achieve their full aims and accepted the award reluctantly. But in the face of the operators' stubborn opposition, they had made real and important gains greatly strengthening the position of the United Mine Workers in the anthracite area.

For all the advances made in the opening years of the century, total union membership rising from 868,500 in 1900 to over 2,000,000 in 1904, and in spite of the more generally sympathetic public attitude shown during the coal strike, there was trouble ahead for organized labor. Employers who had for a time seemed willing to recognize unions, now became alarmed at their growing power. Largely abandoning the program for industrial peace originally sponsored by the National Civic Federation, they were beginning by 1903 to join forces in a vigorous campaign to block any further labor gains.

They encouraged the use of "yellow-dog" contracts obligating employes, as in the old iron-clad oaths, to agree that they would not join any union. They played upon the natural rivalries of immigrant groups to discourage any cooperative action, employed labor spies to inform on labor agitators who would then be summarily fired, and exchanged blacklists of workers charged with radical views. The great employing corporations were ruthless in this renewed anti-union drive and were able, moreover, to bolster its force by successfully calling upon the courts for support in conspiracy indictments and injunctions.

The earlier accords in the machinery and metal trades broke down as employer associations in both instances reverted to their original anti-labor attitudes. Following the action of United States Steel in bluntly refusing to deal with union labor under any circumstances, there was open warfare in the structural iron industry with the workers resorting to violence and dynamite. The packing houses suppressed a strike in which their employes sought collective bargaining; delivery firms in Chicago joined forces to crush completely a teamsters' strike for recognition. In almost every area, organized labor appeared to have been set back as employers who a few years earlier had appeared willing to bargain with the workers, now refused to do so.

There was a change of heart on the part of the National Civic Federation itself. In the face of the increasing breakdown of trade agreements, it appeared to lose its early enthusiasm for unionization. The employer members still professed their friendship for labor but directed their energies primarily toward combatting socialism and the closed shop. Gompers continued to work with them, being no less opposed to socialism, but in spite of his defense of the National Civic Federation's activities, labor lost confidence in its impartiality in industrial disputes.

Openly opposed to all labor organization were the Industrial Alliances that met in national convention in 1903 to form the Citizens' Industrial Association. Their lobbying and propaganda were highly successful in swinging public opinion against labor. After a meeting in 1906 that brought together some 468 delegates, representing almost as many employers' associations, President C. W. Post reported enthusiastically on the progress that he felt was being made. "Two years ago the press and pulpit," he declared, "were delivering platitudes about the oppression of the workingmen. Now all this has been changed since it has been discovered that the enormous Labor Trust is the heaviest oppressor of the independent workingman as well as the common American Citizen. The people have become aroused and are now acting. . . ."

The anti-union campaign was at the same time carried forward even more conspicuously by the National Association of Manufacturers, organized in 1895 but embarking on its first real attacks on organized labor about 1903. Its slogan and war cry was "the open shop," a guarantee of the right to work regardless of union affiliation. This appeal in the name of individual freedom, however, thinly disguised an all-out drive against both union recognition and collective bargaining. The N.A.M. stood for industry's sole and exclusive right in determining both wages and conditions of employment.

"Since the principles and demands of organized labor are absolutely untenable to those believing in the individualistic social order," delegates at the annual convention in 1903 were told by President Parry, "an attitude of conciliation would mean an attitude of compromise with regard to fundamental convictions. . . . The greatest danger lies in the recognition of the union." And one of the early pamphlets of the N.A.M., widely distributed in a propaganda campaign reaching out to the schools and churches as well as to the press and industrial organs, flatly stated that "our government cannot stand, nor its free institutions endure if the Gompers-Debs ideals of liberty and freedom of speech and press are allowed to dominate."

The principle of the open shop, often sustained with a conviction that went beyond all purely economic considerations, was used to justify or condone the most drastic measures in seeking to crush unions. This was perhaps most graphically illustrated in the suppression of the strike of employes of the Colorado Fuel and Iron Company in 1913. The real issue at stake in this dispute was recognition of the United Mine Workers, who had sent their organizers into the territory. Rather than make this concession, the company fiercely fought the strikers with hired detectives, special deputies and the state militia.

Open warfare continued for months in the Colorado mine fields and finally reached a bloody climax when the militia attacked a colony of the strikers at Ludlow. After several rounds of indiscriminate machine-gun fire, the tents in which the workers' families were living were soaked in oil and put to the torch. Women and children huddled in pits to escape the raging flames, and in one of them eleven children and two women were later found burned or suffocated to death. The nation was horrified by this massacre, but still the Colorado Fuel and Iron Company refused to consider negotiations with the union to end the strike.

The company was controlled by the Rockefeller interests and in the investigation of the strike by the House Committee on Mines and Mining, John D. Rockefeller, Jr., was called to the witness stand. In reply to questions as to whether he did not feel that "the killing of people and shooting of children" should not have led to efforts to re-establish labor peace, he implied that rather than give in to the miners, his company was prepared to go to whatever lengths were necessary. The only way that the strike could be settled, he stated, was through unionization of all the mines, which could not be accepted because "our interest in labor is so profound and we believe so sincerely that that interest demands that the camps shall be open camps, that we expect to stand by the officers at any cost." He resented particularly the idea that outside organizers should seek to stir up men who were "thoroughly satisfied with their labor conditions." There could be no surrender. "It was upon a similar principle that the war of the Revolution was carried on," Rockefeller declared. "It is a great national issue of the most vital kind."

This was not an isolated instance of uncompromising opposition to allowing employe organization, and the courts generally sustained employers in making non-membership in a union a condition of employment.

In 1898 Congress had passed a law, the Erdman Act, which prohibited any discrimination against workers by the interstate railways because of union membership. Ten years later, in *Adair* v. *United States,* the Supreme Court held this provision of the Erdman Act unconstitutional as an invasion of both personal liberty and the rights of property. A comparable state statute was outlawed in *Coppage* v. *Kansas* in 1915, and the Supreme Court then proceeded to uphold an injunction granted at the request of the Hitchman Coal and Coke Company, in West Virginia, which prohibited the United Mine Workers from seeking to organize company employes who had been compelled to agree not to join the union under yellow-dog contracts.

These legal obstacles to unionization did not pass uncriticized even in the Supreme Court. Justice Oliver Wendell Holmes strongly dissented. "In present conditions," he argued in the Coppage case, "a workman not unnaturally may believe that only by belonging to a union can he secure a contract that shall be fair to him. . . . If that belief may be held by a reasonable man, it seems to me that it may be enforced by law in order to establish equality of position between the parties in which liberty of contract begins. Whether in the long run it is wise for the workingmen to enact legislation of this sort is not my concern, but I am strongly of the opinion that there is nothing in the Constitution of the United States to prevent it. . . ." His brethren on the Supreme Court were not convinced, however. The decisions upholding and enforcing yellow-dog contracts stood until passage of the Norris–La Guardia Act in 1932 finally reversed public policy.

The courts also sustained the employers in their counter-attack upon union boycotts. The American Federation of Labor had found this weapon highly effective in promoting union recognition. By persuading its members to refrain from buying any goods that did not bear a union label, many recalcitrant employers were brought into line. To meet this situation the American Anti-Boycott Association was established to aid employers in going to court on the ground that such boycotts were conspiracies in restraint of trade and subject to injunction as "malicious" interference with the "probable expectancies" of property rights. Two important cases involving these issues dragged through the courts between 1902 and 1916, and in each instance resulted in a decisive defeat for labor.

In 1902 the United Hatters declared a nationwide boycott of the hats of D. E. Loewe & Company, of Danbury, Connecticut, in support of a strike by a local union to win recognition. The company at once instituted suit charging the United Hatters with conspiring to restrain trade in violation of the terms of the Sherman Act, and claimed triple damages from the individual members of the local union who had gone on strike. After a long period of legal wrangling, the company was upheld in 1916 and allowed total damages and costs assessed at $252,000. The bank accounts of the union members were attached and foreclosure proceedings introduced against their homes, but the fines were eventually paid through contributions from the national union and the A.F. of L.

The Danbury Hatters' case particularly awoke the resentment of labor because of its effect in bringing secondary boycotts under the ban of the Sherman Act and subjecting individual members to damage suits. But even while it was making its tortuous way through the courts, the American Federation of Labor itself became involved in another dispute which had even wider repercussions. In 1906 the metal polishers employed by the Buck's Stove and Range Company, of St. Louis, went on strike for the nine-hour day and appealed for aid. The A.F. of L. responded by placing the company on its "We Don't Patronize" list in the *American Federationist* and advising all union members to boycott its products. J. W. Van Cleave, president both of the Buck's Stove and Range Company and of the National Association of Manufacturers, a bitter enemy of all unions, promptly secured an injunction not only restraining the officers and members of the A.F. of L. from placing his firm on the "We Don't Patronize" list, but also from in any way calling attention to the metal polishers' strike either in writing or orally.

The A.F. of L. refused to heed this sweeping court order. While the offending company was taken off its unfair list, Gompers continued to state that union men could not be coerced into buying Buck stoves and ranges. He was thereupon found in contempt of court and sentenced to a year's imprisonment, two other officers of the Federation also being adjudged guilty and given somewhat lighter sentences. He was never to serve this sentence. Court proceedings continued even after the death of Van Cleave and withdrawal of the original injunction, but the case was finally dismissed by the Supreme Court. Although the A.F. of L. leaders consequently escaped jail, their conviction was nevertheless a shock that aroused labor even more against injunction law than its earlier defeats on this score. Gompers could not be reconciled to the position in which he found himself—a conservative, the friend of employers, the arch foe of labor radicalism, attacked by the government as though he were a revolutionary or an anarchist.

The effect of these decisions, and others in which injunctions were freely granted to employers, appeared to labor to represent a revival of the old conspiracy laws against which it had so often fought. The principles at stake closely paralleled those set forth in the legal cases of the early nineteenth century. Labor felt itself to be fighting again for the basic right to organize and strike against courts which had wholly gone over to the employers' camp in banning union activity as being in restraint of trade. The onetime accepted theory that possible injury to property rights through strikes or boycotts was only incidental to their legitimate purpose of seeking to improve working conditions, was being denied under conditions that seemed to threaten the very existence of unions.

The American Federation of Labor considered it imperative to seek legislative relief from such restrictions. It still did not wish to enter directly into politics, and had no idea of seeking even modification of the economic system. Rejecting renewed proposals of the socialists for adopting their program of government ownership of the means of production, Gompers declared in 1903, "economically, you are unsound; socially you are wrong; industrially you are an impossibility"—and was upheld by a vote of 11,282 to 2,147. But somehow the unions had to be freed from the disabilities under which they were suffering. Protection for the right to organize, to bargain collectively, to strike, to boycott, and to picket had become of immediate and vital concern.

A first step in trying to exercise more effective political pressure in support of such aims was made in 1906 when the A.F. of L. submitted a Bill of Grievances to the President and to Congress. It included most of the traditional demands that labor had been voicing since the Civil War, and sponsored various of the more general measures being promoted by progressives throughout the country. Most important, however, were the demands for exemption of labor unions from the Sherman Act and relief from injunctions which were said to represent a judicial usurpation of power properly belonging to the legislature. "We have waited long and patiently and in vain for redress," the Bill of Grievances concluded. ". . . Labor now appeals to you, and we trust it may not be in vain. But if perchance you may not heed us, we shall appeal to the conscience and support of our fellow citizens."

Congress did not heed labor's spokesmen. With the bills labor sought to introduce sidetracked or pushed aside, the A.F. of L. consequently entered actively into the congressional campaign of 1906. It not only called for the support of all congressional candidates friendly to labor's aspirations, but where neither party had named an acceptable candidate, it advised the nomination of a trade unionist. Two years later

Gompers appealed to both party conventions for support. The Republicans completely ignored him but the Democrats adopted an anti-injunction plank in their platform. The *American Federationist* thereupon took the further step of openly opposing William Howard Taft, assailed as the injunction judge, and coming out definitely in favor of William Jennings Bryan. When Taft was elected and the Republicans continued to pass over labor's demands, further support appeared to be forthcoming for the Democrats. While the A.F. of L. again attacked Taft in the election of 1912, however, it maintained a careful neutrality between Roosevelt and Wilson.

These political tactics were stoutly defended by Gompers as in no sense departing from the A.F. of L.'s traditional non-partisan stand of rewarding labor's friends and punishing its enemies. Legislation was needed to free the unions from existing restrictions, according to his thesis, and the Democrats had shown themselves to be more open-minded and sympathetic than the Republicans. "In performing a solemn duty at this time in support of a political party," the A.F. of L. chieftain declared in 1908, "labor does not become partisan to a political party but partisan to a principle."

How successful such political activities were prior to the Wilson administration was highly dubious. State legislatures adopted a number of measures which materially improved conditions for industrial workers, with special reference to women and children, but as already suggested, they were a response to the awakened sense of social responsibility that typified the whole progressive era rather than the result of political pressures exerted by organized labor. They had grown out of a humanitarian feeling which was not so much concerned over labor's rights—union recognition and collective bargaining—as with the more general aspects of an industrial society that harbored so much poverty, disease and crime.

While labor supported these reforms, moreover, they were not of primary consideration according to the philosophy of the A.F. of L. and Samuel Gompers. Suspicious of the state, Gompers was unwilling to rely upon government for the protection of labor's interests. He favored laws safeguarding women and children in industry, but did not want laws governing either hours or wages for union members. The only effective means for improving general working conditions, in his opinion, was the economic pressure of organized labor. All he asked of the state were guarantees of the right to exercise such pressure.

There was, indeed, no more staunch defender of laissez faire among conservative industrial leaders than the head of the A.F. of L. In 1915 Gompers came valiantly to its defense in an editorial in the *American Federationist,* and the phrases he employed have a strange familiarity in the light of political debates in the 1930's.

"Whither are we drifting," he asked. ". . . If there is no market for cotton those interests demand a law. If wages are low, a law or commission is the remedy proposed. What can be the result of this tendency but the softening of the moral fibre of the people? Where there is unwillingness to accept responsibility for one's life and for making the most of it, there is a loss of strong, red-blooded, rugged independence and will power. . . . We do not want to place more power in the hands of the government to investigate and regulate the lives, the conduct and the freedom of America's workers."

The economic and social reforms enacted during the progressive era were nevertheless important, and directly or indirectly they greatly benefited all workingmen. Child labor laws, placing restrictions on the age at which children might be employed, limiting their hours of work, and otherwise safeguarding health and safety had been adopted in some thirty-eight states by 1912, and protection was afforded women in industry through legislation in twenty-eight states setting maximum hours. More importantly, there had been widespread adoption—in at least thirty-five states by 1915—of workmen's compensation laws providing for compulsory benefit payments for industrial accidents. These latter measures were often inadequate and not always effectively enforced, but they demonstrated significant progress toward ensuring employer responsibility for the health and safety of workers in mines and factories.

A beginning was also made in the passage of general maximum hour laws. The demand for such legislation by the states, that had been pressed so vigorously in the 1840's and again in the 1860's, was not taken up by labor as it had been in these earlier periods. Collective bargaining rather than legal limitation were the means on which the unions principally relied to reduce the working day. As a result of progressive rather than special labor agitation, however, some twenty-five states enacted laws during this era which in the interests of public health and safety limited hours of work for men as well as women. They differed sharply from the earlier maximum hour legislation in that the old clause exempting "special contracts" was finally eliminated. For the first time, state hour laws were enforceable.

The courts had originally blocked the passage of much of this labor legislation, taking the stand that exercise of the state's police power could not be carried so far as to interfere with either the property rights of the employer, or the individual freedom of the worker to conclude whatever contract he desired. In *Lochner* v. *New York,* a case in which a maximum hour law for bakery workers was declared unconstitutional in 1905, the Supreme Court stated that such legislation was barred by the guarantees of liberty in the due process clause of the Fourteenth Amendment. However, the court gradually swung over to a more liberal interpretation of constitutional safeguards, and it finally upheld the maximum hour laws for both men and women, and also accepted the new workmen's compensation laws. When the further attempt was made to enact minimum wage laws, however, the Supreme Court divided evenly on their constitutionality and the validity of such legislation, as passed in seven states, remained in doubt. The issue did not again come up for determination until 1923 and it was then ruled, in *Adkins* v. *Children's Hospital,* that wage restrictions could not be reconciled with liberty of contract. This decision was to stand until 1937 when the Supreme Court finally acknowledged that, under existing conditions of employment, liberty of contract was a fiction which in no way preserved the individual worker's freedom in determining either his hours of work or his wages.

In general, state legislation in behalf of industrial workers, while still lagging far behind contemporary European experiments with both old age pensions and unemployment insurance, had substantial achievements to its credit during the Roosevelt and Taft administrations. On the national stage, as already suggested, there was far less cause for satisfaction. The Bill of Grievances submitted by the A.F. of L. in 1906 appeared to have been permanently tabled by hostile committees in both the House and the Senate. No progress whatsoever was being made in enacting its general provisions for union security. As action in so many cases demonstrated, the injunction and union prosecutions under the

Sherman Act became increasingly powerful weapons in the hands of labor's foes. The attitude of the Democratic House chosen in 1910 was a first sign of a more favorable attitude toward labor. An effective eight-hour day for workers on public contracts was finally passed, an Industrial Relations Commission was set up "to discover the underlying causes of dissatisfaction in the industrial situation," and provision made for establishing a Department of Labor particularly designed to promote the wage earners' welfare. But it was not until the election of 1912 that a real turning point was reached so far as broader legislation by the national government was concerned.

Wilson had attacked what he called "the antiquated and impossible" laws currently governing the relations of employers and employes in "The New Freedom." His inaugural further emphasized the need for legislation that would not only safeguard the workers' lives, improve conditions under which they worked, and provide rational and tolerable hours of labor, but also give them "freedom to act in their own interest." He denied that such laws could be considered class legislation and asserted that they were in the interests of the whole people. Labor rejoiced in such a defense of its position and confidently looked forward to the remedial legislation in respect to injunctions and conspiracy prosecutions for which it had striven so long and so unsuccessfully. "We are no longer journeying in the wilderness," Gompers proclaimed. "We are no longer in the season of mere planting. We are in the harvest time."

The results appeared for a time to bear out this optimism. In 1914 Congress passed the Clayton Act which both strengthened earlier anti-trust legislation and incorporated important clauses affecting the rights of labor. Specifically declaring that "the labor of a human being is not a commodity or article of commerce," the new law stated that nothing in the anti-trust laws should be construed to forbid the existence of unions, prevent them from "lawfully" carrying out their legitimate objects, or hold them to be illegal combinations or conspiracies in restraint of trade. Furthermore, it outlawed the use of injunctions in all disputes between employers and employes "unless necessary to prevent irreparable injury to property, or to a property right . . . for which injury there is no adequate remedy at law."

Gompers hailed this statute as the "Magna Carta" of labor—a final guarantee of the workers' right to organize, to bargain collectively, to strike, to boycott, and to picket. Other opinion varied as to the real efficacy of the new law. Although the *Wall Street Journal* described Congress as "a huddled mob of frightened cowards . . . watching for the labor boss to turn down his thumb," many newspaper editorials, political leaders and even some labor spokesmen pointed out that the cautious phraseology of the Clayton Act showed that labor had really won no new rights and that injunctions had not actually been outlawed. Gompers chose to ignore all such practical considerations as he spread the glad tidings of what he insisted was a great labor victory. Perhaps in order to justify the policies he had followed and to build up the prestige of the A.F. of L., he admitted no doubts as to the full freedom that the unions had theoretically won.

The skeptics were soon shown to have been justified. The guarantees of the Clayton Act proved to be largely illusory once they were subjected to interpretation by the courts. Loopholes were discovered in the supposed exemption of unions from the anti-trust laws; the provisions in regard to the use of injunctions were so interpreted as to provide no real relief. The statement of principle that labor was not a commodity remained, and it had a real significance as marking a change in public attitudes, but it had no practical effect on employer-employe relationships.

Yet there were substantial gains for labor during the Wilson administration and in spite of disappointment over the later interpretation of the Clayton Act, these years were to find organized labor driving ahead on many fronts. It won legislative support on three important issues. Passage of the La Follette Seamen's Act in 1915 remedied many of the most glaring abuses in the employment of sailors and immeasurably improved conditions in the forecastles of American merchant vessels. A demand by railway workers for shorter hours was met the next year when the Adamson Act established an eight-hour day, with time and a half for overtime, for all employes of interstate railways. And congressional enactment of a literacy test for all European immigrants in 1917 was a first step toward the policy of immigration restriction which labor had so long demanded.

The growth of labor unions during the first decade of the new century had been temporarily halted by the industrial counter-attack launched about 1904. The membership of the American Federation of Labor actually declined in 1905 and for the next five years remained almost stationary. It was only 1,562,000 in 1910 in comparison with 1,676,000 six years earlier. Between 1910 and 1917, however, the A.F. of L. gained some 800,000 new members and trade union enrollment as a whole rose to over 3,000,000. It was almost four times what it had been at the opening of the century.

The urge to join a union, in these years as in other periods, came not only from expectation of economic gain through collective action. The hope that he would attain greater security—a square deal and protection from arbitrary discipline—was always highly important, but there was also an often unconscious desire on the part of the individual wage earner to strengthen his feeling of individual worth and significance in an industrialized society. Machinery was more and more making the worker an automatic cog in a process over which he had no influence or control. The complete impersonality of corporate business, with management far removed from any direct contact with employes, further accentuated this loss of individual status. The wage earner could find a satisfaction in membership in such a meaningful social organization as a labor union that was denied him as one among many thousands of depersonalized employes. The desire to take part in some group activity was, indeed, particularly strong during the progressive era. It was a period marked by the rapid growth of social clubs, lodges and fraternal associations. The unions, often including some of the ritual of the fraternal lodges, met a very real need entirely apart from the support they provided for collective bargaining.

The expansion in union ranks, in any event, was brought about both by the increase in membership in old unions and the establishment of new ones. The United Mine Workers had built up a membership of 334,000, by far the strongest union in the country; the building trades— carpenters, painters, masons, bricklayers—had over 300,000 workers in their various unions, and important additions to the organized labor movement were the unions among garment workers.

Activity in this industry had received dramatic impetus from the "uprising of the twenty thousand" among the shirtwaist makers in New York. This strike in the fall of 1909 had so sensationally dramatized the intolerable conditions prevailing in the sweatshops that popular sympathy had swung wholly over to the strikers. Under the leadership of the International Ladies' Garment Workers, they had been able to win all their major demands except a closed shop. This strike was only a preliminary, however, to a further struggle the next year which broke out among the even more sweated workers in the cloak and suit trade. They were largely unorganized but again direction of the strike was taken over by the I.L.G.W.U. With Louis D. Brandeis, later to become an associate justice of the Supreme Court, serving as a mediator, a favorable settlement was again concluded. The garment workers not only won their wage and hour demands but negotiated a "protocol" with their employers which set up machinery for the conciliation of future disputes. The International Ladies' Garment Workers became one of the nation's strongest and most enterprising unions. It was largely made up of immigrants with a heavy majority of women, was somewhat socialistic in its outlook, and greatly concerned over the individual welfare of its members.

The key union among workers in men's clothing was for long the United Garment Workers. In 1914 internal quarrels led a majority of its membership to break away from the A.F. of L. and form the independent Amalgamated Clothing Workers. This union steadily grew in strength and succeeded in concluding trade agreements with manufacturers in all large centers of industry. Like the I.L.G.W.U., it was socialistic in theory but its day-by-day policy was one of increasing cooperation with employers under constructive, broad-minded leadership.

The United Mine Workers, the International Ladies' Garment Workers and the Amalgamated Clothing Workers were industrial unions, including in their membership all workers in the industries which they represented. They remained, however, outstanding exceptions to the general rule of labor organization. There were no unions of any significance in steel, in automobiles, in agricultural machinery, in electrical manufactures, in public utilities, in tobacco manufacture or in meat packing. The very industries that were becoming most important in the economic development of the country, and employed an increasing proportion of industrial workers, were unaffected by the labor activity of these years because the corporations controlling them were so stubbornly anti-union and so powerful that every effort to organize their employes was doomed to failure.

It was the continued low wages and long hours for workers in these mass production industries that largely accounted for the unevenness of the gains that may be attributed to labor during the progressive era. The social legislation of the period, wage advances for skilled workers banded together in the unions comprising the A.F. of L., a changing public attitude and public policy toward unionization, were counteracted by the depressed circumstances of the great hordes of unorganized industrial workers who still accounted for approximately ninety per cent of the total labor force.

XII: THUNDER ON THE LEFT

WHILE THE WAGE EARNERS in the national and international unions were generally willing to accept an economic system under which they appeared to be making slow but definite gains, disturbing currents of a deeper discontent developed during the progressive era among the workers who were outside the bounds of existing trade unionism. New demands were voiced for organization on industrial lines or for the all-inclusive union structure abandoned after the collapse of the Knights of Labor; the adherents of socialism grew in strength and redoubled their efforts to build up an effective political party, and there was radical agitation among the unorganized workers for direct action to secure their share of the benefits made available by an expanding economy.

"The labor men are very ugly and no one can tell how far such discontent will spread," Roosevelt was somewhat fearfully writing Henry Cabot Lodge as early as 1906. "There has been during the last six or eight years a growth of socialistic and radical spirit among workingmen and the leaders are obliged to play to this or they lose their leadership."

The upsurge of radicalism appeared somehow out of place in a period in which the spirit of the country was one of buoyant confidence and such general advance appeared to be underway for the people as a whole. It was a direct reflection, however, of the extent to which the interests of the unskilled workers were being ignored. As the American Federation of Labor continued to neglect industrial organization and fought every radical movement as vigorously as industry itself, the embers of discontent were fanned still more strongly. Fertile ground was provided for a revival of revolutionary activity whose aim was the immediate abolition of the wage system and the complete overthrow of capitalism. For a brief time this movement appeared to threaten the stability and basic conservatism of the entire labor movement. Its spearhead was the Industrial Workers of the World.

Miners, lumberjacks and migratory harvest hands in the West joined forces with socialistic groups representing the unorganized industrial workers of the East in the formation of this new association. The I.W.W. denied that there was anything in common between the working class and the employing class. Viciously attacking the policies of the A.F. of L. and all trade unionism, they called upon the workers to take over themselves possession of the machinery of production.

"Instead of the conservative motto, 'A fair day's wage for a fair day's work,'" their ringing manifesto declared, "we must inscribe on our banner the revolutionary watchword, 'Abolition of the wage system.' It is the historic mission of the working class to do away with capitalism."

The I.W.W. grew out of a secret meeting in Chicago in 1905 which drew together all the radical and dissident elements in the labor movement. These militant western miners, socialists of various persuasions, advocates of industrial unionism and anarchistic exponents of direct action closed their ranks for a unified and direct attack upon capitalism. Events were to prove that they agreed upon little else than their mutual scorn for the program and tactics of the A.F. of L. Accepting the thesis of class struggle as their common starting point, however, they set up an economic organization whose aim was to work on both the political and industrial front for the final emancipation of labor.

The most important group behind the organization of the I.W.W. was the Western Federation of Miners. It had once been affiliated with the A.F. of L. but had withdrawn in 1897 in resentment against what was felt to be the effete East's betrayal of the workers' cause. Permeated with the independent and often lawless spirit of the frontier, the miners had then engaged in a series of strikes in the gold, silver, lead and copper mines of the western states, and in 1903–1904 waged open warfare against the operators in the Cripple Creek area of Colorado. They fought the introduction of strikebreakers; the owners counter-attacked through local vigilance committees and state militia. With each side equally committed to violence, the struggle was dramatically marked by mine explosions, the wrecking of trains, mob outbreaks, individual killings, arrests, imprisonments, and the machine gunning of miners' assemblies. After thirteen months of intermittent fighting, the strike was finally crushed and the vigilantes, deputized sheriffs, police and militia restored something like order to Cripple Creek.

After this defeat, the Western Federation of Miners realized it could not stand alone. It had already formed what was first called the Western Labor Union and then the American Labor Union in an effort to bring together all workers in the western states in a single industrial organization, and the Federation's leaders were now ready to welcome any move toward even broader organization. They hopefully answered the call for the Chicago convention that was to result in formation of the I.W.W. Their delegates numbered only five out of a total of some two hundred at this meeting, but with 27,000 members the western miners were far and away the strongest union represented.

The socialists were the other principal group to send delegates. The Working Men's Party had long since been succeeded by the Socialist Labor Party. Under the domineering leadership of Daniel De Leon, a brilliant orator and pamphleteer known as "the socialist pope," incessant warfare had been waged for a decade against what were considered the timid and pusillanimous policies of the A.F. of L. A master of personal invective, De Leon called the Federation "a cross between a windbag and a rope of sand," while Gompers was intermittently a "labor faker," "an entrapped swindler," and "a greasy tool of Wall St." Unity was never possible in the socialist camp, however, and in 1900 a further split within the ranks led to the creation of still another in the long series of parties professing the socialist faith in one form or another. This faction, which was known simply as the Socialist Party, was to exercise far more influence than any of its predecessors, and under the leadership of Eugene V. Debs polled heavy votes in the presidential elections of the progressive era. The Socialist Labor Party and the Socialist Party were naturally always at odds, but that did not prevent both their leaders being present at Chicago.

While other independent radical unions were officially represented, including the American Labor Union, the United Metal Workers and the United Brotherhood of Railway Employes, individuals rather than organizations were primarily responsible for the establishment of the I.W.W. and the convention was enlivened by the clash of their divergent personalities. In addition to De Leon and Debs, other delegates were William D. Haywood, of the Western Federation of Miners; Father

T. J. Hagerty, a big, black-bearded Catholic priest who was the editor of the American Labor Union's official organ and a militant advocate of industrial unionism; A. M. Simons, the socialist intellectual and editor of the *International Socialist Review;* Charles O. Sherman, the general secretary of the United Metal Workers; William E. Trautmann, a radical leader of the United Brewery Workers and editor of its German language paper, and Mother Jones, a fiery, intrepid, little old lady of seventy-five, with curly white hair and kindly gray eyes, whose zeal as an agitator kept her in the front lines of labor's fighting front for almost half a century.

Among these varied and colorful figures, the most arresting was Haywood. A massive, stoop-shouldered, lumbering giant, his generally tough appearance given an almost sinister cast as a result of the loss of one eye, "Big Bill" Haywood was a powerful and aggressive embodiment of the frontier spirit. He had been cowboy, homesteader and miner, but at the turn of the century left the mines of Silver Creek, Idaho to become an active organizer for labor and the Socialist Party. Described as "a bundle of primitive instincts," Haywood accepted violence as a necessary phase of the labor struggle. He stood forthrightly for direct action. On calling to order the first convention of the I.W.W., he addressed it as "the Continental Congress of the working class" and from the onset clearly revealed that his real interest was in organizing the forgotten unskilled workers and especially the migratory laborers of the West—the "bums" and "red-blooded working stiffs." "We are going down in the gutter," Haywood shouted, "to get at the mass of workers and bring them up to a decent plane of living."

Except for Haywood, none of these convention delegates had more than a corporal's guard of followers to bring into the I.W.W. They spoke for themselves and their individualistic attitudes on labor policy appeared to be irreconcilable in the excitement of convention debate. After giving full vent to their opposition to what they derisively called, "the American Separation of Labor," they nevertheless agreed upon a general program for the I.W.W.

Gompers had nothing but scorn for these leftist maneuvers and the attempt to revive a form of labor organization which he roundly condemned as "fallacious, injurious, reactionary." He struck out particularly at his old foe De Leon whose adherence to the I.W.W. he hoped would

"bring unction to the soul" of its other promoters. "So the trade union
smashers and the rammers from without and the 'borers from within,' "
he wrote, "are again joining hands; a pleasant sight of the 'pirates' and
the 'kangaroos' hugging each other in glee over their prospective prey."

His belief that such strange bedfellows could not long work together
soon appeared to be substantiated. Faction and controversy split the
ranks of the I.W.W. almost immediately. At the 1906 convention a conflict between the more moderate elements, primarily represented by
the Socialist Party, and the outright proponents of revolution led to
wholesale desertions by right-wingers. The next year the Western Federation of Miners itself withdrew, reducing the actual membership of
the I.W.W. to less than 6,000, and then in 1908 a final struggle broke out
over the basic issue of political or economic action. The group favoring
the former policy was led by De Leon and the latter by Trautmann, but
the decisive element at the convention was a delegation of western rebels—"the Overalls Brigade"—which beat its way to Chicago on freight
trains and had scant interest in doctrinaire squabbling.

This faction ousted the De Leonites, who promptly held a rival convention to form a new organization, and then proceeded to amend the
Chicago constitution to their liking. All idea of employing the weapon
of politics was given up. The overthrow of capitalism was to be sought
solely through direct economic action. Openly revolutionary in theory
and practice, committed to strikes, sabotage and violence, the I.W.W.
was pledged never to accept peace with the enemies of the workers.

Only through One Big Union, breaking through all craft lines, it was
now declared, could the workers present an effective united front in the
class struggle. The A.F. of L. had betrayed labor and fallen under the
complete domination of employers.

"Tie 'Em Up," sang the Wobblies:

We have no fight with brothers of the old A.F. of L.
But we ask you use your reason with the facts we have to tell.
Your craft is but protection for a form of property,
The skill that you are losing, don't you see.
Improvements on machinery take your skill and tools away,
And you'll be among the common slaves upon some fateful day.

Now the things of which we're talking we are mighty sure about.—
So what's the use to strike the way you can't win out?

> Tie 'em up! tie 'em up; that's the way to win.
> Don't notify the bosses till hostilities begin.
> Don't furnish chance for gunmen, scabs and all their like;
> What you need is One Big Union and One Big Strike.

Refusing to abandon the right to strike at any time or on any occasion,
the I.W.W. did not approve of trade agreements. Everyday struggles
for wages and hours were only the first line of attack; the decks had to
be kept clear for the final assault. Industrial unions were to provide the
"structure of the new society within the shell of the old" and a workers'
government replace what in a capitalistic society was "simply a committee employed to police the interests of the employing class."

The I.W.W. made its greatest appeal to western miners, construction
gangs, lumberjacks and migratory harvest hands who were not interested
in political action since they seldom had the vote. Ill-paid, homeless,
unmarried; drifting from job to job, largely cut off from the usual ties
of society, they considered themselves victims of an economic system
designed solely to exploit them. They were ready to strike, to resort to
violence, to wage open warfare—not for the nebulous dream of "pie
in the sky" but for down-to-earth ownership of the means of production.
Converts were also won among the immigrant workers of steel mills,
packing plants and textile mills whom the I.W.W. was prepared at all
times to aid. This group was not as rough and ready as the western rebels.
Eastern factory workers did not necessarily accept the revolutionary
implications of the I.W.W. program. But whether they did or not, they
were grateful for the support given to their strikes.

Membership in the I.W.W. never became very great—probably no
more than sixty thousand at its peak. Several hundred thousand union
cards were issued, but casual workers did not remain very long in the
ranks. The significance of the I.W.W., as already suggested, was its
revolutionary leadership. The Wobblies themselves as they came to be
called in the West, often appeared to welcome violence, enjoying a

brawl for its own sake, and they fought the forces of law and order without too much concern over the validity of the issues involved. "Hanging is none too good for them," the *San Diego Tribune* exploded on one occasion in 1912, "they would be much better dead, for they are absolutely useless in the human economy; they are the waste material of creation and should be drained off into the sewer of oblivion there to rot in cold obstruction like any other excrement." Yet without this class of workers, however obstreperous, the West would hardly have developed so rapidly. They did the rough and heavy work: cut the timber, harvested the crops, dug out the minerals. And however mistaken their views may have been, however hopeless their often blind struggle against society, they had courage and militancy that were colorful and exciting.

Their spirit found expression in the I.W.W. songs sung at their union meetings, in harvest camps, on the picket line: "Are you a Wobbly?" "Dump the Bosses Off Your Back," "Paint 'Er Red," "What We Want," "The Red Flag" and "Hallelujah! I'm a Bum!"

> O! I like my boss,
>   He's a good friend of mine,
> And that's why I'm starving
>   Out on the picket-line!
> Hallelujah! I'm a bum!
>   Hallelujah! Bum again!
> Hallelujah! Give us a hand-out
>   To revive us again!

There were I.W.W. strikes in the mining fields, on lumbering projects, in the construction camps of the Northwest; in Pacific coast canneries, eastern textile mills, midwestern steel and meat packing plants, and among streetcar workers, window cleaners and longshoremen. The I.W.W. leaders, and notably "Big Bill" Haywood, who had stayed with the I.W.W. in spite of the withdrawal of the Western Federation of Miners, were ready to back up the unorganized workers—anywhere, anytime. They directed strike activity, manned picket lines, provided relief for the workers' families, agitated and organized with a reckless ardor that made the tactics of the A.F. of L. seem pale and insipid.

When local authorities tried to suppress the activity of the I.W.W. and threw its organizers into jail, "free speech" fights broke out from Walla Walla, Washington to New Bedford, Massachusetts. There was no sooner news of arrests in some particular town than the Wobblies would arrive upon the scene by the hundreds to exercise their constitutional rights and defy the police. When the first contingents were jailed, others took their place until the harassed authorities found the burden upon the community so great that they had no alternative to setting their prisoners free. The Wobblies would pour from the jail triumphant, ready again to agitate, to picket, to battle for their rights.

The West was the scene of the most spectacular strikes and free speech fights waged by the Wobblies, but one of their greatest victories was won in a struggle of textile workers in Lawrence, Massachusetts, in 1912. In spite of eastern fears of an intrusion of frontier violence, however, this strike was marked by rigid discipline. The I.W.W. realized in this instance the importance of winning public sympathy for the workers and did everything possible to maintain order. All idea of revolutionary activity was subordinated to the immediate job. Without any support from other unions, which were jealous of their invasion of an eastern factory town, the I.W.W. leaders in Lawrence directed all their energies toward maintaining the united front among the strikers that ultimately forced the employers' submission.

A reduction in wages for the 30,000 workers in the Lawrence textile mills, about half of whom were employed by the American Woolen Company, brought on the strike. The earnings of the mill hands, largely Italians, Poles, Lithuanians and Russians, averaged less than $9 a week —when the mills were running full time. Moreover in addition to insufficient wages and long hours, a premium system had been introduced to speed up the work under conditions that imposed terrific pressure and tension. The pay cuts were the last straw. The angry workers began spontaneously to walk out on January 12, 1912, as the bells of the city hall rang a general alarm, in a concerted protest that soon involved some 20,000 men and women.

There were some union members in the mills. A few belonged to the United Textile Workers, an A.F. of L. affiliate, and something like a thousand to the I.W.W. The rest were unorganized. Foreseeing the strike, the I.W.W. members had already sent to headquarters for help and Joseph J. Ettor, a member of the general executive board, hurried to Lawrence and was soon joined by another I.W.W. leader, Arturo Giovannitti. These two men at once took over virtual control of the strike, organized it on a wholly realistic basis, and imposed strict discipline. Ettor arranged great mass meetings to keep the strikers united, established picket lines, and saw that relief was given to the needy and suffering families whose sole sources of income had been abruptly cut off. Relief was, indeed, his greatest problem for over half of the city's population of 85,000 were either strikers or their dependents. General committees were formed for each separate national group to distribute supplies, maintain soup kitchens, and provide other aid.

The first suggestion of lawlessness was the discovery, announced in scare headlines in the press, of dynamite planted in various parts of the city. The I.W.W. was at once accused of importing its terroristic methods and such sympathy as had at first been aroused for the strikers turned to angry resentment. "When the strikers use or prepare to use dynamite," the *New York Times* declared editorially, "they display a fiendish lack of humanity which ought to place them beyond the comfort of religion until they have repented."

The strikers protested at once that the dynamite planting was none of their doing. Events were wholly to vindicate them. Before the strike was over it was proved that a local undertaker had planted the dynamite, in an obvious effort to discredit the strikers and particularly the I.W.W., and that the plot had been contrived by persons closely associated with the mill owners themselves. With the arrest of the head of the American Woolen Company, on the charge of being implicated in this scheme, even the most conservative newspapers strongly assailed the strategy of trying to involve the workers in pretended bombing plots. The *Iron Age* spoke of "betrayal of the cause of employers generally," and the *New York Evening Post* condemned "an offense on the part of capitalism which passes the worst acts ever committed by labor unions."

In the meantime the American Woolen Company, still refusing even to consider the workers' demands, tried to reopen the mills. This move

caused a violent clash between strikers and police and during the rioting
an Italian woman was shot and killed. The authorities promptly declared martial law, twenty-two militia companies were called out to
patrol the streets in order to prevent any public meetings or talks, and
Ettor and Giovannitti were arrested as accessories to murder.

Neither the strike committee nor the I.W.W. allowed these developments either to drive them into unwarranted counterviolence or to lessen
their determination to see the strike through. "Big Bill" Haywood took
charge after the arrest of Ettor and Giovannitti, and in spite of his
own and the I.W.W.'s revolutionary policies, he continued to insist upon
an attitude of passive resistance. With such control the workers held
firm. The protection offered by the militia to employes desiring to return
to their jobs did not encourage any defections from the ranks. "In the
spinning room every belt was in motion, the whir of machinery sounded
on every side," wrote a newspaper reporter visiting one of the mills,
"yet not a single operative was at work and not a single machine carried
a spool of yarn."

The problem of feeding the strikers became increasingly difficult,
however, and early in February the committee evolved a plan which
had the double objective of helping to meet immediate needs and
dramatically calling public attention to them. Labor sympathizers in
other cities were asked to provide temporary homes for the children of
the strikers. The response was immediate and several hundred children
were sent to other communities. Alarmed at the effect of this move,
which the head of the United Textile Workers took the lead in denouncing as made solely "to keep up the agitation and further the propaganda
of the Industrial Workers of the World," the Lawrence authorities stated
that no more children would be allowed to leave the city. When the
strike committee undertook to send another group away, the police
forcibly interfered under circumstances that were more successful in
creating sympathy for the strikers than anything else could possibly
have been.

"The station itself," read a report of the Women's Committee of Philadelphia, which was to take care of the children, "was surrounded by
police and militia. . . . When the time approached to depart the children, arranged in a long line, two by two, in orderly procession, with their
parents near at hand, were about to make their way to the train when

the police, who had by that time stationed themselves along both sides of the door, closed in on us with their clubs, beating right and left, with no thought of the children, who were in the most desperate danger of being trampled to death. The mothers and children were thus hurled in a mass and bodily dragged to a military truck, and even then clubbed, irrespective of the cries of the panic-striken women and children. . . ."

This was perhaps the turning point in the strike. Neither the Lowell authorities nor the mill owners could withstand the flood of protests from every part of the country. There were to be further attacks on the strikers and further arrests—the latter totaled 296 during the two months of the strike—but with the picket lines holding firm the American Woolen Company finally admitted defeat and on March 12 offered terms which virtually met all the workers' demands. Wages were to be increased from five to twenty-five per cent, with time and a quarter for overtime; the premium system equitably adjusted, and there was to be no discrimination in rehiring the strikers. At a great mass meeting on the Lawrence Common, Haywood advised acceptance of this offer and the mill operatives agreed to return to their jobs.

A final episode was the trial of Ettor and Giovannitti. For a time it appeared that they would not be given a fair hearing and were likely to be convicted in spite of the lack of any evidence directly implicating them in the murder with which they were charged. The I.W.W. organized a defense committee which collected $60,000 and the workers in Lawrence, declaring that unless the authorities opened the jail doors they would close the mill doors, went on a twenty-four hour protest strike—15,000 strong. In the final outcome, both men were found innocent, and on being released were wildly greeted by crowds who held them in no small part responsible for the victory that the Lawrence textile employes had won under their direction.

Before the trial ended, the two accused men made speeches to the jury setting forth their position, in which they frankly avowed the revolutionary aims of the I.W.W. and their refusal to be intimidated by the police. That of Giovannitti, a poet in his own right whose revolutionary verses are to be found in many anthologies, was eloquent and moving.

"Let me tell you," he declared, "that the first strike that breaks again in this Commonwealth or any other place in America where the work and help and the intelligence of Joseph J. Ettor and Arturo Giovannitti will be needed and necessary, there we shall go again, regardless of any fear or of any threat. We shall return again to our humble efforts, obscure, unknown, misunderstood soldiers of this mighty army of the working class of the world, which, out of the shadows and darkness of the past, is striving towards the destined goal, which is the emancipation of human kind, which is the establishment of love and brotherhood and justice for every man and every woman on this earth."

The I.W.W. had won an astounding triumph in Lawrence. Its membership among the textile workers jumped almost overnight to 18,000, and this renewed vitality appeared to promise still further growth. Alarm was created within the A.F. of L. as to the future development of its aggressive strike tactics, while even greater fears were aroused in the business community over the possible spread of radical doctrines among American workers. "Are we to expect," an article in the *Survey* asked, "that instead of playing the game respectably, or else frankly breaking out into lawless riot which we know well enough how to deal with, the laborers are to listen to a subtle anarchistic philosophy which challenges the fundamental idea of law and order, inculcating such strange doctrines as those of 'direct action,' 'syndicalism,' 'the general strike,' and 'violence'? . . . We think that our whole current morality as to the sacredness of property and even of life is involved in it."

These fears soon proved to be groundless. The I.W.W. had reached the height of its power and influence. As with the old Knights of Labor, its greatest victories were the forerunners of disastrous defeats and of a decline which within a few years would lead to virtual collapse. The I.W.W. was too revolutionary to attract the support of the basically conservative forces of American labor, and in spite of the violence of its propaganda, too cautious to be successful as revolution. The only thing in which it fully succeeded was in arousing popular fears of violence that could not be allayed even by the relatively peaceful tactics of Lawrence.

The next important strike in which the I.W.W. participated was a harbinger of its decline. Trouble developed in 1913 in the silk mills of Paterson, New Jersey, and among other leaders of the Wobblies, Haywood and Ettor were again on hand. This strike was a prolonged and embittered struggle. The Paterson authorities were determined to crush the revolutionary menace of the I.W.W., and it in turn felt that too much depended on a victory in this strike to give in. The brutality of the police in arresting strikers on any pretense, clubbing them into insensibility when they resisted, and breaking up their picket lines was notorious. Yet the strike went on. Among others who were won to sympathy for the silk workers was John Reed, the young Harvard-educated revolutionary who was to write *Ten Days that Shook the World* and be buried beside the walls of the Kremlin. Describing the scene at Paterson, he said that he could never forget "the exultant men who had blithely defied the lawless brutality of the city and gone to prison laughing and singing." But after five grueling months, the exhaustion of their funds and the growing need of their families forced the strikers to surrender. The I.W.W. had to admit defeat.

Succeeding years saw the Wobblies engaged in scores of minor strikes, while their membership greatly fluctuated as local unions broke up and the migratory construction workers and harvest hands drifted in and out of the organization. There were clashes with authority in many instances, and in the western states a mounting tendency to suppress strikes by any means and at any cost. A free-speech fight at Everett, Washington, for example, resulted in seven deaths when deputized sheriffs opened fire on a boatload of Wobblies landing in the harbor.

Upon the outbreak of the European conflict in 1914, the I.W.W. took a decisive stand against war. "We, as members of the industrial army," read a resolution adopted at its convention that year, "will refuse to fight for any purpose except for the realization of industrial freedom." When the United States joined the Allies three years later, it did not modify its position and refused to support the national war effort at the expense of the class conflict. The interests of the workers in their continuing struggle against capitalism were held superior to those of the country as defined by a government which the I.W.W. considered no more than a committee of the employing class. Critical strikes by metal miners at Butte, Montana, and lumber workers in the Northwest dangerously impeded the war program, but the Wobblies maintained that they were not trying to sabotage vital industries but to improve conditions for the workers.

The public reaction was to condemn the I.W.W. as unpatriotic, pro-German, treasonable. In the frenzied atmosphere of war, popular feeling was everywhere whipped up to fever pitch against "Imperial Wilhelm's Warriors." And employers seeing their chance to smash the I.W.W. once and for all, did everything possible to add fuel to these blazing embers of hatred with the enthusiastic cooperation of much of the press. "The outrageous eruption of the I.W.W. in the far West," the *Chicago Tribune* declared, ". . . is nothing less than rebellion." "While the country is at war," echoed the *Cleveland News*, "the only room it can afford I.W.W.'s . . . is behind the walls of penitentiaries."

Such sentiments found concrete expression. In 1917–1918 state after state passed criminal syndicalism laws outlawing the I.W.W. and countless arrests were made under these statutes. The national government also entered the picture under the provisions of the Sedition and Espionage Acts. Federal authorities obtained some 160 convictions against members of the I.W.W. on charges of obstructing the war effort. At a mass trial in Chicago, Haywood and ninety-four others were convicted of sedition and sentenced to jail for terms running up to twenty years. The charges of conspiring against the government were in many instances so flimsy as to be ridiculous, but patriotic fervor was not often restrained by consideration of the constitutional rights of free speech and assembly during the first World War.

When the authorities did not act promptly enough, loyalty leagues and local vigilantes often took the law into their own hands. Brutal clubbings, horse-whippings, tar-and-featherings took place in many communities; there were several instances in which I.W.W. agitators were taken out and lynched by lawless mobs. In July, 1917, some 1200 striking miners at Bisbee, Arizona, of whom less than half were actually I.W.W. members, were forcibly deported from the town by a posse deputized by the sheriff at the instance of a local loyalty league. They were put into cattle cars, taken across the state line and abandoned in the desert. After thirty-six hours without food or water, they were rescued by federal authorities and taken to a detention camp in Columbus, New Mexico.

The energies of the I.W.W. were largely absorbed during these war years in trying to defend what it insisted were its "class war prisoners." Unable to do so successfully, it soon found itself without leaders. Haywood himself eventually skipped bail and fled to Soviet Russia. The organization did not break up—it later experienced recovery of a sort—but it never regained its militant pre-war strength.

Changing economic conditions in the West, marked by the increased use of farm machinery and developing automobile transportation, depleted the ranks of the migratory workers who were such an important element in the membership. The Communist Party, organized as a branch of the Third International in 1919, drew away many of the radical socialists. Finally, what was left of the I.W.W. became far less aggressive with the loss of its old leadership. Emphasis was placed upon preparations for administering control of the means of production rather than revolutionary action to seize such control. "The 'Wobblies' . . . said nothing of revolution or class consciousness, of exploitation . . . or of the necessary overthrow of the capitalist system," a reporter for the *New York World* wrote of an unemployment conference after the war. "They talked instead of 'uninterrupted production,' 'the coordination of industrial processes.' . . ." By the mid-1920's the old fighting I.W.W. had already become a legend.

The impact of the I.W.W. on the labor movement was more important than either its membership or its erratic strike activity would suggest. Apart from such direct results as may have been obtained in improving working conditions in western mines, lumber camps and harvest fields, and occasionally in eastern factories, this revolutionary movement spectacularly centered attention on the desperate needs of vast numbers of unskilled workers and gave a new impetus to industrial unionism which even the A.F. of L. could not entirely ignore. The radical doctrine of class struggle badly shook, for a time at least, the complacency of conservative labor leaders who refused to look beyond the confines of traditional trade unionism.

The I.W.W. was nevertheless a failure. It made no more progress toward abolishing the wage system by inciting class warfare than had the Knights of Labor by their moderate program of education and agitation. The overwhelming bulk of American workingmen remained as fundamentally opposed to I.W.W. philosophy as were their employers or the middle class generally. The American Federation of Labor, which lost no opportunity to discredit and attack its radical rival, continued to dominate the labor movement and revolutionary unionism made no real headway against business unionism. The I.W.W. was a dramatic expression of left-wing sentiment, but it made few converts. American labor could not be convinced that the historic role of the working class was to do away with capitalism.

XIII: THE FIRST WORLD WAR— AND AFTER

As THE SHADOW of impending war fell over the United States and events rapidly drove the country toward participation in the European struggle, American labor was confronted with a grave problem. Was the conflict one in which workingmen had anything at stake? Should the war effort be supported or should labor take advantage of the national crisis to promote its own class interests? The I.W.W. had made its choice in 1914 and stuck to it. The socialists were divided, but true to his convictions Eugene V. Debs continued to attack what he declared to be a wholly capitalistic war—and went to jail. The American Federation of Labor, however, carrying with it the great majority of the nation's wage earners, declared and maintained complete loyalty to the government and its entire war program. As the outstanding spokesman for labor, no public figure was more exuberantly patriotic than Samuel Gompers and no one proved himself to be a more faithful adherent of the Wilson administration.

On the eve of hostilities, organized labor was stronger than it had ever been before and had won for the first time what was in effect official recognition of its role in the national economy. The report of the Commission on Industrial Relations, ascribing much labor discontent to denial of the right to organize, definitely upheld trade unionism as an essential institution for the settlement of industrial disputes; the Clayton Act apparently exempted unions from prosecution under the antitrust laws, and President Wilson had both demonstrated his friendliness on many occasions and declared that no future president would ever be able to ignore the organized labor movement.

Moreover the victory won by labor in 1916 when Congress passed the Adamson Act marked an important extension of governmental authority in the field of labor relations. It was true that Congress had acted under the imminent threat of a railway strike that would have paralyzed the national defense program, and there was widespread resentment against the tactics employed by the railway brotherhoods. But the acceptance of an obligation to safeguard the interests of the workers was nonetheless highly significant.

It was with a new sense of both power and responsibility that the spokesmen of some three million wage earners undertook to define the attitude of labor toward war. The issue was first taken up at a conference held on March 1, 1917—almost a month before hostilities, but at a time when war already appeared imminent—that was attended by representatives of seventy-nine international unions, the railway brotherhoods, and the A.F. of L. executive council. At its conclusion the conferees issued a public statement on "American Labor's Position in Peace or in War" that pledged the full support of all labor organizations should the country become directly involved in conflict with Germany.

It was not an unconditional pledge. Organized labor was determined that such gains as had been made in recent years should be protected in the event of war, and in pledging support to the Wilson administration, insisted on full recognition of its newly attained status. The unions were to be the medium through which government would operate in seeking the cooperation of wage earners, and they were to be given representation on all boards dealing with national defense. Labor was to be free to exercise the right to organize, and while prepared to use all possible restraint, did not agree nor intend to surrender the weapon of the strike. These conditions for labor cooperation were said to be necessary because of the very nature of the aims for which the country was prepared to go to war.

"Wrapped up with the safety of this Republic," the labor leaders asserted, "are ideals of democracy, a heritage which the masses of the people received from our forefathers, who fought that liberty might live in this country—a heritage that is to be maintained and handed down to each generation with undiminished power and usefulness."

The administration was prepared to work with labor on this basis and after our actual entry into the war, tried to pursue a policy in respect to industrial relations that would forestall strikes. Agreements with the American Federation of Labor specifically provided for the enforcement of trade union standards in all government contracts, labor representatives were appointed to all appropriate government agencies, and

Gompers was made a member of the Advisory Commission of the National Council of Defense. "While we are fighting for freedom," President Wilson told the A.F. of L. convention in November, 1917, "we must see among other things that labor is free. . . ."

But industrial peace was not to be so easily maintained during 1917. As prices rose under the stimulus of wartime purchasing without a corresponding increase in wages, there was discontent among the workers and general demands for increases in pay. When such demands were not met, strikes broke out on a scale that exceeded even pre-war years. Before 1917 ended, they reached a total of 4,450, involving over a million workers.

Many of these strikes were instigated by the I.W.W. Under its radical leadership there were threatening outbreaks in the lumber camps of the northwest, among shipyard workers on the Pacific coast, and in the copper mines of Arizona. Labor unrest was by no means limited, however, to workers who fell within the radical fringe of the labor movement. Many of the conservative and patriotic unions affiliated with the A.F. of L. felt justified in making wartime demands and backing them up with strikes that seriously interrupted production in defense industries.

By the beginning of 1918 this situation threatened to block the flow of military supplies overseas. While efforts were constantly being made to resolve labor disputes through special wage adjustment boards and a mediation commission that had been set up by President Wilson in August, 1917, the government felt obliged to intervene still further in order to assure essential industrial output. Both the friendliness of the administration toward organized labor and simple expediency dictated a policy that would win the workers' support rather than one of suppressing strikes by force. Representatives of labor and management were consequently appointed to a War Labor Conference Board, and after it had unanimously agreed upon a set of principles to govern future labor relations, the President appointed upon its recommendation, in April, 1918, a National War Labor Board to serve as a final court of appeal to settle all industrial disputes that could not be resolved through other means. It was composed of five representatives of labor and five of management, with two joint chairmen representative of the public: former President Taft and Frank P. Walsh, who had been chairman of the Commission of Industrial Relations. Somewhat later a further agency, the War Labor Policies Board, headed by Felix Frankfurter, was also established to act as a clearing house to unify departmental labor policies on wages and hours in the war industries.

The general principles upon which the National War Labor Board operated were immensely significant as a reflection of new governmental attitudes toward labor, and also foreshadowed those later to be incorporated in the labor legislation of the New Deal. In return for a general undertaking that there would be no further strikes or lockouts for the duration of the war, the Wilson administration was prepared to accord labor full support for virtually all its traditional demands. The right to organize and bargain collectively through "chosen representatives" was definitely recognized, and was not in any way to be abridged or denied by employers; all existing agreements in respect to union or open shops were to be upheld on their pre-war basis; the eight-hour day was to be applied as far as possible; women entering industry were to be given equal pay for equal work, and there was complete acceptance of "the right of all workers, including common laborers, to a living wage . . . which will ensure the subsistence of the worker and his family in health and reasonable comfort."

With these highly important commitments, strikes tended to subside and such disputes as did develop were in most instances quickly settled. They caused few work stoppages interfering with war production. No need consequently developed to consider such drastic measures as a manpower draft, compulsory arbitration or anti-strike laws. Labor generally upheld its side of the bargain into which it had tacitly entered and Secretary of War Baker declared on one occasion that it had proved to be "more willing to keep in step than capital."

As the principal spokesman for labor, Gompers continued to support the war effort in every possible way and succeeded in completely identifying the A.F. of L. with our foreign policy. He vociferously attacked all pacifist or suspected pro-German groups, promoted the American Alliance for Labor and Democracy as a counter-move to socialist propaganda for peace, and staunchly upheld Americanism. "I want to express my admiration," was President Wilson's warm tribute, "of his patriotic courage, his large vision, and his statesmanlike sense of what had to be done." In the fall of 1918, Gompers went abroad to attend an inter-allied labor conference and he was in Paris during the peace negotiations as a member of the Commission on International Labor Legislation.

Labor policy was reflected in the wartime gains of the workers and the growth of unionism. Wages gradually rose until average earnings in manufacturing, transportation and coal mining topped the $1000 mark, and the unions in 1919 had over a million more members than in 1916—a total of 4,125,000. When the government took over control of the railways, the recognition previously granted only the railway brotherhoods was extended to shopmen, yardmen, maintenance-of-way workers, railway clerks and telegraphers. In other industries where unionization had had hard sledding, there were important advances—among packing-house employes, seamen and longshoremen, electrical workers, and machinists. The war had opened up great opportunities, and American labor had made the most of them.

The conclusion of hostilities at once created a new situation. As wartime restraints were removed and government surrendered such controls as had been exercised by the National War Labor Board, both labor and industry prepared for the inevitable renewal of their historic contest. The precarious wartime truce expired. Labor was militantly determined not only to maintain the gains that had been made during the war but to win further recognition of its rights, and industry was no less bound to free itself from all government control, check any further advance of unionization, and reassert its power. No holds were barred by either antagonist as industrial strife broke out in 1919 on a scale greater than the country had ever before experienced. The strikes that year were to be nationwide in their scope and would directly and dangerously affect, as would those somewhat more than a quarter of a century later, the whole process of national reconversion to peace.

Wages were an immediate cause for many of these disputes. The wartime price rises continued unchecked in 1919—the cost of living would ultimately reach twice the pre-war level—and the workers began to feel the pinch despite the high pay they were still able to command. But the basic issue of union security was far less easily settled than wage adjustments. Many employers were willing to grant or at least compromise wage demands, but saw in any extension of collective bargaining a threat to their management of their own business. They refused to recognize union spokesmen, and concessions that had been made under the pressure of war were widely withdrawn.

The vital importance of this issue of union recognition was brought out in the one attempt the Wilson administration made in post-war years to reconcile the differences between management and labor. The various agencies for handling labor disputes had been promptly scrapped after the Armistice, but as the number of strikes increased, the President summoned a National Industrial Conference, this time composed of representatives of labor, industry and the public, in the hope that some basis could be found for labor peace. Fundamental disagreements at once developed over the nature of collective bargaining and the obligation of an employer to deal with men or groups of men who were not his own employes. The labor representatives insisted on the right "to organize without discrimination" as the only means of assuring recognition of national unions, and the conference collapsed when the public representatives, a group somehow including John D. Rockefeller, Jr., and Elbert H. Gary, chairman of the United States Steel Corporation, upheld those of industry in refusing to grant this concession.

In the meantime, the extent and character of the strikes of 1919 began more and more to alarm the public. They were felt to be not only endangering economic reconversion but threatening the stability of American institutions. The attitude of many people was greatly affected by almost frantic fears of the spread of communism aroused by the Bolshevik Revolution in Russia. Indeed, the influence of the red scare in molding public opinion toward labor strikes in 1919 can hardly be exaggerated. Popular hysteria over the supposed role of Moscow in fomenting disorder in the United States led a great part of the public to believe that most strikes were instigated by Communists on direct orders from the Kremlin. The legitimate rights and justified grievances of the workers were forgotten in a fearful eagerness to make Bolshevism the cause of all labor unrest. Employers made the most of these fears and alarms, waging a ceaseless campaign to identify all strikers as reds. After the high hopes born of the war, labor found itself everywhere on the defensive, hard-pressed to maintain its position, let alone improve it.

There were some grounds for the attitude of the public. The Communist International preached world revolution and had its adherents in the United States. The local Communist Party formed in 1919 attracted many of the radical elements in the labor movement that had formerly been associated with the I.W.W. and other left-wing groups. Its members infiltrated into a number of unions, exercised an influence out of all proportion to their actual numbers, had a part in fomenting several strikes, and occasionally incited violence. But as on previous occasions when an alarmed public saw a radical threat to society in labor uprisings—the railway strikes of 1877, the Pullman strike, and even the coal strike of 1902—communist influence was greatly overemphasized.

Moreover the attempt of conservative employers to fasten the charge of Bolshevism on the labor movement as a whole could not have been wider of the mark. The leadership of the A.F. of L. was as violently hostile to communism as the governing board of the National Association of Manufacturers. Gompers was in the very forefront of the red-baiters who were helping to create the hysterical intolerance of this period. Indeed, his attempt to absolve the labor movement from industry's charges of radical and subversive activity by continually attacking Bolshevism, proved to be something of a boomerang. His irresponsible exaggeration of the red menace intensified the public's fears of social conflict and consequent demand for the forceful suppression of strikes.

In any event, newspaper reports of strike activity, editorial comment, cartoons and the statements of public leaders, all revealed a hardening of the public attitude toward labor as the year progressed. The more sympathetic feeling of the progressive period evaporated as reaction set in against the whole concept of Wilson's New Freedom. There was derisive talk of factory employes riding to work in their cars, buying silk shirts for themselves and silk stockings for their wives, at the very time that they were demanding higher wages. The strikes awoke "unstinted condemnation from almost every walk of life," one newspaper stated; another declared that the only One Big Union the nation would tolerate was "the one whose symbol is the Stars and Stripes."

Popular demand grew for a national policy of strike suppression in the name of economic and social stability. By the close of 1919, strike after strike was collapsing, the *Literary Digest* pointed out, because the power of public opinion had strongly and definitely crystallized in favor of federal, state and local police intervention in support of the employers and against the workers.

A first strike to arouse public opinion in the post-war period was the so-called general strike that broke out in Seattle in February, 1919. It was not actually to prove very important, but the background of violence out of which it grew and the very effort to call out all workers, created national concern and evoked what were already becoming the inevitable charges of Bolshevism.

The incident leading to this strike was a demand on the part of shipyard workers in Seattle for higher wages. When it was bluntly rejected by their employers, the men walked out. The Central Labor Committee in Seattle at this time was controlled by James A. Duncan, an aggressive and radical agitator who had risen to power amid the embittered industrial strife promoted throughout the northwest by the I.W.W. He was an outspoken opponent of the conservative labor policies followed by the A.F. of L., had strongly opposed our entry into the war, and was sympathetic toward Soviet Russia. Seizing the opportunity to make trouble, he called a general strike of all workers in Seattle. Some 60,000 responded and for five hectic days the industrial life of the city was almost paralyzed and its citizens deprived of most of their normal services.

A general strike was a new phenomenon for the United States and the gathering public opposition, both in the Northwest and throughout the country, soon made the participating unions realize that in pursuing such tactics they were forfeiting all popular sympathy. They withdrew their support from the Central Labor Committee and the strike completely collapsed. In the meantime, however, Mayor Ole Hanson had burst into the nation's headlines with sensational statements that the whole thing had been a Bolshevist plot which was crushed only by his own heroic measures.

Even more disturbing was the strike some months later of the Boston police. Discontented with low wages and other aspects of their jobs which they considered unfair, the police had formed a union, which was called the Boston Social Club, and applied to the American Federation of Labor for a charter. Police Commissioner Curtis promptly stated that no members of the force would be allowed to join a union, suspended nineteen of the men who had done so, and began recruiting volunteers to take over should any union activity continue. Outraged at what they considered such unwarranted and arbitrary action, the police took matters in their own hands and on September 9 suddenly went on strike. Boston found itself wholly without police protection that night and its nervous citizens hardly knew what outbreaks of crime and violence to expect. In the event there was a good deal of rowdyism by bands of hoodlums, but no such general lawlessness as had been feared. The next day volunteers and state guards took over the duties of police and complete order was restored.

Settlement of the highly involved issues at stake was not so easy. Charges and counter-charges flew back and forth over responsibility for the strike and the failure to place on duty immediately the volunteer force which had supposedly been trained for just such an emergency. The police commissioner and the mayor were at odds. While the former refused to consider the grievances that had led to the strike or to reinstate any of the men who had taken part in it, the latter showed a good deal more sympathy for the strikers and charged that the whole affair had been miserably mishandled. From A.F. of L. officials came accusations that the police commissioner was more interested in trying to discredit labor than in solving the controversy, and that he had virtually goaded the police on to strike.

Whatever was brought out in support of the police, however, the public generally condemned them for deserting their posts and upheld Commissioner Curtis in his refusal to re-employ them. A "crime against civilization" was President Wilson's sharp comment on the strike, and a future President won nationwide fame by an even more positive statement. Calvin Coolidge, then governor of Massachusetts, was requested by Gompers to remove the police commissioner. He refused. "There is no right to strike against the public safety," read his terse telegram, "by anybody, anywhere, anytime." The public cheered such sentiments to the echo, the Boston police were not reinstated, and Coolidge was started on the road to the White House.

Although the Seattle general strike and the Boston police strike attracted the attention of the entire country, they were local affairs. A great deal more significant in their national, industry-wide implications were strikes in steel and coal. They were defeated under the conditions prevailing in 1919, but they foreshadowed a new pattern of industrial conflict that was to be greatly accentuated after the second World War. The steel strike was especially important. If the steel workers had been successful, the whole labor history of the 1920's might have followed a completely different course. Suppression of the strike, however, postponed effective organization of the workers in this basic industry for another eighteen years.

Conditions in the steel mills fostered universal discontent and underscored what labor leaders declared was an imperative need for unionization if the workers expected any consideration of their grievances. Wages remained low in spite of wartime advances and were steadily falling further behind the continued rise in living costs. A twelve-hour day, six days a week, was still in effect for something over half the labor force, and the average working week was just under sixty-nine hours. Among the highly diversified immigrant groups that made up the majority of employes, living conditions were a bitter travesty upon the promise of a more abundant life which had drawn them to the Land of Opportunity.

Organizational progress on other sectors of the labor front had no parallel in the steel industry. Since suppression of the strikes of the old Amalgamated Association of Iron, Steel and Tin Workers in 1901 and 1910, no further efforts had been toward unionization. While the Amalgamated was still in existence, it was a small craft union that did not touch the interests of the great mass of unskilled workers.

The first step leading toward the strike was the formation, in the summer of 1918, of an organizing committee made up of representatives of twenty-four unions having jurisdiction in the steel industry. Its objective was not only improvement of conditions in the mills but the conquest of this key industry by union labor. The guiding spirit was William Z. Foster, a radical exponent of direct economic action whose early experience in industrial conflict was won in the ranks of the I.W.W. and who later was to become a leading communist. His organizational skill was outstanding and as secretary-treasurer of the associated union committee, he was put in charge of this "one mighty drive to organize the steel plants of America."

Within a year the number of organized workers in the steel mills jumped to 100,000 and an attempt was made to open negotiations with Chairman Gary of the United States Steel Corporation for a trade agreement. When he completely disregarded this request, a strike vote was taken and in behalf of the steel workers, the union committee demanded collective bargaining, the eight-hour day and an increase in wages. Gary's reply to further overtures for the discussion of these demands was blunt and unequivocal. "Our corporation and subsidiaries, although they do not combat labor unions as such," he stated, "decline to discuss business with them." The strike was then officially set for September 22 and by the end of the month close to 350,000 men had quit work in nine states.

The steel industry—the strongest capitalistic power in the world—was ready to meet this challenge and in its determined efforts to break the strike received the full cooperation of local, state and even federal authorities. Thousands of strikebreakers were brought in, particularly large numbers of Negroes; labor spies were hired to do everything possible to stir up animosity and racial antagonism among the different foreign elements in the mills, and deputized guards, local police and state constabularies smashed picket lines and broke up strike meetings with little regard for civil liberties. Violence was held down by the enforcement of martial law in many localities, troops being dispatched to Gary, Indiana, under Major General Wood, but some twenty persons were killed—eighteen of them workers—before the strike was over.

The steel companies also opened up a terrific barrage through newspaper advertisements to discourage the strikers and convince public opinion that the whole thing was a plot hatched in Moscow for the overthrow of American capitalism. The strike was not between the workers and their employers, the steel companies proclaimed, but between revolutionists and America. It could not win for the United States would "never stand for the 'red' rule of Bolshevism, I.W.W.ism or any other 'ism' that seeks to tear down the Constitution." Rumors were even circulated "that the Huns had a hand in fomenting the strike, hoping to retard industrial progress."

So great were the excitement and controversy stirred up under these circumstances that a Commission of Inquiry was set up by the Interchurch World Movement, an organization of Protestant churches, to investigate the strike. It could find no evidence whatsoever of the sinister intrigues the steel companies alleged they had uncovered, and stated that it was far more profitable to consider the workers' uprising in the light of industrial history than "in the glare of baseless excitement over Bolshevism." The repeated emphasis upon the radical, anarchistic, communist aspects of the strike, however, and Foster's left-wing views, succeeded in alienating much popular sympathy for the steel workers in spite of uncontradicted disclosures of the harsh conditions in the mills. The public was all too ready to see Bolshevism at work. The very fact that so many of the steel workers were "hunkies," "dagoes" and "wops," was taken as convincing evidence that they were un-American, revolutionary and controlled by Moscow.

The strike committee could find no way to combat this propaganda successfully. There were withdrawals of support on the part of the sponsoring unions, Foster's leadership was repudiated by the A.F. of L., and discouragement spread through the ranks of the strikers themselves. Late in November the union committee consequently asked the Interchurch Commission to mediate and agreed to accept whatever plan it might suggest for ending the dispute. Gary refused to listen to any peace proposals. The strikers sought "the closed shop, Soviets, and the forcible distribution of property," he declared: ". . . there is absolutely no issue." The strike dragged on but the disheartened men now began to drift back to work. In January, 1920, the leaders gave up. The strike was called off and such men as had not in the meantime been blacklisted returned without having won a single concession.

"The United States Steel Corporation," the Interchurch Commission declared in a final report, "was too big to be beaten by 300,000 workingmen. It had too large a cash surplus, too many allies among other businesses, too much support from government officers, local and national, too strong influence with social institutions such as the press and the pulpit, it spread over too much of the earth—still retaining absolutely centralized control—to be defeated by widely scattered workers of many minds, many fears, varying states of pocketbook and under a comparatively improvised leadership."

The organization of steel was decisive if labor was to unionize other mass-production industries from which it had so far been barred. The business and financial community fully recognized the significance of the 1919 strike as a showdown between the open shop and industrial unionism. The United States Steel Corporation was backed to the hilt. J. P. Morgan assured Gary of his full approval of the stand he had taken in refusing to deal with the unions. Every effort was made—and made successfully—to hold out the bogey of Bolshevism as a justification for refusing even to consider the demands of the workers. The results of the strike were not only back to the twelve-hour day, but back to un-controlled paternalism and anti-unionism in the country's most impor-tant industry.

Even before the end of the steel strike, the conflict in the bituminous coal fields came to a head. The United Mine Workers had concluded a contract with the operators covering the war period, and with the higher prices of 1919 asked for an adjustment in wages that had not been raised since 1917. They proposed a sixty per cent increase in pay and adoption of the thirty-hour week in order to combat the unemployment resulting from the falling-off of wartime need for fuel. The operators not only refused to consider the miners' demands, admittedly excessive, but they insisted that the old contract was still in effect because the war was not yet technically over. A strike that was to involve 425,000 miners was then called for November 1.

The danger to the national economy of any prolonged stoppage in the mining of coal, as on other occasions both before and since 1919, was a matter of grave public concern. The government had already warned that a strike would be illegal under wartime legislation governing the coal industry. To the consternation not only of the United Mine Workers but of American labor generally, the onetime friendly Wilson adminis-tration now took the drastic step of securing an injunction, granted by Judge Albert B. Anderson of the federal district court in Indianapolis, which prohibited any further strike activity by union officials and called upon them to cancel the strike order.

Intervention by the government, in the face of what had been taken by labor as a pledge not to use its wartime authority to suppress strikes, aroused a storm of protest. The American Federation of Labor con-demned the injunction as "an outrageous proceeding . . . which strikes at the very foundation of justice and freedom." It called upon the miners not to give in to government pressure and promised them full support in continuing their struggle.

The acting president of the United Mine Workers in 1919 was a forty-year old labor leader who during the war years had been the union's chief statistician and who was wholly unknown to the public. But John L. Lewis was at once to step into the popular limelight. He did so by calling off the strike. Although he strongly attacked President Wilson for countenancing the use of an injunction, he was unwilling to follow the militant advice of the A.F. of L., and in what later years would seem to make very uncharacteristic action, advised surrender. "We are Americans," Lewis told newspapers in this first instance of his strike leadership, "we cannot fight our government."

The miners themselves, again in what seems an unusual role, refused to follow his orders. They stayed away from the pits in spite of cancellation of the strike order. Before they could be induced to return, further conferences were held in Washington and an understanding reached whereby the operators granted an immediate fourteen per cent wage increase and agreed to leave final settlement of wage demands and other issues in dispute to a special Bituminous Coal Commission. The final award raised the wage increase to twenty-seven per cent, almost half of what the miners had originally asked, but ignored altogether the demand for a thirty-hour week.

The strike had been ended by government action. Even though the miners won considerable gains, the important aspect of the controversy was the application of injunction law. A vital precedent had been established. In his willingness to comply with the government's orders, however, Lewis showed a keener realization of how far public opinion was prepared to go in suppressing strikes than the leaders of the A.F. of L. The resentment that had been displayed in the case of the steel strike was even more intensified when the coal miners threatened the nation with a fuel famine just as winter drew on.

President Wilson declared the coal strike to be "wrong both morally and legally." Congress endorsed his position, and editorials throughout the country applauded the use of the injunction. "Neither the miners nor any other organized minority," the *Chambersburg Public-Opinion* commented, "has the right to plunge the country into economic and social chaos. . . . A labor autocracy is as dangerous as a capital autocracy." "When enormous combinations of workingmen," the *Philadelphia Public Ledger* said, "deliberately enter upon a country-wide plan to take the country by the throat and compel the employers in that particular field of industry to yield to the demands of the men, they are engaged in an unlawful conspiracy." And the *Chicago Daily News* bluntly stated: "The public is weary of industrial strife. It is determined to protect itself."

The issue of Bolshevism was of course raised again. Senator Poindexter said that the strike was the penalty paid for an over-lenient governmental policy towards "anarchists and murderous communists." After its settlement the *New York Tribune* declared that the firm policy finally adopted by the administration was both an example and a warning: "Tell this in Russia, proclaim it on the streets of Moscow, sear it into the mind of all domestic disintegrators."

Although the strikes of 1919 resulted in a sharp setback for labor and there was a feeling of embittered disillusionment with what was regarded as betrayal at the hands of the Wilson administration, the wartime advance in unionism was not yet halted. Labor was still militant in spite of defeats. In many important areas it succeeded in winning the wage increases for which it fought, and there was continued expansion in union membership. Among the 110 unions now affiliated with the A.F. of L., machinists, non-operating railway workers, textile operatives and seamen showed especially important gains, and in such industries as food and clothing both unskilled and semi-skilled workers were being organized.

The A.F. of L. nevertheless found itself in an increasingly difficult position. The government support on which it had counted in pursuing its program of business unionism had given way to a revival of injunction law, and consequently there was strong pressure to adopt more aggressive tactics. The Federation leadership still refused, however, to be drawn into political action and in the face of new suggestions for a labor party, expressly reaffirmed the traditional non-political objectives that had always governed A.F. of L. policy. At a conference in December, 1919, a new "Labor's Bill of Rights" was proclaimed that called for union recognition, a living wage and restrictions on the use of injunctions, but beyond this the Federation would not go.

Circumstances soon made such a program more than ever difficult.

Before the close of the next year, a sudden, sharp depression struck the country. The collapse of the inflationary post-war boom led to tumbling prices all along the line, business failures, industrial stagnation, universal wage cuts, and unemployment on a large scale. By midsummer 1921, an estimated five million workers had lost their jobs. Industry took quick advantage of these circumstances to intensify its anti-union campaign. Injunctions and arrests broke a strike of the seamen's union and subsequent blacklisting reduced it to less than a fifth of its wartime strength. The packing house employes were so badly defeated that the industry reverted to the open shop. And in 1922 the railway shopmen, under fire from all sides, suffered an even more significant reverse.

The latter strike broke out when the Railway Labor Board, set up to govern employe relations after the railroads had been returned to private ownership in 1920, abrogated agreements that had been negotiated during the war, abolished overtime, and authorized wage cuts totaling $60,000,000. The railway brotherhoods were not affected by these pay reductions and the maintenance-of-way workers agreed to arbitration, but the members of the six shop craft unions were incensed at the board's apparent submission to employer pressure. A strike was called and on July 1, 1922, the shopmen walked out, 400,000 strong.

From the very first they found the going hard. With the Railway Labor Board declaring their action an outlaw strike, the brotherhoods cooperating with management to keep the trains running, and President Harding warning against any interference with the mails, public sympathy was almost entirely against the shopmen. The popular attitude was perhaps most graphically revealed by the fact that among the strikebreakers brought in under the protection of deputized guards and militia, were hundreds of college boys. But this was not all. On September 1, as the strike appeared in any event about to collapse, the government stepped in to deliver the coup de grace. Attorney General Daugherty obtained from Judge James H. Wilkerson, of the federal district court in Chicago, what has often been described as "the most sweeping injunction ever issued in a labor dispute."

It prohibited picketing of all sorts, strike meetings, statements to the public, the expenditure of union funds to carry on the strike, and the use of any means of communication by the leaders to direct it. No one was permitted to aid the strikers "by letters, telegrams, telephones, word of mouth . . ." or to persuade anyone to stop work by "jeers, entreaties, arguments, persuasion, rewards or otherwise." Daugherty intended to break the strike at any cost. "So long and to the extent that I can speak for the government of the United States," he told the press, "I will use the power of the government within my control to prevent the labor unions of the country from destroying the open shop."

This drastic move caused vehement debate throughout the country. Not only newspapers sympathetic to labor but many others, perhaps influenced by partisan considerations in a good many cases, assailed the injunction as wholly unwarranted and a denial of freedom of speech. The *New York Evening Post* declared that it had been watching the impending defeat of the strike with a sense that it was well deserved, but that this was "a blow below the belt." The *Newark News* referred to the injunction as "gag law" and the *New York World* criticized it severely as "a clumsy step." On the other hand, conservative Republican papers tried to defend administration policy. The *New York Tribune,* the *Philadelphia Inquirer,* the *Boston Transcript* and the *Chicago Daily News* agreed that however broad the injunction, it was no broader than the lawlessness of the shopmen in threatening to paralyze all railroad transportation. The last word on the part of labor's enemies was perhaps spoken by the *Manufacturers' Record.* The injunction, it declared, merely commanded the workers "to cease their adulterous intercourse with lawlessness."

For the railway shopmen government intervention was the final straw. They eagerly seized upon a proposal by President Willard of the Baltimore and Ohio for separate settlements with individual roads and came to terms as best they could. The more friendly attitude of some lines enabled them to retain their organization for some 225,000 workers, but 175,000 were forced into company unions. Government intervention had swung the scales in favor of the employes and railway labor had suffered a disastrous blow.

The whole labor movement continued to lose ground during the 1921–1922 depression, and under the demoralizing influence of unemployment was unable to command the strength to defend itself as the capitalistic counter-attack, reinforced by injunction law, gathered steady momentum. Some unions were completely crushed; others suffered heavy losses. Labor had come out of the war strongly organized, determined to extend its gains, and confident that with friendly government protection it would be able to raise the standard of living for all American workers. Between 1920 and 1923, however, union membership as a whole fell from its peak figure of a little over 5,000,000 to approximately 3,500,000.

XX

XIV: LABOR IN RETREAT

XXXXXXXXXXXXXXXXXXXXXXXXXXXXXXXXXXXXXXXXXXXX

THE SEVEN YEARS from 1922 through 1929 were a period of expanding production, further concentration of economic power, rising national income and a conservative retreat to the laissez-faire principles governing our economy in the nineteenth century. Business largely dominated government and there were no new advances along the path of social and economic reform plotted out by pre-war progressives. Prosperity and a soaring stock market, speculation and two cars in every garage, were all that seemed to matter. A complacent people happily accepted in 1928 President Hoover's confident pronouncement that "we in America are nearer to the final triumph over poverty than ever before in the history of any land."

The 1920's were also "the era of wonderful nonsense." The younger generation was in revolt; speakeasies, bottleggers and gangsterism flourished mightily, and newspaper sensationalism fastened public attention upon million dollar prize fights, long distance marathons, the Scopes monkey trial, Lindberg's trans-Atlantic flight, bathing beauty contests. . . . The American scene was vivid, colorful, exciting.

The country's thirty-odd million non-agricultural workers played their full part in national development and generally shared in the mounting prosperity. Wages rose, and while two cars in every garage may have remained a distant dream, there was more left over in the average workingman's budget after payment for food, shelter and clothing than ever before in all our history. Wage earners were swept along with the general public in the orgy of installment buying of automobiles, vacuum cleaners, washing machines and electric refrigerators; and they paid their share of the cool $10,000,000,000 that was being spent annually for amusements and recreation. They even made their occasional flyers on the stock market, with William Green broadcasting upon "The

Worker and His Money" for the Wall Street investment firm of Halsey, Stuart and Company.

"A workman is far better paid in America than anywhere else in the world," wrote an enthusiastic French visitor, André Siegfried, in 1927, "and his standard of living is enormously higher. This difference, which was noticeable before the War, has been greatly accentuated since, and is now the chief contrast between the old and the new continents. . . ."

Looking upon the American scene as a whole, indeed, more and more wage earners appeared in the process of being absorbed into what was commonly called the middle class. With not only higher pay making possible conveniences and luxuries heretofore beyond their reach, but shorter working hours providing new leisure for the enjoyment of other aspects of life, working people were no longer set off in a distinct category as they perhaps once had been. Their recreation and amusements conformed increasingly to a general nationwide pattern. The automobiles that every Sunday crowded the country's motor roads; the huge weekly attendance at moving picture theaters; the growing audience for the new phenomenon of radio broadcasting were all manifestations of this growth of a more uniform society. If factory employes did not pay as much for their clothes as those in higher income brackets, they wore the same models. The sons and daughters of working people went to the great state universities in closer fulfillment of the century-old dream of equal education. In scores of ways, the workers were taking over the customs, the mores and the aspirations of the people generally. Social democracy appeared to have attained a new validity as the American way of life.

This process was aided by the curtailment of immigration. The status of industrial workers had been traditionally depressed by the annual influx of ignorant, penniless and unskilled immigrants. The adoption of the quota system in the mid-1920's, cutting down the annual number of alien arrivals from some five million to a bare 150,000, had an immense effect not only economically but also socially on the position of the worker. New paths of advancement were opened up by this curtailment of the traditional labor surplus, not necessarily paths leading out of the wage earning class to the employer class, but nevertheless promising a more assured status in our evolving society.

It was largely overlooked in the 1920's, however, that there were still glaring inequalities in the way these material and social gains were distributed among the workers, just as there were in the general distribution of prosperity in the country at large. Many segments of labor did not appear to have been invited to the feast of plenty that was provided by economic expansion, and even those groups of workers who profited most from the upward trend of wages, could still feel that their share of the awards of prosperity were by no means commensurate with the far greater profits being made by business.

More important, unemployment was by no means banished from the land and in some areas was unusually high. Technological advance, which was constantly enabling industry to produce more goods with fewer workers, led to declines in factory pay rolls in many basic industries. New machinery and labor saving devices in road construction, textiles, the rubber industry and electrical equipment, to cite a few instances, cut the necessary labor for given output anywhere from twenty-five to sixty per cent. It was estimated that in manufacturing, railroads and coal mining, the labor of 3,272,000 fewer workers was necessary to maintain old rates of production, and that increased economic activity called for the addition of only 2,269,000. This left a net decline in employment in these industries of over 1,000,000. New opportunities in trade and service industries helped to offset this situation, but there was nevertheless persistent unemployment throughout the 1920's which was estimated to have ranged in terms of man-years from ten to thirteen per cent of the total labor supply. At least two million persons were probably out of work even in 1928.

The insecurity of the industrial worker in respect to his job which resulted from such conditions could never be wholly compensated by high wages while he was at work. In their study of *Middletown*, the Lynds found the fear of being laid off a constant obsession among the working-class families they interviewed even though the community was a prosperous one. The job was the thing in which they were interested much more than wages or hours. Whatever the general statistics of employment, the individual out of work faced the always bleak prospect of trying to find something else to do before his meager savings melted away altogether.

As for the status of organized labor—rather than that of wage earners generally—conditions in the 1920's had a paradoxical effect. In flat contradiction of what had been its record in every previous period of national prosperity, the labor movement lost ground. Not only was no further progress made in organizing the unskilled workers in the mass production industries, but existing trade unions steadily declined in membership. We have seen that under the impact of the depression in 1921, the total enrollment in American unions fell from over 5,000,000 to approximately 3,600,000. What was far more significant, however, was the failure during succeeding years to make up any of these losses. At the peak of 1929 prosperity, total union membership was 3,443,000—less than it had been in any year since 1917.

In the happy light of continued good times and generally rising wages for those who had work, this did not seem to matter. While job insecurity may have deterred some employes from joining unions in the face of employer opposition, many of them apparently felt that unions were no longer as necessary as they had formerly believed them to be. What profit strikes or other agitation for collective bargaining when the pay envelope was automatically growing fatter and a more abundant life seemed to be assured with our rapid approach to the final triumph over poverty?

There was no way for the workers to foresee in the halcyon atmosphere of these days that just over the horizon was another depression, a more devastating, long-lived depression than even those of the 1830's, the 1870's or the 1890's, when fifteen million helpless workers would find themselves thrown on the streets, selling apples at corner stands, queueing up before soup kitchens, crowding the breadlines. But its gathering shadows were soon to extinguish the "golden glow" of the 1920's and startlingly reveal the inherent weakness in labor's position. While the entire country was to suffer grievously from the sudden collapse of the New Economic Order, the impact of depression was once again to fall most heavily upon wage earners.

The economic recovery that succeeded the brief collapse of 1921 found industry determined to prevent organized labor from recapturing the position it had attained during the war. The anti-union campaign revived in 1919 was intensified, and a new emphasis placed upon upholding the open shop. Theoretically, the open shop still implied nothing more than the right of the employer to hire whomever he chose, regardless of membership or non-membership in a union. But as in the early 1900's, it actually meant not only a policy whereby union members were almost invariably subject to discrimination, but refusal to recognize the union even if a majority of the employes belonged to it. The open shop, that is, became more than ever a recognized technique for denying the whole process of collective bargaining in the relations between employer and employe.

To promote the drive against unions, open shop associations were formed throughout the country in the 1920's, as they had been during earlier periods of industrial counter-attack. Fifty such employer groups were set up in New York, eighteen in Massachusetts, twenty in Connecticut, forty-six in Illinois, seventeen in Ohio and twenty-three in Michigan. Local chambers of commerce, manufacturers' associations and citizens' alliances further supported the campaign, and behind them stood the National Association of Manufacturers, the National Metal Trades Association and the League for Industrial Rights. With an inspiration born of the heightened nationalism of these postwar years, a conference of these various associations, meeting in Chicago in 1921, formally named the open shop the "American Plan." The traditional values of rugged individualism were set against the subversive, foreign concepts of collectivism. "Every man to work out his own salvation," the proponents of the American Plan proclaimed, "and not to be bound by the shackles of organization to his own detriment."

Full advantage was also taken of every indication of corrupt union leadership and racketeering to convince both workers and the public that they were being duped by the supposed advantages of collective bargaining. And both corruption and racketeering could be found in some unions during the feverish days of the 1920's. Unlawful collusion between union leaders and employers, extortion by labor bosses, and outright graft were exposed in the building trades and service industries of such cities as New York, Chicago and San Francisco. In some instances gangsters, sensing an opportunity for even greater profit than bootlegging, moved in on the unions and fleeced both employers and employes by intimidation and violence. The conservatives' attack upon labor unions, however, made no distinction between these occasional examples of corrupt and anti-social policies and the over-all picture of responsible leadership in the great majority of unions. When labor leaders were not luridly depicted as Bolsheviks plotting revolution, they were described as conscienceless spoilsmen, taking advantage of union members in every possible way to build up their own power and wealth.

"The palatial temples of labor," John E. Edgerton, president of the N.A.M. grandiloquently declared in 1925, "whose golden domes rise in exultant splendor throughout the nation, the millions of dollars extracted annually by the jewelled hand of greed from the pockets of wage earners and paid out in lucrative salaries, tell the pitiful story of a slavery such as this country never knew before." The employers of the nation were summoned to fulfill their duty "to break the shackles that have been forged upon the wrists of those who labor" and to free their employes from "the false leadership of designing pirates who parade in the guise of the workingmen's friend."

Nor was propaganda the only weapon employed in fighting unionism and promoting the open shop. Many employers continued to force yellow-dog contracts upon employes, to plant labor spies in their plants, to exchange black lists of undesirable union members, and openly follow the most discriminatory practices in hiring workers. It was the old story of intimidation and coercion, and when trouble developed in spite of all such precautions, strong-arm guards were often employed to beat up the trouble-makers while incipient strikes were crushed by bringing in strike-breakers under protection of local authorities.

In the coal fields, for example, unionism found itself particularly hard-pressed with factionalism and conflict within labor's own ranks making it highly vulnerable to employer attacks. Coal was a sick industry, failing to share in the country's general prosperity as a result of competition from new sources of power, and the mine owners were doubly determined to meet the problem of cutting production costs by beating down labor. They sought to undermine wage agreements already signed with the miners, and even more dangerously for unionism, began shifting production from the central bituminous field to non-unionized mines in such states as West Virginia, Kentucky, Tennessee and Alabama where they could operate without union restraints upon wages and hours.

The United Mine Workers were confronted with a knotty dilemma.

When strikes broke out in the non-unionized fields, there were insistent demands for help. Should the union violate its contracts in the central bituminous field by declaring a sympathetic strike, or should it stand by passively and allow conditions to deteriorate in the non-union mines and ultimately drag down the entire industry? John L. Lewis insisted upon maintaining contractual agreements. He refused assistance to all strikes not authorized by the union and proposed to meet the problem of the non-union mines by organizing the workers in the south and bringing them under disciplined control.

His program failed. The United Mine Workers steadily lost ground in the unionized fields, even though it concluded and maintained further agreements with operators, and organization in the non-unionized mines made no headway. The union agents were received in a manner somewhat at variance with traditional southern hospitality. They were tarred-and-feathered, ridden out of the company controlled mining towns on rails, beaten up by armed guards and sometimes murdered. Increasing strikes and disorder led in some mining communities to virtual civil war with an ugly record of violence, shootings and assassination.

The more radical elements among the United Mine Workers bitterly resented the failure of Lewis to call a general strike in support of the non-union miners. They helped to stir up discontent against a policy that was said to be both betraying the unorganized workers and destroying the union itself. There was rebellion among his own lieutenants and outlaw strikes even within union ranks. When Lewis countered by violently attacking his opponents as Communists, insisting upon complete submission to his authority and expelling local leaders who countenanced unauthorized walk-outs, there was widespread dissatisfaction among the rank and file who saw in his maintainence of contracts only surrender to anti-union operators.

Lewis managed during these difficult days to retain control of the union but it was badly split and in no position to maintain the influence that it had formerly exercised in the mine fields. The operators were able to whittle away the gains won through earlier national strikes, and the demoralization that marked the non-union mines spread into the organized areas of the central bituminous field. In 1922 the United Mine Workers had attained a strength of 500,000—some seventy per cent of all coal miners. The story of decline is perhaps most graphically revealed in a membership that had shrunk ten years later to 150,000.

In seeking to combat the anti-union campaign of employers, whether in the coal fields or elsewhere, labor could not look for any aid or support from government or the courts. The validity of yellow-dog contracts, so widely enforced in the southern coal mines, was still upheld; there was no legal redress for discrimination against union members, and successive court decisions wholly invalidated the supposed safeguards of the Clayton Act against injunction law.

Early in 1921, the Supreme Court stated in *Duplex Printing Press* v. *Deering* that nothing in the act legalized secondary boycotts or protected unions from injunctions that might be brought against them for conspiring in restraint of trade. Later that same year, in the notable case of *Truax* v. *Corrigan,* any hope of legal relief for labor was even more effectively killed. Arizona had passed a law that sought to do away altogether with injunctions in labor disputes and the Supreme Court in effect declared it to be unconstitutional. In preventing an employer from obtaining an injunction, it was decreed, the state took away his means of securing protection and thereby deprived him of property without due process of law. With such encouragement, employers resorted to injunctions even more frequently than in the days before passage of the Clayton Act. In 1928 the American Federation of Labor submitted a list of 389 that had been granted by either federal or state courts in the preceding decade, and this was obviously far from complete because of the large number unrecorded in the lower courts.

Perhaps the most revealing of all court decisions in this period was that in the previously noted case of *Adkins* v. *Children's Hospital* which was handed down in 1923. In invalidating a minimum wage law as a violation of constitutional safeguards of liberty of contract, it marked an abrupt reversal of the earlier trend toward sustaining such legislation, but it was even more significant because of a reassertion of the old concept that labor was a commodity. While the Supreme Court conceded "the ethical right of every worker, man or woman, to a living wage," it declared that the employer was not bound to furnish such a wage and that there was no warrant for the state to seek to establish it by legislation. Since in principle "there can be no difference between the case of selling labor and the case of selling goods," the court said, any attempt to compel the employer to pay a stated wage "is so clearly the product of a naked, arbitrary power that it cannot be allowed to stand under the Constitution of the United States."

Even Chief Justice Taft—the "injunction judge"—protested this conclusion and pointed out that individual employes were not on a level of equality in contracting with employers and were "peculiarly subject to the overreaching of the harsh and greedy employer." Associate Justice Holmes also dissented, with sharp criticism of the court's one-sided support of "the dogma Liberty of Contract."

Although both government and courts theoretically recognized the desirability of labor unions, even President Harding declaring that the right of workers to organize was "not one whit less absolute" than that of management and capital, they were consistently restricting the activity for which unions were formed. The one exception to such repressive policies during the 1920's was the passage and approval of the Railway Labor Act of 1926. This measure provided for the formation of unions among railway workers "without interference, influence or coercion," and set up special machinery for the settlement of all railway labor disputes. In upholding this law, the Supreme Court declared that the legality of collective action on the part of employes would be "a mockery if representation were made futile by interferences with freedom of choice." But rights upheld for railway workers were not extended to other classes of employes until the 1930's.

Confronted with legal restrictions on union activity and adverse court decisions, organized labor once again began to feel, as it had when it submitted its "Bill of Grievances" in 1906, that more direct political pressure would have to be exercised if it was to win any freedom of action in combatting the employers' anti-union campaign. The drive for a labor party that had first developed in 1919 when "Labor's Bill of Rights" was drawn up, gathered increasing force with further revelations of the Supreme Court's attitude. Even the A.F. of L. was unable wholly to resist the pressure for some sort of unified political action.

This agitation had first come to a head in 1922 when a Chicago meeting of some 128 delegates from various farm, labor and other liberal groups formed the Conference for Progressive Political Action. William H. Johnston of the powerful International Association of Machinists was a leading figure in this movement; the railway brotherhoods, smarting under the restrictions of the old Railway Labor Board and the revival of injunction law, backed it vigorously, and support was also forthcoming from twenty-eight national unions, eight state labor federations, several mid-western farmers' parties, the Women's Trade Union League, and the Socialists. When two years later both the Republicans and the Democrats nominated highly conservative candidates, Calvin Coolidge and John W. Davis, these progressives offered an independent nomination to Senator La Follette of Wisconsin. On the condition that no attempt be made to run candidates for other offices than the presidency and vice-presidency (Senator Wheeler of Montana being given the latter nomination), La Follette accepted this proposal and the Conference for Progressive Political Action formally entered the 1924 campaign.

The platform, declaring that the principal issue before the country was the control of government and industry by private monopoly, was in large measure a carry-over of the progressive principles of pre-war years. It called for public ownership of the nation's water power and of railroads, the conservation of natural resources, aid for farmers, tax reduction on moderate incomes, downward tariff revision, and remedial labor legislation. "We favor abolition of the use of injunctions in labor disputes," it was stated, "and declare for complete protection of the right of farmers and industrial workers to organize, bargain collectively through representatives of their own choosing, and conduct without hindrance cooperative enterprises."

The American Federation of Labor was at first opposed to the Conference for Progressive Political Action, but when both major parties ignored labor's demands, it took the unprecedented step of endorsing the La Follette candidacy. The Republican and Democratic parties, declared the executive council, have "flouted the desires of labor" and are "in a condition of moral bankruptcy which constitutes a menace and a peril to our country and its institutions." In spite of this attack on the major parties, however, the A.F. of L. aligned itself with the Progressives of 1924 very cautiously. In keeping with his policy during the political flirtations of pre-war years, Gompers tried to make it clear that the Federation made no commitments except to support La Follette as "a friend of labor" in this single campaign and was not countenancing a third party as such. While recognizing the need for legislation to free labor from the restrictions represented by injunction law, he reaffirmed his faith in "voluntarism" by declaring that "we do not accept government as the solution of the problems of life."

Even with these qualifications and reservations, many A.F. of L. leaders refused to go along with the action of the executive council. John L Lewis and William Hutcheson, of the Carpenters, gave their support to Coolidge, and George L. Berry, of the Printing Pressmen, at the last moment shifted over to the camp of John W. Davis. Although the A.F. of L. had so far departed from its traditional policy as to come out openly for a presidential candidate of a third party, its support was somewhat left-handed and only $25,000 was raised as a campaign fund.

La Follette secured nearly five million votes—a substantial indication of popular discontent with both Republican and Democratic conservatism—but he carried only his home state of Wisconsin. The labor vote had not been delivered and the progressives' failure was widely interpreted as labor's failure. "The radical movement of this year," wrote the Washington correspondent of the *Seattle Times*, "represented the first attempt on the part of organized labor, through its governing bodies, to secure separate political action. The radical failure seems likely to end the possibility, for a good many years, of labor endorsement of a third-party presidential ticket." There was "no such thing as a labor vote," the *New York Herald Tribune* stated in analyzing the election returns, and the *Washington Star* agreed that "the workingmen of this country have not joined the insurgency against the established parties." More succinctly and colloquially, the *Philadelphia Bulletin* simply stated that "labor's incursion into politics was a dud."

The A.F. of L. apparently read very much the same meaning into the election. It promptly withdrew its support from the Conference for Progressive Political Action and reasserted its opposition to a third party. The entire movement collapsed. While in succeeding years labor continued to press for relief from injunctions, no further direct forays were made into politics. With even the Socialist vote falling off heavily, wage earners appeared ready to accept, with the rest of the country, the conservative political pattern that continued to characterize the national scene until the advent of the New Deal.

It was shortly after this unsuccessful campaign—in December, 1924—that the grand old man of the A.F. of L., Samuel Gompers, died at the age of seventy-four. In his later years it had become increasingly difficult for him to carry on his work. Nothing except death, however, could make him surrender the power he had held so securely ever since the Federation had been established forty years earlier. His control had momentarily appeared to be threatened in 1921 when Lewis entered the lists as a presidential candidate, but Gompers had put down this incipient rebellion as he had so many others. He was the acknowledged leader of organized labor and there was no real rival to his pre-eminence in this field. Both the successes and the failures of the A.F. of L. largely reflected the application of the conservative, pragmatic philosophy he so consistently upheld.

Labor mourned his death and so also did the business community. Newspaper editorials were an interesting commentary on the extent to which his moderate policies had won confidence and were accepted as forestalling more radical tendencies on the part of the nation's workers. Gompers was said to have held trade unionism to a straightforward, non-political path by the sheer force of his personality, and he was generally applauded for having consistently tried to bridge the gap between capital and labor. His death was termed a loss to America primarily because it opened up the possibility of a split within the A.F. of L. that might enable extremist elements to come into power.

When the choice of the Federation for its new president fell upon William Green, the business community consequently breathed a sigh of relief. For Green too stood for conservatism in labor policies, and assurance seemed to be made doubly sure by an immediate statement to the press that it would be his "steadfast purpose to adhere to those fundamental principles of trade-unionism so ably championed by Mr. Gompers." The country at once felt that there was no need for concern over possible socialistic or other third party deviations from the traditional A.F. of L. program. "Labor is safe under his leadership," the

Richmond Times Despatch declared in a typical comment upon Green's election; "capital has nothing to fear, and the public is fortunate in having him as spokesman of a highly important group of citizens."

Green was born in Coshocton, Ohio, in 1873. Like so many labor leaders, he was a second generation American, the son of Welsh immigrants, and as a boy had followed his father into the coal pits in Ohio. Joining the United Mine Workers, he was chosen a sub-district union president in 1906 and started upon a gradual climb to the high councils of organized labor. As leader of the miners in Ohio, he was sent to the state legislature as a trade union representative, and then elected secretary-treasurer of the United Mine Workers in reward for his faithful services. When in 1913 Gompers decided that the miners should be represented on the executive council of the A.F. of L., he turned to Green and appointed him an eighth vice-president. As death one by one removed the higher officers, Green slowly rose in scale to third vice-president. It was from this post, with the backing of Lewis, that he was raised to the pinnacle of the A.F. of L. presidency.

He appeared in 1924 a rather undistinguished figure without the forceful, dramatic characteristics that in different ways marked Gompers, Mitchell and Lewis. Sober and sedate—he had taught Sunday School as a young man and originally hoped to train for the ministry—he was not one to drink beer with the boys in the Gompers' tradition. His teetotalism was rather a reminder of Terence Powderly. Secretary of Labor Perkins was later to describe him as "the mildest and most polite of men" and his plump figure, round, humorless face, soft voice and quiet manner did not add up to a very arresting personality. But Green was a great joiner, belonging to the Elks, the Odd Fellows and the Masons, and his pleasant, affable manner and general friendliness made him popular. He was also respected for his unquestioned integrity and conscientious, hard-working devotion to the concerns of union labor.

In 1917 Green had declared himself, as a result of his own experience with the United Mine Workers, to be wholly in favor of industrial unionism, and this was one reason for the support Lewis gave him. "The organization of men by industry rather than by craft," Green had stated, "brings about a more perfect organization, closer cooperation. . . . It is becoming more and more evident that if unskilled workers are forced to work long hours and for low wages, the interests of the skilled are constantly menaced thereby." But in his new office all this was forgotten. Craft unionism as opposed to industrial unionism was to remain the basic policy of the A.F. of L., and no real attempts would be made during the 1920's to press for union recognition among the unskilled workers in mass-production industries.

In proving himself to be quite as conservative as Gompers had been, Green appeared no more willing than his predecessor to recognize the possible need for changes in the A.F. of L. policy to meet changing circumstances. He continued to uphold the concept of voluntarism which Gompers had so stoutly defended with that emphasis upon "strong, red-blooded, rugged independence" which might well have come from President Hoover himself. It was not until 1932, when the impact of the depression had undermined many A.F. of L. principles, that Green finally gave up his opposition to such forms of state intervention as old-age pensions and unemployment insurance.

The conservatism if not timidity of the A.F. of L. weakened all organized labor in the face of the anti-union drive of employers in the 1920's. But yellow-dog contracts and injunctions were not the only barriers in the path of unionization. The labor movement was also being killed by kindness. Industry complemented its aggressive enforcement of the open shop with a developing program of welfare capitalism. It sought to discourage trade unionism by making working conditions so favorable that the workers would no longer consider unions of any value, at the same time increasing production and industrial efficiency through closer labor-management cooperation.

Industry had long since tried to promote greater production per worker, to reduce labor turnover, and generally to improve technical standards through a process of "rationalization" in industrial management. During the progressive era, a program developed by Frederick W. Taylor had begun to be widely adopted. Time and motion studies, the development of piece work, increased productivity on the assembly line, and "scientific" adjustment of employe relations were the subject of universal experimentation. In the post-war era "Taylorism" won even wider attention in the constant search to reduce manufacturing costs. Trade unionism had no place in this program of industrial efficiency, but employers recognized the need for some substitute that would help to create the idea of "one big family" working cooperatively in the mutual interests of industry and labor. They thought they had found it in shop councils, employe representation plans, and most specifically, company unions.

An early move along such lines was a program adopted by the Colorado Fuel and Iron Company after the strike that had culminated in the bloody massacre at Ludlow in 1914. The Rockefeller interests had refused to recognize the United Mine Workers, and instead instituted a company union that was to provide "industrial democracy" without the dangerous implications of any association with the organized labor movement. The Rockfeller experiment was followed by many other corporations, 125 setting up company unions in one form or another during the war, and the open-shop campaign of post-war years led to still further emphasis upon this trend toward employer-controlled substitutes for outside unions. By 1926 the number of company unions had increased to over 400, with a membership of some 1,369,000, or about half the membership of unions affiliated with the A.F. of L.

As personnel managers made further studies of the labor problem (almost three thousand books on the subject were published in the first five years after the war) other measures were adopted to strengthen the role of the company unions and win employe allegiance. Scores and then hundreds of corporations set up profit-sharing schemes, paid out bonuses in company stock, or otherwise sought to give the workers a direct financial interest in corporate activities. It was estimated in 1928 that over a million employes owned or had subscribed for over a billion dollars worth of stock in the companies by which they were employed. Group insurance policies, which were forfeited should the employe change his job, were also introduced and some five million industrial workers were insured under such plans by 1926. At the same time, various old-age pension programs were established, free clinics set up to help maintain health standards, and employe cafeterias and lunchrooms installed. Under the direction of personnel departments or company unions, picnics, glee clubs, dances, sports events and other recreational activities were also sponsored for plant employes, while hundreds of company magazines rang all the changes on goodwill and friendly human contacts between labor and management.

The amplifications of welfare capitalism knew no limits and it succeeded to a very considerable extent in improving working conditions and indirectly increasing employe income. Its immediate benefits for the worker were very real. Yet the entire program remained wholly subject to the control of the corporation sponsor, and there was no reality to employe representation under such conditions. It was not without significance that those corporations which most generously provided for the workers' welfare were also those most strongly anti-union in their basic policies. How quickly welfare capitalism might collapse—and especially its stock distribution program—should prosperity give way to depression was hardly realized at the time. Few of the members of company unions understood how dependent they had become upon their employers for the favors they were receiving in lieu of union recognition and the advantages of genuine collective bargaining.

This lesson would be learned after 1929, but in the meantime welfare capitalism won many victories. "The assertion may be boldly made," S. B. Peck, chairman of the Open Shop Committee of the National Association of Manufacturers, declared, "that the decreasing membership in most of the unions and the great difficulty they are experiencing in holding their members together, is due to the fact that the employers—notably the once so-called 'soulless corporations'—are doing more for the welfare of the workers than the unions themselves." The Committee on Education and Labor of the Seventy-Sixth Congress reported, in 1926, that the N.A.M. had done its work in combatting unionism so well that it was able to settle back "to the quiet enjoyment of the fruits of their efforts during the years of prosperity."

The consequences of the double-edged program of seeking to suppress bona fide labor unions and building up employe allegiance through the benefits of company unions and welfare capitalism, were seen not only in declining membership for the A.F. of L. but in a greater measure of industrial peace than the country had enjoyed for many years. This does not mean there were no strikes. Those on the part of the depressed textile workers, for example, were persistent, hard-fought and marked by violence and bloodshed. In such southern mill towns as Gastonia and Marion, North Carolina, and Elizabethton, Tennessee, open clashes between strikers and state troopers led to heavy death tolls. The overall record, however, was one of a steadily declining number of labor

disputes. During the war period, the total number of strikes had averaged over 3000 a year and involved well over a million workers annually.
By the mid-1920's, such figures had been halved. At the close of the
decade, the annual number of strikes was around 800 and engaged only
some 300,000 workers, or slightly more than one per cent of the aggregate
labor force.

Far from seeking to revive labor militancy, the American Federation
of Labor made every effort to encourage labor-management cooperation.
Green was destined to accept proudly in 1930 the gold medal of the
Roosevelt Memorial Association for his outstanding services in allaying
industrial strife. While the A.F. of L. could not countenance company
unions, it passively acquiesced in many other aspects of welfare capitalism. Content with the gains that its own membership was making as
wages rose in response to the demand for skilled workers, little effort
was made to broaden the scope of union activity. At the close of the
1920's the organized labor movement appeared to be accepting as com-
placently as any other element in our national economy the promise of
assured economic advance.

It has been said that the nation's workers generally experienced a
greater rise in wages during the 1920's than in any comparable period.
Annual earnings, indeed, rose between 1921 and 1928 from an average
of $1,171 to $1,408. In terms of actual purchasing power, for there was
no comparable rise in living costs, this has been estimated to represent a
gain of more than twenty per cent.

Both actual wages and their rate of increase were nevertheless very
uneven. The hourly rate for bricklayers in New York rose, between 1920
and 1928, from $1.06 to $1.87 and that of newspaper compositors from
92 cents to $1.20, but in the case of bituminous miners, there was a de-
cline in the hourly rate from 83 cents to 73 cents, and for mule spinners
in the cotton mills a drop from 83 cents to 63 cents. The gains of the
1920's went primarily to the skilled workers and trade union members.
Millions of working class families still had incomes of less than $1000 a
year even in 1929.

As far as hours of work were concerned, the general picture shows
substantial improvement. The eight-hour day generally prevailed and

it was estimated that since the opening of the century, the working week for wage earners had been cut from fifteen to thirty per cent. But wide discrepancies appear when available statistics are broken down. While a 43.5 hour week was the average in the building trades, for instance, a 60-hour week was still being maintained for blast furnace workers in the steel mills.

Factors other than wages and hours also affected the well-being of the nation's workers in these as in other years. The speed-up in industrial processes added to the strain and nervous tension under which men operating machines and working on the assembly line constantly labored. For many factory employes the substitution of wholly mechanical operations for the exercise of individual skills meant monotony and boredom that were not always compensated by higher wages and shorter hours. While this was nothing new in the history of industrialization, it was more than ever true during the 1920's.

With the march of the machine also holding over the worker's head the constant threat of losing his job, the industrial workers of the country were consequently still far from attaining that security and well-being that was the goal of organized labor. The gains that had been made were more precarious than impersonal statistics might suggest, especially since those that might be attributed to welfare capitalism were wholly unprotected by any contractual understanding. So far as organizational strength and aggressive trade unionism had been sacrificed in accepting labor-management cooperation in place of genuine collective bargaining, the wage earners had seriously undermined their hard-won capacity to protect their own interests. They were almost wholly dependent on the continued willingness and ability of employers to treat them fairly.

This was the situation when depression gradually engulfed the country after the sudden collapse of the stock market in 1929. The story is a familiar one: the shock to national confidence as billions of dollars of security values melted away, the frantic assertions that conditions were fundamentally sound, and the slow strangulation of business as the cracks in our industrial system slowly widened and the whole structure seemed threatened with collapse. The depression was another historic turn in the economic cycle, but its impact on society was greater than that of any depression in the past.

Before it had run its course, farm prices fell to forty per cent of their previous levels, the value of exports declined to a third of their former peak, industrial production was almost halved, and the balance sheet of corporate enterprise revealed a deficit of $5,650,000,000. In three years, a national income estimated at $82,885,000,000 had dropped to $40,074,000,000. Even more significant—and far more devastating—unemployment rose to over seven million by the close of 1930, and then in another two years to something like fifteen million.

Statistics, however, give only an inadequate idea of the dire effects of the depression. They can hardly depict the scrimping and saving forced upon millions of middle-class families, the privations and hardships caused those in lower income groups, and the cruel suffering of the unemployed workers and their families. The bread lines, the tramp jungles so ironically called Hoovervilles that sprang up in the outskirts of countless cities, the army of young men and boys wandering back and forth across the country in hopeless search for jobs, were a tragic commentary upon the glowing mirage of the era that was to abolish poverty.

The country's wage earners stood by helplessly as the depression cut into production and paralyzed normal trade, causing many factories, mines and workshops to close down altogether. Early in 1930 a series of industrial conferences had been held in Washington at which employers promised to uphold wages and maintain employment. The workers accepted these pledges in good faith. Like the rest of the country, they could not believe that prosperity had so suddenly collapsed and were still hopeful that recovery was just around the corner. But there were no collective bargaining agreements in the mass production industries —steel, automobiles, electrical equipment—to compel observance of wage scales. Pay checks were gradually cut, and then all too often replaced by blunt notices of dismissal.

The whole program of welfare capitalism also went abruptly by the board as employers were forced to withdraw the benefits that in the piping days of prosperity had often been granted in the place of wage increases. Profit-sharing schemes, employe stock ownership, industrial pensions and even workers' health and recreational projects were rapidly discarded. Circumstances forced retrenchment, but in many cases it was carried out at the expense of the workers while full dividends were still being paid on common stock. The company unions were powerless to protect their members' interests. Reliance upon welfare capitalism had proved to be a delusion.

Organized labor seemed to be completely demoralized. The national unions did not even try to exercise any direct pressure upon the government in favor of recovery measures, and their strength had been so sapped by the retreat before welfare capitalism that concerted action along economic lines was out of the question in the face of nationwide unemployment. Strike activity was at a minimum and in 1930 fell to a new low point when less than 200,000 workers were involved in all work stoppages. Continued declines in union membership were also the general rule. The total number of organized workers fell by 1933 to less than 3,000,000—or the approximate level of 1917.

In some ways the most surprising phenomenon of the depression years was this apathetic attitude on the part of industrial workers while the unemployment figures steadily mounted and the bread lines lengthened. There was no suggestion of revolt against an economic system that had let them down so badly. There was no parallel of the ugly railway strikes of 1877 or Debs' Rebellion in 1894. In Park Avenue drawing rooms and the offices of Wall Street brokers, there was a great deal of talk of "the coming revolution," but the unemployed themselves were too discouraged and too spiritless to be interested.

Writing in *Harper's* in mid-summer 1932, George Soule found that while there was a distinct drift on the part of intellectuals into the radical camp, with rising interest in communism, no such trend could be discovered in the ranks of labor. "The masses are in a desperate condition all right," he wrote, "but unfortunately there is no sign that they feel the slightest resentment. They just sit at home and blame prohibition. . . . Like the Republican administration, they are awaiting nothing more drastic than the return of prosperity." In another article in the same magazine, Elmer Davis also commented with astonishment on "the quiet acceptance of the situation by men who have lost their jobs and everything else through the operation of the policies that were to abolish poverty."

There was one unexpected occasion when Green, addressing the A.F. of L., "dropped his gentle manner," as described in the *Literary Digest*, "to let loose a verbal blast as thunderous as a crash of coal in the Ohio mine where he used to swing a pick." Unless a shorter work day and shorter work week were adopted to increase employment, he told a cheering audience, "we will secure it through force of some kind." Asked by eager reporters just what he meant by force, he quickly explained that he meant economic force. Even this vague hint of labor militancy, however, awoke concern. "Is this the time for industrial war?" asked the *Boston Transcript*. Any suggestion of trying "to coerce industry by the strike method" was deeply deplored by the *Washington Post*. The *Herald Tribune* felt that Green had suffered "an attack of nerves."

But this outburst was an exception to the generally cautious attitude of the American Federation of Labor. Maintaining until the end of 1932 its strong opposition to unemployment insurance, it urged nothing more concrete in the way of government action to promote recovery or relieve unemployment than "the stabilization of industry" through adoption of its program for increasing jobs by a shorter work week.

The press praised this attitude. "Today labor stands patient and hopeful," the *Cleveland Plain Dealer* wrote. ". . . Never has there been a period of depression so free from labor strife. Unemployment has harassed it. Closed factories have taken away its livelihood. But, in the face of enormous hardship, labor has showed its good citizenship and sturdy American stamina. Labor deserves a salute." Whether the workers themselves were satisfied with this generous salute instead of jobs may be open to question. The *Philadelphia Record*, reflecting a more realistic attitude than that of the *Plain Dealer*, declared that the Federation's stand against unemployment insurance was a ghastly jest. "Liberty to starve?" it asked, "Is that what Mr. Green fights for?"

The consequences of government inaction and labor passivity were with every passing month more graphically reflected in the increasing number of jobless workers dependent upon state or private charity. The vaunted campaign to spread the work did not seem to have any effect other than to reduce the workers' income, seldom opening up any opportunities for those who had already been laid off.

Some of the states attempted to pass legislation that would improve working conditions. New workingmen's compensation laws were adopted in a number of instances, fourteen states approved old age pensions, and Wisconsin pioneered with a new Labor Bill of Rights and unemployment insurance. Early in March, 1932, a highly significant victory for organized labor as a whole was won through the passage by Congress of the Norris–La Guardia Act. This measure at long last declared it to be public policy that labor should have full freedom of association, without interference by employers; outlawed yellow-dog contracts, and prohibited federal courts from issuing injunctions in labor disputes except under carefully defined conditions. Although at least one congressman rose to state that this bill represented a "long march in the direction of Moscow," it was overwhelmingly supported in both the House and Senate and received widespread popular approval. For all the importance of the Norris–La Guardia Act in pointing the way to the labor policies of the New Deal, however, it did not meet the immediate problem of the nation's wage earners. It held no solution for unemployment.

As conditions reached their nadir in the summer of 1932, the presidential campaign offered a first practical opportunity for political protest against the failure of the Hoover Administration to cope adequately with the depression. Franklin D. Roosevelt, as Democratic nominee, clearly demonstrated his sympathy for the working masses of the country and for "the forgotten man at the bottom of the economic pyramid." He repeatedly stressed the imperative need to provide direct relief and vigorously advocated unemployment insurance. Yet the American Federation of Labor declared its neutrality in the presidential campaign. Willing to endorse friends of labor among the congressional candidates, it refused to announce itself in favor of either Hoover or Roosevelt. There can be no question that industrial workers helped to swell the great popular majority that Roosevelt won in 1932, but the A.F. of L. did not officially have any part in his election.

The campaign over, no further developments took place in respect to labor problems and economic conditions continued to deteriorate. The American Federation of Labor urged a thirty-hour week and expanded public works; it finally came out in favor of unemployment insurance. But no positive action was taken to promote such measures. Labor was waiting, like the rest of the country, to see what the new President would do.

XXX

XV: THE NEW DEAL

XXXXXXXXXXXXXXXXXXXXXXXXXXXXXXXXXXXXXXXXX

". . . A HOST OF UNEMPLOYED CITIZENS face the grim problem of existence, and an equally great number toil with little return. Only a foolish optimist can deny the dark realities of the moment. . . . Our greatest primary task is to put people to work."

When Franklin D. Roosevelt came into office in March, 1933, his stirring inaugural held out a promise of action in coping with the national emergency that created throughout the nation a new feeling of hope and confidence. The government was at long last prepared to accept the responsibility of extending that measure of direct aid to agriculture and labor, as well as industry, which alone could restore the disrupted balance of our national economy. As the President spiritedly declared that "the only thing we have to fear is fear itself," the country felt that it had found the leadership for want of which it had been floundering helplessly in the deepening morass of depression.

There was nothing in Roosevelt's immediate program that applied directly to labor except his promise to put people to work. Social security —with unemployment and old-age insurance—was already under consideration, but the labor provisions that were to be written into the National Recovery Administration codes, the Wagner Act and the Fair Labor Standards Act were not envisaged when he entered upon office. They evolved gradually out of the needs of the times. A basic understanding and sympathy for the rights of labor were nevertheless inherent in the emerging philosophy of the New Deal. For the first time in our history a national administration was to make the welfare of industrial workers a direct concern of government and act on the principle that only organized labor could deal on equal terms with organized capital in bringing about a proper balance between these two rival forces in a capitalistic society. Heretofore labor unions had been tolerated, they were now to be encouraged.

264

The advent of the New Deal was thus to prove a momentous watershed in the history of the labor movement. Age-old traditions were smashed; new and dynamic forces released. Greater gains were to be won by wage earners than in any previous period in our history, and both the economic and the political power of labor was immeasurably enhanced. The struggles, hardships and defeats of a century appeared to have culminated in the possibility of complete attainment of the workers' historic objectives.

The premise upon which New Deal policy toward labor was based had already been set forth in the general recognition of its right to organize written into the Norris–La Guardia Act. When the Roosevelt administration adopted the over-all experiment in economic control of the National Industrial Recovery Act, somewhat dubiously based upon the powers of Congress to regulate interstate commerce, a first step was taken toward implementing this right to organize in the famous—or as viewed in some quarters infamous—Section 7(*a*).

This important move in support of labor's interests was an end result of highly complicated manoeuvering. In March, 1933, a bill was introduced into Congress by Senator Black and Representative Connery to establish the thirty-hour week that the A.F. of L. had been demanding as a means of spreading work and relieving unemployment. Roosevelt was very skeptical of its value unless there was included in it some provision for maintaining wages. In behalf of the President, Secretary of Labor Perkins consequently suggested amendments that would have combined with the reduction in work hours a guarantee of minimum wages. The theory underlying the new bill was not unlike that promoted by Ira Steward in the 1860's—except that increasing the pay through decreasing the hours was subordinated to wage stabilization. There was as yet no idea of going any further. "When I talked with the President in April, 1933, about the Black bill," Secretary Perkins has recorded, "his mind was as innocent as a child's of any such program as N.R.A."

The idea of minimum wages awoke a storm of opposition from business interests and was not too enthusiastically supported by labor. In place of such a limited approach to the problems of depression, it was urged in both camps that the administration raise its sights and institute a far broader recovery program. The United States Chamber of Commerce proposed that business should be freed from the restrictions of the anti-trust laws and encouraged to work out its own salvation. As a spokesman for labor, John L. Lewis advocated that the controls over production, prices and wages that he had been demanding in coal mining should be extended to industry as a whole. As scores of such plans began to arouse increasing interest both in and out of Congress, several independent groups of presidential advisers began to try to work out specific measures. Little real progress was being made, however, and Roosevelt decided to intervene. Withdrawing administration support from the Black–Connery bill, in which at best his interest had been lukewarm, he called upon his advisers to get together on a common program, shutting themselves up in a locked room if necessary until they could come to agreement.

The plan finally adopted and incorporated into the National Industrial Recovery Act was to allow industry to write its own codes of fair competition, but to compensate labor for granting industry such a free hand by providing special safeguards for its interests. Section 7(a) of the new measure, drawing in part from provisions of the Railway Labor Act of 1926, stipulated that the industrial codes should contain three important provisions: employes should have the right to organize and bargain collectively through representatives of their own choosing, free from interference, restraint or coercion on the part of employers; no one seeking employment should be required to join a company union or to refrain from joining any labor organization of his own choosing; and employers should comply with maximum hours, minimum rates of pay and other conditions of employment approved by the President. Considering the new law as a whole, the ideas underlying the Chamber of Commerce program, labor's traditional demand for union recognition, and certain modified provisions of the Black–Connery bill were brought together in a single omnibus measure, and to this over-all plan was further added, under a separate title, a vast public works program authorizing appropriations of $3,300,000,000.

The basic purpose of the National Industrial Recovery Act, as approved in June, 1933, was in the President's words, "to put people back to work." It was at once to ensure reasonable profits for industry by preventing unfair competition and disastrous overproduction, and living wages for labor by spreading work through shorter hours. Roosevelt termed the law "the most important and far-reaching legislation ever enacted by the American Congress."

The N.R.A. was virtually to collapse through internal stress and strain even before it was finally outlawed by the Supreme Court—a generally unlamented victim of early New Deal enthusiasm. Nevertheless its implications for labor went far toward justifying Roosevelt's statement. The guarantee of collective bargaining and establishment of wage and hour controls by congressional action, in spite of loopholes that were to develop in enforcement of the law, represented the most forward steps ever taken by government in the field of industrial relations. And these steps were not to be retraced even when other provisions of the N.R.A. went by the board. The New Deal picked up the shattered fragments of Section 7(a) and put them together again, far more carefully, in the Wagner Act and the Fair Labor Standards Act. There was to be no retreat under Roosevelt from this progressive advance in safeguarding the interest of industrial workers.

In June, 1933 the N.R.A. was hailed enthusiastically throughout the country. It is true that such a conservative organ as the *Manufacturer's Record*, looking with a jaundiced eye upon any concessions to labor whatsoever, was soon to state that "labor agitators . . . are trying to establish a labor dictatorship in this country," but this critical note was lost in the general chorus of excited approval for the new recovery program. In the bright dawn of its inception, the N.R.A. started off under the dynamic direction of General Hugh Johnson amid a fanfare of patriotic oratory and popular demonstrations. As symbols of code acceptance, Blue Eagles were soon being proudly displayed the length and breadth of the land.

Labor joyfully acclaimed Section 7(a). "Millions of workers throughout the nation," William Green declared, "stood up for the first time in their lives to receive their charter of industrial freedom." Countless unions were overnight aroused from the doldrums of depression lethargy. Confident in the protection of the law, organizers set out to restore the depleted strength of moribund locals, form new ones, and invade territory from which they had formerly been barred. In the coal fields, placards at the mine pits announced "President Roosevelt wants you to join the union." The workers themselves often did not wait for the official emissaries from A.F. of L. headquarters but set up their own locals, and then applied for charters from the parent organization. The burst of labor activity had no precedent except perhaps the dramatic growth of the Knights of Labor half a century earlier.

When the A.F. of L. met for its annual convention in October, President Green confidently announced that an unofficial count showed over 1,500,000 new recruits added to its ranks, recouping the losses of over a decade and bringing total membership to close upon four million.[1] He envisaged a goal of ten millions, eventually twenty-five.

The greatest gains were in the so-called industrial unions,[2] and particularly in those that had suffered most heavily during the depression. Within a few months the United Mine Workers recouped 300,000 members and concluded new agreements in the formerly non-union coal fields of Kentucky and Alabama; the International Ladies' Garment Workers added 100,000 to its rolls, recapturing lost territory in New York and runaway shops in other parts of the country, and the Amalgamated Clothing Workers made up its earlier losses with some 50,000 recruits. But this was not all. Under the spur of Section 7(a), the A.F. of L. even appeared to be ready, with the new slogan of "Organize the Unorganized in the Mass Production Industries," to invade territory from which it had formerly held aloof. Nearly 100,000 workers were said to have been organized in the automobile industry, 90,000 in steel, 90,000 in lumber yards and sawmills, and 60,000 in rubber.

It was soon to develop, however, that this burst of activity among the unorganized workers had a very precarious foundation and the proud boasts of President Green were not wholly justified. The traditional skepticism of the A.F. of L. toward industrial unionism, reinforced

[1] These figures were a broad estimate. It might be noted at this point, however, that all general statistics on union membership are only approximate because of widely different practices in reporting enrollment. Real exactitude is never possible. See Leo Wolman, *Ebb and Flow in Unionism*, National Bureau of Economic Research, Washington, 1936.

[2] In distinction to craft unions, whose jurisdiction was limited to one or several allied trades, industrial unions exercised a jurisdiction over all or most occupations, skilled or unskilled, within an entire industry. They were sometimes called vertical unions at this time.

by the determination of old-line craft union leaders to retain control of
the labor movement, blocked any campaign to organize the workers
in mass production along industrial lines. The accepted technique was
to form so-called federal unions, directly affiliated with the A.F. of L.
itself, until jurisdictional problems could be worked out and the new
union membership in steel, automobiles, rubber and other industries
gradually absorbed into existing unions. Between 1932 and 1934, the
number of federal charters outstanding rose from 307 to 1798. This was
not the form of organization, however, that met the real need of unskilled workers and very soon the initial flurry of activity in the mass
production industries began to subside.

Such evidence of failure gave rise to an insistent demand on the part
of the more progressive leaders within the A.F. of L. for a change of
tactics. They called for a more aggressive campaign to bring the unorganized workers into the fold and the immediate granting of industrial
union charters in automobile and steel, in rubber, aluminum and radio.
When the conservative oligarchy in control of the A.F. of L. rejected
these demands, a widening breach between adherents of craft unions
and industrial unions led to what was to prove a critical split in the ranks
of labor. Its unity was shattered at the moment of its greatest opportunity. The labor insurgents set up their own Committee for Industrial Organization, under circumstances to which we shall return, and a new
chapter was opened in labor history.

In the meantime, the older unions had also discovered that the high
promise of their new charter of liberties was not to be realized without
further struggles. Pending adoption of the N.R.A.'s industrial codes, all
employers were asked to subscribe to the President's Re-Employment
Agreement—a blanket code in which a forty-hour week was prescribed,
minimum wages were set at either $15 a week or 40 cents an hour, and
child labor abolished for all those under sixteen. More permanent agreements were then to be drawn up by the trade associations, with the
workers' interests supposedly protected by a labor advisory board in
each industry. In the final analysis, however, the trade associations
generally acted independently and employes had no real part in the
formulation of the permanent codes. A majority of them established the
forty-hour week, with minimum wages from $12 to $15 a week, but while
some ninety-five per cent of the nation's industrial workers were ulti-

mately given this protection, labor's rights in other respects were largely ignored. The safeguards for collective bargaining were either not definitely recognized or were gradually whittled away. The automobile manufacturers, for example, succeeded in having inserted in their code a clause that enabled them to select, retain or advance their employes "on the basis of individual merit." In theory such a right could hardly be disputed, but for anti-union employers it provided the means to discriminate against union members on any convenient pretext. President Roosevelt subsequently ordered that interpretations of Section 7(a) should not be included in any code. It did not interfere with the bona fide right of the employer to hire whom he chose, he asserted, but it clearly prohibited the exercise of this right as a device to keep employes from joining a union.

As industry began to recover and fearful employers crept cautiously out of the cyclone cellars into which they had been driven by the depression, further resentments developed over the concessions granted labor in return for management's freedom to control production and fix prices. The *Iron Age* warned of the dangers of what it chose to call "collective bludgeoning" and *Steel* stated that with organized labor "baring its teeth," every effort should be made to retain the open shop. Viewing fearfully predictions of a membership of 10,000,000 in the A.F. of L., the *Commercial and Financial Chronicle* declared that the country would then have "an organized body, or class within the State, more powerful than the State itself. That in itself would mean the extinction of freedom and independence. In the end oppression would prevail everywhere. . . ." Responding to such dire warnings, some employers bluntly refused to comply at all with the labor provisions of the codes and others sought every possible means to evade the spirit if not the letter of the law.

One of the principal weapons used in combatting the clear intent of Section 7(a) was the company union. Employes could not be required to join such an organization, but their employers were still free to exercise every possible kind of pressure in making it seem advisable. And this was done so effectively that enrollment in company unions rapidly rose from 1,250,000 to 2,500,000. The N.R.A. not only tacitly approved such unions, stating that the government had not endorsed "any particular form of organization," but encouraged them by allowing proportional

representation in collective bargaining. Even when a national union
enrolled a majority of workers in a plant, it was not accepted as spokesman for the whole labor force and management could still deal with any
other employe group. Such an interpretation of the law was attacked by
labor as completely nullifying the whole principle of collective bargaining. The N.R.A. was bitterly assailed as the National Run Around and
the Blue Eagle was said to have changed into a vulture.

As the old lines of industrial strife were again tightened, the N.R.A.
thus found itself caught between two fires: the recalcitrant attitude of
many employers and the militant demands of labor. First a National
Labor Board, then special boards in certain industries, and finally in
July, 1934, a National Labor Relations Board were set up to handle the
growing volume of industrial disputes. They failed to win the confidence
of either management or labor and often appeared to be working at
cross purposes with the N.R.A. itself. The National Labor Relations
Board stood for important principles. Its support for majority representation, secret elections and bona fide collective bargaining, together
with its refusal to acknowledge company-dominated unions, were to
provide a basis for the policies of the later board under the same name.
The original N.L.R.B., however, was hampered and restricted under
the operation of the National Recovery Administration and had no
power to enforce its decisions.

To defend their interests, the workers felt more and more driven to
strikes. The number of industrial disputes rose precipitately in the latter
half of 1933—almost as many in this six month period as in all of 1932
—and the next year saw the total rise to 1,856. Almost 1,500,000 workers
—more than seven per cent of the total labor force—were involved. In
steel, automobiles, and textiles, among the longshoremen of the Pacific
coast and the lumber workers of the northwest, in scores of other industries, strikes were either threatened or broke out on a scale comparable to that of the early 1920's. Many of these strikes were for wage
increases but a great number of them, at least a third, were for union
recognition.

Government did what it could to allay this unrest, setting up special
advisory boards and mediation commissions which tried to get the
strikers back to work while further investigations were made in the
industries concerned. The outbreaks among steel and automobile work-

ers were prevented from developing into national strikes at the last moment; mediation settled the longshoremen's strike after San Francisco had been briefly gripped by what was fearfully called a general strike. But the workers went back to their jobs dissatisfied and highly skeptical of government policy.

The most serious and violent strike was that of the textile workers. Employers were widely disregarding code provisions and the Cotton Code Authority did nothing to enforce them. Demanding a thirty-hour week without reduction in the minimum $13 wage, abolition of the stretch-out and recognition of the United Textile Workers, the mill employes walked out in mass during August, 1934—110,000 in Massachusetts, 50,000 in Rhode Island, 60,000 in Georgia, 28,000 in Alabama. By the end of the month, somewhere between 400,000 and 500,000 men and women were estimated to be on strike in twenty states—the largest single strike in labor history to that time. In the south, where "flying squadrons" rushed from one mill town to another to call out the workers and set up picket lines, there were inevitable clashes with the police and special sheriff deputies. At the height of the struggle some 11,000 national guardsmen in eight states were under arms to preserve order.

On September 7, after President Roosevelt intervened and promised the appointment of a new Textile Labor Relations Board to study conditions in the industry, the union leaders called the strike off. Was it strategic retreat or surrender? Opinion was varied and the labor policy makers were both praised and assailed for ordering the textile workers back. But it was soon apparent that there was to be no real peace in the industry. The employers continued to discriminate against union members, returning strikers were often barred from the mills in southern towns, and demoralization spread further throughout the workers' ranks.

The gains that labor had made in the early days of the N.R.A. seemed to be fading away. The obdurate attitude of employers unwilling to accept code provisions or carry out bona fide collective bargaining, the failure of the government to safeguard the workers in strike settlements, and the inability or reluctance of the A.F. of L. to give the mass production workers the support that might have enabled them to organize effectively, combined to dash labor's high hopes. Although union membership in 1935 was a million greater than it had been two years earlier, it was below the four million mark that Green had so proudly announced for the A.F. of L. alone at the close of 1933. Hundreds of thousands of the new recruits had fallen by the wayside and some six hundred federal unions disbanded. The organized strength of the automobile workers dwindled to 10,000; the burst of activity in steel subsided with a residue of only 8,600 members in the Amalgamated Association of Iron, Tin and Steel Workers, and of the several hundred thousand who had joined the United Textile Workers during the textile strike, only 80,000 remained with the union. The dramatic movement touched off with the adoption of Section 7(*a*) had lost its momentum.

By the beginning of 1935 the failure of the N.R.A., not only to solve the problem of labor relations but to provide for successful business organization, could no longer be disguised. It was being openly attacked on all fronts in sad contrast to the exuberant fervor of the parades and flag waving with which it had first been greeted. An original impetus had been given to recovery, but the psychological effect of that shot in the arm had worn off. Big business was generally in revolt against the labor provisions in the codes. Little business felt itself squeezed to the wall both by the revival of monopoly and by union demands. Labor was convinced that it had been betrayed. With the whole program bogging down because of inner contradictions, the country was no longer willing to support a system of economic controls that could not be successfully administered and appeared to bear most heavily on the consumer. It was with relief rather than regret that the public accepted the announcement in May, 1935, that the Supreme Court had delivered the coup de grace to the entire set-up by declaring, in the famous Schechter poultry case, that the National Industrial Recovery Act was unconstitutional.

This development completely swept away such safeguards for labor as had been written into Section 7(*a*). However, an amendment to the Railway Labor Act had definitely extended them to railroad employes, and a drive to secure them on a firmer basis for all other workers had already been launched. As early as March, 1934, Senator Wagner introduced a bill to close the loopholes that enabled industry to cripple labor's strength by setting up company unions and refusing to bargain collectively with any other group. He had temporarily withdrawn this measure on the President's plea for a further trial period under existing legislation, but reintroduced it early in 1935. Just eleven days before the N.R.A. was declared unconstitutional, it passed the Senate.

The Wagner bill had strong support from labor and the collapse of the N.R.A. naturally intensified the demand for its immediate acceptance by the House. "I do not mind telling you," an unusually militant Green testified before one congressional committee, "that the spirit of the workers in America has been aroused. They are going to find a way to bargain collectively. . . . Labor must have its place in the sun. We cannot and will not continue to urge workers to have patience, unless the Wagner bill is made law, and unless it is enforced, once it becomes law."

Roosevelt had no part in developing this new measure and on the evidence of both Secretary Perkins and Raymond Moley, he did not particularly like it when it was described to him. It was Senator Wagner's work. But with the N.R.A. out of the picture, Moley has reported, the President "flung his arms open" and suddenly embraced it. Labor could not be completely let down and here were the means to re-enact a stronger Section 7(a) so far as collective bargaining was concerned. With administration support, the measure now promptly passed the House. It was signed by Roosevelt on July 5.

Although the general policy of the Wagner Act—or as it was officially called the National Labor Relations Act—had been foreshadowed by Section 7(a) of the National Industrial Recovery Act, the new law heavily underscored the basic change in governmental attitude toward labor. Not only were old ideas of a laissez-faire attitude in industrial relations again ignored; the Roosevelt administration now upheld the right of wage earners to organize without making any such corresponding concessions to management as had been incorporated in the N.R.A. It was prepared to strengthen the bargaining position of the workers, and consequently their ability to obtain a larger share of the national income, over against whatever claims might be put forward by industry. The justification for this position was that only through government support could labor meet management on anything like equal terms in our industrialized society, and that the time had come when the scales, always so heavily weighted in favor of industry, should be redressed in favor of the workers. Every unfair labor practice banned in the Wagner Act applied to employers and it imposed no restraints whatsoever on the unions.

Roosevelt declared the purpose of the law to be the creation of a better relationship between labor and management but he tacitly acknowledged its one-sidedness. "By preventing practices which tend to destroy the independence of labor," he stated, "it seeks, for every worker within its scope, that freedom of choice and action which is justly his."

To assure such freedom, labor's right to organize was not only expressly reaffirmed, but all employer interference was explicitly forbidden. It was to be an unfair labor practice for an employer to restrain or coerce his employes in exercising their rights, to try to dominate or even contribute financially to the support of any labor organization, to encourage or discourage union membership by discrimination in hiring and firing, or to refuse to bargain collectively. Moreover, representatives designated for collective bargaining by a majority of the employes in an appropriate unit, whether it was an employer, craft or plant unit, were to have exclusive bargaining rights for all employes. The new legislation, that is, definitely undertook to outlaw the company-dominated unions that had flourished under the N.R.A., and to foster and to promote the growth of a bona fide unionism.

The administration of the Wagner Act was placed in the hands of a new National Labor Relations Board, made up of three members, with sole authority to determine the appropriate bargaining unit and to supervise the elections wherein employes chose their exclusive representatives for dealing with employers. The board could also hear complaints of unfair labor practices, issue "cease and desist" orders where they were found to be justified, and petition the courts for enforcement of its orders. The N.L.R.B. was not concerned with the substance of disputes over wages and hours, or any other issues affecting conditions of work, but solely with the practical encouragement and facilitation of collective bargaining.

"It should be clearly understood," President Roosevelt said in explaining the quasi-judicial functions of this administrative agency, "that it will not act as mediator or conciliator in labor disputes. The function of mediation remains, under this Act, the duty of the Secretary of Labor and of the Conciliation Service of the Department of Labor. . . . It is important that the judicial function and the mediation function should not be confused. Compromise, the essence of mediation, has no place in the interpretation and enforcement of the law."

At the time of its passage, the Wagner Act had widespread support. Conservative elements within the business community criticized the one-sidedness of the law, freely predicted union irresponsibility under its provisions, and were generally alarmed at what they considered the dangers to management control. But public opinion polls repeatedly emphasized popular sympathy for labor's aspirations in these days. There was a general feeling that the workers were fully entitled to government protection even at the expense of management, and confidence that they would not abuse their new privileges.

Whatever the pro's and con's of the new legislation, however, its implications were tremendous. At long last the general expressions upholding labor's right to organize—in the Clayton Act, the Norris–La Guardia Act, the National Industrial Recovery Act—were given reality. Labor had for over a century fought for freedom from legal restraints which hampered its activity. It had struggled against conspiracy laws, against enforcement of yellow-dog contracts, against judicial interpretations of liberty that actually nullified the individual worker's freedom, against the arbitrary use of injunctions. The Wagner Act not only removed past obstructions to union activity but erected substantial barriers to any interference on the part of employers to the full mobilization of labor's economic strength.

The battle to realize the full benefits of the new law, however, had still to be fought. While many employers were ready to accept its provisions and bargain collectively with their employes in good faith, there were others so implacably opposed to unionization that they were determined to continue their resistance to it at all cost. In many quarters labor had to push its campaign for organization against as fierce opposition as it had ever faced. The workers again fell back on strikes to win the union recognition that many companies withheld in spite of all governmental guarantees.

The excuse often advanced for refusing to meet the new legal requirements of collective bargaining was that the Wagner Act was unconstitutional. Advised by their lawyers that the Supreme Court would almost certainly invalidate it as going beyond the powers of Congress over interstate commerce, on which its provisions were based, anti-union employers did not hesitate to violate the law and instituted scores of injunctions to prevent the National Labor Relations Board from enforcing it. They launched an attack on labor which was especially aimed at unionization in steel, automobiles, rubber and other mass production industries. They still tried to maintain their control over company unions. Labor spies, stool pigeons and agents provocateurs were hired to ferret out any evidence of union activity, sow seeds of distrust and suspicion among the workers themselves, and furnish the information which would enable the employers to get rid of all those who might be classed as agitators. Strong arm squads were maintained in some instances to discourage union membership by more forcible methods, and outside organizers were beaten up, run out of town and threatened with further violence should they ever show up again.

The report of the La Follette Civil Liberties Committee was a shocking revelation of the disregard of legal and constitutional rights that so widely characterized industrial relations between 1933 and 1937. A first installment, made public in December, 1937, disclosed that some 2,500 corporations, the list reading "like a bluebook of American industry," had long followed the practice of hiring labor spies from agencies specializing in industrial espionage. The records of such firms as the Pinkerton and Burns agencies, the Railway and Audit Inspection Company, and the Corporations Auxiliary Company showed that they had furnished in the three year period under review a total of 3,871 agents to report on union activities, stir up discontent among employes and generally block labor organization. In carrying out their secret activities, individual operatives had become affiliated with ninety-three unions, and a third of the Pinkerton detectives had actually succeeded in becoming union officials. It was further stated that a selected list of companies, representative but not inclusive, had spent from 1933 to 1936 a total of $9,440,000 for spies, strikebreakers and munitions, the General Motors Corporation alone footing a bill of $830,000.

"The public cannot afford to let this challenge presented by industrial espionage go unnoticed," the La Follette committee concluded. "Through it private corporations dominate their employes, deny them their constitutional rights, promote disorder and disharmony, and even set at naught the powers of the government itself."

When this same committee investigated the Little Steel strike of 1937, disclosures of the weapons that had been accumulated for industrial war were even more startling than those of industrial espionage. The Youngstown Sheet and Tube Company had on hand 8 machine guns, 369 rifles, 190 shotguns and 450 revolvers, with 6,000 rounds of ball ammunition and 3,950 rounds of shot ammunition, and also 109 gas guns with over 3,000 rounds of gas ammunition. The Republic Steel Corporation had comparable equipment, and with purchases of tear and sickening gas amounting to $79,000, was described as the largest buyer of such supplies—not excepting law enforcement bodies—in the United States. Senator La Follette declared that the arsenals of these two steel companies "would be adequate equipment for a small war."

There was also brought to light one especially notorious example of industrial techniques in combatting unionism, first developed by the Remington Rand Company and then widely publicized by the National Association of Manufacturers under the name of the Mohawk Valley formula. This formula blueprinted a systematic campaign to denounce all union organizers as dangerous agitators, align the community in support of employers in the name of law and order, intimidate strikers by mobilizing the local police to break up meetings, instigate "back to work" movements by secretly organizing "loyal employes," and set up vigilance committees for protection in getting a struck plant again in operation. The underlying purpose behind the Mohawk Valley formula was to win public support by branding union leaders as subversive and threatening to remove the affected industry from the community if local business interests stood by and allowed radical agitators to win control over workers otherwise ready and anxious to cooperate with their employers.

The evidence made public by the La Follette Committee unveiled previously hidden aspects of industrial warfare. Even the most conservative newspapers, while suggesting that the committee's investigation had been one-sided and its report undoubtedly exaggerated, recognized a state of affairs that could not be condoned and came to the defense of labor's civil liberties. The disclosures, indeed, played a highly important part in convincing many corporations of the wisdom of abandoning practices which could not stand the light of day.

Labor was in the meantime combatting this anti-union campaign with its own militant tactics. Widespread industrial unrest continued throughout the whole period in which the basic principles underlying the Wagner Act were at stake. In 1937 strikes rose to a peak even higher than that of 1934. They totaled 4,720 and engaged almost two million workers.

The constitutionality of the Wagner Act was still undetermined as this new wave of unrest rose to a dramatic climax in the sit-down strikes of General Motors automobile workers, but the Supreme Court finally acted on April 12, 1937. In a series of decisions, of which the most important was that rendered in the case of *National Labor Relations Board* v. *Jones and Laughlin Steel Company,* the law was sustained. This was a spectacular victory for the New Deal and for organized labor, reflecting the change in the attitude of the court that dramatically punctuated the struggle over its reorganization initiated earlier in the year by President Roosevelt. The regulation of labor relations as they might affect interstate commerce was declared to be clearly within the province of Congress under the commerce clause, and the contention that the rights of either employer or employe were invaded by the provisions of the act was flatly rejected.

"Employees have as clear a right to organize and select their representatives for lawful purposes," Chief Justice Hughes stated in the five-to-four decision in *N.L.R.B.* v. *Jones and Laughlin,* "as the respondent has to organize its business and select its own officers and agents. Discrimination and coercion to prevent the free exercise of the right of employees to self-organization and representation is a proper subject for condemnation by competent legislative authority. Long ago we stated the reason for labor organizations. We said that they were organized out of the necessities of the situation; that a single employee was helpless in dealing with an employer; that he was dependent ordinarily on his daily wage for the maintenance of himself and his family; that if the employer refused to pay him the wages he thought fair, he was nevertheless unable to leave the employ and resist arbitrary and unfair treatment; that union was essential to give laborers opportunity to deal on an equality with their employer. . . ."

Its authority established, the National Labor Relations Board was finally in a position to apply the law effectively. It interpreted broadly the provision that it was an unfair labor practice for an employer to interfere with, restrain or coerce employes in the exercise of their rights. Not only were such old practices as yellow-dog contracts, blacklisting and other overt forms of discrimination outlawed, but the employment of labor spies and anti-union propaganda were prohibited. Company-dominated unions were disestablished, both union shops and closed shops upheld, interference forbidden with peaceful picketing.

The majority of cases coming before the board in regard to unfair labor practices were actually handled without prejudice to the interests of industry. It of course remained true that wholly unjustified charges might often be brought up, and that management could not counter with any complaints of unfair practices on the part of the unions. The over-all record of the N.L.R.B. was nevertheless quite a different one from that presented by a generally hostile press which lost no occasion to attack the board for its supposed partiality to labor.

Between 1935 and 1945, a total of 36,000 cases involving charges of unfair labor practices and 38,000 concerned with employe representation were handled. Considering them as a whole, 25.9 per cent were withdrawn without any action being taken, 11.9 were dismissed by regional directors, 46.3 were settled by informal procedures leading to mutual agreement, and only 15.9 required official hearings. The latter cases led to the disestablishment of some 2,000 company unions and the reinstatement of 300,000 employes, with back pay aggregating $9,000,000, where employers were found guilty of discrimination against bona fide union members.

In addition to hearing cases of unfair labor practices and issuing cease and desist orders when it found them justified, the National Labor Relations Board during this period from 1935 to 1945 also held some 24,000 elections, in which 6,000,000 workers participated, to determine collective bargaining units. The C.I.O. won 40 per cent of these elections, the A.F. of L. 33.4 per cent, independent unions 10.5 per cent, and in 16.1 per cent no bargaining unit was chosen. It should be remembered that the board had nothing whatsoever to do with disputes over wages and hours, but in respect to the issues that it was authorized to handle, its activities greatly helped to stabilize industrial relations.

The protection given labor's right to organize and bargain collectively was the most important phase of the pro-labor policy that was generally followed under the New Deal. Once embarked on its course, the Roosevelt administration went far beyond any previous administration in encouraging the growth of unions and accepting the basic role they played in the development of our national economy. But the Wagner Act was not the only New Deal measure which aided labor or contributed to the improved status of industrial workers.

The insistence of the President, from his earliest days in office, upon the obligation of government to cope directly with the fundamental problems of unemployment and relief clearly demonstrated a sympathetic understanding of the needs of the nation's wage earners that was in line with the most progressive principles of American democracy. The public works program included in the National Industrial Recovery Act was principally intended as a means to prime the pump of industry, but both the Civilian Conservation Corps and the Federal Emergency Relief Administration had as their direct objectives relief for the great army of unemployed. They represented an approach to the vital problem of human needs that differed sharply from that of President Hoover, who had long held out against direct relief as undermining individual initiative and self-respect. The Roosevelt administration was to be much more realistic in recognizing the position in which the unemployed found themselves and the necessity of government aid until a revived industry could provide normal opportunities for employment.

This was further borne out in the program that culminated in the Works Progress Administration. This agency was set up not only to aid the unemployed but to provide them with jobs that would enable them to retain their self-respect. The slow pace of recovery, and the recession that developed in 1937, were to involve the government far more deeply in this undertaking than had been originally contemplated. The well-being of industrial workers was nevertheless considered more important than possible economies, and the administration held to its course in spite of all criticism of the tremendous expense involved.

A much more far-reaching measure, considered by Roosevelt "the cornerstone of his administration," was the Social Security Act with its comprehensive provision for unemployment insurance, old age insurance, and other aid for the needy. The principles underlying this law had been opposed by the American Federation of Labor, as we have seen, until the reversal of its traditional policy on unemployment insurance at the 1932 convention. It then came out in support of governmental action. The President's own interest, however, most effectively sustained the drive for social security. "In his own mind," Secretary Perkins has written, "it was *his* program."

Roosevelt instituted studies on the best method of providing for social security early in 1933, talked continually with his advisers of what he termed "cradle to the grave" insurance long before the phrase became current in England, and appointed a Committee on Economic Security in his cabinet to reconcile differing views on how the whole program should be handled. A proposed bill was placed upon his "must list" in 1934 and when Congress failed to act that year, he renewed his insistence upon its adoption at the next session. Final action was then taken and in August, 1935 the Social Security Act was overwhelmingly approved.

The new law had three major parts: First, unemployment compensation was to be handled through the states by remission of ninety per cent of a national payroll tax to every state adopting an insurance program meeting federal specifications. Second, old age pensions were to be administered directly by the federal government from funds secured through equal taxes upon employers and employes which were to start at one per cent of the latter's wages and gradually rise to three per cent. Third, other assistance for the needy was to be provided through grants to the states for the aged and blind, dependent children, and the crippled and disabled, while federal funds were also allocated for maternal and child health services, child welfare work, the rehabilitation of the disabled, and general public health.

This social security program was limited in its scope because of the exclusion of several categories of employes; its benefit payments were not over-generous by any standards, and it fell far short of the "cradle to grave" insurance about which Roosevelt liked to talk. The United States still lagged behind other countries that had long since developed more comprehensive plans. The new law was nevertheless another epochal development in the history of a nation so long wedded to laissez-faire concepts of the role of government in economic and social matters. That social security won the support of industry, labor and the public was a highly significant indication of how the stress of economic circumstances had changed popular attitudes since the depression.

"The experience of these years," Green wrote, "showed that the very disaster of the crisis compelled the government to assume responsibilities and discharge functions within the field of private endeavour which had been regarded as outside its scope. The national government, acting in behalf of all the people, was compelled to care for the needy and unemployed."

In addition to direct relief for the unemployed and social security, the New Deal was also committed to the improvement of working conditions first attempted in the wage and hour provisions of the N.R.A. codes. Other means to attain this goal were at once sought when the National Industrial Recovery Act was declared unconstitutional. A first step was passage of the Walsh-Healey Public Contracts Act, establishing the forty-hour week and minimum wages for all employes of contractors making supplies for the government. But this measure was obviously limited in its scope and the real question was how a more general measure could overcome the constitutional objections that had been brought not only against the N.R.A. but also against minimum wage legislation by the states. Secretary Perkins explored the possibilities of a new approach to the problem but the attitude of the Supreme Court seemed an insuperable barrier.

The issue entered into the 1936 campaign. The Republicans came out in favor of minimum wage legislation through state laws or interstate compacts, but the Democrats declared they would continue to seek national legislation "within the constitution." It was not until the Supreme Court battle had been fought out early in 1937, however, that Roosevelt gave the go-ahead signal for the introduction of a bill providing for maximum hours, minimum wages and, as an almost last minute addition, the abolition of child labor which had first been sought in the N.R.A. codes.

The Fair Labor Standards bill, as it came to be known, met vigorous opposition, reflecting in part the political animosities growing out of the court struggle, and it was at first given only very equivocal support even by labor. Many of the conservatives in the A.F. of L. were still opposed to wage legislation in principle, fearing that minimum wages would become maximum wages, and President Green took an unyield-ing stand against what he considered important shortcomings in the administration's proposals. With spokesmen for the American Federa-tion of Labor and the National Association of Manufacturers in dubious alliance, few New Deal measures faced harder sledding.

Roosevelt repeatedly and emphatically stressed the importance of the bill both in messages to Congress and in fireside chats to the country. "A self-supporting and self-respecting democracy," he declared in May, 1937, "can plead no justification for the existence of child labor, no economic reason for chiseling workers' wages or stretching workers' hours." But entirely apart from justice to the wage earners themselves, the provisions of the proposed bill were supported as an essential means for sustaining and building up national purchasing power.

The importance of high wages from this point of view was of course no new idea. Labor had always maintained that only when the workers were paid enough to enable them to buy the products of their own in-dustry could our economic system function successfully. The assertion of this principle goes back at least as far as the statement of the Mechan-ics' Union of Trade Associations in 1827 on wages, consumption and manufacturing output. But the argument made slow headway and in the early 1930's was only gradually beginning to gain the acceptance that is today almost commonplace. The purchasing power theory in support for high wages had been traditionally overshadowed by the counter argument that by increasing costs of production, high wages actually narrowed the market for manufactured goods and consequently slowed down production.

When Congress failed to act on the Fair Labor Standards bill in the summer of 1937, Roosevelt returned to the attack on this broad front and after calling a special session in November, again demanded prompt passage.

"I believe that the country as a whole," he stated, "recognizes the need for congressional action if we are to maintain wage increases and the purchasing power of the nation against recessive factors in the general industrial situation. The exploitation of child labor and the undercutting of wages and the stretching of the hours of the poorest paid workers in periods of business recession has a serious effect on buying power. . . . What does the country ultimately gain if we encourage businessmen to enlarge the capacity of American industry to produce unless we see to it that the income of our working population actually expands sufficiently to create markets to absorb that increased production?"

After successive delays, redrafts of the original bill to meet labor's objections, and the exercise of strong administration pressure, the opposition finally gave way. The Fair Labor Standards bill was passed in June, 1938. It established a minimum wage of 25 cents an hour rising to 40 cents an hour in seven years, a forty-four-hour week to be reduced to forty hours in three years, and prohibited the labor of children under sixteen in industries whose products entered into interstate commerce. A movement whose origins may be traced back to the demands for a legislative ten-hour day voiced by labor over a century earlier had come to fruition. The state had entered more directly and comprehensively into the control of wages and hours than would have been believed even remotely possible prior to the depression. It was a development in its way as far-reaching as the government's new support for collective bargaining. Again nothing could have more directly contravened the principles of laissez-faire economy, which such labor leaders as Samuel Gompers, and even William Green, had upheld no less zealously than the most conservative of capitalists. But maximum hour and minimum wage legislation was now generally approved—accepted as necessary—by most people.

Government had swung over to the support of the interests of labor and so had the courts. The series of cases in which the Wagner Act, Social Security and the Fair Labor Standards Act were upheld marked a judicial reversal of earlier decisions which gave the final stamp of approval to New Deal policies. The view that laws affecting union membership or prescribing minimum wages violated constitutional guarantees of liberty of contract was abandoned when the Supreme Court stated that "regulation which is reasonable in relation to its subject and is adopted in the interests of the community," could not be construed as violating the due process clause of either the fifth or fourteenth amendments.

Moreover the courts now went on wholly to exempt unions from prosecution under the anti-trust laws and to reverse other restrictive policies by generally upholding the right to strike, to boycott and to picket. Whereas during even the progressive era labor found supposedly guaranteed privileges repeatedly curtailed by the Supreme Court, its position was now being constantly bolstered by favorable decisions. Peaceful picketing was declared in one notable case, *Thornhill* v. *Alabama*, for example, to be a legitimate exercise of free speech within the area guaranteed by the constitution.

So far, indeed, did the Supreme Court go that in 1945 a majority decision in *Hunt* v. *Crumboch* upheld the right of a union, under highly complicated circumstances, to exercise a boycott that virtually drove the firm against which it was directed out of business. To Justice Jackson this case gave occasion for a significant review of judicial policy toward labor.

"With this decision," he stated in a vigorous dissenting opinion, "the labor movement has come full circle. The workingman has struggled long, the fight has been filled with hatred, and conflict has been dangerous, but now workers may not be deprived of their livelihood merely because their employers oppose and they favor unions. Labor has won other rights as well, unemployment compensation, old-age benefits and, what is most important and the basis of all its gains, the recognition that the opportunity to earn his support is not alone the concern of the individual but is the problem which all organized societies must contend with and conquer if they are to survive. This Court now sustains the claim of a union to the right to deny participation in the economic world to an employer simply because the union dislikes him. This Court permits to employes the same arbitrary dominance over the economic sphere which they control that labor so long, so bitterly and so rightly asserted should belong to no man."

Whatever the validity of Justice Jackson's views and the later problems that would arise in regard to the sometimes arbitrary assertion of labor's rights, the general program of the New Deal in encouraging the growth of strong unions and otherwise sustaining the position of organized labor was still applauded by the nation as a whole in the mid-1930's. Repeated public-opinion polls revealed strong support for each of the successive labor measures adopted by Congress between 1933 and 1938. President Roosevelt was undoubtedly justified at this time in asserting his belief that a majority of the people were glad "that we are slowly working out for labor greater privileges and at the same time greater responsibilities."

The continued strikes of these years, and particularly those of 1937, clearly showed that no final solution had been found for industrial relations and a pronounced reaction to the pro-labor policies of the New Deal was soon to set in. In spite of both labor disturbances and a growing demand for modification of the Wagner Act, however, Roosevelt was to remain convinced that the increased strength of unionism would in time lead to greater industrial stability. He believed thoroughly in the principle of collective bargaining. "It must remain," he declared, "as the foundation of industrial relations for all time." He was prepared not only to help labor to maintain its gains but to advance them still further.

"Only in free lands," he stated in an important address to the convention of the International Brotherhood of Teamsters in 1940, "have free labor unions survived. When union workers assemble with freedom and independence in a convention like this, it is a proof that American democracy has remained unimpaired; it is a symbol of our determination to keep it free."

Labor was still suffering from growing pains, in his opinion, and more responsible leadership was bound to emerge and make possible a larger degree of cooperation with equally responsible management. When warned on one occasion that the unions might become too powerful, he was quoted as replying, "Too powerful for what?" His attitude was that their power should prove an antidote for that of big business. His faith in labor and in the vital importance of free labor unions was not to be shaken.

The basic importance of the New Deal program did not lie in immediate gains or losses for labor but in its recognition that this whole matter of working conditions was no longer the concern of employe and employer alone, but of society as a whole. Democratic capitalism could hardly hope to survive unless the great army of workers could obtain through concerted effort the freedom and the security that as individuals they were powerless to defend in an industrialized society. The New Deal's policy was pro-labor, but it was pro-labor in order to redress the balance that had been tipped in favor of industry. It looked primarily toward the wellbeing of the workers, but in the conviction that upon their wellbeing rested that of the entire country.

XXX

XVI: RISE OF THE C.I.O.

XXXXXXXXXXXXXXXXXXXXXXXXXXXXXXXXXXXXXXXXXXX

WHILE ORGANIZED LABOR was making such pronounced gains during the period of the New Deal, conflict within its own ranks shattered the relative unity that it had formerly maintained. As the controversy over industrial versus craft unionism within the American Federation of Labor led to insurgent revolt and establishment of the Committee for Industrial Organization, the ground was laid for a continuing rivalry which in some measure may actually have stimulated union growth, but also served to diffuse labor's energy through internal feuds and dissension.

The issues in dispute were comparable to those which had arisen when the A.F. of L. challenged the Knights of Labor half a century earlier. Should union organization be pursued principally in the interests of the skilled workers, or should it aim to include more effectively the great mass of unskilled workers? The Knights had sought to meet the problem by promoting one all-inclusive union, but economic circumstance gave far greater validity to the program of the new unionism of the A.F. of L. with its emphasis on closely disciplined crafts. Industrial unionism could not be successfully promoted in any form in the 1880's because the unskilled workers, their ranks constantly replenished by immigration, had such meager bargaining power. But changed conditions in the 1930's underscored both the importance and the practicality of building up out-and-out industrial unions. Failure to meet the needs of unorganized workers in the mass production industries had greatly weakened the whole labor movement, and the opportunity to organize them was better than ever before with government support and the curtailment of immigration greatly enhancing their potential bargaining power.

Craft unionism versus industrial unionism, however, became increasingly overshadowed in the quarrel between the A.F. of L. and the C.I.O.

by the drives for power on the part of the two factions and the mounting rivalry between their leaders. The issues originally at stake gave way to the fierce interplay of union politics and the clash of ambitious personalities. Charges and countercharges flew back and forth between William Green and John L. Lewis.

"In the midst of our common effort to better the welfare of all workers," Green was to write, "came forth a man who sought other ends. Consumed with personal ambition, he gave the lie to the democratic process after it had rejected his leadership. He raised the voice of dualism and disunity, a voice which while pretending to unite sought to disrupt; a voice which while declaiming democratic ideals sought dictatorship."

Lewis struck back savagely at what he considered the obstructive attitude of the A.F. of L. and the blind conservatism of its leadership. The organizing efforts of the Federation were said to represent "twenty-five years of unbroken failure," and its president was charged with being unable to either understand what was happening to the national economy or to rise to the opportunities of the hour. "Alas, poor Green," Lewis told reporters as the verbal brickbats were flying back and forth in 1936, "I knew him well. He wishes me to join him in fluttering procrastination, the while intoning *O tempora, O mores!*"

In taking over command of the campaign for industrial unionism and directly defying the oligarchy in control of the A.F. of L., Lewis soon revealed himself to be the most aggressive and colorful figure that American labor had ever known. His spectacular success in reviving the United Mine Workers during the early days of the New Deal, increasing its membership from 150,000 to 400,000, attracted nationwide attention. The magazine *Fortune* wryly commented that "he made a noise like the whole labor movement," and in time the noise was to rise to a deafening roar. It was characteristic of popular attitudes toward Lewis in this period that he was invariably described, whether by friend or foe, in gaudy superlatives. He was either an unexampled hero or an unspeakable villain.

Philip Murray, destined to succeed him as president of the C.I.O., declared that he was "without a peer in the realm of America"; in the days of the united front with communism, Earl Browder hailed him not merely as the greatest of American trade union leaders but "as a leader of world democracy," and Huey Long could pay him no higher compliment than to single him out as "the Huey Long of labor." The chorus of condemnation, on the other hand, reached its peak during the days of war. When *Fortune* held a poll in 1943 on who were the most harmful individuals in the United States, seventy per cent of the ballots bore the name of John L. Lewis.

Both his family background and early life were closely associated with the labor movement. His parentage, like that of William Green, was of Welsh mining stock and when his father emigrated to the United States in 1875, the family settled in the small coal town of Lucas, Iowa, where Lewis senior promptly joined the Knights of Labor. John L. was born in 1880 and went into the pits at the age of twelve. After restlessly roaming the mining regions in several states as a boy and young man, he took up labor politics in 1909. Elected president of a United Mine Workers local in Panama, Illinois, he became state legislative agent for the union, then a field representative for the A.F. of L., and successively chief statistician, first vice-president and finally president of the United Mine Workers. At the time of the coal crisis in 1919, as we have seen, he won national headlines for his refusal to lead the miners in a strike against the government. Subsequent years found Lewis desperately on the defensive as the coal operators hammered away at his union, radical elements promoted a revolt against his leadership, and the strength of the U.M.W. gradually dwindled. It was his prompt seizure of the chance presented by the N.R.A. to recoup both his and his union's fortunes that first demonstrated the shrewd tactical sense and astute opportunism, reenforced by defiant courage, which were to make him a national leader.

No public figure other than President Roosevelt was more familiar to the American people as he pursued his stormy, turbulent career after 1933—militantly challenging the world of industry ("They are striking me hip and thigh . . . right merrily shall I return their blows"), vilifying his enemies within the labor movement, making and breaking alliances as he shifted the grounds of his attack, and defying the government in self-centered pursuit of his own ambitions. Innumerable articles attempted to find the answer to the question he once asked: "What makes me tick? Is it power I am after, or am I a Saint Francis in disguise, or what?" An elemental force, a consummate actor, a consecrated leader, a self-willed opportunist . . . what was John L. Lewis? If the answer was indeed a Saint Francis, the disguise could hardly have been more complete. Cartoonists had a happy field day drawing the jutting jaw, the glowering scowl, the bushy eyebrows of this mighty protagonist of labor.

No consistent philosophy could be discerned in the tortuous windings of his career. He paid eloquent tribute at one time to Herbert Hoover's "genius for constructive industrial statesmanship"; eagerly embraced the New Deal and threw the full weight of his influence behind Roosevelt in 1936; dramatically broke with the President four years later to stake retention of his office in the C.I.O. on the election of Wendell Willkie. In politics and within the labor movement, it was "off ag'in, on ag'in, gone ag'in—Finnigin" for this erratic individualist whose only definite lodestar so often appeared to be the interests of John L. Lewis. Whether he believed in a laissez-faire or a regulated economy might often be in doubt, but there was no question but that he always believed in himself.

To the interviewers who flocked to discuss national problems with him in 1936 and 1937, he talked pompously of industrial democracy, but completely failed to clarify what the term meant. It was apparent only that he had no idea of trying to overturn or seriously disturb the existing economic system. He had no long range program or ultimate ideal, and from that point of view his policy conformed to the traditional opportunism of Samuel Gompers and the A.F. of L. rather than the reformist zeal of Terence V. Powderly and the Knights of Labor. He believed that labor should play a greater role in affairs of government but his flirtations with the idea of a third party seemed to be inspired not so much by the desire to promote any specific program as the desire to promote John L. Lewis. When asked about the future of labor, his answers were lost in hazy and verbose platitudes. "It would be unwisdom to paint a picture that would only alarm our adversaries of tomorrow," he told one inquiring reporter. "Neither can I bond the purity of motive or the administrative rectitude of the labor movement of tomorrow."

On the platform, in public meetings and over the radio, Lewis showed a flare for the dramatic that inevitably arrested public attention. He well knew his ability as an actor ("My life is but a stage," he said on one occasion) and he would alternately cajole, denounce, threaten, pontificate with equal self-assurance. His sense of his own importance was magnificent.

He performed prodigies of valor in building up the United Mine Workers and in organizing the C.I.O. Labor was to owe him an immense debt. But his insatiable lust for power helped to betray the solidarity of trade unionism and his defiance of government during the Second World War was a highly important factor in alienating the public sympathy that labor enjoyed in the early days of the New Deal. Whatever the losses he suffered in either public or labor support, however, Lewis could never be relegated to the background. With his miners standing firmly behind him, accepting his dictatorial control of their union because he got results, he continued to play an important role in labor politics.

The discontent with the fumbling policies of the A.F. of L. that was to give Lewis his chance to lead the movement for industrial unionism came to a head at the annual convention of the Federation in San Francisco in 1934. With the drifting away of union members in textiles and steel, in automobiles and rubber, the demand for industrial charters to replace federal charters became increasingly vocal. The leaders of industrial unions within the A.F. of L. attacked the policy that required new unions to be subordinated to the jurisdictional claims of existing craft unions. They vigorously reasserted their conviction that only the organization of all workers—the skilled and the unskilled—in single industry-wide unions could meet the needs of workers engaged in mass production.

The old-line craft union leaders were not convinced. The very fact that in previous years the membership in existing industrial unions had increased 130 per cent, while that of craft unions had gained only 10 per cent, simply emphasized for them the dangers of granting the new industrial charters which the insurgents demanded. They insisted that such a departure from traditional practice would destroy the foundations upon which the A.F. of L. had been built. Wage earners could not be successfully organized, it was reiterated, except by bringing them into "the respective national and international unions where jurisdiction has been established."

The controversy was temporarily resolved at San Francisco by a compromise engineered by moderates on both sides of the issue. It was agreed that charters would be granted for unions in automobiles, rubber, cement, radio and aluminum, and an intensive drive initiated to organize the steel industry, but that the rights of existing craft unions would be fully protected and all jurisdictional disputes submitted to an executive council enlarged to include representatives of the industrial unions.

This was at least a partial success for the insurgents and a hopeful augury for labor, but the succeeding year saw little or nothing done to carry out the agreement. The A.F. of L. leadership had not in reality been aroused from its complacent conservatism. The craft union leaders, and especially those of the building trades, had not been persuaded of the need for industrial unionism. They still saw only dangers to their own hold on power in any broadening of the bases of the labor movement. They continued to postpone and delay any action along the lines to which they had supposedly agreed. The next convention of the Federation, held at Atlantic City in 1935, met against a background of growing union demoralization in the mass production industries and an executive council report that "we did not deem it advisable to launch an organizing campaign for the steel industry."

Lewis came to Atlantic City demanding action. The situation in steel was for him one of particular concern. He had succeeded in organizing the workers in the captive coal mines belonging to that industry and was convinced that this new union redoubt could not be held unless the steel workers were also organized. This time he was determined, together with other leaders favoring industrial unionism, to compel the executive council to live up to its promises—or else.

The issue was placed fairly before the convention in majority and minority reports submitted by its resolutions committee. The former declared that since it was a primary obligation of the A.F. of L. "to protect the jurisdictional rights of all trade unions organized upon craft lines," industrial charters would violate the agreements that had always existed between the Federation and its craft affiliates. The latter insisted that in any industry where the work performed by a majority of the workers fell within the jurisdictional claim of more than one craft union, industrial organization was "the only form that will be acceptable to the workers or adequately meet their needs."

On the one side in this embittered controversy were William Green, cautiously following the policies bequeathed him by Samuel Gompers in spite of earlier advocacy of industrial unionism; the hard-boiled and hard-hitting head of the carpenters, William L. Hutcheson, firmly resolved to keep all workers in wood or its substitutes within the comfortable fold of his own union; Daniel J. Tobin, the pugnacious leader of the teamsters who scornfully characterized the unskilled workers in the mass-production industries as "rubbish;" Matthew Woll, of the photoengravers, whose conservatism was exemplified by his role as acting president of the old and moribund National Civic Federation, and the dignified, scholarly John P. Frey, head of the Metal Trades Department of the A.F. of L. This was the Old Guard, ready to fight industrial unionism with all the weapons at its command.

Lewis led the insurgents and had the support of some of the most progressive and forceful labor leaders of the day. Among them were Charles P. Howard, calm, persuasive head of the Typographical Union and the actual author of the minority report; Philip Murray, the somewhat retiring and soft spoken, but extremely able, *alter ego* of Lewis in the United Mine Workers; Sidney Hillman, the Lithuanian-born needle trades leader, who harbored a fund of nervous energy and ambition beneath his quiet manner and who had just brought the formerly independent Amalgamated Clothing Workers into the A.F. of L., and David Dubinsky, one of the shrewdest of trade unionists and president of the effervescent International Ladies' Garment Workers.

The debate among these chieftains over A.F. of L. policy continued for several days, the issue sharpened by attack and counterattack on the floor of the convention. Its peak was reached when Lewis, excoriating tactics that resulted in the new unions "dying like the grass withering before the autumn sun," vehemently assailed what he regarded as the betrayal of the promises made at the preceding convention.

"At San Francisco they seduced me with fair words," he thundered, "Now, of course, having learned that I was seduced, I am enraged and I am ready to rend my seducers limb from limb, including delegate Woll. In that sense, of course, I speak figuratively." He called upon the convention delegates to make a contribution to the welfare of their less fortunate brethren, to heed their cry from Macedonia, to organize the unorganized and make the Federation into the greatest instrument that had ever been forged to befriend the cause of humanity. And he solemnly warned that if they let slip this opportunity, the enemies of labor would be encouraged "and high wassail will prevail at the banquet tables of the mighty."

But for all his eloquence, his appeals and his warnings, Lewis was unable to make the delegates see why they should modify traditional policies. The majority were unmoved by the threat of being rended limb from limb, even figuratively. Their ears were closed to all cries from Macedonia. They were not disturbed by the picture of high wassail at the banquets of the mighty. When the final vote was taken, the program for industrial unionism went down to defeat through a vote of 18,024 to 10,933 in favor of the majority report of the resolutions committee favoring craft unions.

Shortly afterward an incident occurred which appeared to symbolize the break that this crucial vote meant. The details are somewhat obscure. But in the course of further wrangling over procedure, Hutcheson so far departed from parliamentary decorum as to call Lewis a term which bystanders identified as "bastard." The rejoinder of the miner's chieftain was an uppercut, with all the force of some 225 pounds behind it, which caught the equally burly czar of the carpenters squarely on the jaw. The assailants were separated and the danger of a free-for-all happily averted, but the altercation hardly served to placate feelings, already so touchy, in the two camps into which labor had been divided.

Immediately after the A.F. of L. convention, the advocates of industrial unionism met to consider further action. They were unwilling to accept a decision that once again put off any effective organizational work in the mass production industries and on November 9, 1935 took the first steps to set up their own Committee for Industrial Organization. As originally constituted it was made up of Lewis, Howard, Hillman and Dubinsky, together with Max Zaritsky, of the Cap and Millinery Department of the United Hatters; Thomas F. McMahon of the United Textile Workers; Thomas H. Brown of the Mine, Mill and Smelter Workers, and Harvey C. Fremming of the Oil Field, Gas Well and Refining Workers. It was the declared intent of this committee to work within the framework of the A.F. of L. rather than to set up an independent organization. Its functions were to be "educational and advisory" in an effort to promote the recognition and acceptance of "modern collective bargaining" in the mass production industries. In spite of such statements, however, the leaders of the C.I.O. were at once accused by Green of going against the majority decision of the A.F. of L. convention. Their sole motive, he was repeatedly to declare, was to force acceptance of their own views. The answer of Lewis was to bid further defiance to the executive council.

"Dear Sir and Brother," he wrote Green on November 23: "Effective this date I resign as vice-president of the American Federation of Labor."

The C.I.O. at once began to lay plans for its own organizing campaign and early in January, 1936, submitted to the executive council of the A.F. of L. for a final time the old demand for industrial charters in steel and automobiles, rubber and radio. But there was no break in the ranks of the Old Guard. More fearful than ever of what the aggressive tactics of the new committee might mean to the established position of craft unions in the A.F. of L., the members of the executive council now countered with an order for the immediate dissolution of the C.I.O. It was fomenting insurrection, they charged, and was a dual organization created only to serve the interests of "a few self-seeking individuals."

Throughout the next few months angry controversy raged between the leaders of the A.F. of L. and those of the C.I.O. and the cleavage in labor's ranks steadily widened. Green alternately pleaded and threatened in trying to bring the rebels back into the fold. Lewis adamantly went his own way. Finally in late summer, the A.F. of L. executive council suspended the ten unions that had in the meantime affiliated with the C.I.O. Far from submitting to such discipline, however, Lewis declared that the council had acted without authority. "I fear his threats," was his answer to Green's charges on one occasion, "as much as I believe his promises." When the Federation met for its 1936 convention at Tampa, Florida, delegates from the C.I.O. unions were conspicuously absent. The countermove of the A.F. of L. was to vote by an overwhelming but meaningless majority that their suspension should remain in effect until "the breach be healed and adjusted under such terms and conditions as the Executive Committee may deem best."

The C.I.O. marched ahead with its own organizing program. New unions in steel, automobiles, glass, rubber and radio joined the original members. In increasing alarm, the A.F. of L. again denounced the movement as threatening to destroy the whole basis of labor federation and assailed its leaders for betraying the union cause. In March, 1937, amid the nationwide excitement caused by organizational drives in both steel and automobiles, the executive council made the decisive move of ordering all C.I.O. unions expelled from state and city federations of the A.F. of L.

Toward the close of 1937, again under the influence of moderate leaders in both camps, belated efforts were made to find some basis for peace. They were foredoomed to failure. The A.F. of L. proposed the return of the original C.I.O. unions and the merger of its new ones with existing A.F. of L. unions. The C.I.O. demanded admittance of its entire membership, now grown to some thirty-two unions, with full voting power. Each organization was looking toward domination in any proposed merger and neither A.F. of L. nor C.I.O. leaders were willing to make the concessions that might have enabled them to work together. The issue was no longer, if it ever had been in reality, industrial unionism versus craft unionism. It was a contest for power. The welfare of labor as a whole was sacrificed to the rivalries of stubborn, self-willed ambition.

In the opinion of many observers, it was at this time that Lewis first dangerously overplayed his hand and lost what might have been the chance to control a united labor movement. For the C.I.O. membership had actually outstripped that of the A.F. of L. At the close of 1937 it totaled some 3,700,000 as against its rival's 3,400,000, and whatever the terms of merger, the industrial unions would have dominated a reconstituted A.F. of L. But the growing power of the C.I.O. apparently convinced Lewis that he could win even greater victories without sharing responsibility, and he was stubbornly determined to go his own way. Not again would such a favorable opportunity present itself for restoring labor unity.

After the failure of these peace negotiations in the fall of 1937, the A.F. of L. confirmed the action of its executive council in expelling all C.I.O. members, except for the Ladies' Garment Workers who were soon to return to the fold. Then in May, 1938, Lewis and his lieutenants took the final steps to transform what had originally been only an organizing committee into a permanent Congress of Industrial Organizations. These moves, however, were only formalities. The rift in the house of labor was already complete.

The C.I.O. was to continue to promote industrial unionism and uphold the interests of the great mass of unskilled workers but it did not in actual fact differ very much from the A.F. of L. In spite of the attacks made upon it, and the charges that it was fostering communism, it was no less conservative in its basic principles than the parent organization. Unlike such earlier opponents of craft unionism as the Knights of Labor, the Socialist Trade and Labor Alliance and the I.W.W., the C.I.O. was wholly committed to advancing the interests of wage earners through collective bargaining within the existing structure of democratic capitalism. It was prepared to put more emphasis on political action than the A.F. of L. had in the past, but this was a logical outgrowth of the larger role that government was playing in the regulation of labor relations. There was no reflection of a radical or revolutionary demand for any change in our political system.

In actual structure the C.I.O. also followed the general pattern of the A.F. of L. except that it did not have special departments. The older organization had long since found it necessary to set up a Building and Construction Trades Department, a Metal Trades Department, a Railway Employees' Department and a Union Label Trades Department, but with its major unions industrial in scope, there was no need for such divisions within the C.I.O. It did, however, establish state and city industrial union councils comparable to the A.F. of L. state federations of labor and city centrals. The authority of the C.I.O. in dealing with the member unions has proved in practice to be more extensive than that of the A.F. of L. and its executive council has intervened far more often in local union affairs.

Generally speaking, the C.I.O. conformed to the established traditions of American labor, rather than the more class-conscious traditions of European labor. Its startling impact on the labor movement was primarily due to the fact that it was more alert to the needs of the unskilled workers than the A.F. of L. and more active and aggressive in promoting them.

The response to the C.I.O.'s vigorous campaign for industrial unionism, set in motion soon after its revolt against the dilatory and delaying
tactics of the A.F. of L. in 1935, was immediate and nationwide. Here
was what the great body of workers in mass production industries had
been waiting for and they flocked to join unions that really met their
needs and freed them from the discriminatory controls of federal unions.
As organizers went out from the new C.I.O. headquarters, supported
by funds made available through contributions from the miners, needle
workers and other sympathetic unions, they were greeted with enthusiasm. With the energetic, skillful leadership of Lewis and Murray,
Hillman and Dubinsky, progress was phenomenal.

The key drive of the C.I.O. among the nation's steel workers was
launched in June, 1936 with the establishment of the Steel Workers'
Organizing Committee. Under Murray's direction it took over the
nearly defunct Amalgamated Association of Iron, Steel and Tin Workers,
set up district headquarters in Pittsburgh, Chicago and Birmingham, and
soon had some four hundred organizers distributing union literature,
holding mass meetings, canvassing from house to house in the steel
towns of Pennsylvania, Ohio, Illinois and Alabama. With average annual
wages among the workers as low as $560, compared with a minimum
$1500 standard of living budget, they found fertile ground for effective
union propaganda. The steel industry, whose obdurate anti-unionism
could be traced from Homestead through the great steel strike of 1919,
was prepared to meet this new challenge with full recognition of its
significance. Page advertisements were inserted in papers throughout
the country by the Iron and Steel Institute which declared that the companies' own employe representation plans fully met the needs of the
workers, that the C.I.O. was trying to intimidate and coerce them into
joining the union, and that radical and communist influences were again
at work.

Lewis took to the radio in a nationwide hook-up to counteract this
propaganda barrage and warned not only the steel operators but all
industry that the drive sponsored by the C.I.O. to unionize the industrial workers could not be withstood.

"Let him who will, be he economic tyrant or sordid mercenary," he
shouted into the ether, "pit his strength against this mighty upsurge of
human sentiment now being crystallized in the hearts of thirty million

workers who clamor for the establishment of industrial democracy and for participation in its tangible fruits. He is a madman or a fool who believes that this river of human sentiment . . . can be dammed or impounded by the erection of arbitrary barriers of restraint."

Within a matter of months, the industry which had successfully beaten back unionism on so many occasions found itself on the defensive. Thousands of workers flocked to join the Steel Workers' Organizing Committee. Former company unions in many instances simply transformed themselves into locals of the new union, and when management sought to regain control by promising wage increases tied to the cost of living, their members bluntly rejected any such agreements. By the close of 1936, the S.W.O.C. could boast of the establishment of some 150 union lodges with a total membership of over 100,000. It had become strong enough to demand recognition and collective bargaining, strong enough to threaten a nationwide strike should the steel industry refuse to heed the workers' demands.

While preparations for such a move were still underway, however, an unexpected and dramatic announcement was made on March 1, 1937. As a result of secret negotiations which had been proceeding for some time between Lewis and Myron C. Taylor, chairman of the board of directors of the United States Steel Corporation, an agreement had been reached whereby "Big Steel" recognized the S.W.O.C. as the bargaining agent for its members, granted a ten per cent wage increase, and accepted an eight-hour day and forty-hour week. Even though the company still maintained a technical open shop policy, it was a tremendous victory for unionism and one that had few if any parallels in the whole history of the organized labor movement. A citadel had fallen before the onslaught of the C.I.O. and its submission graphically revealed what was to become the new pattern of labor relations in the mass production industries as a whole.

"Big Steel" had surrendered, it was believed, under the pressure of banking interests that had clearly read the handwriting on the wall ever since passage of the Wagner Act. With a majority of the company's employes (more accurately, those of its chief subsidiary, the Carnegie-Illinois Steel Company) already enrolled under the banners of the Steel Workers' Organizing Committee, they foresaw a strike that would cripple operations at a time when production was just getting back into stride and new orders were piling up on the company's books. The corporation that had at one time declared its unalterable opposition to union labor was induced to accept peacefully a trend which could no longer be successfully withstood. Enlightened self-interest triumphed over stubborn prejudice.

Over a hundred independent companies followed the lead of United States Steel and by May the S.W.O.C. membership had leaped ahead to over 300,000. But there were still important hold-outs. The companies known as "Little Steel"—Republic, Youngstown Sheet and Tube, Inland Steel and Bethlehem—refused to come to terms with the S.W.O.C. and began to mobilize their forces to resist any further union pressure. Under the leadership of Tom M. Girdler, the tough, reactionary, virulently anti-labor president of Republic, the battle lines were drawn.

The reply of the leaders of the S.W.O.C. was a strike call and during May some 75,000 workers in the plants of "Little Steel" walked out in a concerted move to compel recognition of their union. The companies fought back and through their strong control over the steel towns did so successfully. Citizens' committees were formed to support a campaign of intimidation and violent coercion; back-to-work movements were organized with the protection of local police and special deputies; and attacks upon the picket lines, tear gassing of union headquarters, arrests of strike leaders, and the use of militia to protect strikebreakers gradually broke down the morale of the workers.

Violence flared up in a score of steel towns and reached a peak in a bloody clash at the South Chicago shop of the Republic Steel Company. On May 30 a line of some three hundred pickets was halted by the police, some missiles were thrown, and the police opened fire. The unarmed workers broke ranks and frantically fled for safety from the hail of bullets, but they left ten of their number dead on the street and over a hundred injured. While some twenty-two of the police were also wounded in the affray, not a single one suffered any critical injury.

The "Memorial Day Massacre," as it was at once called by union labor, awoke widespread public sympathy for the strikers. Later investigations, including careful study of moving picture films, clearly revealed that they had not provoked the attack. But the sentiment in the steel towns themselves still remained strongly anti-union and with such support the companies were too well entrenched for the workers to hold out. Propaganda, force and terrorism broke the strike and the C.I.O. suffered its first defeat.

It was to prove a Pyrrhic victory for "Little Steel." Four years later the National Labor Relations Board ordered the companies concerned to recognize what had by then become the United Steelworkers of America, reinstate all employes who had lost their jobs through participation in the strike or because of union membership, and to accept collective bargaining. Stubbornly resisting labor pressure up to the last moment, "Little Steel" was finally forced to capitulate through government intervention. By then—1941—the C.I.O. had succeeded in organizing 600,000 steel workers and virtually the entire industry was covered by union contracts.

In the meantime an even more dramatic and violent revolution had taken place in the automobile industry. There had been seething unrest among its workers since the advent of the N.R.A. and the failure of the incipient strikes of 1934. In spite of high hourly rates, seasonal lay-offs held down annual wages to an average of less than $1,000 while another widely held grievance was the speed-up on the assembly line. For the worker whose sole task was to stand by a conveyor belt and put a wheel on a passing chassis, set a fender or simply tighten a bolt, the tense strain of working under increasing pressure sometimes became almost unbearable. But every attempt to secure modification of such conditions by concerted protest was beaten down by management. The automobile industry had developed its spy system so extensively that union activity appeared to be blocked before it could get started.

Nevertheless unionization was not given up. The United Automobile Workers had been established through a merger of the federal unions originally set up by the A.F. of L. and its organizers were actively at work. Still, progress was slow. Growing discontented with the meager support of the Federation, the new union thereupon broke away from the A.F. of L. in 1936 and threw in its lot with the C.I.O. Homer S. Martin was elected as president and preparations made for a revitalized organizational campaign that was eventually to make the United Automobile,

Aircraft and Agricultural Implement Workers the largest industrial union in the country.

Martin was young and idealistic, with little experience as either a worker or union member. After graduating from a small Missouri college, he had entered the Baptist ministry and in 1932 become pastor of a small church in a Kansas City suburb. His outspoken sympathy for the workers soon led to his losing his position, and he took a job in a Chevrolet factory where he began to preach unionism with evangelical zeal. Fired as a trouble maker, he devoted all his time to union work and rose to be vice-president of the struggling U.A.W. Described in appearance and manner as an almost typical Y.M.C.A. secretary—friendly, quiet, bespectacled—Martin took over control of the union after his election to the presidency and infused it with a new spirit. What he lacked in experience, he made up in energy. Under the impact of his inspirational appeals, which turned union meetings into something very much like old-fashioned revivals, the automobile workers joined up in rapidly increasing numbers.

There were some scattered strikes during the summer of 1936 and by late fall the United Automobile Workers—some 30,000 strong—was coming out in the open, prepared to demand recognition from the giants of the industry—General Motors, Chrysler, and Ford. "We don't want to be driven; we don't want to be spied on," was the workers' new refrain. But the companies, defying the provisions of the Wagner Act, were not yet willing to make any concessions. When Martin asked the officers of General Motors for a conference on collective bargaining, William S. Knudsen, vice-president, merely suggested that if the workers had any grievances they should take them up with local plant managers. The reply of the union was a strike which began in the Fisher Body plants of the company at Flint, Michigan, in January, 1937 and then gradually spread to Detroit, Cleveland, Toledo, and other parts of the country. Production in General Motors came to a standstill with some 112,000 of its 150,000 workers idle.

This strike was something new under the sun. It took the form in Flint of a sit-down. There had been some earlier use of this radical technique, notably among the rubber workers at Akron, but the General Motors strike marked its first use on a really wide scale. The automobile workers refused to leave the plant; they just sat at their work benches.

It was not an act of violence but one of passive resistance, doubly effective in that such a strike could be broken only by the forcible removal of the workers from company premises.

Excitement ran high in Flint and neighboring Detroit. General Motors management and the Flint Alliance, a company-sponsored association supposedly made up of loyal employes, assailed the sit-down as an unlawful invasion of property rights and called for the immediate ejection of the strikers. Martin countered with charges that General Motors proposed to invade the property rights of the workers.

"What more sacred property right is there in the world today," he demanded, "than the right of a man to his job? This property right involves the right to support his family, feed his children and keep starvation away from the door. This . . . is the very foundation stone of American homes . . . the most sacred, most fundamental property right in America."

The C.I.O. at first looked upon the strike with misgivings and was anything but enthusiastic over the sit-down. Deeply involved in the organizing drive in steel, whose success was considered basic to the whole program of industrial unionism, the outbreak in automobiles was highly embarrassing. But support could not be withheld and the C.I.O. undertook to do everything it could to aid the General Motors employes. "You men are undoubtedly carrying on through one of the most heroic battles that has ever been undertaken by strikers in an industrial dispute," Lewis declared. "The attention of the entire American public is focussed upon you. . . ."

The latter part of his statement was unquestionably true, and became even more so as violence broke out in Flint and the strikers showed their stubborn determination not to be dislodged from the occupied plants. The cutting off of all heat—even though it was the dead of winter—made no difference. When the police tried to rush Fisher Body Plant No. 2, they were met by a hail of missiles—coffee mugs, pop bottles, iron bolts and heavy automobile door hinges. When they then returned to the attack with tear-gas bombs, the strikers retaliated by turning streams of water on them from the plant fire hoses. The forces of law and order were finally compelled to make a hasty retreat in what the exultant workers promptly termed the "Battle of the Running Bulls."

The strike dragged on from week to week as the General Motors employes continued to sit it out with food and other supplies brought in to them through the picket lines. Discipline was rigid. "Brilliantly lighted," reads a contemporary description by a union organizer, "this vast plant was heavily guarded inside and outside—to keep strikebreakers and other interlopers from entering and to protect the building and its contents. Especially did these strikers guard the company's dies. No liquor was permitted on the premises, and smoking was prohibited on all production floors. Forty-five men were assigned to police patrol duty inside. Their word was law."

Both the company and the Flint Alliance now demanded that the state militia be mobilized to clear the plants since the police had failed to do so. But Governor Murphy of Michigan, sympathetic with the automobile workers and fearful of the bloodshed that would certainly result, refused to take this step. Finally, however, General Motors obtained a court order setting 3:00 P. M. on February 3 as the deadline for evacuation of the plants under penalty of imprisonment and fines. The strikers were undismayed. "We the workers," they wired the governor, ". . . have carried on a stay-in strike over a month to make General Motors Corporation obey the law and engage in collective bargaining. . . . Unarmed as we are, the introduction of the militia, sheriffs or police with murderous weapons will mean a blood-bath of unarmed workers. . . . We have decided to stay in the plant."

Realizing that the strikers meant what they said, Murphy frantically summoned a peace conference. John L. Lewis rushed to Detroit ("Let there be no moaning at the bar when I put out to sea," he cryptically told reporters as he entrained in Washington) and began negotiations with Vice-President Knudsen, whom Governor Murphy had prevailed upon to meet him. But the morning of February 3 arrived without any settlement having been reached. The sit-downers were barricaded in the factories, armed with iron bolts and door hinges, and protected against the expected tear and vomiting gas with slight cheesecloth masks. Outside the besieged plants, thousands of sympathetic workers and members of women's emergency brigades milled about as sound trucks blared forth the slogan of "Solidarity Forever."

The zero hour approached—and passed. Governor Murphy refused to order the national guardsmen to enforce the court order. In spite of mounting popular pressure, he remained unwilling to make a move that would have precipitated violence on an unpredictable scale.

The next day President Roosevelt added his request for a continuation of negotiations to that of Governor Murphy, and the Lewis-Knudsen talks (with other representatives of both General Motors and the strikers present) were resumed. For a full week, while the sit-downers grimly held the fort, the conference proceeded until at long last, the weary, haggard governor was able to announce that agreement had been reached. General Motors undertook to recognize the United Automobile Workers as the bargaining agent for its members, to drop injunction proceedings against the strikers, not to discriminate in any way against union members, and to take up such grievances as the speed-up and other matters.

It was not a complete victory for the union. The U.A.W. had sought sole bargaining privileges for all General Motors employes, a uniform minimum wage and the thirty-hour week. But as in the case of the S.W.O.C. settlement with "Big Steel," another anti-union stronghold had been captured. Organized labor had taken the first step toward what was to become the complete unionization of the entire automobile industry. Whatever might be said of the legality or ethics of a sit-down strike, the results spoke for its effectiveness.

With the success of the automobile workers in General Motors, sit-down strikes spread through union ranks in all parts of the country. The employes of the Chrysler Corporation soon followed suit, and after a relatively brief sit-down in comparison with the forty-four day strike at General Motors, succeeded in winning recognition for the union and a collective bargaining agreement comparable to that exacted from General Motors. Indeed, only Ford continued to hold out among the automobile companies, successfully resisting all attempts of the United Automobile Workers to organize its plants for another four years.

Other industries also felt the impact of labor's new weapon. Between September, 1936, and June, 1937, almost 500,000 workers were involved in sit-down strikes. Rubber workers, glass workers and textile workers sat at their benches; striking Woolworth clerks stayed behind their counters but would not wait on customers; pie bakers, opticians, dress-makers and apartment house janitors sat down. The longest strike of this kind was that of some 1800 electrical workers in Philadelphia. Two bridegrooms sat out their honeymoons and the wives of six other married strikers greeted their returning husbands with newly born babies.

As workers throughout the country eagerly took up this militant strategy to force anti-union employers into line, they enthusiastically sang their song of revolt:

> When they tie the can to a union man,
> > Sit down! Sit down!
> When they give him the sack, they'll take him back,
> > Sit down! Sit down!
>
> When the speed-up comes, just twiddle your thumbs,
> > Sit down! Sit down!
> When the boss won't talk, don't take a walk,
> > Sit down! Sit down!

These strikes aroused increasing popular resentment. Conservative newspapers grew hysterical in condemning such a flagrant invasion of property rights and there was little support for the sit-downs from any quarter. While Upton Sinclair wrote from California that "for seventy-five years big business has been sitting down on the American people, and now I am delighted to see the process reversed," even among labor sympathizers there were few to echo this sentiment. The A.F. of L. explicitly disavowed the sit-down and while the C.I.O. had supported the automobile workers, official approval was never given to its general use. After lively and acrimonious debate, the Senate resolved that such strikes were "illegal and contrary to public policy," and the courts eventually outlawed them as constituting trespass on private property.

For all the excitement it occasioned during the first half of 1937, the sit-down strike in fact proved to be a temporary phenomenon and was abandoned almost as quickly as it had been adopted. It had been the quick and ready response of new and impatient union members fighting for recognition in the strongholds of anti-unionism and embittered by the refusal of employers to comply with the provisions of the Wagner Act. When the law was sustained and the N.L.R.B. empowered to hold elections for collective bargaining units, the sit-downs were given up.

Before this happened, however, the strikes of early 1937 had greatly aroused public opinion and labor as a whole bore the brunt of popular condemnation of the sit-down. Gallup poll reports showed that an overwhelming majority of persons interviewed opposed the use of labor's new weapon, while seventy per cent of those questioned were convinced that new regulatory laws were needed to curb the unions. Sit-down strikes might be explained as no more contrary to law than the refusal of industry to heed cease-and desist orders issued by the N.L.R.B., but they awoke fears and alarms that were not easily stilled.

The immediate consequences of C.I.O. activity throughout 1937 were, in any event, immense gains for all affiliated unions. If the dramatic victories won in steel and automobiles were the most important fruits of the general assault upon the mass production industries, there were other developments that played their part in revolutionizing the labor scene. Organized drives among the rubber workers, radio and electrical workers, lumbermen and longshoremen, among others, served to build up strong and powerful unions. The campaign of a new Textile Workers' Organizing Committee, under the skillful management of Sidney Hillman, was particularly significant in that it succeeded in organizing many southern mills where the A.F. of L. had failed to make any appreciable headway. Thousands of new converts for unionism were won in company towns where labor organizers had never before dared to show themselves, and within a year the union had signed hundreds of collective bargaining agreements throughout the industry.

More important than the actual strength of C.I.O. unions at the close of 1937—600,000 mine workers, 400,000 automobile workers, 375,000 steel workers, 300,000 textile workers, 250,000 ladies' garment workers, 177,000 clothing workers, 100,000 agricultural and packing workers—was the broader base for organized labor as a whole that its campaign had finally achieved. The C.I.O. had successfully organized the unskilled workers into industrial unions, and broken through the narrow lines of craft unionism fostered by the A.F. of L. It had welcomed as the Federation had never done, immigrants, Negroes, and women, disregarding lines of color, sex or nationality.

The C.I.O. influence, moreover, extended to the entire labor front. The A.F. of L., as previously suggested, soon found that it could not ignore the unskilled workers while its rival made such giant strides in organizing them. It had, of course, never done so altogether. The lines between skilled, semi-skilled and unskilled workers had, indeed, become so blurred with the advance of the machine and the assembly line that many A.F. of L. unions included all types. There had also always been industrial unions in the Federation, as we have seen in tracing the growth of organization among coal miners and workers in the garment industry. But the example of what had been done in steel, automobiles and other mass production industries aroused the A.F. of L. to the need of expanding its own organization to prevent the C.I.O. from wholly monopolizing the new opportunities for unionization. Thousands of workers whose skill was no greater than that of the rank and file of the industrial unions were drawn into such multiple-craft or semi-industrial A.F. of L. unions as the machinists, the boilermakers, the meat cutters, the restaurant employes, the hod carriers and common laborers, and the teamsters. Galvanized into more strenuous activity than ever before, the Federation admitted new recruits wherever it could find them, and if its development was not as dramatic as that of the C.I.O., there were large gains in membership. Even with the defection of the unions that went over to the rival organization, A.F. of L. enrollment at the close of 1937, as we have seen, was about a million greater than in 1933.

The A.F. of L. and the C.I.O. continued to strive to build up their strength in jealous competition. The former reached out to set up new industrial unions, the latter did not hesitate to charter craft unions. As labor leaders increasingly realized that there was no one formula for organization, and that different working conditions demanded different approaches to union problems, debate over the old issues that had led to the split in the labor movement became wholly academic. While the C.I.O. had a majority of industrial unions in the mass production industries and the A.F. of L. included by far the larger proportion of what might still be called craft unions, old distinctions were largely broken down and both organizations, becoming more and more alike, were prepared to welcome all comers.

The unhappy by-product of these developments was the spread of jurisdictional quarrels between competing unions. The A.F. of L. carpenters fought the C.I.O. woodworkers, the C.I.O. automobile workers fought the A.F. of L. machinists, and A.F. of L. and C.I.O. longshoremen, textile workers, electrical workers, packing house workers and retail clerks battled indiscriminately. The heavens rang with charges of union raiding, scabbing, and mutual betrayal. The bitterness of these family squabbles often exceeded that of labor-capital disputes. The recriminatory attacks of the two organizations upon one another, and sometimes union battles within either the A.F. of L. or C.I.O., were on occasion more violent than labor attacks upon industry. Strikes broke out again and again for no other cause than a quarrel over jurisdiction, to the great loss of the workers immediately concerned and to the immense harm of all organized labor.

In their efforts to win recognition for their respective unions, the A.F. of L. and the C.I.O. brought the National Labor Relations Board into their feud. The goal of this agency was absolute impartiality in handling elections for the unions to be designated as employe bargaining agents, but it was hampered again and again by attacks made upon it not by industry but by labor. The very fact that it was criticized so severely in both labor camps was perhaps the best proof of its success in maintaining impartiality, but such criticism nevertheless provided ammunition to those who were assailing it on the broader grounds of exceeding its authority and displaying an anti-industry bias. Labor's internal squabbles were not only dissipating its own strength, but threatening to undermine the governmental agency set up to encourage union recognition.

The solidarity which had been the bright dream of nineteenth century labor leaders was lost. It may well be argued that a too closely unified labor movement would have held out the risks of over-centralized authority and the nationwide control of the workers by dictatorial leaders who would have ignored democratic procedures. Diversity in the ranks of labor is an assurance against such a dangerous development. Nevertheless the position of organized labor, from either its own or the public point of view, was not as securely established as it might have been had statesmanship prevailed in the original dispute over craft versus industrial unionism, or in the later efforts for reunion between the A.F. of L. and the C.I.O. It was widely felt at the close of the 1930's that not until a greater measure of unity was restored would organized labor be able to act with the responsibility that was so highly important if it was to play its full part in upholding the stability of our economic system and broadening the bases of social democracy.

XXX

XVII: LABOR AND POLITICS

XXXXXXXXXXXXXXXXXXXXXXXXXXXXXXXXXXXXXXXXXXX

THE ROLE OF LABOR in politics took on a new significance with the New Deal. With government intervention in industrial relations on such a broad scale, the maintenance in office of a national administration and congress sympathetic toward labor's aspirations became of more vital import than ever before. The limited objectives sought by the lobbying activities of the A.F. of L. in the days when Samuel Gompers opposed minimum wages, old age pensions and unemployment insurance as "softening the moral fibre of the people," no longer met the needs of the nation's workers. The new industrial unions were especially dependent upon the protection afforded them by New Deal legislation and were consequently ready to do everything in their power to assure the continuance of a pro-labor administration in Washington.

The pronounced swing toward more extensive participation in politics was not, however, entirely due to this desire for effective enforcement of the new labor laws. There was a growing awareness of the larger issues involved in the Roosevelt program. Labor generally felt that the New Deal represented the progressive forces in American democracy, carrying forward a tradition of popular government in the interests of the common people that stemmed from the days of Jackson. All the implications of democratic capitalism were accepted in this support for the New Deal. Labor did not think in terms of an industrial commonwealth or a socialist state. Its goal was to bring about those conditions in our economic and social life that would enable the system of free enterprise to operate successfully with the largest possible degree of social justice.

It was natural that in this burst of political activity, the C.I.O. should be far more aggressive than the A.F. of L. The liberal and insurgent spirit characterizing its advocacy of industrial unionism was carried over to the promotion of social reform. While there was not actually any far departure from the old tradition of rewarding labor's friends and punishing its enemies, the C.I.O. was to go much farther in trying to make this policy effective. Unlike the A.F. of L., which continued in upholding non-partisanship in presidential elections, it was prepared to come out in vigorous support of Roosevelt.

There was also greater recognition by the industrial unions making up the C.I.O. membership than on the part of the more strongly established craft unions in the A.F. of L. of the extent to which all wage earners had become dependent upon government. The experience of the depression had convinced them of the need for additional controls over the economic life of the nation.

"With the guarantee of the 'right to organize,' such industries may be unionized," Lewis wrote in regard to mass-production enterprises, "but, on the other hand, better living standards, shorter working hours and improved employment conditions for their members cannot be hoped for unless legislative or other provisions be made for economic planning and for price, production and profit controls. Because of these fundamental conditions, it is obvious to industrial workers that the labor movement must organize and exert itself not only in the economic field but also in the political arena. . . ."

To carry forward such a program, the C.I.O. leadership was instrumental in establishing Labor's Non-Partisan League in 1936, and also supported the formation of the American Labor Party in New York. The primary purpose behind these moves was the re-election of Roosevelt, and every effort was made to win the support of both A.F. of L. and C.I.O. unions. The first president of the Non-Partisan League was George L. Berry, of the Printing Pressmen's Union, an A.F. of L. affiliate. But while many state labor federations and member unions did cooperate with the league, the A.F. of L. itself would not officially have anything to do with it. The executive council was divided on political issues. William Hutcheson headed the Republican Labor Committee and Daniel Tobin the Democratic Labor Committee. While Green personally backed Roosevelt, he condemned the Non-Partisan League as a dual movement in politics just as the C.I.O. was a dual movement in economic organization.

There was never any question, however, as to where either the C.I.O., or the new industrial unions stood. Heavy contributions were made to the Non-Partisan League's campaign fund, the United Mine Workers alone advancing $500,000, and Lewis called for unequivocal support for the New Deal. "Labor has gained more under President Roosevelt," he declared, "than under any president in memory. Obviously it is the duty of labor to support Roosevelt 100 per cent in the next election."

The Democrats had appealed for labor's backing and had every reason to expect it. The Roosevelt administration had grappled directly with the issues created by the depression and shown a primary concern with getting people back to work, raising wages and promoting union organization. "We will continue to protect the worker," the Democratic platform pledged, "and we will guard his rights, both as wage earner and consumer. . . ." The Republicans also promised to uphold the right to organize, but neither their previous record nor general attitude were any assurance that labor's broader aims would receive from them the support which had been obtained under the New Deal.

The campaign of 1936 was a bitter one. The divisions of opinion created in American society crossed party lines and aligned class against class as had not happened since Populism challenged the conservative rule of the dominant business community forty years earlier. With former President Hoover and the Liberty League charging that the administration sought "to introduce the foreign creeds of Regimentation, Socialism and Fascism," Roosevelt struck back no less vigorously with the counter-charge that the "economic royalists" considered government as a mere appendage of their own affairs. "Government by organized money," he declared, "is just as dangerous as government by organized mob."

The votes of labor—of A.F. of L. as well as C.I.O. union members—played an important part in enabling Roosevelt to sweep the country in 1936. The wage earners had aligned themselves with other liberal elements in the country in a nationwide popular response to a dynamic program of recovery and reform. Labor was endorsing agricultural relief and business reform as well as a new order of industrial relations and social security; it was endorsing a measure of economic recovery reflected in rising business activity and higher farm income as well as lessening unemployment and increased wages.

The campaign activities of the Non-Partisan League and the vote won for Roosevelt in New York by the American Labor Party appeared to demonstrate the value of direct labor action in politics. The

C.I.O. developed a broad and comprehensive legislative program, and in a new Declaration of Purpose, the Non-Partisan League stated that it would attempt in future elections to insure both the nomination and the election of candidates pledged to support labor and other progressive measures. It was ready to work "with every progressive group whose purpose is to secure the enactment of liberal and humanitarian legislation."

The Non-Partisan League entered into local elections in several states during the next few years, seeking to capture control of the Democratic Party in Pennsylvania, playing an active role in New Jersey politics, and throwing its support behind a campaign for a labor administration in Detroit. In New York, the American Labor Party drew largely from the socialist-minded members of the needle trades unions, but it also attracted enough liberal supporters outside the ranks of labor to rally 500,000 votes for the re-election of Mayor La Guardia in 1937. On the national stage, there was continued activity in backing up New Deal legislation, supporting Roosevelt's program for the reorganization of the Supreme Court, and promoting further reform measures all along the line. The Non-Partisan League entered into the congressional elections of 1938 and energetically tried to defeat all opponents of the New Deal and to elect its adherents regardless of party affiliation.

An important part was played in this political activity of the late 1930's—although his role was to be even more significant with the formation of the C.I.O.'s Political Action Committee in 1944—by Sidney Hillman. A strong proponent of "constructive co-operation" between labor and management, he also urged broad participation by wage earners in politics to assure the basic conditions that would make such cooperation feasible. Few unions have been more politically conscious than his Amalgamated Clothing Workers. Sometimes characterized as the very embodiment of "social engineering" union leadership, at once highly practical and idealistic, Hillman was one of the foremost labor strategists of the day with a broad and visionary view of the society he believed could be created in America.

"Having realized our dreams of yesterday," he told a union convention in 1938, "let us dedicate ourselves to new dreams of a future where there will be no unemployment; a future where men and women will be economically secure and politically free."

The possibilities of developing an even more active political role for labor than represented by the Non-Partisan League were widely debated at this time. The old issue of formation of a labor party, which had so often been raised in the past, was once again revived. The League was seen in some quarters as the possible nucleus for a movement in which labor, the farmers and other liberal groups might be brought together in a coalition that would either capture control of the Democratic machine or set up an independent third party should it prove desirable.

These ideas did not make any real headway, however. The A.F. of L. would have none of them and the C.I.O., while repeatedly calling for a constructive program of economic security, did not go so far as to endorse independent political action. Past experience with third party movements was discouraging for further experiment along these lines, and the friendly attitude toward labor of the New Deal appeared in any event to make it inadvisable. The workers as a whole appeared to endorse Green's stand that labor was not a sect or a class, but a cross-section of the nation with such diverse interests that a labor party would have no real validity. As throughout the nineteenth century, there was no binding tie like a common belief in socialism or any other positive philosophy. The possible threat of a third party was always in the background, however, should wage earners find that they could not exercise sufficient influence on the major parties—and especially the Democrats—to assure support for their basic aims.

Third party or no third party, conservative and anti-New Deal forces became increasingly alarmed over the effect of the political pressure labor was exerting in the late 1930's. To combat such influences, the program of the C.I.O. was singled out as radical and un-American. Charges were made that left-wing elements were wholly in control of the Non-Partisan League and forcing it to follow the Communist party line. The National Association of Manufacturers and other employer groups seized every opportunity to press such attacks. One pamphlet widely circulated by various anti-union groups had the engaging title "Join the C.I.O. and Help Build a Soviet America." The active leaders of the Non-Partisan League and the American Labor Party, including

Hillman and Lewis, were assailed for their supposed sympathies with communism and willingness to promote policies dictated from Moscow.

There were some fitfully burning embers where the opponents of the C.I.O. saw such dense clouds of smoke. The radical elements always present in the labor movement, and which in the past had been represented by Chicago anarchists, left-wing socialists and the I.W.W., were now generally enrolled in the Communist camp. Their labor front had originally been the Trade Union Educational League, founded by William Z. Foster after the failure of the steel strike in 1919, and subsequently the Trade Union Unity League set up some ten years later to promote industrial unionism independently of the A.F. of L. The shift in the Moscow party line in the mid-1930's, which swung Communist support to a united democratic front against fascism, then led to abandonment of dual unionism and a return to older socialist techniques of boring from within. The Communists were prepared to do everything they could to encourage industrial unionism and hoped to win control, or at least to dominate, the C.I.O. and its political affiliates.

Lewis did not hesitate to draw upon their experience and organizing skill in building up the C.I.O. and the Non-Partisan League. He needed help from every quarter. "We have to work," he stated, "with what we have." While he fully recognized that the Communists would seek to use the new unions for strengthening their own position, he nevertheless thought that he could disregard their politics so long as they were aiding him in promoting industrial unionism. As a result of such hospitality, Communists or fellow travelers won important positions in some unions and even in the high councils of the C.I.O. itself. There was to be continued internal strife within the United Automobile Workers as the left-wing and conservative factions struggled for power, and Communist sympathizers largely succeeded in winning control in the Electrical, Radio and Machine Workers; the Transport Workers, the Maritime Union, the State, County and Municipal Workers, the Fur and Leather Workers, and the Woodworkers of America. Their zeal and enterprise —in parliamentary strategy, organizational "leg-work," and the pressures exerted by "goon squads" of toughs in local elections—gave them an influence out of all proportion to their actual numbers.

There was no more question at this time than in previous periods of the basic conservatism and loyalty of the great bulk of union members,

whether allied with the A.F. of L. or the C.I.O. Communist leadership
in a union did not mean that its members conformed to the party line,
but rather that they accepted direction from any quarter which brought
results. Just as anti-revolutionary workers had welcomed the aid of
I.W.W. organizers twenty-five years earlier, so those engaged in the
strikes of the 1930's were quite willing to accept Communist help. The
high command of the C.I.O. distrusted the Communists because it
well knew that they put the welfare of the party ahead of everything
else, but so long as they were cooperating in promoting labor's aims, it
continued to take advantage of their assistance. If Lewis appeared to be
flirting too dangerously with them at times, if not actually working in
close alliance, other leaders in the C.I.O., such as Murray and Hillman,
were strenuously to combat their influence. They fully realized that
however small the Communist nucleus in the labor movement might be,
it was so tightly knit and so closely disciplined that it was always a
threat to democratic unionism.

The political support that the left-wing was prepared to give Roosevelt and the New Deal as part of the program for a united front, added
further confusion to the labor scene. The anti-New Deal forces made
the most of Communist backing for Roosevelt in attacking his administration for what they declared were its socialistic and radical policies.
But while the President could repudiate Communist support as such,
he continued to need that of organized labor. It was consequently greatly
to his interest to have a united movement strong enough to throw out
the Communists, dominate the radical minority, and independently
rally the progressive forces of the nation behind his policies. Since 1937
he had continually urged a reconciliation between the A.F. of L. and
the C.I.O. with such ideas in view, and in 1939 he again called upon both
organizations to make a real effort to settle their differences.

Upon Roosevelt's insistence, peace negotiations were resumed that
year and representatives of the A.F. of L. and the C.I.O. tried to get
together. The issue of craft unionism versus industrial unionism had
long since lost any real validity, as we have seen, but the rival drives
for power had been intensified by the conflicts of the past few years.
Lewis put forward an ambitious proposal for the merger of the A.F. of L.,
the C.I.O. and also of the railway brotherhoods. It was wholly impractical, for the railway brotherhoods were not remotely interested in

such a project, and Lewis was immediately charged with not acting in good faith.

The A.F. of L. counter-offer was for readmission of the C.I.O. unions in the parent organization but without recognition of their extended jurisdiction. Lewis adjourned the meeting without giving a definite answer to this proposal, but was soon declaring that peace was "impossible" because of the obstructive attitude of the A.F. of L. leaders who were pursuing a policy of "rule or ruin." The truth of the matter was that neither side was willing to make real concessions. In spite of their professed acceptance of the need for labor unity, both the A.F. of L. and the C.I.O. put their own interests first. Green continued to express his "passion for peace," but it was to be upon his own terms. Lewis was perhaps more frank in stating, "we must expand our movement."

The internal difficulties confronting labor, whether born of Communist intrigue or jurisdictional squabbling, were in no way resolved in 1939. In the meantime, however, far more important developments on the world scene were to have their inevitable repercussions on both labor and national politics. Russia and Germany concluded their famous pact in late August and immediately afterward Europe was plunged into war by Hitler's attack on Poland. The United States found itself menaced by the growing possibility of being drawn into the raging struggle against fascism, and popular attention was increasingly diverted from domestic problems to the larger issues of foreign policy. The country was critically divided into opposing camps on the overshadowing question of whether aid to the allies could keep war from our shores, or whether we should seek to maintain an isolationist position as the only means to safeguard our own peace.

As expressed in resolutions adopted by both the A.F. of L. and the C.I.O., labor was wholly opposed to our entering the war but was prepared to back up Roosevelt's policy of extending aid to the allies and building up our own national defense. There were differing viewpoints within union ranks, however, as among other elements in the population, while the Communist party line had abruptly shifted from the united democratic front to virulent isolationism. The Roosevelt administration was attacked as vigorously as it had formerly been defended. With the approach of the election of 1940, the question of how labor would vote consequently became of utmost importance. In these circumstances the position of Lewis was to attract nationwide attention, and it was a strange, unpredictable role that he chose to play.

In the aftermath of Roosevelt's re-election in 1936, Lewis had grandiosely assumed that the Democrats had won their sweeping victory not merely because of labor's support but because he—John L. Lewis—had been largely instrumental in delivering the labor vote. The C.I.O. and its Non-Partisan League, according to this thesis, had saved the New Deal and Roosevelt consequently was under a direct obligation to pay off his political debt by subscribing fully to C.I.O. policy. Success had gone so much to Lewis' head that he appeared to think that the President should be at his beck and call, and in the midst of the sit-down strikes at the General Motors plants early in 1937, he made his position clear.

"For six months the economic royalists represented by General Motors," Lewis told reporters, "contributed their money and used their energy to drive this administration out of power. The administration asked labor for help and labor gave it. The same economic royalists now have their fangs in labor. The workers of this country expect the administration to help the workers in every legal way and to support the workers in General Motors plants."

It was an arrogant statement and Roosevelt showed his resentment at the assumption that he stood in any way committed to the C.I.O. He did not let it interfere with his efforts to bring about peace in the automobile industry, which he felt to be in the public interest, but he rejected the idea of political bargaining in what had been his close cooperation with Lewis in the past. Smarting under at least an implied presidential rebuke, the C.I.O. leader began to nurse a grudge and it was deepened when in the course of the fierce struggle between the S.W.O.C. and the "Little Steel" companies, Roosevelt flared out in a statement calling down a "plague o' both your houses." After brooding over this further rebuff, Lewis took the occasion of a Labor Day radio speech, in which he recounted the deaths and injuries suffered during the steel strike, to return to the attack.

"It ill behooves one who has supped at labor's table and who has been sheltered in labor's house," he pontifically proclaimed, "to curse with equal fervor and fine impartiality both labor and its adversaries when they become locked in deadly embrace."

There was another aspect, however, to this growing rift between Roosevelt and Lewis. With the continuing triumphs of the C.I.O. and his own mounting fame, Lewis began to have political ambitions. Some time after the third term possibilities for Roosevelt had become a matter of widespread discussion, in late 1939 or early 1940, he went to the President with a proposal. Frances Perkins has related the story in an account of a conversation in which Roosevelt told her and Daniel Tobin, of the A.F. of L. teamsters' union, of how Lewis had proposed a way to get around all objections to a third term.

"Mr. President, I have thought of all that and I have a suggestion to make for you to consider," Mrs. Perkins quotes Roosevelt, who in turn was quoting Lewis. "If the vice-presidential candidate on your ticket should happen to be John L. Lewis, those objections would disappear. A strong labor man would insure the full support, not only of all the labor people, but of all the liberals who worry about such things as third terms."

It was a suggestion that did not appeal to the President. He let it slide. But there is another account of this incident, probably apocryphal. It has Lewis proposing to Roosevelt that as the "two most prominent men in the nation" they would make an invincible ticket, and the President blandly asking, "Which place will you take, John?"

Whatever part frustrated ambition may have played in Lewis' political stand, he had allowed himself to become convinced by 1940 that Roosevelt was no longer the great champion of industrial democracy to whose support he had summoned all labor four years earlier. He now charged the administration with betraying the workers' cause and refusing to give labor representation in either the cabinet or any policy-making government agency. At a United Mine Workers convention in January, he dramatically broke all former ties with the President. "Should the Democratic National Committee," he told his startled audience, "be coerced or dragooned into renominating him, I am convinced . . . his candidacy would result in ignominious defeat."

Lewis was playing a dangerous game. His course appeared to suggest that having failed to transform the Democratic Party into an out-and-out labor party, with himself as possible successor to Roosevelt, he had formed the idea that Labor's Non-Partisan League might develop into a third party which could provide the necessary vehicle for his own political preferment in 1944. The whole issue was deeply involved in his feuding with other C.I.O. leaders and his close association with left-wing and Communist groups. It was also bound up with the position he had taken on foreign policy. For with the outbreak of war in Europe, Lewis had swung over to the isolationist camp and was in angry opposition to the whole program of aid to the allies. The extent to which foreign policy rather than personal pique and political frustration accounted for his desertion of Roosevelt remains, however, a question which perhaps even Lewis himself could not honestly answer.

In any event, he openly opposed the President as the 1940 campaign got underway. The New Deal had completely failed to bring about economic recovery, he declared, and it was in fact entirely responsible for the prolongation of the depression. For a time he did not indicate whether opposition to Roosevelt meant support for Wendell Willkie, nominated by the Republicans, but such doubts as to where he stood were resolved in a radio speech on October 25th which had been carefully timed for full dramatic effect.

"I think the re-election of President Roosevelt for a third term would be a national evil of the first magnitude," Lewis stated. "He no longer hears the cries of the people. I think that the election of Mr. Wendell Willkie is imperative in relation to the country's needs. I commend him to the men and women of labor. . . .

"It is obvious that President Roosevelt will not be re-elected for a third term unless he has the overwhelming support of the men and women of labor. If he is, therefore, re-elected, it will mean that the members of the Congress of Industrial Organizations have rejected my advice and recommendation. I will accept the result as being the equivalent of a vote of no confidence and will retire as president of the Congress of Industrial Organizations in November."

The men and women of labor were not, however, to have their political opinions made up for them by Lewis. The labor vote could no more be delivered in 1940 than in previous years. Ignoring the warnings of the C.I.O. president, many of his associates came out openly for the Democratic candidate, and union after union adopted resolutions favoring a third term. The majority of the A.F. of L. leaders and unions also endorsed the President, and there can be no question that the votes of wage earners contributed heavily, as they had in his two earlier elections, to Roosevelt's third triumph. The vote in mining districts where the leadership of Lewis was generally followed automatically, showed that even members of the United Mine Workers refused to heed his advice in national politics.

In happy contradiction of the Lewis pronouncement, Green declared after the election that working men and working women had voted for Roosevelt because "they believe he is the friend and the champion of social justice and economic freedom."

Lewis had completely over-reached himself. In gambling the presidency of the C.I.O. on the willingness of labor's rank and file to follow him, he had not only taken himself completely out of politics but had sacrificed control of the organization he had done so much to build up. For he fulfilled his pledge to retire from the presidency of the C.I.O. at its next convention. He was still able to exert a powerful influence in labor councils, but it was the close of a chapter in his spectacular career. For all the defiant independence and dramatic posturing that were to mark his later activities, and in spite of the excitement he was to cause as a war and post-war strike leader, he could not recapture the power and prestige of his days as president of the C.I.O.

He remained, of course, head of the United Mine Workers and its members continued to follow wherever he led so far as union affairs were concerned. It was a merry chase. Lewis was soon to take them out of the C.I.O. and then in time back into the A.F. of L. The miners could never be sure just where they stood. Lewis made up his own mind and gave short shrift to the ideas of associates or followers. At the close of 1947, the miners were again to find themselves in the labor wilderness when their erratic chieftain walked out of the A.F. of L. for the second time with a casual abruptness that was startling even for him. Reporters summoned to the United Mine Workers headquarters were shown a message scrawled in blue crayon on a two-by-four inch slip of paper which read: "Green, AFL. We disaffiliate, Lewis. 12/12/47."

The new C.I.O. president in 1940 was Philip Murray, the hero of the S.W.O.C. organizing campaign and for so many years the able and loyal lieutenant of Lewis in the United Mine Workers. His background had a marked similarity to that of both Green and Lewis in that his family was

of British coal mining stock. Murray, however, was himself born abroad
—in Lanarkshire, Scotland in 1886—and did not come to the United
States until he was sixteen. He then followed the family tradition of
entering the mines. Two years later he had his first difficulties with
management and lost his job as a result of taking part in a strike. "I've
never had a doubt since then," he has written, "of what I wanted to do
with my life."

In 1916 he was chosen president of District Number 5 of the United
Mine Workers and four years later vice-president of the international
union. He was known as an extremely able administrator and organizer,
but perhaps most of all for his faithful support, in good times and bad,
of the policies laid down by his chief. He had shown no great interest in
broad ideas of social reform, but believed thoroughly that something
that went with any system of free enterprise was the right of the worker
to a decent wage. Labor organization and collective bargaining were
essential, in his opinion, to secure this goal.

Quiet and self-effacing, Murray was for long considered little more
than a shadow of Lewis. When he became president of the C.I.O. he
was to reveal, however, a tough-minded and stubborn independence that
enabled him to set his own course and to follow it even when it led to a
break with the man whom he most admired and for whom he continued
to profess a deep affection. Murray had qualities, as time was to show,
that made him stand out as a labor leader of strong convictions who
was also able to inspire great personal loyalty.

He gave a first and unexpected demonstration of his independence
when he insisted as a condition for assuming the C.I.O. presidency that
the convention adopt a forthright resolution condemning communism
and all foreign ideologies. In view of the shadowy alliance that Lewis
had maintained with the left wing, Murray was determined to set the
record straight. He did not intend to embark upon a purge of all Communists and fellow travelers, nor did he desire to disrupt the labor movement by extravagent red-baiting. But he was wholly opposed to communism and refused to let the C.I.O. become a front for subversive
political activity. In the same independence of spirit, he rejected the
isolationism that was being preached by both Lewis and the Communists. While still opposing American entry into the war, he was prepared
to support Roosevelt's foreign policy and program for national defense.

It was his own decision. "The convictions which I recommend," he was to tell the C.I.O. convention a year later, "have not come to me as a result of pressure from any group within or without. I am one individual, as you know, who resents the exercise of pressure from individuals or groups. I stand upon my individual integrity as a man."

After the election of 1940, the country in general swung more strongly behind the program of national defense. The successive measures taken by the Roosevelt administration to extend aid to the allies, particularly the adoption of lend-lease, became the all-important issues confronting the nation. The division between isolationists and interventionists grew even more embittered, but the imperative necessity to build up our own security could hardly be denied by any school of thought other than outright pacificists. Mounting war orders from abroad had long since provided a spur to the economic recovery that the New Deal had been unable to achieve, and the demands of the defense program were now to stimulate even greater production all along the economic front. The United States felt itself in imminent danger of being drawn into the war, but it was in the meantime beginning to enjoy unparalleled prosperity.

Labor felt the impact of these developments in many ways. Increased production brought about a rapid decline in unemployment, which had remained at dangerously high levels in spite of everything done by the Roosevelt administration, and also served to stimulate wage increases. The growing need for skilled workers in the defense industries was a new characteristic of the labor market contrasting sharply with conditions that had prevailed for over ten years. Between April, 1940, and December, 1941, total non-agricultural employment rose from thirty-five to over forty-one million, and wage rates generally increased about twenty per cent. In the durable goods industries that were basic to the defense program, average earnings spurted from $29.88 to $38.62 a week. War had come to the rescue of American industry and the strength of organized labor, as enrolled in both the A.F. of L. and C.I.O. unions, enabled wage earners to share substantially in the mounting profits of wartime business.

Labor was prepared to cooperate fully in building up the United

States as "the great arsenal of democracy," but remembering the defeats and setbacks of the 1920's, was also insistent that the benefits attained under the New Deal should not in any way be prejudiced. Further than that, it asserted the right to press forward the campaign to extend union recognition and collective bargaining, and as the cost of living rapidly rose under wartime conditions, demanded further wage increases to maintain the purchasing power of labor income. With industry booming and union strength growing, the stage was consequently set for further struggles between management and labor over their respective roles in our expanding economy. The year 1941 was to prove one of the most tumultuous in labor history.

In most instances labor was pursuing reasonable and constructive policies; and industry, accepting the principles of collective bargaining, met it half way in concluding mutually advantageous agreements on wages, hours and working conditions. The "Little Steel" companies and the United Steelworkers of America finally came to terms, and Henry Ford completely reversed his anti-union policies to sign a contract unreservedly recognizing the United Automobile Workers and even going so far as to grant it a closed shop. But such progress in allaying the causes of industrial strife was soon overshadowded by the outbreak of fresh disputes. In some instances they arose out of excessive and unwarranted union demands, but in others from the obduracy of employers refusing to accept the implications of the new industrial order.

Almost hysterical fear of the growing strength of the unions led a few companies not only to refuse new wage demands but to try in every possible way to clip labor's wings. This group refused further concessions looking toward union recognition, attacked the closed shop as undemocratic and un-American, and circumvented the legal requirements of collective bargaining wherever they could. They covered their anti-union activity in many instances with a mantle of patriotism, insisting that their objectives were merely to maintain uninterrupted industrial production.

The needs of national defense, indeed, tended to make the public impatient of labor's demands and its cause was in no way helped by widespread internal squabbling. The angry recriminations of rival leaders, jurisdictional strikes and highly publicized exposures of a few instances of union racketeering and graft weakened public confidence in the responsibility of organized workers in the face of the mounting national emergency. And it was true that some of the new, insurgent unions were unable to maintain discipline among their thousands of freshly recruited members. Their belligerent attitude toward employers and insistence upon wage increases and other concessions were on occasion as destructive of industrial peace as the anti-union policies of reactionary business.

The number of labor disputes in 1941 reached a higher total than in any previous year with the single exception of 1937. There were strikes in the automobile industry, in the shipyards, in transportation, in the building trades, in textiles, steel and coal mining. Hardly an industry escaped work-stoppages which at least for a time seriously interfered with production. In all, there were 4,288 strikes involving over 2,000,000 workers—almost twice the number of disputes and four times the number of workers as in the previous year. Approximately 8.4 per cent of the nation's employed industrial wage earners took part in these outbreaks and 23,000,000 man-days of work were lost.

A number of strikes were fomented by Communists. Until Germany's invasion of Russia, the party line remained one of virulent opposition to aid to the allies and there were radical left-wing efforts to sabotage the program of national defense. After June, 1941, this attitude was to change in another overnight shift of policy, but Communist-instigated strikes, which responsible labor leadership did its best to control, accounted for no small part of the labor disturbances in the first half of the year.

The threat to the defense program in these work stoppages led to the creation, as early as March, 1941, of the National Defense Mediation Board. This was a tripartite body, representative of labor, management and the public, with authority to seek the adjustment of disputes in the defense industries through either mediation or voluntary arbitration. Its powers did not include enforcement of its decisions, and while it was successful in restoring industrial peace in many instances, more drastic action was to prove necessary on several notable occasions.

A strike on the part of aviation workers at Inglewood, California, led to seizure of a North American Aviation plant by the War Department before a negotiated compromise could be effected, and the Navy Department moved in on a strike of shipyards workers at Kearny, New Jersey, after the Federal Shipbuilding and Dry Dock Company rejected a proposed settlement granting the union maintenance of membership. The climax both of labor disputes and of the troubles of the National Defense Mediation Board was to be reached, however, in a coal strike that so seriously interrupted production as to threaten the whole defense program.

The major issue at stake was establishment of the union shop in the so-called "captive" coal mines operated by the steel industry. The Defense Mediation Board had wavered on the validity of incorporating such a demand in union contracts and when the mining dispute came before it for action in the fall of 1941, it refused to accept the union shop as a basis for a contract. Lewis consequently ignored the board and in the face of President Roosevelt's plea that as a loyal citizen he should come to the aid of his country, called a strike in the captive coal mines on October 27 that threatened to close down almost the entire steel industry.

His defiance of the government had wider significance than protection of the rights of coal miners. Lewis was seeking to win back his shattered prestige by a dramatic labor victory, and he was also demonstrating the opposition which as an outspoken isolationist he felt toward the whole Roosevelt program in foreign affairs. He had pitted himself against the President in the political arena in 1940, and now a year later he was prepared to challenge him in the economic sphere. The fight for the union shop was to be made a test of power, and in complete disregard of the needs of the country and public opposition to his tactics, Lewis was ready to go his own way.

Roosevelt promptly went on the air after the strike was called to declare that the country had to have coal and that national production could not be hampered "by the selfish obstruction of a small but dangerous minority of labor leaders." There were suggestions that he was finally ready to accept anti-strike legislation already being proposed in Congress. But in the meantime Lewis had been negotiating with Myron C. Taylor, of the United States Steel Corporation, and an agreement was reached whereby the union shop issue was again to be reviewed by the Defense Mediation Board without either party obliged to accept its rulings. Lewis was confident that his demands would now have to be approved because of the country's urgent need for coal, and he called off the strike for a temporary truce period while the board again took the case under consideration.

It gave its decision on November 10—and it was nine to two against the union shop. Only the two C.I.O. members dissented from a report which was upheld not only by the representatives of management and the public, but by those of the A.F. of L. Ninety-five per cent of the 53,000 workers in the captive coal mines were already members of the United Mine Workers, but the position taken was that a union shop was a matter for collective bargaining rather than government order, and it was unjustifiable for the Defense Mediation Board to force 2,500 men to join a union against their will.

A principle was at stake and a showdown between Lewis and the President appeared to be unavoidable. The miners' leader refused to modify orders renewing the strike at the expiration of the truce, and he was backed up by the C.I.O. in spite of the internal feuds within that organization. Its representatives on the Defense Mediation Board promptly resigned, and a resolution of the convention then in session upheld Lewis' stand. For his part, Roosevelt declared that under no circumstances would the government order a union shop, insisted upon further negotiations between the miners and the steel companies, and at the same time made preparations for government seizure of the mines should an agreement not be reached. Congress was currently debating amendments to the neutrality legislation and partly to assure support for his foreign program by Congressmen who felt he was dealing too leniently with labor, the President pledged that regardless of what Lewis might do, coal would be mined—"the government proposes to see this thing through."

There was a week of feverish negotiations with the country clamoring for a settlement but neither the miners nor the steel companies would give in on the union shop. On November 17 the strike was again on. The workers in the captive mines laid down their tools and soon sympathetic strikes in other areas swelled the total of idle men in the coal pits to some 250,000. The steel industry was hamstrung in the face of a national emergency rapidly coming to a climax. It was reported that Roosevelt was finally ready to act, with 50,000 troops ordered to take over the mines, and the situation grew hourly more tense. Then suddenly and unexpectedly, on November 22, the strike was called off. Lewis had accepted a proposal of the President for binding arbitration of the union shop issue by a three man tribunal—Lewis himself, President Fairless of the United States Steel Corporation, and as the impartial member, John R. Steelman of the United States Conciliation Service.

Had Lewis capitulated? The secret of his abrupt move was the position of the third man on the tribunal. Steelman was a friend of labor and he was known to be sympathetic toward the union shop. The miners' chieftain felt certain of what his decision would be—and events were to prove him wholly justified. It was Roosevelt who had given in. The appointment of the new arbitration tribunal was in effect repudiation of the Defense Mediation Board and acceptance of Lewis' demands. The strike had been called off, coal would be mined, but governmental authority had been brazenly flouted. The grave national emergency had convinced the President that the defense program could not be further jeopardized, even if it meant letting Lewis have his way. The precedent established was to have grave consequences.

Public reaction to the coal strike was a growing intensification of the anti-labor feeling that had been sweeping the country ever since the early strikes had broken out in defense industries. The work stoppages of the first half of the year, and especially those that were felt to be Communist-inspired, had greatly aroused a nation feverishly arming for a threatened war. Newspaper editorials, the statements of national leaders and public opinion polls, all showed a pronounced stiffening of attitudes toward labor. In and out of Congress, there was a demand for new legislation to restrict the power of the unions and safeguard the public interest against further interruptions to industrial production. The coal strike, and the shocking spectacle of Lewis arrogantly defying the National Defense Mediation Board and the authority of the President, merely brought matters to a head. Anti-labor laws of varying severity had already been passed in twenty-two states and some thirty bills to curb unions were introduced in Congress.

Against the background of uncertainty over the coal strike, and other labor disturbances including a narrowly averted railroad strike, the House approved one of these anti-labor measures on December 3 by a vote of 252 to 136. It would have banned all strikes in defense industries involving the closed shop or growing out of jurisdictional disputes, and any others unless approved by a majority of workers in government-supervised elections after a thirty-day cooling off period. The bill was denounced by Green as "an instrument of oppression"; Murray declared that "nothing more subversive to American democracy has ever been prepared." It appeared probable that its terms would be modified by the Senate, and the President was believed to favor a milder measure, but there was little doubt that some law would be speedily enacted to meet what was generally being called "the national menace" of continued strikes paralyzing defense.

The country was angry. Even the friends of labor, fearing that the popular feeling against unions might lead to curtailment of basic rights guaranteed by the Wagner Act, called for greater moderation on the part of both A.F. of L. and C.I.O. leaders. "The union movement in this country is no longer an infant requiring protection," the *New Republic* editorialized. "It has grown up physically, and if it is to conduct itself like a responsible adult it must be controlled by the same social discipline which governs the rest of the community."

How far the pendulum might have swung against labor in the face of this public reaction in 1941 can hardly be known. For new events suddenly interposed with dramatic force. On December 7—the very day that the arbitral tribunal announced that Lewis had been granted a union shop in the captive coal mines and while the House anti-strike bill was pending in the Senate—Japan struck at Pearl Harbor. The nation found itself at war.

XVIII: THE SECOND WORLD WAR

THE ATTACK upon Pearl Harbor created overnight a spirit of national unity that the country had perhaps never before known. With the outbreak of hostilities in the Pacific and the almost immediate declarations of war by Germany and Italy, everything was forgotten except the imperative needs of national defense. The controversy between isolationists and interventionists came to a sudden end, political differences were buried, and labor leaders unitedly pledged their absolute loyalty to the national cause. "When the nation is attacked," Lewis declared, "every American must rally to its defense. All other considerations become insignificant. . . ."

This fine fervor of patriotism was not always to be sustained on such a lofty level. While there was throughout our conflict with Germany and Japan consistent support for the war effort on the part of all groups within American society, industry, labor and agriculture each sought at the same time to protect its interests as the wartime economy threatened to upset the normal balance of national life. Labor was necessarily concerned over union security, representation on government agencies and the relationship between wages and prices. It was determined to maintain its pre-war strength and influence. There were to be strikes, particularly those called by John L. Lewis, that for a time seriously endangered the flow of military supplies.

Nevertheless the over-all labor picture was a highly favorable one. Responsible union leadership did its best to hold strikes to a minimum, and when they did break out, sought to get the men back to work with the least possible interruption to production. Even including the coal strikes, the number of man-days idle because of wartime work stoppages averaged only one tenth of one per cent of the total available working time in all industry—the best record since such statistics have been available except for 1929 and 1930. The time lost by strikes was no more than the equivalent of one day per worker throughout the period from 1942 through 1944.

A greater threat to industrial output than strikes, in fact, was posed by the recurrent problems of labor shortages, turn-over and absenteeism which were a natural consequence of wartime conditions. Civilian employment was to rise to 53,000,000, with some 6,000,000 women largely replacing the men drained off for service in the armed forces, but in some areas a critical need for skilled workers persisted despite everything done to meet it. The War Manpower Commission worked out a complicated system of labor priorities and draft deferments, but there were times when the alarms of army and navy procurement officers, and exaggerated newspaper headlines, seemed to suggest that the situation was wholly out of hand.

In 1944 Roosevelt even felt it necessary to recommend a national service act that would in effect have made it possible to draft industrial workers. Congress was reluctant to take this step, however, and the increasingly favorable course of military operations soon led to abandonment of such a radical program. The war was to come to an end without any such rigid controls being exercised over the labor force.

Well before the outbreak of hostilities, labor had insisted on its right to be represented in government agencies determining the economic policies made necessary by the national emergency. For a time the administration appeared reluctant to meet the full desires of the unions on this score, and labor repeatedly claimed that it was being ignored on policy-making levels. As a result of such persistent pressure by the A.F. of L. and the C.I.O., however, the nation's workers eventually received a measure of official recognition in the operation of the wartime economy that went far beyond that extended during the First World War and that served as a striking demonstration of its new influence.

In 1941 Sidney Hillman—selected by the President because he was considered "just half way between John Lewis and Bill Green"—had served as a co-director, teamed with William S. Knudsen, in the Office of Production Management. When this agency gave way to the War Production Board, under the chairmanship of Donald M. Nelson, a number of labor advisory committees were appointed, and labor representatives served as vice-chairmen in charge of Manpower Requirement and Labor Production. During the war production drive launched in

1942, labor-management committees were also set up in defense industries throughout the country to promote still further a cooperative approach in turning out the ships and airplanes, tanks and munitions, that the country needed so desperately. In some quarters these committees were opposed—the President of the National Association of Manufacturers stated on one occasion, "The managers of industry are making our system work. Why experiment?"—but they proved to be of very real value in helping employers and employes to get together in speeding up production and settling minor grievances. Within a year, some 1,900 were in operation in plants employing nearly four million war workers, and the total would later swell to 5,000.

Labor was also represented on the Labor-Management Policy Committee of the War Manpower Commission; both the Office of Price Administration and the Office of Civilian Defense had labor policy committees, and the presidents of the A.F. of L. and the C.I.O. served on the six-man Economic Stabilization Board. In the lower echelons of the war effort, union members were appointed to price and rationing boards, played an important part in developing the program of civilian defense, and had an influential role in all war relief activities.

Far more important than any of these posts, however, and basic to the whole wartime program affecting industrial relations, was the representation of labor on the National War Labor Board. This was the agency charged not only with the settlement of disputes between workers and management, but with general control over wages and hours. Its history was largely synonymous with that of labor during the whole war period.

The genesis of the War Labor Board was a conference of labor and business leaders summoned by President Roosevelt almost immediately after Pearl Harbor to avert the anti-union legislation pending in Congress and establish a basis for wartime cooperation that would minimize possible strikes. It met in Washington on December 17, 1941, and after prolonged discussions agreement was reached on a three-point program: no strikes or lockouts for the duration of the war, peaceful settlement of industrial disputes, and the creation of a labor board to handle all controversies that otherwise failed of solution. It had not proved possible in the course of this meeting to arrive at an understanding mutually acceptable to labor and management on the basic issue of union security that had wrecked the National Defense Mediation Board. Roosevelt forcefully cut the Gordian knot by insisting that it be left to future settlement by the new War Labor Board.

This board was then created by executive order in January, 1942. It was tripartite in form and composed of twelve members—four representing management, four labor, and four the public—under the chairmanship of William H. Davis, former head of the Defense Mediation Board. Alternate members and associates were later added in the same ratio. The primary function of the W.L.B., as originally constituted, was to take over, generally after certification by the Secretary of Labor, any unsettled industrial dispute that "might interrupt work which contributes to the effective prosecution of the war." Its decisions were to be accepted as binding by both industry and labor.

The authority given the War Labor Board meant in effect a wartime suspension of the normal processes of collective bargaining. Labor gave up its right to strike as an ultimate sanction in upholding its interests and it was the board that was finally to decide the terms and conditions of employment. Moreover its settlements were to be arrived at by tripartite decisions, in which the public representatives would necessarily have the last word when management and labor could not agree.

The War Labor Board got off to a good start in 1942 when it found a solution to the issue of union security in the so-called maintenance of membership agreements. Neither a closed nor a union shop were to be enforced. Union members or those who joined a union, however, were required as part of any contract made in their behalf to remain union members for the life of the contract, and they were subject to discharge from their employment if at any time they failed to maintain good union standing. Management representatives on the War Labor Board protested this arrangement and were never to be wholly reconciled to it, but they at least passively acquiesced after provision had been made for an initial fifteen day escape period during which any employe could withdraw from a union wholly without prejudice. Once arrived at, the principle of maintenance of membership was to be consistently upheld throughout the war. It ultimately applied to the status of some three million workers, or approximately twenty per cent of those covered by union agreements.

Nothing could have contributed more substantially to industrial peace than such assurance that union security and individual freedom of action would be alike safeguarded, and the result of the War Labor Board's policy on this fundamental issue was directly reflected in the decline of strikes during 1942. At the close of the year, President Green was able to claim with justification at the annual A.F. of L. convention that labor had "maintained the finest record of continuous, uninterrupted production ever achieved." And this record was recognized by all national leaders, civilian and military. In a message to the convention Roosevelt declared that labor's cooperation in the war effort spoke for itself—"it is splendid."

A more difficult issue than union security soon developed, however, as wartime price increases led to heightened demands for wage adjustments in line with the rise in the cost of living. The War Labor Board first sought to meet this issue on an individual basis and wage advances were allowed where circumstances seemed to warrant them. But the government was gravely concerned over inflationary trends and in April, 1942, adopted an over-all program for price and wage stabilization in an effort to maintain economic stability. It became necessary for the W.L.B. to seek some sort of formula that would reconcile justifiable increases in pay with the basic need to hold wages as a whole in line. Roosevelt had given no specific directive on this issue for it was felt to be impracticable to freeze wages altogether. It was consequently left to the board to promote wage stabilization as best it could with due regard to existing inequities and substandard rates.

The first opportunity for the War Labor Board to establish a general policy arose with the demand on the part of employes of the Little Steel companies, in July, for wage increases amounting to a dollar a day. After lengthy hearings, it was decided that any advance should be limited to an equivalent of the increase in the cost of living between January, 1941, a time of relative price stability, and May, 1942, when the anti-inflation program had officially gone into effect. On the basis of the Bureau of Labor Statistics' cost of living index (later called consumer price index), this amounted to fifteen per cent. Such an increase in wages was consequently awarded the Little Steel workers, amounting to forty-four cents a day rather than the dollar a day they had originally demanded.

This was the so-called Little Steel formula. It was to remain the basic criterion that the War Labor Board sought to follow in the settlement of all wage disputes. It was adopted on the assumption that the stabilization program would bring to an end "the tragic race between wages and prices" that had first got under way in 1941. Had such a premise proved to be well founded, the task of the board in adjusting wage disputes would have been relatively simple. Prices were not held so rigidly in line, however, and the W.L.B. was to be constantly engaged in trying to reconcile its formula with increased living costs that exceeded the figures on which it was based.

Application of the Little Steel formula was soon to be extended, by government directive, beyond the dispute cases to which it was first applied. After passage of the Economic Stabilization Act in October, 1942, the War Labor Board was ordered, as part of the anti-inflation program, to limit all wage increases throughout industry, except where substandard or flagrantly inequitable conditions prevailed, to the fifteen per cent increase in straight-time hourly earnings that it had granted the steel workers. For the remainder of the war, the board consequently had two distinct functions: the settlement of dispute cases and approval of voluntary wage agreements. In both categories the Little Steel formula, originally intended as a cost-of-living adjustment, was frozen as the top limit for all wage adjustments.

Labor was prepared to support the general stabilization program and so long as prices were held down effectively, had no quarrel with the Little Steel formula. But as successive breaks developed in the dykes erected to stem the inflationary tide, its application aroused increasing resentment. By early 1943 the consumer price index had risen to 124, as compared with 115 when the formula was set up, and the unions further charged that actual living costs had risen even more than this index showed. The wage earners began to feel that they were being forced to bear the brunt of higher prices while farmers and other producers were profiting from them.

The government recognized the dangers in this situation but rather than permit an upward adjustment in wages, sought to roll back prices. President Roosevelt issued his famous hold-the-line order in April and every effort was made to stabilize an equitable price-wage relationship. These control measures were relatively successful. The consumer price index rose only one more point until the close of 1944, and even in August, 1945 stood no higher than 129. But the fact remained that while prices had been held in line, they had not been rolled back. The advance in living costs remained well in excess of the wage increases permitted under the Little Steel formula.

As a consequence of such developments, labor grew increasingly restive during 1943 and the unusual record of industrial peace during the previous twelve months was not to be repeated. Before the year ended, nearly two million workers had been involved in work stoppages, or more than twice the number during 1942, and the total man-days idle was 13,500,000 in comparison with 4,183,000. While this still amounted to little more than one-seventh of one per cent of total working time, it marked a serious deterioration in the situation.

For the most part these strikes were local outbreaks on the part of dissatisfied workers and were not authorized by union leaders within either the A.F. of L. or the C.I.O. But they were all the harder to control. Impatient over what was often the long delay by the War Labor Board in settling dispute cases, or irritated by minor grievances which were not satisfactorily adjusted, the workers would often take matters in their own hands and spontaneously quit work. Wartime conditions made for strain and tension, with angry resentment over what under other circumstances would have been trivialities. Working under heavy pressure for long hours, and living in wartime housing developments where congestion and overcrowding led easily to frayed nerves, it was not surprising that men and women sometimes felt driven to lay down their tools or abandon their machines in protest against what they considered management's failure to consider their complaints. Sometimes such strikes were no more than "quickies." Once the workers had let off steam by asserting themselves, the disputes would be quickly settled and work resumed without any serious interruption to production.

An exception to such brief and unauthorized outbreaks was the series of coal strikes engineered by Lewis during the summer of 1943. They constituted a challenge to the government's wage policy and to the authority of the War Labor Board that was to have serious and widespread repercussions.

As the time approached in April for the renewal of the annual contract between the United Mine Workers and the coal operators, Lewis put forward new wage demands. There was nothing picayune about them. He insisted upon a $2 a day increase for his 530,000 miners, including portal-to-portal pay for time traveling underground, and he refused to consider any compromise. The dispute was taken over by the War Labor Board. Lewis refused to recognize its authority. Scornfully attacking it as "prejudiced" and "malignant," he defiantly stayed away from the hearings. If his demands were not accepted, he let it be known, there would be no agreement and a very unfortunate situation would be automatically created. He would not of course call a strike in wartime, but "the miners were unwilling to trespass upon the property of the coal operators in the absence of a contract."

The members of the United Mine Workers needed no further instructions. As they began to quit work even before the official expiration of existing contracts on April 30, the country found itself confronted with a stoppage in coal production that could not fail to have disastrous effects upon the whole war economy should it be very much prolonged. The crisis was even more serious than that in the fall of 1941, and Roosevelt felt called upon to act promptly in trying to avert a complete and devastating strike. He gave orders for government seizure of the coal mines and on May 2 went on the air to appeal to the strikers to go back to work.

Full responsibility for the breakdown in contract negotiations was placed on the shoulders of the officers of the United Mine Workers. Lewis had been a party to labor's no-strike pledge, the President declared, and in refusing to have anything to do with the War Labor Board, the agency officially charged with the peaceful settlement of industrial disputes, he was defying governmental authority. Roosevelt expressed his sympathy for the miners and promised measures to roll back the prices of the commodities they had to buy. He reminded them, however, that every man who stopped mining coal was obstructing the war effort, gambling with the lives of American soldiers and sailors, and endangering the future security of the whole people. Production had to go on. The mines would be operated by the Secretary of the Interior under the old contract, according to his pronouncement, but any new agreement approved by the War Labor Board would be made retroactive. "Tomorrow the Stars and Stripes will fly over the coal mines," Roosevelt concluded. "I hope every miner will be at work under that Flag."

Roosevelt had made his appeal—and within a few days the miners were back at work. But it was not because of anything the President had said. Just twenty minutes before the President went on the air, Lewis had announced a fifteen-day truce (later extended to thirty days) to try to work out a new contract in cooperation with Secretary Ickes. He had not surrendered, hardly retreated. He merely granted a temporary respite without withdrawing any of his demands.

The controversy went on for the next six months, punctuated with alternate work stoppages and truces. Eventually the mines were returned to private operation in the expectation that a settlement could be worked out between operators and the union without further government intervention, but the terms proposed for this accord were rejected by the War Labor Board as violating the Little Steel formula. At no time did Lewis show the slightest willingness to accept the authority of the Board or take into consideration public interest in the production of coal. The situation came to a final crisis at the close of October when for a fourth time, half a million miners laid down their tools and obeying the unspoken orders of Lewis, stayed away from the pits. The government again seized the mines and Secretary Ickes was now instructed to conclude a special wage agreement, again subject to the approval of the War Labor Board, which was to be limited to the period of government operation.

The original issues at stake had long since been forgotten by the public and the picture could hardly have been more confused. There had been repeated clashes between miners and operators, miners and the government, and even between the War Labor Board and the Secretary of the Interior. But Lewis still dominated the scene. His stubborn, intractable stand in the face of the imperative need for coal overshadowed every other phase of the conflict. The President was widely criticized for temporizing on the issue and for not taking more drastic action, but Lewis was the villain of the piece in the eyes of the general public. Although labor sympathized with the coal workers and welcomed the strike because it dramatized the failure to hold prices down, even its spokesmen assailed the miners' chieftain. The C.I.O. executive committee publicly condemned his attitude toward the War Labor Board and what was called "his personal and political vendetta against the President of the United States."

With the second seizure of the mines, a settlement was finally worked out between Lewis and Secretary Ickes. It was a highly complicated compromise. Largely through inclusion of portal-to-portal travel and an increase in miners' working time, $1.50 a day was added to wages. Since the Little Steel formula for basic rates was nominally upheld, the War Labor Board reluctantly approved this agreement. However, Lewis had forced the government's hand and if he had not actually won as much as he claimed, he appeared to have achieved a great victory. Only after the new agreement had been signed, moreover, did he order the miners back to work.

Lewis held his position by being tough. As in the earlier strike on the eve of Pearl Harbor, he stubbornly insisted that a national emergency was no excuse for exploiting the miners. Their demand for higher wages was deemed a matter of simple justice superior to any considerations of coal production or national defense. The miners themselves unhesitatingly followed his orders. When Lewis told them to work, they worked; when he told them to stay home or go fishing, they stayed home or went fishing. The orders they accepted were those of the president of their union, not those of the President of the United States.

The whirling gusts of popular anger whenever they went out on strike did not affect their attitude. Hard-pressed by a rise in living costs that had outstripped their wages, working hard and dangerously, fully realizing that such gains as they had made in the past had been won by fighting for them, isolated in the scattered coal towns from the direct impact of public opinion, the miners felt their course wholly warranted despite its effect in halting essential production on which all industry was dependent.

While the coal controversy was dragging on in the late spring and summer of 1943, public resentment over this threat to the war effort and over other work-stoppages that seemed to be getting out of hand, caused a strong anti-labor tide to set in. President Roosevelt in June declared the miners' attitude to be "intolerable," proposed raising the draft age for non-combatant service in order to provide the means for inducting them into the army, and warned that the coal strikes had "stirred up the anger and disapproval of the overwhelming mass of the American people." The latter comment was if anything an understatement. The press almost universally denounced non-patriotic labor leadership in the coal fields, and saw in the spread of strikes in other areas a breakdown of the no-strike pledge that had seemed to assure full labor co-operation in the war effort.

This was not warranted on the basis of the continued observance of the no-strike pledge by the overwhelming majority of workers and the strenuous efforts of responsible labor leadership to hold outlaw strikes in check. The newspapers seldom took into account the justified grievances of labor. But at the same time there were elements in the picture, in addition to the coal strikes, that reenforced popular criticism of union policies and intensified the demand for adoption of the labor curbs that had been pending in 1941.

It is true that on many occasions during the war years, unions acted arbitrarily or capriciously in trying to safeguard the interests of their members. There had long been a tendency in some quarters to build up or maintain labor monopolies by blocking the introduction of labor saving devices or low-cost methods of production. Examples of "feather-bedding," the practice whereby unions insist upon the employment of extra workers who are not really needed, or stand-bies whose only function is to protect vested union privileges, were notorious in some trades and occupations. Management and the public had to bear the brunt of jurisdictional strikes and interunion quarrels that led to work stoppages wholly beyond their control and serving only to promote the selfish interests of this or that labor faction. And finally the public could not help being even more gravely concerned over the failure of union labor to provide any guarantee that essential public services, on which the entire community was dependent, might not be wilfully interrupted by strikes even when the demands of war made their continued operation a matter of vital national security.

The propaganda of anti-union employers made the most of every instance of union irresponsibility and magnified the danger of industry-wide strikes. Organized labor could hardly expect its opponents not to take advantage of its shortcomings, mistakes and failure to take public opinion into due consideration. But even though the faithful observance of collective bargaining agreements was actually increasing, there was no denial that wartime labor sometimes seemed to show an apparently callous disregard of the national interest. In any event, the temper of the country in 1943 was reflected by a renewed drive in Congress and in the state legislatures to enact laws that would protect the public from strikes or other labor excesses, and support was too widespread for it to be easily dismissed as solely the work of die-hards in the National Association of Manufacturers or the United States Chamber of Commerce.

The most important of the restrictive bills proposed in Congress was a measure sponsored by Representative Smith and Senator Connally. It had powerful backing, and in the midst of the excitement occasioned by the coal strikes, was hastily approved during June by decisive majorities in both the Senate and the House. The bill provided, in the first instance, statutory authority for the War Labor Board. In the event that the board's intervention in a labor dispute proved unsuccessful, the President was then empowered to take over control of any plant or industry where a halt in production threatened the war effort, with criminal penalties for any persons who thereafter instigated or promoted a strike. When the government did not find it necessary to move in, strikes were not subject to such a drastic ban, but they were restrained by a thirty-day cooling-off period during which a strike vote was to be taken among all employes concerned by the National Labor Relations Board. Finally, the Smith-Connally bill prohibited all union contributions to political campaign funds.

The hurried vote for this measure was largely the result of angry public resentment against any strike in time of war, fanned to flames by the domineering tactics of John L. Lewis. Although there was need to provide against wartime threats to industrial production, Congress had actually gone much further. It ignored the widespread observance of the no-strike pledge through the bill's criminal provisions, while paradoxically providing under other circumstances for strike votes that would have absolved labor from its voluntary commitment not to strike. The unions were to be disciplined, that is, through curtailing their exercise of a recognized right even though they had agreed to hold it in abeyance for the war period and were generally doing so. The A.F. of L. executive council bitterly declared that the bill was "born of hatred and malice on the part of reactionary congressmen," while Murray told an approving C.I.O. convention that the country was witnessing "the most vicious and continuous attack on labor and labor's rights in the history of the nation."

President Roosevelt vetoed the Smith-Connally bill. He approved some of its provisions, recognizing the need to guard against irresponsible unionism, but he was particularly opposed to the provision for thirty-day cooling-off periods and strike votes. He tried to impress upon Congress that it ran wholly counter to the no-strike program sponsored by the government and generally supported by labor, despite the arbitrary stand of the United Mine Workers, and that it would be conducive to labor unrest rather than industrial peace. In the temper of the times, however, Congress paid no attention to his objections and immediately over-rode his veto. *The New York Times* described what was officially called the War Labor Disputes Act as "a hasty, ill-considered and confused measure," but it was on the statute books for the duration of the war.

The Smith-Connally Act had given statutory authority to the War Labor Board and in the face of the unrest in labor ranks, which was hardly allayed by the new law, it found its problems in settling industrial disputes more and more difficult. Labor had a strong case for wage increases beyond the limits of the Little Steel formula in the admittedly high cost of living. This had been tacitly recognized, however reluctantly, in the approval given to the agreement that finally concluded the coal strike. The representatives of management on the board declared that a union had only to strike with sufficient vigor to win the reversal of declared public policy, and characterized the action that had been taken on Lewis' demands as appeasing labor and sacrificing the stabilization program. The fact remained, however, that the gap between wages and prices gravely prejudiced the workers' standard of living while the country as a whole was enjoying a high degree of wartime prosperity.

Moreover there was an instance early in 1944 of the government going beyond the Little Steel formula in settlement of a wage dispute that fell outside the province of the War Labor Board and yet could not fail to influence its policies. This was a threatened railway strike that was only narrowly averted after government seizure of the lines.

Railway labor relations, in time of war as well as in time of peace, were subject to the amended Railway Labor Act of 1926 which provided that in the event no settlement of a dispute could be reached through mediation or arbitration under the aegis of the National Mediation Board, it should be taken under consideration by a special Emergency Board appointed by the President with no strike action for a thirty-day cooling-off period. After the failure of preliminary steps in the fall of 1943 to reconcile the divergent views of railway labor and management on wage adjustments, an Emergency Board was duly appointed by the President. Its award virtually met the railway unions' demands but in going beyond the increases permitted under the Little Steel formula, was disapproved by the Office of Economic Stabilization. The railway workers thereupon voted for a strike to go into effect on December 30.

President Roosevelt at once proposed that the whole issue be referred to him as an arbitrator between the Emergency Board and the Office of Economic Stabilization for a final and binding decision. The non-operating unions and two of the operating unions accepted this proposal, but it was rejected by the Locomotive Firemen, the Railway Conductors and the Switchmen's unions. They refused to withdraw their strike notices. Orders were promptly given and executed for seizure of the railroads by the government. "The war cannot wait and I cannot wait," Roosevelt declared. "American lives and American victory are at stake."

Before matters came to a head, announcement was made of the arbitral award for the unions which had assented to presidential intervention. The Emergency Board rather than the Office of Economic Stabilization was upheld and wage advances that went over and beyond the Little Steel formula were justified by the President as being made in lieu of overtime and vacation pay to which the railway workers were otherwise entitled. In the light of concessions so fully meeting their demands, the unions that had refused presidential arbitration, as well as those which had agreed to it, accepted the new award and the former withdrew their strike notices. There had been no real interruption of the railway service and on January 18, 1944, the lines were restored to private operation after a brief period of wholly nominal government control.

With the railway workers as well as the coal miners winning substantial wage increases, however disguised as compensation for travel time or vacation pay, the War Labor Board found itself in turn compelled to resort to what now became known as fringe benefits to meet labor's demands. By this time almost all the country's workers had received the maximum increase under the Little Steel formula, and while it was still to be upheld so far as straight-time hourly rates were concerned, these concessions importantly supplemented take-home pay. They included vacations and holidays with pay, allowance for travel time and lunch periods, bonus and incentive payments, and adjustments for shift differentials. Moreover by holding that establishment of health and insurance funds was a legitimate subject for collective bargaining not subject to its review, the War Labor Board also opened the way for still further indirect wage increases.

These fringe benefits were immensely important during the war in helping to allay industrial unrest and avert the strikes that would almost surely have broken out had the Little Steel formula been more rigidly maintained in the face of prices that had risen well beyond the level on which it was based. But they had a more lasting significance in helping to set up an entirely new pattern in employment practices. Vacations with pay, to cite a single example, was a highly important innovation for industrial workers that was to win increasingly widespread acceptance. Moreover, War Labor Board policies in several other respects served to improve the status of the country's wage earners. The board upheld equal wages for equal work for women employes, consistently sought to remove other inequities in pay among workers in the same or different plants, and generally lent its influence to the formulation of more consistent and uniform wage policies.

In carrying out its functions during the war, the W.L.B. altogether approved some 415,000 voluntary wage agreements, involving twenty million employes, and imposed settlements in approximately 20,000 dispute cases affecting nearly as many workers. It was a gigantic, time-consuming task for which there was no precedent, and while the board was often to be subject to criticism for delays in handling these cases, it worked on the whole with great efficiency in view of the huge volume of work piled up after 1943.

Neither executive orders nor the Smith-Connally Act gave it the power directly to enforce its decisions in the dispute cases. When its own authority and such pressures as it could bring to bear through other agencies proved to be ineffective, however, the board could recommend the seizure of any war plant by the President and the consequent application of direct sanctions to compel compliance with its orders. Its decisions were generally accepted by disputants without recourse to such measures. On only forty occasions did the President have to order plant seizures—twenty-six times because unions defied the board's orders, twenty-three times because employers proved recalcitrant, and once when neither the union nor management would agree to the decision.

The most dramatic case of employer defiance was that of the Montgomery Ward Company which denied the jurisdiction of the War Labor Board on the ground that the mail order business did not directly involve the war effort. When it spurned an order to recognize a C.I.O. union as the bargaining agent for its employes, Roosevelt ordered seizure of the company's plant and outspokenly criticized its officers for their reckless disregard of the government's program to maintain industrial harmony. President Sewell Avery, whose attitude toward unions was reflected in his view that the closed shop and the Constitution were incompatible, obstinately refused to acknowledge the government's right to take over company property. Before the issue was settled, the country was treated to the engaging spectacle of Avery's bodily removal from his office by two stalwart members of the army's occupying force.

The War Labor Board was criticized by industry for failing to maintain the Little Steel formula more strictly and granting concessions that amounted to unjustified wage increases. Labor attacked it on an exactly opposite count for being unwilling to take price rises into sufficient consideration through a too inelastic interpretation of the Little Steel formula. The public often held its delays in hearing cases and issuing orders responsible for labor unrest and unnecessary work stoppages. However, the full record of this important experiment in tripartite labor arbitration, as previously suggested, was a successful one. Strikes were held down— to a total approximately one-third that of pre-war years; the stabilization program was sustained far better than was realized until after the breakdown of the board's controls at the close of the war, and labor's fundamental rights were sympathetically safeguarded. Indeed, the War Labor Board's sponsorship of maintenance of membership; its approval of vacation pay, health and insurance funds, and equal pay for women, and the nationwide effect of its general surveys of rate structures, represented highly significant long term gains for all wage earners.

The influence of the War Labor Board, superimposed upon that of the National Labor Relations Board, which still conducted elections for appropriate bargaining units and protected unions from unfair employer practices, served to accentuate the vitally important role that government had come to play in industrial relations. Organized labor had grown very strong, but it was more than ever dependent upon government in maintaining its power. Union leaders fully realized that not only the wartime position of labor but its future status in time of peace were to a very great extent subject to the attitude that might be taken toward labor in Washington. The importance of political action on the part of union members throughout the country to assure the continuance of a sympathetic administration appeared to be even greater than during the days of the New Deal.

With another presidential campaign in 1944, there was consequently a renewed labor drive in support of President Roosevelt and of congressional candidates who could be counted upon in the post-war period to uphold the gains that labor had made since 1933. The passage of the Smith-Connally Act certainly seemed to suggest that the experiences of 1919 might well be repeated unless the workers exerted really decisive political influence. While the A.F. of L. maintained its traditional nonpartisanship and did not enter directly into the 1944 campaign, the greater number of its constituent unions endorsed Roosevelt and worked actively for his re-election. The C.I.O. not only declared official support for a fourth term for the President, but formed a nationwide Political Action Committee with the avowed purpose of getting out the labor vote.

This move had been decided upon by the C.I.O. executive committee the previous summer as a result of the losses sustained by progressive and pro-labor forces in the mid-term elections of 1942. Under the energetic direction of Sidney Hillman as chairman, with R. J. Thomas, new head of the United Automobile Workers, serving as treasurer, the C.I.O.-P.A.C. planned a national door bell-ringing campaign to educate the workers in regard to their political responsibilities, publicize the labor records of members of congress, and encourage a heavy registration that would build up the progressive vote. Roosevelt was specifically endorsed by the national organization, but local branches were left free to take whatever action they chose in recommending congressional candidates.

The P.A.C. campaign was financed during its earlier phases by contributions from unions totaling some $670,000. After the nomination of presidential candidates, these funds were frozen and further activity supported by individual contributions to avoid the possible penalties of the Smith-Connally Act. The door-to-door canvass to bring out voters was its most important activity, but the P.A.C. also published and distributed a mass of campaign literature—millions of copies of pamphlets, leaflets and fliers. Their effectiveness was recognized by friends and foes alike. "Far and wide the slickest political propaganda produced in the U.S. in a generation" was *Time's* terse comment. The pamphlets emphasized that the primary task facing the nation was a complete and speedy victory over the Axis powers, and then put forward a broad program of social reform for the post-war years: full employment, fair wages, protection for the rights of labor and the farmer, adequate housing, help for the veterans and social security. The P.A.C. was out to enlist popular support, not only among members of the C.I.O. unions but from all labor unions, for direct political action to secure these aims.

This campaign, against the background of the strikes that had broken out in 1943, created a general alarm among conservatives and anti-union business interests. The P.A.C. expressly disavowed any idea of forming a third party, but the threat of possible labor domination in the political sphere intensified the fears that had already led to the Smith-Connally Act's ban upon contributions to political campaign funds. Unions were still in popular disrepute. Public opinions polls in 1944 showed a sixty-seven per cent majority of those interviewed favoring additional curbs upon their activity, and newspaper comment was becoming increasingly hostile.

The P.A.C. sought a hearing at both the Republican and Democratic conventions, as had labor groups since the days of Samuel Gompers, but its closest ties were naturally with the Democrats who had so notably promoted labor's aims and were in turn greatly dependent upon labor's political support. Its influence was said to have been very important in the choice of a running mate for President Roosevelt. Failing to secure the nomination of Henry Wallace, it blocked that of James F. Byrnes and opened the way for Harry Truman. Hillman was reputedly one of the most powerful figures behind the scenes in these political maneuvers, and reports of his ascendant role were accorded nationwide currency by the published story that Roosevelt had given an order "to clear everything with Sidney." Although denied by all concerned, this tale was picked up by the press and used overtime by the President's opponents.

The P.A.C. was attacked as radical, un-American and dominated by the Communists who in this wartime campaign were strongly supporting Roosevelt's re-election. A long report by the Dies Committee on Un-American activities concluded with the charge that the whole movement was "a subversive Communist campaign to subvert the Congress of the United States to its totalitarian program." The president of the Union Pacific Railroad solemnly warned that the P.A.C. was "a pernicious innovation that has literally snaked its way into American politics," while Governor Bricker of Ohio declared that it was seeking "to dominate our government with radical and communistic schemes."

The fact that Hillman happened to be foreign-born and a Jew led to other intolerant attacks. Addressing the C.I.O. convention after the election, he was to state that the widespread attempt to smear the P.A.C. had been one of "lies on the top of lies, lies in the newspaper chains the editors of which I am sure are now ashamed to read their own editorials. . . . No slander was too base, no appeal to prejudice too bigoted, no tactics too unprincipled for them to employ." It was a generally justified charge and investigation by the F.B.I. proved the accusations of communism leveled against Hillman to be wholly without foundation.

Many leaders of the A.F. of L., as well as affiliated unions, cooperated with the C.I.O.-P.A.C. Other liberal groups either worked with it directly or with an allied National Citizens Political Action Committee. Labor support for Roosevelt was clearly indicated in a nationwide poll of some 140 A.F. of L. and C.I.O. union newspapers with a total circulation of six million. In sharp contrast to comparable polls of the metropolitan press, it showed that among all these labor papers, only one supported Dewey and only eleven upheld the A.F. of L's official neutrality. The majority that again swept Roosevelt into office was unquestionably swelled by the P.A.C.'s vigorous action in marshalling the workers' vote. It was also claimed that the committee was primarily responsible for the election of 17 senators, 120 representatives and 6 governors whose candidacies were locally sponsored.

After the close of the campaign, the C.I.O. reaffirmed its opposition to a third party but approved the continuance of the P.A.C. as an independent non-partisan instrument to promote united political activity on a nationwide basis. "Labor has long recognized," President Murray reported, "that the gains which it wins through economic action can be protected, implemented and extended only if it develops a progressive program of legislation and secures its enactment through effective participation in the political life of the nation."

When the war finally drew to a close after the advance of allied armies against Germany and successful operations in the Pacific, organized labor had undergone what in retrospect was a phenomenal development. It had at once made a signal contribution to the winning of the war, and on its own account made spectacular progress in building up its economic and political influence. As during the First World War, the national emergency had proved to be a time of opportunity, and labor had made the most of it.

Its contribution to victory was demonstrated by the magnificent record of industrial production which would have been impossible had the nation's workers not played their full part in the amazing transformation of our economy to meet the needs of national defense. Between July, 1940, and July, 1945, the combined efforts of management and labor that constitute American industry turned out 200,000 combat planes, 71,000 naval ships, 5,000 cargo ships, 9,000 pieces of heavy artillery, almost 2,000,000 heavy machine guns, 12,000,000 rifles and carbines, 86,000 tanks, 16,000 armored cars, 2,400,000 army trucks, almost 6,000,000 aircraft bombs, 537,000 depth charges. . . . The production of coal rose to the record total of over 600,000 tons a year; electric energy output increased from 130,000 million to 230,000 million kilowatt hours, and the fabrication of steel ingots mounted from 47,000,000 to 80,000,000 tons.

The role of labor in these spectacular achievements was praised by American leaders both at home and abroad. From General Eisenhower and Admiral King, from both the Secretary of War and the Secretary of the Navy, from Donald Nelson of the War Production Board, and Paul V. McNutt of the War Manpower Commission came repeated tributes to the stupendous job labor had done in helping to make our army and navy such a superbly equipped fighting force. It was the determination of American workers to preserve their heritage for coming generations, President Roosevelt declared, that made possible "the greatest production achievement in the world's history."

As for its own position, organized labor's gains during the war period represented an increase of nearly fifty per cent in union membership. At the close of hostilities, total enrollment exceeded 14,000,000, with the A.F. of L. reporting some 6,800,000 members, the C.I.O. an approximate 6,000,000, and the remainder accounted for by the railway brotherhoods, the United Mine Workers and other independent unions. In the great mass-production industries that a decade earlier had been completely unorganized, collective bargaining agreements covered virtually the entire labor force. Although the breach between the A.F. of L. and the C.I.O. had not been closed, sometimes hampering the collaboration that might have given even greater effectiveness to labor pressure in safeguarding the workers' interests, the organized strength of the American labor movement was far more strongly consolidated than it had ever been before.

At the same time, the rapidity and extent of these gains had not only alarmed business interests that saw a threat to management controls, but awakened as we have seen widespread fears among other elements in the population as to whether labor would use its new-found power with due regard for the public welfare. The excesses of some unions and the aggressively militant spirit among many rank-and-file workers, overshadowing the stability in industrial relations that had more generally resulted from the extension of collective bargaining, intensified the widespread demand for further curtailment of the privileges accorded labor which had already found expression in the Smith-Connally Act. With industry prepared to give its full backing to every move to curb their strength, the unions were actually in a more vulnerable position than their wartime growth suggested.

Labor stood at a momentous crossroads as the guns fell silent in Europe and the Pacific. Clearly a high degree of statesmanship was demanded if it was to hold its lines, recover public confidence, and play its part in the stabilization of the national economy and maintenance of industrial peace.

XXX

XIX: LABOR IN THE POSTWAR SCENE

XXXXXXXXXXXXXXXXXXXXXXXXXXXXXXXXXXXXXXXXXXX

THE END OF THE WAR was almost as great a challenge to the American people as had been its start. An economy wholly geared to the single purpose of providing the manpower and materials essential to victory over Germany and Japan had somehow to be readjusted to the no less demanding needs of peace. The problem facing the nation was how to effect this transition without allowing unemployment to plunge the country into immediate depression, or permitting inflationary pressures to set off a chain reaction of rising prices and rising wages that might encourage an equally dangerous cycle of boom and bust.

Labor was gravely concerned. Even before the end of hostilities there had been fear that peace would mean unemployment and lower wages, and also the further release of those anti-union forces seeking to curb union strength. After V-J Day, this feeling of insecurity was heightened by the universal predictions, concurred in by labor, business and government economists, that unemployment might well rise to ten million by the spring of 1946. Both the A.F. of L. and the C.I.O. maintained that such a breakdown in the national economy could be prevented only through active support for a program of full employment and wage increases to sustain national purchasing power and create an expanding market for industrial goods.

When the immediate consequence of peace proved to be a decline in weekly take-home pay because of a return to the forty-hour week, and widespread lay-offs as factories shut down for retooling, labor's insistence upon wage increases was stiffened. Critics saw in these demands nothing more than a move "to treat the economic pool as a grab-bag," but the workers themselves felt that they were being called upon to carry the burden of reconversion while government was actually aiding business through tax refunds and other indirect assistance. Moreover prices were rising. The limited wage adjustments that had been permitted by the War Labor Board were wholly inadequate as the relaxation of former controls spurred on the advance in living costs. Hourly rates should be raised, union after union demanded, to maintain the wartime level of take-home pay in actual purchasing power.

When industry generally rejected these demands, labor's answer was to strike. The workers were resolved to defend their interests while they were still strong enough to do so, before possible depression and unemployment weakened union ranks. There was an over-all strategy behind this movement, largely developed by the C.I.O., and labor leaders knew very well what they were about. They talked in terms of national policy and continually emphasized consumer purchasing power as well as labor's rights.

The situation differed very much from that in 1919. Then too labor was prepared to struggle desperately to maintain wartime gains. But it had no such well-defined and correlated aims. With the possible exception of that in steel, the strikes that broke out in 1919 were scattered, sporadic and sometimes almost spontaneous uprisings without either effective organization or effective leadership. They had led to violence and counter-violence. Finally, in an atmosphere of mounting hostility to the unions, government had given its support to industry. In spite of some temporary gains, organized labor was thrown wholly on the defensive and forced into the gradual retreat that marked the 1920's.

The cohesive power of the strong unions of 1945 wholly changed this picture and the industries involved in postwar strikes did not even try to maintain production. The struggle was no less grim than in 1919, but it was an endurance contest rather than a slugging match. Although more workers were to be simultaneously on strike in early 1946 than ever before, bloodshed was for the first time in the history of critical labor disputes largely avoided. Emotions were violently aroused, but there was little physical violence. As strike followed strike in oil, automobiles, steel, electrical equipment, farm machinery, coal and railroads, the tremendous implications of the nationwide organization of industrial workers that had taken place since 1933, were borne home with dramatic force. Here was an entirely new challenge to the national economy. It was not the threat of violence, sabotage, industrial warfare in the old sense, but of a paralysis of economic life through peaceful but far more effective work-stoppages on a nationwide scale.

The Truman administration had been compelled to face the critical problem of developing a new labor policy immediately after the defeat of Japan. Labor could no longer be expected to observe its wartime no-strike pledge, and it was the hope of the President that a return to the normal processes of collective bargaining could be effected without endangering reconversion. Government controls were consequently relaxed and wage increases were permitted so long as they did not affect existing prices. Largely deprived of its former authority, the War Labor Board was transferred to the Department of Labor. It soon began to wind up its activities, and was replaced at the beginning of 1946 by the National Wage Stabilization Board. Truman appealed to both labor and industry to abide by their basic wartime agreements and seek whatever adjustments were necessary through peaceful negotiation.

The administration attitude remained one of sympathy for labor in spite of its withdrawal of support from the War Labor Board. The position taken was that unions were entitled to safeguards that would counteract their feeling of insecurity, that industry could afford to make reasonable wage concessions without raising prices on manufactured products, and that collective bargaining could be relied upon to work these issues out. "Wage increases are imperative," the President stated on October 20, "to cushion the shock to our workers, to sustain adequate purchasing power and to raise the national income. . . . Fortunately there is room in the existing price structure for business as a whole to grant increases in rates."

It was a statement of policy widely criticized as continuing the political favoritism of the New Deal. Senator Taft angrily characterized it as surrender to the C.I.O. But while the President's foes might attack his program as one of appeasement, his support for labor in the post-war period fundamentally conformed to the philosophy that accepted a responsibility on the part of government to protect the nation's millions of industrial workers against unemployment, and to use its influence to raise their standard of living. The importance of sustaining national purchasing power was quite as basic in Truman's thinking as it had been in that of Roosevelt. The wellbeing of labor was considered essential for the wellbeing of the country as a whole.

To what extent the wage increases proposed by the President could be permitted without upsetting the stabilization program was nevertheless highly debatable. Truman's position was bolstered by governmental economic surveys that purported to show that industry could advance wages as much as twenty-four per cent and yet make reasonable profits. Corporation records for the war period showed earnings some two and one half times the pre-war average, and John R. Steelman, Director of War Mobilization and Reconversion, was to report in October, 1946, that profits, after taxes, were at the highest point in history. Business spokesmen, however, flatly denied the validity of these reports, set forth a quite different analysis of the situation, and declared that higher wages meant greatly increased costs that could not possibly be absorbed within the existing price structure.

Wherever the truth lay in what was to develop into an interminable debate over wages and profits, the fact remained that leaving the issue to collective bargaining did not work out successfully. Both labor and industry had perhaps grown rusty in the practice of this technique during the period of government control, and in any event they showed little disposition to get together. Labor demanded increases up to thirty per cent over existing hourly rates; industry stated that anything like such concessions were impossible unless it was allowed to pass them on to the public in the form of higher prices. When the unions then requested the right to examine company records in order to prove the thesis that wages could be advanced without raising prices, management struck back vigorously at what was termed an attempt to intrude upon its functions and open the door to labor control over business operations. All proposals along these lines were viewed as a challenge to industry that had to be resisted in the name of free enterprise.

The opposition to labor's demands was also strengthened by the fact that many companies were in a position to welcome a test that was accepted as inevitable sooner or later. The right to obtain refunds on earlier excess profit taxes for any losses sustained during 1946, provided an important compensation for the possible effects of curtailed production. But if industry was ready to defend itself, labor was even more determined to attack. Disputes multiplied on an ever broadening front and the National Labor Relations Board was overwhelmed by requests for strike votes in accordance with the terms of the Smith-Connally Act. By October, 1945, some eight hundred such petitions were pending with no question whatsoever of what the outcome of the vote would be in the great majority of cases.

Confronted by the failure of collective bargaining and such growing evidence of serious industrial unrest, President Truman turned, as President Wilson had under similar circumstances in 1919, to a labor-management conference. Representatives of the unions and of management were summoned to Washington on November 5, 1945, to try to formulate "a broad and permanent foundation for industrial peace and progress." They duly met and conferred, but with little more success than the Wilson conference had been able to achieve. It proved possible to reach a general understanding on the basic principle of collective bargaining, which marked a very real advance over the situation in 1919, but not on any agreement on procedures that might have broken the existing impasse. Apart from recommendations for expanding the Conciliation Service of the Department of Labor, the conference had no practical results.

Its failure had not been unexpected for even while its sessions were in progress, the tide of strikes that had been foreshadowed in the early fall began to come to full flood. Oil refinery workers, lumberjacks, glass workers; machinists and shipyard workers in San Francisco; building service operators and longshoremen in New York; truck drivers in the Midwest; and coal miners in Pennsylvania were in the vanguard of an uprising that now engulfed the entire country. The picket lines in scores of cities carried placards demanding union security and take-home pay the equivalent of wartime wages. The slogan of the day was "Fifty-two for Forty or Fight."

Then on November 21, some 200,000 workers in General Motors plants in twelve states walked out, swelling the nationwide strike total to 500,000, and a week later an ominous vote portended the imminent turn-out of 750,000 steel workers. As labor and management packed their bags in Washington on the last day of November, the nation found itself confronted with a crisis that threatened to stall the entire reconversion program.

The General Motors strike was not only important in itself but for its broader significance in outlining the pattern for the whole series of strikes that so widely disrupted the national economy in early 1946. It had started earlier than originally contemplated. The high strategy of the C.I.O. favored a first test in steel as the basic industry on which all manufacture so greatly depended, but unrest among the automobile workers and union politics had forced the hand of the United Automobile Workers. General Motors bore the brunt of the first really large-scale labor assault of the post-war period.

Although R. J. Thomas was at this time head of the U.A.W., the General Motors strike itself was conducted under the dynamic leadership of Walter Reuther, a rising power in the auto workers union who was soon to battle his way to the presidency. Not quite forty, he was a veteran in labor struggles and in early efforts to organize workers in the Ford plants, had been brutally beaten up by the "brass-knuckle-men" of the company's service department. In appearance more like a prosperous young industrialist than a hard-fighting labor leader; fastidious, well-dressed and serious minded, Reuther had already proved himself to be both devoted to the cause he had adopted and highly ambitious. Neither a smoker nor a drinker, little given to social diversions, he was forever working at his job with a concentrated, single-minded energy that was to lead to his gradual emergence as one of the strongest leaders in the whole labor movement.

His ideas were broad and comprehensive, carrying him far beyond the immediate problems of business unionism. Only by "making progress with the community," Reuther believed, could labor retain the gains that had already been made. His views owed something to socialist theory but he was vigorously opposed to the Communist faction within the U.A.W., which he was to continue to combat after his elevation to the presidency and finally drive out of power. His basic attitudes conformed to the best traditions of American progressivism. Reuther was convinced that organized labor should play a large role in the political as well as the economic life of the country.

"The kind of labor movement we want," he once stated, "is not committed to a nickel-in-the-pay-envelope philosophy. We are building a labor movement, not to patch up the old world so men can starve less often and less frequently, but a labor movement that will remake the world so that the working people will get the benefit of their labor."

This philosophy was to underlie his direction of the General Motors strike. The union's demand was for a thirty per cent wage increase and it was Reuther's contention, bulwarked with statistical evidence, that it could be granted without forcing any rise in automobile prices. He declared that he did not favor any wage increase that was beyond the range of industry's ability to hold the price line. He was thinking in terms of national purchasing power and economic stabilization rather than merely high pay for automobile workers. When General Motors declared that no increase greater than ten per cent was possible and that the union's terms were "not an offer for arbitration but a demand for abdication," Reuther's reply was his famous demand for a "look at the books." The company's outraged rejection of any such proposal then led to a collapse of bargaining negotiations and the General Motors strike was on.

In the light of these developments, and the pending strike in steel, Truman was brought face to face with the failure of his post-war labor policy. He still hoped to keep government intervention in industrial relations at a minimum, but felt driven to take some action that might at once help to restore labor peace and sustain the general stabilization program in the face of the mounting threat of inflation. He proposed thirty-day cooling off periods before any strike could be called, with submission of the issues in dispute to presidential fact-finding boards that would publicly report on all relevant information. Moreover he took up labor's suggestion and declared that such fact-finding boards should be empowered to examine industrial records.

Neither labor nor industry welcomed this proposal. The former attacked it as prejudicing the right to strike; the latter was unwilling to open company records to governmental "fishing expeditions." With so little support from any quarter, Congress refused to take any action on the President's recommendations.

Truman nevertheless decided to go ahead on his own authority so far as the appointment of fact-finding boards was concerned, and six were established between November 27, 1945, and January 17, 1946. The first one was in the oil refinery workers strike, where the government had already taken over the struck plants, but the most important was in the General Motors dispute and was set up on December 12. Management refused to cooperate in the latter instance. When Truman stated that "ability to pay is relevant," General Motors withdrew from the board's hearings. There was no sign of a break in the automobile strike as both the union and the company stood by their original proposals. The deadlock went into its sixth week with the workers still idle and the company's plants wholly shut down. Tension heightened as attack and counter-attack on the motives of the two parties to the dispute further deepened the mistrust and hostility dividing workers and management.

In the meantime, strikes were spreading in other industries as the C.I.O. unions developed their strategy of a nationwide offensive against the mass production industries. The dispute involving 40,000 oil refinery workers was still unsettled; soon after the turn of the year, 300,000 meat packers walked out and the government took over the struck plants; workers in seventy-eight plants of General Electric, Westinghouse and the electrical equipment division of General Motors next added 180,000 to the strikers' ranks, and finally on January 21, the 750,000 steel workers struck in accordance with their earlier vote. Including the General Motors employes, the number of men simultaneously on strike throughout the nation spiraled to a staggering total of almost 2,000,000. Headlines on newspapers from coast to coast underscored the gravity of the industrial crisis and the public clamored for decisive action to restore some measure of industrial peace. Steel particularly held the spotlight. Its virtually complete halt in production was causing additional thousands of workers to be laid off as other industries felt the impact of spreading industrial paralysis.

Truman stood by his fact-finding program. In spite of popular demands for more direct action, he waited while investigations in the various industries concerned led to the gradual development of a pattern for possible strike settlements which would at once meet the legitimate demands of the workers and serve to hold the price line. As eventually worked out, the new policy was to permit wage increases that matched the thirty-three per cent rise in living costs that was estimated to have taken place since 1941, and allow price relief for any company granting such increases if its earnings fell below pre-war averages. Application of this program meant that over and above the wage increases already granted under the Little Steel formula, further advances were to be authorized ranging from 17½ to 20 per cent in various industries as compared with the 30 per cent generally demanded by the unions. This new formula provided in practice for an average 18½ cents per hour increase, and made possible a reasonable adjustment of straight-line rates to higher living costs even though weekly take-home pay, because of the loss of overtime, would still remain materially below wartime levels.

The new wage-price policy was formally announced on February 14, and even before this date settlements along such general lines had been worked out in the oil refinery and meat packing disputes. Its application to steel, however, was to prove even more decisive in breaking the industrial impasse. In this dispute the differences between the United Steelworkers and their employers, for whom President Fairless of the United States Steel Corporation acted as spokesman, had already been gradually narrowed down and President Truman directly proposed the 18½-cent-an-hour compromise. But while the union was at once willing to accept this figure, the industry refused until given more definite assurance of price relief. When the new wage-price policy was put into effect, with specific provision in the case of the steel industry for an advance of $5 a ton on steel prices, the last obstacle to agreement was removed. After a three weeks' strike that had forced the banking of furnaces throughout the country and cut production to six per cent of capacity, union and management came to terms on the basis of the President's formula.

The General Motors strike still remained to be settled and altogether it dragged on four months, costing the workers an estimated $130,000,000 and the company $600,000,000, before a new contract was finally signed with an 18½-cent-per-hour increase. The electrical workers were also long in coming to terms with their employers, but here too an eventual solution was reached at the now accepted basis for general wage adjustments. By mid-March the number of strikers throughout the country had fallen to less than 200,000 and the crisis facing the nation at the opening of the year had been resolved. The reconversion program had been seriously set back, but the resiliency of the national economy rapidly asserted itself.

The question remained, however, whether too heavy a price had been paid for industrial peace. Workers in other industries than those involved in the strike wave naturally demanded increases to bring their wages up to the level recommended by the fact-finding boards and their employers had little alternative under the circumstances to granting them. The National Wage Stabilization Board had some 4,000 such voluntary agreements submitted for its approval during April and the average

increase for industrial wage earners as a whole in this period was estimated at about eleven per cent.

Could efforts to maintain an effective price control program stand the
inflationary pressure of even these relatively limited wage advances?
There were evident danger signals. President Truman nevertheless remained confident. "A bulge in the line," he admitted in characterizing his
new wage-price policy, "but if you all cooperate with me, there will
be no break-through."

The end was not yet, however. Hardly had these first strikes ended
with such pronounced gains for labor than the inevitable breakdown
took place in negotiations for a new contract for the coal miners. Lewis
could hardly be expected to stand aside, and with his usual shrewd sense
of timing, he was now prepared to go the C.I.O. one better in his demands. Wage increases were as always the real crux of the matter, but
when the operators agreed to accept the new Presidential formula, he
insisted on additional safeguards for working conditions and royalty
contributions of seven cents a ton on all coal that was dug, to be paid
into a general miners' welfare fund. When management balked, declaring that the royalties would cost $60,000,000 annually, Lewis abruptly
walked out of the conference. "Good day, gentlemen," he was reported
as saying. "We trust that time, as it shrinks your purse, may modify
your niggardly and anti-social purposes." On April 1, some 400,000
miners in the drab little towns of western Pennsylvania and West Virginia, Alabama and Kentucky, Illinois and Iowa were once again on
vacation from shaft, tipple and breaker house.

The pattern of earlier coal strikes was closely repeated. Offers and
counter-offers got nowhere, attempted mediation wholly failed, a temporary truce soon broke down, and the square-jawed, obstinate miners'
chieftain, who had succeeded through his tactics in raising pay in the
coal fields from $15 to $63 a week in the past thirteen years, grimly stuck
to his demands in customary defiance of operators, government and
public opinion. With coal above ground dwindling to three weeks'
supply, the steel industry was able to operate at little more than half
normal capacity. A nationwide embargo was declared on freight trans-

portation, and cities from coast to coast were compelled to decree brown-outs to conserve fuel for public utilities.

When negotiations that had been renewed during a twelve-day truce in May again collapsed, the growing emergency forced the government to intervene and the mines were seized under authority of what Lewis denounced as "the infamous Smith-Connally statute." Further efforts to reach a settlement were then shifted, as during war days, to the office of the Secretary of the Interior and an agreement between the government and the union was finally concluded. The miners were awarded an 18½-cents-per-hour increase in wages, federal safety regulations were to be enforced throughout the mine fields, and a five-cent-a-ton royalty was to be paid into a welfare fund jointly administered by the operators and the union. Lewis had made some concessions in respect to the welfare fund, but in general he had achieved another startling triumph. The union proudly announced "the greatest economic and social gains registered by the U.M.W. in a single wage agreement since the birth of the union in 1890."

This settlement had been reached against the background of still another strike which in its dramatic implications overshadowed all others in this turbulent year. Wage negotiations had broken down between the railway workers and the carriers. The elaborate machinery of the Railway Labor Act had once again failed to avert a crisis that even more than the work-stoppages in steel and coal threatened the health, welfare and safety of the people. A railway strike in our closely knit economy could not fail to have almost disastrous effects, and yet it appeared to be imminent unless government found in time some means to prevent it. An emergency board finally succeeded in working out terms acceptable to the non-operating unions and two of the railway brotherhoods, which agreed to arbitration of the wage issue and deferment of their demands for rules changes, but this time the Railroad Trainmen and Locomotive Engineers—nearly 300,000 strong—refused to go along with them. Strike orders were issued to take effect on May 18.

Truman at once gave orders for seizure of the railroads as had Roosevelt in 1943. They were taken over the day before the strike was scheduled and the President succeeded in winning a five-day postponement of any stoppage. But while all the other unions agreed in this interval to accept the board's award of immediate wage increases, the trainmen and engineers would not budge from their position on the immediate need for rules changes in addition to wage adjustments. On May 23 the strike went into effect. All railroad transportation came to a halt as the engineers completed their runs and refused to take out any more trains.

The next day the President went on the air in a nationwide broadcast appealing to the trainmen and engineers to disregard the orders of their union leaders and go back to work. "The strike," he declared, "is a strike against your government. . . . It must meet the challenge or confess its impotence." The men were then presented with an ultimatum. They were offered the same terms as had been accepted by the other unions, but if they had not returned to work by four the next afternoon, the government would undertake to operate the railroads and provide the protection of the armed forces "to every man who heeds the call of his country in this hour of need."

Still the recalcitrant union leaders, Alvanley Johnston of the Locomotive Engineers and A. F. Whitney of the Railroad Trainmen, made no move to call their men back to work. Measures were promptly prepared for enforcing the most drastic strike action that had been contemplated since the injunction proceedings a quarter of a century earlier, and the entire country waited excitedly as the ultimatum deadline approached and the President went before Congress to ask specific authority for his policy. It was a special joint session—tense and expectant.

Truman began by denouncing the strike leaders for their lack of patriotism. The breakdown in negotiations, he declared, was wholly due to the "obstinate arrogance of two men." He asked for temporary power to apply for an injunction against strike leaders in any emergency threatening the public welfare, with authority to deprive the strikers themselves of their seniority rights and to draft them into the armed forces should they strike against the government. At this point in his speech he was suddenly interrupted. A clerk handed him a hastily written note and amid hushed silence he quietly announced: "Word had just been received that the rail strike has been settled on terms proposed by the President." But when the almost hysterical cheers that greeted this announcement died down, Truman continued calmly with his prepared statement. In no way modifying his stand, he told Congress that while the measures he proposed might appear drastic, the situation demanded such steps to meet an immediate crisis.

Had the President known that the strike was called off before he appeared before Congress? His action was to arouse intense controversy, with Senator Morse charging that White House advisers had known before noon that the two brotherhoods had decided to capitulate and that the President had withheld vital facts so as to contribute to the anti-labor hysteria upon which he was counting for passage of his bill. "One of the cheapest exhibitions of ham acting I have ever seen," was the senator's blunt characterization of the interrupted speech. The timing of events, however, was so close as to defy accurate analysis. The actual agreement between the unions and the carriers was signed at 3:55 P. M., the strike officially called off at 3:57 and Truman's announcement made at 4:10.

The House at once responded to the President's appeal and hastily passed a bill embodying his proposals by the overwhelming majority of 306 to 13. But with the railway strike itself now settled, strong opposition developed in the Senate. In an ironical shift of usual alignments, conservative Republicans, and notably Senator Taft, took the lead in denouncing the administration labor measure as unfair to the workers and a violation of their civil liberties. At their instigation, the House bill was first basically amended, and then as opposition still persisted, allowed to die in committee.

Attacks on the Truman program were vehement in liberal and labor circles. The President was accused of turning completely against the unions. He was bitterly assailed at the C.I.O. convention as "the Number 1 strikebreaker of the American bankers and railroads," while the infuriated leader of the Railroad Trainmen, A. F. Whitney, acidly called him "a political accident." The full use of the $47,000,000 in the union's treasury was pledged for Truman's defeat should he seek re-election.

There were a few other actual or threatened strikes during the summer of 1946. Highly involved maritime disputes, in which seamen and longshoremen belonging to both A.F. of L. and C.I.O. unions on the Atlantic and Pacific coasts participated, were for a time especially disturbing. But a complete tie-up of all shipping was averted at almost the last moment. Other controversies ranged from a demand on the part of unionized T.W.A. airplane pilots for a salary level of $20,000, to a Holly-wood jurisdictional quarrel that found the Make-up Artists and Hair Stylists lined up against the Motion Picture Costumers. The strikes in major industries had died down, however, and the country was able to breathe more easily.

The record of the twelve month period since V-J Day had been a shattering one. No less than 4,630 work stoppages had been reported and the total number of workers who had been on strike exceeded five million, with 120,000,000 days of idleness. Yet for all the interruptions these strikes imposed on the reconversion program, both production and employment were actually to achieve new peacetime levels. Instead of millions of workers seeking non-existent jobs, as had been so generally predicted would be the case, the demobilized members of the armed forces were largely absorbed by industry. The employed civilian labor force had risen by the end of 1946 to the all-time record of 55,000,000.

The success that attended industrial reconversion was not to be matched in the program to hold the line against inflation. Having won wage increases, labor was prepared to support enthusiastically continued price controls. Industry, on the other hand, strongly favored their abandonment, arguing that production was being held back and that equilibrium could best be established in the national economy by allow-ing free rein to natural competitive forces. But would prices remain stable during the period that production would need to catch up with consumer demand for goods that had been unavailable during the war? Labor declared that if the cost of living rose further, new wage in-creases would be necessary. The settlements in early 1946, President Murray of the C.I.O. expressly warned, had been accepted "only under the pledge and assurance of the present Administration that the price line would be held."

The stabilization program still seemed to be working in midsummer despite the admitted bulge in the line. The consumer price index was ten points higher than it had been when President Roosevelt announced his hold-the-line order in April, 1943, but the rise since final victory over Japan had been only four points in spite of such concessions as had been made to support wage increases. This relative stability in price-wage relationships, however, was to be short-lived as the opponents of existing regulation hammered away at the government's policy.

The political duel between the administration and its political foes led to heated charges and counter-charges over responsibility for what was happening as the O.P.A. controls were first suspended, then partially re-established and finally allowed to lapse. By October, 1946, in any event, the whole stabilization program was history and living costs were rising spectacularly. The consumer price index had already jumped seven points in July and four more in September. At the close of the year it was twenty points over mid-summer levels. Standing at 153, the rise in six months had been greater than in the entire three-year period in which O.P.A. controls had been in effect.

Industry attributed a large share of responsibility to labor because of wage increases; labor maintained that industry was to blame because of its greed for profits. In mounting antagonism, both groups tended to forget that a thirty-four per cent increase in food prices was by far the largest contributing factor in mounting living costs. The debate was embittered and wholly inconclusive. The only fact emerging from the fog of controversy was the indubitable one of soaring inflation.

In spite of repeated warnings that under these circumstances further wage increases would be an open invitation to additional price rises, labor grew increasingly restless. Union after union began to prepare the ground for new demands as the only means of keeping up with advancing living costs. With both automobile workers and steel workers asking for reconsideration of existing contracts, the stage was set by the autumn of 1946 for another challenge to industry. The dubious honor of initiating this second round of wage demands was not, however, to fall to the C.I.O. unions. Lewis suddenly took the ball. In November the nation found itself again confronted—and for the eighth time in five years—with a crisis in coal.

Every effort to negotiate a contract between the miners and operators to replace the one concluded with the government earlier in the year had broken down. "We do not propose," Lewis had stated in rejecting the operators' offers, "to be driven like dumb beasts to the slaughter house of slow strangulation by your proposal." The United Mine Workers took the position that changes in the price-wage relationship now forced a revision of the government contract, and put forward new demands for both wage increases and reduction in the working day. Secretary of the Interior Krug refused to consider reopening the contract. He insisted that it was valid for the full period of government operation of the mines and denied that the miners had any legal right to go out on strike. When Lewis persisted in his stand and the miners began to quit their jobs with the familiar slogan of "no contract, no work," Krug applied to Judge T. Alan Goldsborough, of the federal district court in Washington, for an injunction to restrain all strike activity.

The issue presented was critical. Determined this time not to give way before Lewis, the government contended that the miners' action in staying away from the pits was a strike seriously endangering the public welfare and properly subject to injunction proceedings. The union protested vigorously that any such move was wholly contrary to the provisions of the Norris–La Guardia Act, which prohibited the use of injunctions in labor disputes, and that its strike was not against the government because the Department of Interior's control over the mines was nominal. As the work stoppage continued in the face of a temporary restraining order, settlement of the basic question shifted to the courts. The entire country waited anxiously for the outcome of the most clearcut struggle yet to develop between the President of the United States and the president of the United Mine Workers.

The legal proceedings were complicated but the final result was that Judge Goldsborough ruled that the Norris–La Guardia Act did not apply to a case in which the government was party to the dispute, and that in the exercise of its sovereign power the government could enjoin the union to save society from "a public calamity." When Lewis still refused to obey court orders, he was cited for contempt and after formal trial on December 4, found guilty. The United Mine Workers was fined $3,500,000 and Lewis himself $10,000.

In the intensely emotional atmosphere created by these developments, the debate over the use of the injunction was even fiercer than earlier controversies over the attitude of the miners. Lewis declared in court that he could not acquiesce "in what must be described as the ugly recrudescence of 'government by injunction,'" and labor generally upheld his stand for all his personal unpopularity in both the A.F. of L. and the C.I.O. On the other hand, Judge Goldsborough's characterization of the strike as "an evil, demoniac, monstrous thing . . . a threat to democratic government itself" won a wide popular response. For a time the miners still stayed away from the pits, but three days after his citation for contempt, Lewis ordered them back to work in another of his temporary truces. Arrangements were being made for the prompt appeal of the case to the Supreme Court, and he stated that he wished it to be free in its deliberations "from public pressure superinduced by the hysteria and frenzy of an economic crisis."

The Supreme Court ultimately upheld Judge Goldsborough both in issuing the injunction and in finding Lewis and the United Mine Workers in contempt for disobeying it. The principle was clearly affirmed, although by a five to four decision, that the Norris–La Guardia Act could not bar the government from seeking an injunction where a strike threatened the national welfare and security. The fine imposed upon the United Mine Workers was, however, reduced to $700,000 on condition that the strike was permanently called off, and on March 19 Lewis finally gave such orders.

He had been compelled to back down temporarily but his bargaining power with the coal operators was not substantially impaired. When the expiration of the Smith-Connally Act forced return of the mines to private control on June 30, 1947, he succeeded in winning a new contract raising wages, reducing work hours and increasing the royalty contribution to the miners' welfare fund.

Before final settlement of the coal controversy, the second round of wage demands had been taken up by other unions under circumstances somewhat parelleling the situation a year earlier. The cost of living had risen an additional eighteen per cent since early 1946, and with the inflationary trend still continuing, the workers again felt that their interests were being ignored while business profits mounted. The demand now generally put forward was for a further advance of about twenty-three per cent, and labor again insisted—with such economic analyses as the famous report by Robert R. Nathan seeking to demonstrate that business profits had actually risen fifty per cent—upon the ability of industry to grant such concessions without raising prices. Management simply reiterated its view that additional wage increases inevitably meant higher prices. The country appeared to be caught in a vicious inflationary cycle. Whether industry made greater profits or labor secured higher wages, the consuming public found itself paying ever mounting prices. There seemed to be little question that the workers themselves were suffering more as consumers than they were gaining as highly paid workers, but the immediate pressure of the cost of living drove them remorselessly to make new demands.

Nevertheless both labor and management were in a more conciliatory mood in 1947 than in 1946. The issue of union security, which had been as much at stake in the earlier year as wages, was no longer so vital. Labor had demonstrated its power. And neither party to the perennial wage dispute wished to see another outbreak of strikes that was so harmful to all concerned. As a consequence, collective bargaining succeeded in bringing about acceptable compromises in the major industries with settlements representing an average 15-cent-per-hour increase.

While this was a substantial advance, it still did not mean that labor had recovered its wartime status. Continuing inflation partially nullified its gains. The Secretary of Labor was to state in his annual report that while average weekly pay in manufacturing rose between June, 1946, and June, 1947, from $43.31 to $49.53, it actually declined five per cent in purchasing power. "The increase in living costs," he declared, "erased all the gains of the 1946–47 wage increases and a great part of the wage earners' gains since Pearl Harbor." Over against average annual earnings of approximately $2,000, moreover, the Bureau of Labor Statistics reported that in June, 1947, the average budget for a family of four, sufficient to provide for health and reasonable comfort, ranged in cities throughout the country from $3,004 to $3,458.

Following these wage settlements, there were disputes leading to strikes among seamen and longshoremen, and also shipyard workers, that again became inextricably involved in inter-union controversies. A strike of telephone workers for a time tied up communications when an unsuccessful demand was made for nation-wide agreements. But the general picture during 1947 was one of relative industrial peace. In the first six months, the time lost through work stoppages amounted to only 0.5 per cent of total working time, in comparison with 2.4 per cent in the comparable period of 1946. Succeeding months witnessed no national or industrywide strikes whatsoever.

For all such improvement in the general situation, a public that had watched organized labor bring the reconversion program almost to a halt was not content to let things stand as they were. The anti-union sentiment that had been manifest during the last years of the war had been greatly intensified by the strikes that had broken out in the major industries in 1946 with such apparently complete disregard of the public interest. If this hostility toward labor was again fostered by a few reactionary elements still opposed to union organization in principle, the American people widely held the position, as repeated public opinion polls demonstrated, that labor leadership had failed to demonstrate responsibility commensurate with its power. National strikes threatening public health and safety, whether in coal, railroads, steel or other major industries, were felt to be too dangerous to be tolerated. There was a growing conviction that somehow the means had to be found to prevent any arbitrary domination over the nation's economic order by an organized minority even though it was as widely representative as labor. In the past government had been compelled to assert its authority over big business; it was now called upon to meet a comparable challenge on the part of big unions.

This popular demand for the assertion of more effective controls over labor unions was again reflected in Congress. The movement to amend the Wagner Act, which admittedly outlawed only unfair labor practices committed by employers, first came to a head during the 1946 crisis which had threatened to bog down the whole reconversion program. In February, the House hurriedly passed a rigidly restrictive bill introduced by Representative Case. With the easing of the immediate strike danger, further action on this measure was postponed. When the coal and railroad strikes again aroused public apprehension, however, the Senate took up and approved the House measure. On May 29 the Case bill was sent to the President. Among other features it set up a Federal Mediation Board, prescribed a sixty-day cooling off period before any strike could be called, decreed loss of their rights under the Wagner Act for any workers who in these circumstances left their jobs, banned both secondary boycotts and jurisdictional strikes, and authorized the use of injunctions to prevent violent or obstructional picketing.

President Truman vetoed this bill. Although it was not as stringent as his own emergency proposal for drafting strikers, he felt that as a

permanent measure it imposed unwarranted restrictions on the unions
and actually dealt with the symptoms of labor disputes rather than their
causes. Any long-range program for assuring industrial peace, the President told Congress, should continue to safeguard the basic principle of
union security. This he did not feel was accomplished by the proposed
legislation, and he urged further consideration of the whole program.

Congress did not pass the Case bill over his veto but it still had no
intention of letting the issue go by default. Republican victories in the
mid-term elections of 1946 strengthened the anti-labor forces, and with
the turn of the year the drive to curb the unions gathered new momentum. The election, indeed, was interpreted in some quarters as a direct
popular mandate to take drastic action to redress the balance that had
swung so much in labor's favor during the previous fourteen years. Not
only did Congress adopt new legislation, but restrictive laws were
also to be enacted during 1947 in some thirty states.

Labor was at once aroused to the threat to its interests and there were
repeated calls for united action to combat what was termed a "deliberate
and monstrous movement . . . to cripple, if not destroy, the labor
movement," but the legislative mill finally ground out what was to become the Taft-Hartley Act. The more rigid provisions of this measure
as first passed by the House were substantially amended in the Senate,
but even then it went far beyond anything that the friends of labor
thought justified. President Truman vetoed it. He asserted that the proposed bill was designed to weaken labor unions, would encourage rather
than discourage strikes by depriving the workers of legal protection for
their fundamental rights, and make government "an unwanted partici-
pant at every bargaining table." Its provisions, he stated, were "shocking—bad for labor, bad for management, bad for the country." But Congress was resolved this time to have its way. Amid vehement attacks on
the President's attitude and bald charges of misrepresentation, his objections were swept aside and on June 23, 1947, the bill was passed over
his veto.

The Taft-Hartley Act was a long and immensely complicated measure
among whose scores of provisions it was difficult to discern any very
definite pattern. Its declared purpose was to restore equality of bargaining power between employers and employes. To that end the basic rights
guaranteed labor in the Wagner Act were not withdrawn, but com-

pensated by guaranteeing comparable rights to employers. Or to express it in another way, whereas the earlier legislation had condemned only unfair employer practices, the new law dealt also with unfair union practices. Henceforth the unions were not to be allowed to coerce employes, to refuse to bargain collectively, to charge excessive membership fees, or to engage in either secondary boycotts or jurisdictional strikes. On the other hand, while employers were still constrained to recognize and bargain with duly certified unions, they were permitted full freedom of expression for their views in respect to union organization, short of threats of reprisal or promise of benefits, and they could also themselves call for elections for bargaining units.

The new act, however, went beyond this attempt to equalize bargaining power by imposing additional curbs importantly affecting union security. Not only were closed shops expressly banned but rigid and highly complicated restrictions were placed about union shops. Moreover unions were required to give sixty-day notice for the termination or modification of any agreement and were made suable in federal courts for breach of contract. They were prohibited from making contributions or expenditures in political campaigns, and their officers were required to file affidavits that they were not members of the Communist Party.

In Title II, an elaborate formula provided for dealing with national emergency strikes. Whenever such a strike affected an entire industry, or a substantial part of it, and was found to imperil national health and safety, the President was authorized to appoint a board of inquiry and on receiving its preliminary report, apply through the Attorney General for an injunction restraining all strike activity for sixty days. If no settlement was reached in this interval, the injunction was to be extended for twenty days, and a secret ballot held among all employes involved as to their willingness to accept the final offer made by their employers. Should these moves still fail to bring about settlement, the law provided no further action other than the submission by the President of a full report to Congress "with such recommendations as he may see fit to make for consideration and appropriate action."

Finally, certain administrative changes were made such as enlargement of the National Labor Relations Board and appointment of a general counsel to handle the prosecution of all unfair labor practices.

A new and independent Federal Mediation and Conciliation Service was also established with authority to step into any dispute threatening a substantial interruption of commerce.

Throughout the original period of congressional debate, and particularly in the interval between veto and re-passage, the issues involved in this legislation had been heatedly debated throughout the country. The full strength of employer associations, spearheaded by the National Association of Manufacturers, was thrown behind the drive for the bill's enactment. The A.F. of L. and the C.I.O. fought back uncompromisingly and refused to make any concessions in their demand for its complete defeat. Both industry and labor sent their spokesmen to congressional hearings, bought radio time to set forth their respective views to the public, and inserted full-page advertisements outlining their positions in the press.

Its proponents' contention was that the proposed measure went no further than to restore some measure of justice in labor relations. "This bill," said Senator Taft, "simply reduces special privileges granted to labor union leaders." Labor, on the other hand, interpreted it as a vindictive attack on all unionism. The A.F. of L. declared that "the forces of reaction in this country want a showdown with free American labor."

There was a basic weakness in labor's position. The campaign to win public support and build up opposition to any legislation infringing on union security had been started too late. Holding anti-union employers and the N.A.M. wholly responsible for the movement to amend the Wagner Act, neither the A.F. of L. nor the C.I.O. had taken fully into account the extent of public concern over what was considered labor irresponsibility. The almost universal feeling of frustration among the people as a whole when industrywide strikes interfered with basic public services was largely ignored. And more important, labor presented no alternative to the Taft-Hartley Act. It was unwilling or unable to adjust its strategy to the changed circumstances of the post-war era and to accept the need for any modification of the provisions of the Wagner Act. A more conciliatory policy might well have directed popular opinion in support of moderate amendments that would have protected the public interest without infringing upon union security. Public-opinion polls in September revealed that fifty-three per cent of those questioned, and who had heard of the Taft-Hartley Act, believed that it should be either revised or repealed. But labor policy failed to win or effectively hold such latent support.

The importance of the Taft-Hartley Act lay in its shift of emphasis. It did not go so far as to reverse the basic policies inaugurated by the New Deal. Far from marking a return to the laissez-faire theories of the 1920's, government intervention in industrial relations was carried even further than in the Wagner Act. But such intervention was no longer entirely in the interests of labor. The new law placed definite restraints upon its organized activities for the first time since the New Deal had come into office. In spite of a declared intent to safeguard the interests of employes, employers and the public alike, its underlying spirit reflected a desire to curb the unions.

Court interpretation, possible amendments and the way the law was administered would obviously affect the final test of its efficacy. As enacted in June, 1947, however, the Taft-Hartley Act appeared to deny much of the experience in collective bargaining of the previous decade, to substitute legal procedures for the free search for mutually acceptable agreements, and to threaten the union security for which labor had been so long struggling. It was in no sense "the slave labor bill" that it was hysterically termed by its union critics, but the whole was greater than the sum of its parts in its potentially adverse effect on the status of the nation's wage earners.

XX: MID-CENTURY

ALTHOUGH THE SHADOW of Taft-Hartley continued to hover over the organized labor movement as the years approached and passed the mid-century mark, there was no interruption in the continued improvement of the wage earners' status in American society. While the unions could not sustain the rapid pace of their growth in the late 1930's and early 1940's, membership expanded to an approximate eighteen million and the proportion of workers whose terms of employment were covered by collective bargaining agreements was steadily increasing. Against a background of unexpectedly stable economic conditions, influenced to an indeterminate extent by armament expenditures and foreign aid, union activity also succeeded in bringing about further gains in the general average of wages and in additional fringe benefits.

The power and influence of organized labor were under these circumstances acknowledged—economically if not politically—as never before. With few exceptions management regularly engaged in collective bargaining as the normal method for determining wages and working conditions. In sharp contrast with conditions prevailing in earlier periods of history, even the most conservative spokesmen of business accepted the basic role of the unions in the national economy and in the broader concerns of American society. Their growth in power and prestige, the editors of *Fortune* declared, "is itself one of the significant features of the modern free-enterprise system."

The campaign waged against the Taft-Hartley Act by both the C.I.O. and the A.F. of L. was never for a moment relaxed even though these mid-century developments showed how far it was from being the "slave labor" bill its critics maintained. All possible pressure was brought upon Congress for repeal and this issue became one of the most clear-cut points of dispute between conservative and liberal elements in existing political alignments. As the presidential election of 1948 approached, the two major parties were forced to take a stand and the basic political pattern of the 1930's was reflected in the Democrats' insistence upon Taft-Hartley's outright appeal and the Republicans' avoidance of any more direct statement than a declaration of the party's support for "continuing study to improve labor-management legislation."

The unexpected victory of President Truman at once raised labor's hopes that repeal could be effected. They proved to be illusory. Congress remained under the control of a conservative bloc made up of Republicans and Southern Democrats who had little sympathy for organized labor's demands, and Senator Taft took the lead in strongly opposing any substantial change in the existing law. One modification was made in 1951. The actual experience in holding union shop elections had so clearly demonstrated employee attitudes on this issue (some 87 per cent of the workers supporting the union in such elections as were held) that, in the interest of saving the funds expended in supervising elections, Congress amended the law to permit union shop agreements without worker polls. Otherwise Taft-Hartley remained intact in spite of everything said or done by its labor foes.

It was again an issue in the election of 1952. Once more the Democrats called for repeal and the Republicans were unwilling to go any further than to propose such amendments to the law as time and circumstances might prove to be desirable. However, labor continued to press for action in spite of the Republican victory. President Eisenhower's appointment of Martin P. Durkin, former president of the United Association of Journeymen Plumbers and Steamfitters, as his Secretary of Labor (it was said the cabinet was made up of nine millionaires and a plumber!) and his statement to Congress on February 2, 1953, that experience had shown the need for corrective measures in respect to Taft-Hartley were interpreted as keeping the door open for amendments to the law even though hope of its repeal had to be abandoned.

Yet again nothing was done. Durkin drew up nineteen amendments and, in the belief that he had the President's approval for them, published a draft message for their submission to Congress. Eisenhower denied he had promised to support them. In angry resentment of what he declared was the repudiation of an agreed-upon policy, Durkin thereupon resigned from the cabinet. Although Eisenhower tried to explain his position and reassure organized labor of his sympathy, union leaders were convinced that the conservative forces surrounding the President had forced him to go back on his promises. It was not enough for him to state, as he did at the A.F. of L. convention in September, that he had "a very great comprehension of what organized labor has done for this country." His failure to back up his own Secretary of Labor in amending Taft-Hartley affronted union forces. Leaders in both the A.F. of L. and the C.I.O. reaffirmed their resolution to exercise all possible political influence in securing more friendly legislation.

There was still no real evidence, however (except for a possibly restrictive influence on new organizing campaigns in some areas), that the Taft-Hartley Act had substantially retarded the growing strength of the labor movement. The injunction provisions of the law as applied to national emergency strikes were rarely invoked and what were often described as its "union busting" clauses did not have the consequences that labor had feared. The labor-management conflicts of these days revealed the growing strength of the major unions rather than any decline in their bargaining power.

A first major dispute in which the Taft-Hartley Act was involved occurred in the perennially restless coal industry where in spite of the settlement in 1947, strikes continued intermittently under the still aggressive leadership of John L. Lewis. A new controversy between the miners and the operators centered about the charge made by Lewis that the operators had "dishonored" their contracts in respect to the health and welfare fund. Settlement of this issue, after a month-long strike in 1948, nevertheless did not restore peace in the coal fields, and Lewis grew increasingly concerned over the generally unsettled conditions in the industry. In order to bring further pressure upon the operators for higher wages and a more favorable contract, he called the miners out in a series of so-called "memorial" work stoppages, nominally protesting against the death and injury rate in mining. Production was being constantly interrupted throughout 1949; and, while new agreements were concluded with some operators in December, unauthorized strikes nevertheless continued.

President Truman finally invoked—on February 6, 1950—the national emergency provisions of Taft-Hartley in an effort to bring the United Mine Workers into line, and a temporary injunction was issued against any further strikes. The union officials sent out orders calling the men back to work; they were largely ignored. Contempt proceedings were then instituted against the U.M.W., the government asserting that the union order calling off the strike had been given only "token compliance" by the union. A federal court refused to sustain the proceedings on the ground that lack of good faith in the issuance of the union orders had not been proved. In this impasse Truman sought authority from Congress to seize the coal mines; but, before any action was taken, new agreements were reached—in March—between the operators and the union. While something like order was restored, the experience with Taft-Hartley had proved, to say the least, very inconclusive.

In these same years—1949 and 1950—a number of other significant strikes took place, most notably in automobiles and on the railroads, but the Taft-Hartley Act was not applied. Workers in the Chrysler plants were out for one hundred days before the company and United Automobile Workers finally came to terms; railroad employees became involved in an even longer-lasting controversy that carried over into 1951. The government in the latter instance took over the railroads and in the face of continued "sick" walkouts, the Secretary of the Army threatened at one time to dismiss all workers who did not stay on the job. Government control was finally relinquished in 1952 after a settlement that among other features granted a union shop for non-operating employees.

The most lively dispute centering about Taft-Hartley was occasioned by the steel strike of 1952—the longest and costliest in the history of that industry. It developed against the tense background of war in Korea and an emergency situation that led the government to re-establish controls over both wages and prices. Popular concern recalled the situation that had existed during the war from 1941 to 1945.

Negotiations for a new contract between the industry and the United Steelworkers broke down at the close of 1951; but, with reference of the dispute to the new Wage Stabilization Board, the union agreed to hold any strike action in abeyance until the Board made its report. The award announced three months later was acceptable to the steel workers, but the industry denounced its recognition of the union shop and refused to accept the proposed wage increases without compensatory increases in the price of steel. The Economic Stabilization Director would not consent to price increases and, with the collapse of further negotiations, the United Steelworkers prepared to go on strike.

Industry at once insisted that the emergency provisions of the Taft-Hartley Act should be applied, but in view of the fact that the workers had refrained from striking for three months, President Truman refused to invoke the law. Instead he took the drastic step, on April 8, 1952, of seizing the steel plants as the only practical means of maintaining production during the emergency. "I feel sure," he stated, "that the Constitution does not require me to endanger our national safety by letting all the steel mills close down at this particular time."

His action awoke a storm of protest and controversy. The steel industry promptly took the issue to the courts and the legal battle was fought out against a background of preliminary injunctions against government operation of the plants, temporary stays of the court order, intermittent work stoppages, and further futile negotiations. Finally on June 2 the Supreme Court ruled that the seizure of the mills was an unconstitutional exercise of executive authority and the President perforce ordered their return to the owners. The steel workers—some 650,000 strong—at once resumed their strike and production was closed down throughout the industry.

It was not until July 26—after nearly two months—that the steel companies and the union finally came to terms with a settlement that largely conformed to that originally proposed by the Wage Stabilization Board. It was estimated that the strike had cost the industry some $350 million and the workers had lost $50 million in wages. The strike had not only crippled the steel industry, however. It had caused the shutdown of many steel-using plants and brought automobile assembly lines to a temporary halt. The supply of materials for the military forces in Korea was for a time seriously endangered as the political battle continued to rage over Truman's refusal to invoke Taft-Hartley and his attempt to take over the steel companies.

If the troubles in steel dominated the labor scene in 1952, the most spectacular strike of 1953 was that which broke out on New York's docks and wharves. The ramifications of this dispute could not have been more complicated. It involved directly a conflict between the International

Longshoremen's Association and the New York Shipping Association over wages and hiring practices; but, before peace was finally restored, a Senate investigating committee had described the waterfront as a "lawless frontier" plagued by corruption, communism and gangsterism; the state authorities of both New York and New Jersey had intervened; the American Federation of Labor, after expelling the I.L.A. on charges of extortion and racketeering, had chartered a new longshoremen's union, and President Eisenhower invoked the Taft-Hartley Act. None of these moves, however, ended the violence and gangsterism which appeared to bear out everything the Senate investigating committee had said of the "lawless frontier."

In these circumstances the National Labor Relations Board attempted to resolve the embittered rivalry that had developed between the old I.L.A. and the new union chartered by the A.F. of L. by holding elections to determine the proper bargaining agent on the waterfront. It was won by the old I.L.A.—reorganized and with backing from John L. Lewis—but the election results were invalidated on charges of intimidation and duress. A series of wildcat strikes provided a hectic background for these events, that had carried over into 1954; and, on condition that they would be ended, the National Labor Relations Board agreed to new elections. They were held in May and in spite of all the charges that had been made against it, and the continued opposition of the A.F. of L., the old union was again victorious. On August 27, 1954, the N.L.R.B. officially accepted it as the longshoremen's approved bargaining agent and the A.F. of L. abandoned its attempts to build up a new union. Although there were still some further work stoppages, a two-year agreement barring strikes or lockouts was finally concluded in November. Whether the pledges of good behavior on the part of the old I.L.A. and the measures adopted by the New York and New Jersey commissions to maintain order would successfully mend the situation still remained to be seen, but for the time being an uneasy calm descended upon the embattled waterfront.

The turbulent warfare among the longshoremen, as well as such strikes as those in coal, steel, automobiles, and railroading, always made good newspaper copy. The settlements reached without work stoppages naturally passed unnoticed and were, in fact, far more the rule than the exception. The statistics for the first half dozen years after the adoption of the Taft-Hartley Act, indeed, revealed a gradual decline in nationwide strike activity and a reduction in the time lost through work stoppages. The annual total of man-days idle in the years 1947–1951 averaged 40 million (in comparison with 116 million in 1946); rose to 55 million in 1952, were approximately halved the next year, and then further declined in 1954 to 22 million—which represented no more than about one-fourth of one per cent of total working time for all wage earners.

In no one of the strikes in this period did labor suffer a significant reverse. The ultimate settlement in each important instance represented further wage increases and the cession by management in many cases of additional fringe benefits. With mounting prosperity the unions were in a position to insist upon such demands and the employers could do little more than fight a limited, rear-guard action. Again and again there were incorporated into the new agreements—in addition to wage increases—provisions for better working conditions, insurance benefits, vacations with pay, and, most importantly, extended pension funds.

One of the most interesting of all collective bargaining agreements concluded during this period—and one which was to provide a precedent for many subsequent ones both within and without the industry —was that signed in May, 1950, by General Motors and the United Automobile Workers. It established a generous pension system, special insurance benefits, annual "improvement factor" increases in wages, and also cost-of-living adjustments based on price changes recorded by the Bureau of Labor Statistics. Moreover this contract was to run for five years. Perhaps no single event at mid-century so fully demonstrated the spectacular progress made in the relations between labor and management as this broad and comprehensive agreement.

In general the course of labor's gains was reflected in the basic fact that in the mid-1950's something like two-thirds of all non-agricultural workers—an approximate 30 million—were covered by collective bargaining agreements. The average weekly earnings of those in manufacturing industries had risen to some $75, which after adjustment to changes in the value of the dollar and prevailing price levels represented an increase since 1939 of something more than 50 per cent. And again to such gains must be added the manifold fringe benefits that were now the rule rather than the exception.

Although organized labor remained most concerned with economic action to uphold the interests of union members, it continued to be deeply involved in political activity. The drive spearheaded by the C.I.O.'s Policy Action Committee and the A.F. of L.'s Labor's League for Political Education to elect a Democratic administration in both the 1948 and 1952 elections was a case in point. Moreover labor campaigned aggressively for a further broadening of social security and an increase in minimum wage rates, as well as for revision of Taft-Hartley. Its successes here were significant if not dramatic. The Social Security Act was extended to cover an increasing number of workers in respect to old-age and survivors insurance benefits, and monthly payments on such accounts were substantially increased. Minimum wage levels were also advanced and in 1955 Eisenhower proposed a further increase from the prevailing 75 cents an hour to 90 cents. Labor's demand was for an hourly rate of $1.25 and a compromise between these figures appeared to be clearly in order.

Labor's concerns were not bounded, however, by bills affecting the workers' status or even by legislation dealing with other more general national issues. They extended beyond domestic horizons. Foreign policy became of ever greater importance for wage earners as well as other elements in American society as the country's great expectations for a durable peace were shattered by conflict with Communist imperialism and the harsh impact of cold war.

Both the A.F. of L. and the C.I.O. strongly supported the basic policy followed by the Truman Administration, and subsequently that of President Eisenhower. The resolutions adopted at their annual conventions, as well as at those of many international unions, endorsed the Truman Doctrine, gave emphatic support to the Marshall Plan, called for the full development of the Point Four program, and sustained American participation in the North Atlantic Treaty Organization. There was no move made in seeking to contain communism which did not receive labor's wholehearted approval, and again and again labor leaders took the initiative in calling for greater popular realization of the dangers confronting the nation.

Writing in the *American Federationist* in January, 1948, George Meany, at that time secretary-treasurer of the A.F. of L., emphasized that, in order to win the peace, the United States must seek to keep its sister democracies free. Upholding the Marshall Plan as the best means of halting the forward surge of totalitarianism in Europe, he emphasized that its annual cost would be no more than the nation willingly spent in just sixteen days of war. In a later article he upheld the North Atlantic Treaty. "In this grave hour," he stated, "the people of America can be fully assured that in American labor the cause of democracy at home and abroad has a most devoted, determined and dynamic champion."

Comparable statements were made by the leaders of the C.I.O., with Walter Reuther as well as Philip Murray consistently upholding the Truman-Acheson policy, urging further action to strengthen the United Nations, and emphasizing the importance of Point Four. Reuther called on one occasion for "a broad program of social action to back the country's defense and foreign aid programs." An article in the *C.I.O. News* stated that, with adequate support, Point Four could be developed so that it would not only help two-thirds of humanity, but also provide additional jobs in the United States.

After the outbreak of war in Korea in 1950, the A.F. of L. adopted a resolution declaring that, in the light of this conflagration, the paramount task confronting the free labor movement was to deter and if need be decisively defeat Soviet imperialism. The C.I.O. also took occasion "to reaffirm its complete support of our government and the United Nations in the struggle against Communist aggression . . ."

In its own immediate sphere of activity, American labor continued to cooperate fully with the International Labor Office; withdrew its representatives (the C.I.O. but not the A.F. of L. had originally joined) from the World Federation of Trade Unions when it appeared to be falling completely under Communist influence, and cooperated in 1949 in the formation of the new International Confederation of Free Trade Unions. At the same time, vigorous action was taken on the home front to free the labor movement of any taint of communism.

The latter issue came to a head at the C.I.O. convention in 1949 when the organization faced up squarely to the "left-right" issue and moved to eliminate all Communist leadership within union ranks. The constitution was revised to make Communists ineligible for any executive office within the C.I.O. and to provide for the expulsion by a two-thirds vote of any national union following the Communist line. Immediate action was taken in the case of the United Electrical, Radio and Machine Workers, and three committees were set up to examine the policies of ten other unions charged with being under Communist domination. With one exception, they too were expelled during the next year.

The C.I.O. organized new unions to replace those thrown out and succeeded in making up all membership losses. The officials of the Communist-controlled unions, Philip Murray declared, had been following a policy "of harassment, of opposition and of obstructionism" in adherence to the Communist program, but they constituted no more than "a small but noisy clique" within C.I.O. ranks.

The Korean crisis confronted organized labor with a number of issues comparable to those faced during the Second World War. The reinstitution of government controls over the national economy, with establishment of a Wage Stabilization Board as an arm of the Economic Stabilization Agency, introduced new factors into the whole program of collective bargaining. As in the years 1941–1945 labor was ready to cooperate fully with government. Working closely together, the A.F. of L. and the C.I.O. set up a United Labor Policy Committee to advise the administration on labor policies in an effort to provide a sound basis for industrial peace during the national emergency. Its immediate purpose was to work out agreements among the major unions in regard to manpower problems, production, wages, prices and the appointment of union officials to public offices.

Considerable friction developed in carrying through this program and for a time collaboration between organized labor and the government was severely strained. In protest against what was said to have been the slight attention paid to labor's views and the adoption of a policy forbidding any wage increases amounting to more than 10 per cent over the levels existing in January, 1950, the United Labor Policy Committee called for the withdrawal of the labor members from the Wage Stabilization Board and the resignation of other labor representatives on government agencies. The "walkout" lasted some two months, but the issues in dispute were finally settled. Labor then accepted representation on a new National Advisory Board on Mobilization Policy and also returned to a reorganized Wage Stabilization Board.

The United Labor Policy Committee, which had played the major role in all these developments and demonstrated an unusual degree of union cooperation, was suddenly broken up in August, 1951, with the withdrawal of the A.F. of L. members. By that time, however, there was considerable justification for the statement that it had "to a large extent accomplished its purpose." For in spite of all the difficulties encountered and the flare-up of controversy over representation on government agencies, organized labor had continued to support the national defense effort. Strike activity in the latter part of 1950 and in 1951 actually fell to very low levels.

Entirely apart from developments in the promotion of the workers' security, whether through peaceful collective bargaining or strike activity, and from the growing participation of labor in both domestic politics and matters of foreign policy, the month of November, 1953, was to prove an unusually notable one in the annals of American labor. On the ninth, Philip Murray, president of the C.I.O. since the resignation of John L. Lewis, died suddenly of a heart attack; on the twenty-first, William Green, president of the A.F. of L. for nearly thirty years, passed away with almost equal unexpectedness. Within a brief span of twelve days organized labor had been struck two harsh blows, and both the C.I.O. and the A.F. of L. were confronted with the difficult task of choosing new leaders.

There was a sharp struggle within the C.I.O. before the presidency was offered to Walter Reuther, the brilliant, hard-hitting, dynamic head of the United Auto Workers. His star had steadily risen in recent years. There remained something enigmatic about his own ambitions, although earlier reports that he hoped to develop a labor third party had subsided, but never any question about his complete, single-minded devotion to labor's cause. Reuther was a logical successor to the post first held by Lewis.

The A.F. of L. chose as its new head Secretary-Treasurer Meany. Relatively little known outside union ranks, George Meany had started his career as an apprentice plumber and had a long record of activity in organized labor—union business agent, secretary of the New York Building Trades Council, state president of the A.F. of L., and secretary-treasurer of the national federation since 1939. A large, heavy man, weighing some 228 pounds, he was described as "a cross between a bull-dog and a bull." He looked like an old-fashioned, conventional labor leader, generally pictured either smoking a big cigar or chewing determinedly on an unlighted one; but he hardly conformed to type in the breadth of his interests. Fond of dancing, a fair pianist, he was also very much interested in sports and the first A.F. of L. president to be a golfer.

In his contacts with other union leaders and representatives of management, Meany was blunt and outspoken, sometimes truculent. One of the few A.F. of L. officials willing and able to stand up against Lewis, he had successfully challenged the latter's stand in 1947 on the signing of non-Communist affidavits (which Lewis was unwilling to do) and carried the day so far as the A.F. of L. was concerned. He could be as tough as circumstances demanded.

Throughout his career he had always stood for progressive principles —not always wholly conforming to official A.F. of L. policy—and he was a hard fighter in behalf of every cause he took up. He was a consistent opponent of any sort of racial or religious discrimination. More political-minded than most A.F. of L. officials, Meany had long been interested in community affairs and believed union members should play a larger role in all such activities.

The new heads of both labor federations were men of vigor, determination and—as already suggested—unusually broad interests. It soon became apparent that organized labor had gained fresh strength with their advent to power. They provided a new stimulus to invigorated organizing campaigns on the part of both the A.F. of L. and the C.I.O., and in their public statements of policy continued to take a strong stand in seeking to marshal labor's strength in support of liberal policies at home and effective internationalism abroad.

Over the horizon, moreover, was a further development to which they also gave new impetus. This was the long-discussed, periodically predicted, and always postponed merger of the A.F. of L. and the C.I.O. The original issues in dispute between the two great national organizations had long since largely disappeared, and internal political differences were being gradually smoothed over. The simultaneous change in national leadership consequently seemed to provide a unique opportunity for finally bringing traditional rivalries to an end and uniting the major forces of labor in a single national federation.

The relative balance between the A.F. of L. and the C.I.O. had shifted somewhat with the passing years. Of the estimated national total of some 18 million union members, the A.F. of L. claimed 9.5 million and the C.I.O. about 6 million, with 2.5 million belonging to the Railway Brotherhoods, the United Mine Workers, and other independent unions outside the ranks of either federation. The emphasis the C.I.O. placed upon industrial unionism had continued to act as a catalyst in arousing the A.F. of L. to the need for greater organizing activity in the mass-production industries and in developing more vigorous policies all along the line. Moreover, just as the two organizations had drawn together in matters concerning economic action, so had the C.I.O.'s example inspired the A.F. of L. to play a larger role in the field of political action. Cooperation had become increasingly the rule, with the C.I.O.-P.A.C. working closely with Labor's League for Political Education.

A first significant step toward a possible merger, wherein a number of individual unions had already pointed the way, was the conclusion among the constituent unions of the A.F. of L. and the C.I.O. in June, 1954, of a two-year no-raiding agreement. The facts showed that the widely prevailing union piracy, and consequent jurisdictional strikes, were a fruitless and costly waste of time and energy from every point of view. Meany and Reuther had the vision and the authority to take the steps that could lead to a cessation of this union warfare and to friendlier relations along the entire labor front. By 1955 some eighty of the A.F. of L.'s 110 unions and all but two of the C.I.O.'s thirty-three had ratified the no-raiding agreement.

In the meantime there was also in operation a joint unity committee with Meany and Reuther again playing dominant roles. The no-raiding agreement gave very real promise that something concrete might come of its deliberations, and there were also straws in the wind in the developing moves for individual consolidation on the part of a number of rival C.I.O. and A.F. of L. international unions. Whether the merger talks were really succeeding was nevertheless not known outside of the closest labor circles. It was with dramatic suddenness that the joint committee announced on February 9, 1955, that full agreement had been reached on the part of the representatives of both the A.F. of L. and the C.I.O. for the union of the two organizations.

The proposed merger, it was stated, would preserve the integrity of each affiliated national and international union, with the no-raiding agreement continued on a voluntary basis, and also maintain the identity of the C.I.O. through the creation of a special Council of Industrial Organization analogous to the existing special departments within the A.F. of L. The new federation would thus recognize in every respect that there was a place in the ranks of organized labor for both industrial and craft unions and that the determining factor in every instance would be the most effective organizational means for safeguarding the rights of the workers involved.

Consolidation held out the promise of effective action in meeting a number of labor's major problems. It greatly strengthened the forces that were combatting Communist infiltration, racketeering and racial discrimination. The report of the unity committee specifically stated that the merged federation would make every effort to protect the American trade union movement "from any and all corrupt influence and from the undermining efforts of the Communist agencies and all others who are opposed to the basic principles of our democracy and of free and democratic trade unionism."

What had always been the most ticklish problem in a proposed merger—that of leadership in a new organization—was settled by the professed willingness of the C.I.O. to step aside in favor of the A.F. of L. Once the merger was finally ratified by the two organizations—an almost foregone conclusion in view of the support accorded the unity committee and favorable action by the executive committees of both the A.F. of L. and the C.I.O.—it was expected that George Meany would become the president of the new federation with a nationwide and industrywide membership of some 15 million organized workers.

In concluding their historic statement announcing a final agreement for the consolidation of the A.F. of L. and the C.I.O. into a united trade union movement, Meany and Reuther jointly declared:

"We feel confident that merger of the two union groups which we represent will be a boon to our nation and its people in this tense period. We are happy that, in our way, we have been able to bring about unity of the American labor movement at a time when the unity of all the American people is most urgently needed in the face of the Communist threat to world peace and civilization."

The proposed merger was hailed, and not only within the ranks of labor, as promoting the cause of free and democratic trade unionism.

Except for a statement on the part of the president of the National Association of Manufacturers that the merger "should be outlawed," and the occasional expression of conservative fears that it would mean a labor monopoly, even the organs of the business community endorsed the move and thought it would make for industrial peace. The *Wall Street Journal* denied that the merger would of itself enhance the monopoly status of labor in any way, and *Nation's Business,* while suggesting that it might mean "a political powerhouse," pointed out its potential advantage for industry in minimizing jurisdictional disputes.

Among other newspapers, the *New York Times* characterized the merger as a "feat of statesmanship," the Washington *Post and Times-Herald* referred to it as an "effective demonstration of the maturity and responsibility that labor has attained," the *Christian Science Monitor* spoke of labor's "growing maturity and a sense of responsibility," and the Washington *Star* expressed the belief, echoed in other papers, that the merger should contribute "to a long-term stability of labor-management relations." Perhaps nothing could have more clearly reflected how conservative attitudes toward labor organization had changed in the past two decades than the response that the A.F. of L.-C.I.O. merger generally elicited throughout the country.

Shortly after the merger announcement, Meany wrote a significant article in *Fortune* outlining organized labor's new goals and aspirations. He dealt generally with the existing position of unions, the continued need for further improvement in the workers' status, and the importance of both economic and political action. Because of labor's ever increasing stake in government policies, he declared, "we shall remain in politics."

What more specifically did labor want? In answer to this question Meany wrote:

"We do not seek to recast American society in any particular doctrinaire or ideological image. We seek an ever rising standard of living. Sam Gompers once put the matter succinctly. When asked what the labor movement wanted, he answered, 'More.' If by a better standard of living we mean not only more money but more leisure and richer cultural life, the answer remains, 'More.'"

At the same time, Reuther was making even clearer that he also wanted "more" for wage earners by introducing into the bargaining for new agreements between the United Automobile Workers and the major manufacturers the revolutionary conception of a guaranteed annual wage. This was his immediate aim and he expressed his full confidence that, difficult as the problems might be, they could be worked out to the mutual benefit of both the automobile industry and its employees. He did not maintain that a guaranteed annual wage—or guaranteed annual employment as it was sometimes called—could in any sense be considered a cure-all for industrial relations, but he stated his conviction that it could become "an important lever for raising the sights of business leadership so that their planning takes into account the needs of the workers in their plants and of the entire community for a steady flow of income and purchasing power."

Opposition to the guaranteed wage and doubts as to its practicality nevertheless appeared, in the spring of 1955, to be widespread throughout the business community. The *Journal of Commerce* reported on March 1 the crystallization of such feeling among top management in the nation's leading industries. It remained to be seen whether agreement could be reached on this new issue with Reuther insisting in the face of all opposition that the guaranteed annual wage was "both economically sound and morally right."

There was no question of his determination to fight the issue through. "This is a crusade," Reuther declared, "a crusade to gear economic abundance to human needs. We plan to take management up on the mountains and we would like to give them a little bit of the vision we have. We would like to show them the great new world that can be built if free labor and free management and free government and free people can cooperate together in harnessing the power of America and gearing it to the basic needs of people."

In the negotiations he conducted with the automobile industry for new contracts in the early summer, Reuther succeeded in making remarkable progress toward acceptance of this new union objective. The leading companies, indeed, agreed upon the principle of a guaranteed annual wage, and the United Automobile Workers won greater gains—without the threatened strikes—than even the most optimistic union members had anticipated. The Ford Company, promptly followed by General Motors, pioneered with contracts that provided guaranteed pay for at least half a year and at figures closely approaching normal rates.

There were problems other than that of a guaranteed annual wage that still concerned labor. The widespread existence of "right to work" laws in many states (seventeen in 1955) was believed to be a dangerous threat to union security in their discrimination against both the closed shop and the union shop. This legislation was possible under the provision in the Taft-Hartley Act which stated that if state laws were more restrictive of union security than federal legislation, the state laws prevailed. Although the new Secretary of Labor, James P. Mitchell, called upon the states to repeal these laws, organized labor felt the only practical way to combat them was to eliminate the provision in Taft-Hartley which made them possible.

Perhaps even more important to union members were the possible implications of what was being called "automation"—or the operation of machines by machines—in creating further technological unemployment. Labor did not oppose automation as such but felt it essential that provision be made to cushion the shock of a too rapid displacement of factory workers either through a guaranteed annual wage or some other protective measure. This was an issue in which labor felt itself entitled to have a voice not only from the point of view of job security but because of the need for the full employment essential for increasing mass purchasing power.

It was clear that on these problems, as well as in respect to amendment of the Taft-Hartley Act, organized labor was determined to exercise all its economic and political strength—reinforced by the merger of the A.F. of L. and the C.I.O.—in doing everything possible to defend and advance the interests of all wage earners. The future goal of "more" was to be kept steadily in mind.

In concluding his article for *Fortune*, Meany was nevertheless able to look back upon the past with a sense of great achievement. The standard of living for American wage earners, he wrote, had doubled since 1900 and their working time had been reduced by one-third. He looked forward confidently to further progress along these lines within the framework of that system of free enterprise which had made possible labor's favorable status in American society.

XX

XXI: POSTSCRIPT

XXXXXXXXXXXXXXXXXXXXXXXXXXXXXXXXXXXXXXXXXXXX

THROUGHOUT AMERICAN HISTORY certain basic factors have deeply affected the organized labor movement. The freedom and opportunity
of life in the United States have prevented the development of any real
class consciousness. A general surplus of workers resulting from the
continual flow of immigrants has until recent years tended to make
effective labor organization unusually difficult, with differences in race,
language and religion proving for a time almost insuperable barriers
to cooperation in the mass production industries. And management was
for long strongly opposed to labor unions not only on grounds of economic advantage but because of a pervasive laissez-faire philosophy
that, despite monopolistic practices in industry, denied the right of workers to combine for concerted action.

The American labor movement, again owing to the circumstances
of life in the United States, has never had a consistent philosophy conforming in any way to the patterns discernible in European countries.
In the first stages of the industrial revolution, American labor leaders
thought in vague terms of the creation of a cooperative commonwealth
in which the workers themselves would ultimately own the means of
production. These utopian programs appeared to seek escape from the
implications of industrialism rather than an adjustment to its harsh
realities and the workers rarely gave them wholehearted support. Believing in the opportunities of American life both for themselves and
even more for their children, they had a basic faith in democratic capitalism. They were concerned almost exclusively with improving their
economic position and social status within the existing structure of
society.

At no time has American labor been seriously affected by the tenets
of Marxian socialism or importantly diverted from its fundamentally
conservative attitude on political and economic issues. The occasional

instances of radical activity, whether violence on the part of the I.W.W. or propaganda and intrigue by Communists, have served only to underscore the moderation which has marked the views held by an overwhelming majority of American workers. Nor has the impact of present-day economic developments served in any way to dim the confidence with which labor looks to the future under a system of free enterprise. Recent polls among wage earners reveal that they not only still believe in the possibilities of both individual and group advancement in the United States, but that a majority are convinced that their children will have a more abundant life than they have had themselves.

For these reasons, every attempt to form a labor party has proved unsuccessful. Without any definite goal such as socialism to unite them, wage earners have historically been as diversified in their political allegiance as the members of any other group in American society. So far as any generalization is possible, however, it may be said that their influence has been thrown on the side of social reform and progressive advance. The basic aims of labor have proved to be broader than the immediate interests of wage earners as a class. There has been opportunism, narrow selfishness, irresponsibility in the American labor movement, as in every economic or political movement, but strong democratic convictions are implicit in the thinking of almost all trade unionists. They have looked toward the gradual evolution of a society in which the opportunities and rewards of American life will be available for the people as a whole on a basis of increasing equality.

The failure of both the National Labor Union and of the Knights of Labor to establish a strongly unified labor movement led to new departures at the close of the nineteenth century. Emphasis was placed on practical business unionism. The A.F. of L. resolutely put aside objectives either more comprehensive or more distant than the immediate improvement of working conditions for its own trade union membership. This program was well adapted to the circumstances of that day and the A.F. of L. succeeded for the first time in building an enduring national federation among American wage earners. But the opportunities opened up by the New Deal made possible another shift in organizational approach and also led to a revived interest both in politics and in reforms that can be effected only by political action. While the C.I.O., established as a rival organization to press the claims of industrial as opposed to craft unionism, took the lead along such lines, the A.F. of L. also broadened its outlook and changed its policies. The philosophy of many present-day labor leaders is closer to that of William Sylvis and Terence Powderly than to that of Samuel Gompers. In spite of natural differences within labor ranks, there is a large measure of agreement on common aims that reach beyond the issues presented either by union security or by wage-hour agreements. And while labor still opposes a third party, it is far more politically active than ever before, and successfully so.

Indeed, labor has become so strong in recent years, again both economically and politically, that the way in which it uses its power has become of paramount importance. There are tremendous potentialities for both good and harm in union activity, and the future of free enterprise depends quite as much on responsible labor leadership as on responsible leadership in industry.

Continued improvement in the status of wage earners should materially help to safeguard our economic and social institutions. Only through enhanced purchasing power resulting from higher wages, and broader participation in social activities as a consequence of shorter hours, can labor as a whole play its part in maintaining the stability of the American way of life. It may be truthfully said that labor's gains are in the long run gains for the nation as a whole. Yet the great unions of today, if for no other reason than their size, can also constitute a threat to democratic society through the arbitrary exercise of their economic power. Labor monopoly can no more be condoned than industrial monopoly. Policies that ignore the public interest are as dangerous when they are the policies of organized workers as when they are those of organized businessmen. Democracy cannot allow any single group, however broadly based, to attain uncontrolled dominance in the economic or political sphere.

The postwar period has been an unusual one in many ways. Its outstanding characteristic—the continued dominance of foreign affairs as a result of the rising threat of Communist imperialism—has directly affected industrial relations quite as much as other phases of domestic life. The mounting production that owes so much to the needs of national defense and foreign aid, and the consequent inflationary pressures that have so deeply influenced the national economy, have had an immensely important part in strengthening the position of labor. For prosperity has to a very considerable degree limited the issues immediately in dispute between management and employees to a division of industrial earnings that have been large enough to provide at one and the same time substantial—and sometimes record—corporation profits and also steadily rising wages. In these fortunate circumstances a reasonably balanced economy has been maintained by the countervailing forces of big industry and big labor—together with big retailing enterprise and big agriculture. And there has been the further pervasive and sometimes more problematic influence of big government in promoting social security.

How the existing balance of these countervailing forces might be affected by economic decline and possible depression is another matter altogether, and further uncertainties are found in the future role of big government. In the mid-1950's, however, organized labor seemed ready to rely largely—if not altogether—on its own economic power to protect the interests of union members. While it fully realized the importance of friendly legislation, as the continuing campaign against the Taft-Hartley Act and state "right to work" laws suggested, the new approach was to seek federal legislation along more general lines that would maintain the basic principles first established by the Wagner Act rather than spell out more specific government safeguards.

The disputes that have arisen between management and labor in recent years have at times caused serious interruptions in the nation's economic life. They have led on occasion to government intervention. It has had to be recognized that where the failure of employers and employees to resolve their differences have endangered the public welfare, the state has a responsibility or obligation to use its power to protect the interests of the people as a whole. The laissez-faire concepts of an earlier age have been completely discarded. Yet the attention attracted by the few strikes that have assumed really dangerous proportions or called for government intervention, it may be repeated, tends to obscure the overwhelming number of cases in which collective bargaining has worked successfully, and in which agreements have been reached between management and labor without resort to strikes or work stoppages.

The steadily expanding scope of such collective bargaining, the increasing acceptance of arbitration or mediation when negotiations temporarily collapse, the general observance of union contracts, and the diminishing violence when strikes do break out attest to a growing sense of responsibility on the part of both management and labor. Industrial relations remain one of the most acute issues in modern society. Nevertheless the growing maturity of unions—especially in the case of the new industrial unions—continues to hold out the highest promise that the long campaign of American labor for recognition of its rights is working to the advantage not only of the nation's wage earners but to that of the people as a whole.

One thing further appeared clear in the mid-1950's. The existence of free, democratic unions was a powerful bulwark in the defense of a free society. In the face of the totalitarian threat represented by communism, there was no stronger influence working to uphold the fundamental principles of American democracy than the organized labor movement. It had unmistakably aligned itself, as demonstrated by the support it accorded liberal policies both at home and abroad, with those forces whose persistent goal was the creation of a free and secure America in a free and secure world.

XXX

BIBLIOGRAPHICAL NOTES

XXXXXXXXXXXXXXXXXXXXXXXXXXXXXXXXXXXXXXXXXXX

The literature of the labor movement is immense and the following bibliographical notes attempt no more than a limited review of those sources—both primary and secondary—that seem significant to the present author and have proved most helpful in writing this history.

A basic work for any study of American labor has long been John R. Commons and associates, *A Documentary History of American Industrial Society,* 10 vols., Cleveland, 1910. This is supplemented by the same author's *History of Labour in the United States,* 2 vols., New York, 1926, to which were later added two more volumes: Don D. Lescohier and Elizabeth Brandeis, *History of Labor in the United States, 1896-1933, Working Conditions,* New York, 1935, and Selig Perlman and Philip Taft, *History of Labor in the United States, 1896-1932, Labor Movements,* New York, 1935.

A number of other general histories, largely derived from these pioneer studies, include Mary Beard, *A Short History of the American Labor Movement,* New York, 1920; Marjorie R. Clark and A. F. Simon, *The Labor Movement in America,* New York, 1938; Selig Perlman, *A History of Trade Unionism in the United States,* New York, 1922; Samuel P. Orth, *The Armies of Labor,* New Haven, 1921; and Anthony Bimba, *The History of the American Working Class,* New York, 1927. No one of these books brings the story down to date or is really very satisfactory.

Other studies that include interesting material on historical backgrounds, although that is not their major objective, are H. A. Millis and R. E. Montgomery, *Organized Labor,* New York, 1945; Norman J. Ware, *Labor in Modern Industrial Society,* Boston, 1935; Frank Tracy Carleton, *Organized Labor in American History,* New York, 1920; and David J. Saposs, *Readings in Trade Unionism,* New York, 1926.

A later and very readable history, although largely concentrating on a few of the more important unions, is Herbert Harris, *American Labor,* New Haven, 1938; and even more recent is Philip S. Foner, *History of the Labor Movement in the United States,* New York, 1947. The latter book carries the record only to 1881 and is Marxist in its approach, but it is an interesting attempt to break away from Commons' interpretation and highly valuable for its wealth of quotations from contemporary labor sources. Although written twenty years ago, Selig Perlman, *A Theory of the Labor Movement,* New York,

1928, is still very valuable. The basic statistical data on unions are to be found in Leo Wolman, *The Growth of American Trade Unions*, Washington, 1924, and *Ebb and Flow in Trade Unionism*, Washington, 1936.

The proceedings of the various labor associations, labor journals, the autobiographical writings of labor leaders, contemporary and other special articles and individual union histories, some of which will be cited under their appropriate topical headings, of course supplement this more organized and easily available material. Government reports are often very important, particularly the *Monthly Labor Review* and other publications of the Bureau of Labor Statistics. For a comprehensive bibliography, reference may be made to *A Trade Union Library*, published by the Industrial Relations Section, Princeton University, Princeton, New Jersey.

The Colonial Period

Chapter I

There is far more material available on slavery and indentured servants in colonial society than on the status of free workers. There is some helpful information in Commons, *A Documentary History of American Industrial Society*, but perhaps the most useful study for this period is Richard B. Morris, *Government and Labor in Early America*, New York, 1946. Marcus W. Jernegan, *Laboring and Dependent Classes in Colonial America*, Chicago, 1931, is also very helpful. Other general sources which treat labor conditions briefly are James Truslow Adams, *Provincial Society*, New York, 1927; Carl Bridenbaugh, *Cities in the Wilderness*, New York, 1938; Curtis P. Nettels, *The Roots of American Civilization*, New York, 1939; John C. Miller, *Origins of the American Revolution*, Boston, 1943; Claude Van Tyne, *The Causes of the War for Independence*, New York, 1922; and Thomas J. Wertenbaker, *The First Americans*, New York, 1927.

Early Labor Societies and the Workingmen's Parties

Chapters II–IV

A great deal of source material is available on these topics in Commons, *Documentary History*, but the activities of the workingmen's parties are best studied through contemporary newspapers and the author has relied heavily upon the *Working Man's Advocate*, published in New York from 1829 to 1836. Morris, *Government and Labor in Early America* has valuable information on the beginnings of unionization; Commons, *History of Labour in the United States*, treats it comprehensively, and there is some supplementary material in Ware, *Labor in Modern Industrial Society.* An occasional illuminating sidelight is thrown on the story in Frank Tracy Carleton, *The History and Problems of Organized Labor,* Boston, 1920, and an unusual short study is John Bach McMaster, *The Acquisition of the Political, Social and Industrial Rights of Man in America,* Cleveland, 1903. A recent and fascinating book dealing in part with the role of the workingmen in the rise of Jacksonian democracy is Arthur M. Schlesinger, Jr., *The Age of Jackson,* Boston, 1945. A number of subsequent articles, such as William A. Sullivan, "Did Labor Support Andrew Jackson?" *Political Science Quarterly,* December, 1947, dispute his point of view.

Mid-Century and National Organization
Chapters V–VII

The continuing story of the labor movement through these years may again be traced in the general labor histories, but a more detailed account of the status of workers in this period is Norman J. Ware, *The Industrial Worker, 1840-1860,* New York, 1924. There is also some material in Louis M. Hacker, *The Triumph of American Capitalism,* New York, 1940, and Allan Nevins, *The Emergence of Modern America,* New York, 1927. Post–Civil War developments are recorded in three books centered upon the life of the president of the National Labor Union: James C. Sylvis, *The Life, Speeches, Labor and Essays of William H. Sylvis,* Philadelphia, 1872; Jonathan Grossman, *William Sylvis, Pioneer of American Labor,* New York, 1945; and Charlotte Todes, *William H. Sylvis and the National Labor Union,* New York, 1942. There is also authentic first-hand material on this period in Terence V. Powderly, *Thirty Years of Labor,* Columbus, 1890.

The story of the strikes and violence during the depression of the 1870's is most graphically portrayed in newspapers and magazines of the time, particularly *The New York Times,* the *New York Tribune* and *Harper's Weekly,* which the author has used extensively. There are also several longer contemporary accounts, notably J. A. Dacus, *Annals of the Great Strike,* Chicago, 1877. Two more recent and also important books on strike activity which begin with events in this period are Samuel Yellen's *American Labor Struggles,* New York, 1936, and the dramatic but much less objective *Dynamite,* by Louis Adamic, New York, 1931. Anthony Bimba is the author of *The Molly Maguires,* New York, 1932.

The Knights of Labor
Chapter VIII

The most complete account of the Knights of Labor is found in Norman J. Ware, *The Labor Movement in the United States*, New York, 1929, but the autobiographical writings of its Grand Master Workman, Terence V. Powderly, are also highly valuable: the previously cited *Thirty Years of Labor* and the recently published *The Path I Trod*, New York, 1940. Interesting material is also to be found in Samuel Gompers, *Seventy Years of Life and Labor*, 2 vols., New York, 1925. More general accounts of this period, such as Ida Tarbell, *The Nationalizing of Business*, New York, 1936, deal at some length with the Knights of Labor; and its history is of course recounted in Commons and the other labor histories.

The American Federation of Labor
Chapter IX

The importance of this topic leads to extended treatment in all labor histories and it is the subject of a special monograph by Lewis W. Lorwin entitled *The American Federation of Labor*, Washington, 1934. The autobiography of Samuel Gompers, previously cited, is of course basic, and is supplemented by Rowland H. Harvey, *Samuel Gompers*, Stanford University (California), 1935, and Louis B. Reed, *The Labor Philosophy of Samuel Gompers*, New York, 1930. From this point on, moreover, the annual *Proceedings* of the A.F. of L. and the *American Federationist* become important source material.

Homestead and Pullman
Chapter X

In addition to sources dealing directly with either the Knights of Labor or the A.F. of L., the turbulence of the 1890's has received extended study. The most vivid material, as in earlier periods of labor unrest, is found in newspapers and magazines (the *Chicago Tribune* gave over its whole front page to the Homestead strike), but both Yellen in *American Labor Struggles* and Adamic in *Dynamite* have exciting accounts. Two other books dealing with specific labor disturbances are Almont Lindsay, *The Pullman Strike*, Chicago, 1942, and Henry David, *History of the Haymarket Affair*, New York, 1936. The role of the Pullman strike's leader is told in McAllister Coleman, *Eugene V. Debs*, New York, 1931.

Two studies of labor's political activity during this period are Nathan Fine, *Labor and Farmer Parties in the United States*, New York, 1928, and Chester McArthur Destler, *American Radicalism, 1865-1901*, New London (Connecticut), 1947, but neither gives a very clear picture. Further references may be found in Fred A. Haynes, *Third Party Movements Since the Civil War*, Iowa City, 1916, and Morris Hilquit, *History of Socialism*, 1903.

Progressive Period

Chapter XI

The general labor story of these years is found in such books as Selig Perlman and Philip Taft, *History of Labor in the United States, 1896-1932* (the continuation of the Commons' history); Lorwin's *The American Federation of Labor;* and the studies of Samuel Gompers already cited. An interesting chapter on labor is found in Harold U. Faulkner, *The Quest for Social Justice*, New York, 1931. The coal strike is fully treated in Elsie Gluck's *John Mitchell—Miner*, New York, 1929; reference should also be made to Mitchell's own book, *Organized Labor*, Philadelphia, 1903, and there is further material on the strike in Henry F. Pringle, *Theodore Roosevelt*, New York, 1931.

Two valuable books on legal issues affecting labor during the progressive period are Edward Berman, *Labor and the Sherman Act*, New York, 1931, and Felix Frankfurter and Nathan Greene, *The Labor Injunction*, New York, 1930.

The general condition of the workers is broadly portrayed in the *Final Report and Testimony of the Commission on Industrial Relations*, 11 vols., issued as Senate Document 415, Sixty-Fourth Congress, First Session, Washington, 1916. Public opinion toward labor matters is best studied through the contemporary press and the useful compilations of editorial views in the *Literary Digest*. One among many interesting contemporary discussions is Washington Gladden, *The Labor Question*, Boston, 1911, and there is a good deal of material in the *Autobiography of Lincoln Steffens*, 2 vols., New York, 1931, and Ray Stannard Baker, *American Chronicle*, New York, 1945.

The Industrial Workers of the World

Chapter XII

The story of the rise and fall of the I.W.W. is authoritatively and objectively told in Paul F. Brissenden, *The I.W.W.*, New York, 1919, and John S. Gambs,

The Decline of the I.W.W., New York, 1932. An important contemporary source is the autobiography of William D. Haywood, *Bill Haywood's Book,* New York, 1929. The strike stories are told in both Yellen and Adamic, but again contemporary accounts, which crowded both newspapers and magazines, give the real flavor of such a sensational outbreak as the Lawrence strike. More general and important accounts of labor radicalism dealing with the I.W.W. include David J. Saposs, *Left-Wing Unionism,* New York, 1926, and Mary D. Savage, *Industrial Unionism in America,* New York, 1922.

The First World War and the 1920's

Chapters XIII–XIV

The history of labor during the First World War is most adequately presented in Gordon S. Watkins, *Labor Problems and Labor Administration in the United States During the World War,* Urbana (Illinois), 1919. Other official and non-official accounts of wartime activities on the home front, such as Preston W. Slosson, *The Great Crusade and After,* New York, 1930, and Frederick L. Paxton, *American Democracy and the World War,* 2 vols., Boston, 1939, also touch on labor relations, but the labor histories themselves naturally provide more comprehensive treatment. The dramatic events of 1919 are best followed in contemporary newspapers, the *Literary Digest* again proving highly useful in its compilations of editorial opinion. The steel strike is treated in detail not only in the report of the Senate Committee on Labor and Education, but that of the Interchurch World Movement. The story from the point of view of its leader is told in William Z. Foster, *The Great Steel Strike,* New York, 1920.

For the 1920's there is a wealth of background material on economic conditions as they affected the status of labor in government reports, notably that on *Recent Economic Changes in the United States,* issued in 1929 by the President's Conference on Unemployment. It is most usefully summarized in George Soule's excellent *Prosperity Decade,* New York, 1947. Both Perlman and Taft, *History of Labor in the United States, 1896-1932,* and Lorwin, *The American Federation of Labor,* are also useful for this period, and there are interesting sidelights on labor relations in Thomas S. Cochran and William Miller, *The Age of Enterprise,* New York, 1942. The policies of the A.F. of L. are also discussed in such books as Louis B. Reed, *The Labor Philosophy of Samuel Gompers,* previously noted; William E. Walling, *American Labor and American Democracy,* New York, 1926; and William Green, *Labor and Democracy,* Princeton, 1939.

The story of the miners is told in John L. Lewis, *The Miners' Fight for American Standards,* Indianapolis, 1925. Other special labor topics are taken up in Harold Seidman, *Labor Czars,* New York, 1938; Lewis Lorwin, *Labor and Internationalism,* Washington, 1920; R. W. Dunn, *Company Unions,* New York, 1927; G. S. Mitchell, *Textile Unionism in the South,* Chapel Hill, 1931; William Z. Foster, *Misleaders of Labor,* New York, 1927, and Savel Zimand, *The Open Shop Drive,* New York, 1928.

At this point there might also well be noted a number of special histories of individual unions although the material treated covers a much broader span than the 1920's. Among such books are Robert R. Dunn, *Labor and Automobiles,* New York, 1929; McAllister Coleman, *Men and Coal,* New York, 1943; B. R. Brazeal, *The Brotherhood of Sleeping Car Porters,* New York, 1946; Vernon H. Jensen, *Lumber and Labor,* New York, 1945; Joel Seidman, *The Needle Trades,* New York, 1942; Jacob Loft, *The Printing Trades,* New York, 1944; Benjamin Stolberg, *Tailor's Progress,* New York, 1944, and Donald B. Robinson, *Spotlight on a Union, The Story of the United Hatters,* New York, 1948.

The New Deal and the C.I.O.

Chapters XV–XVII

The advent of the New Deal, revival of unionism and development of the C.I.O. have brought out more labor studies for the 1930's than are available for any other period. The general economic background is best treated in Broadus Mitchell, *Depression Decade,* New York, 1947; and government labor policy, apart from the wealth of information in *The Public Papers and Addresses of Franklin D. Roosevelt,* is usefully summarized in Carroll R. Daugherty, *Labor Under the N.R.A.,* Boston, 1934; Lewis L. Lorwin and Arthur Wubnig, *Labor Relations Boards,* Washington, 1935; and Joseph Rosenfarb, *The National Labor Policy,* New York, 1940. The most valuable source from among the writings of members of the Roosevelt cabinet is Frances Perkins, *The Roosevelt I Knew,* New York, 1946.

The anti-union drive in the mass-production industries is graphically revealed in the report of the La Follette Civil Liberties Investigation; Senate Committee on Education and Labor, Hearings on Senate Resolution 266, Seventy-Fourth Congress, First Session, and Senate Resolution 60, Seventy-Fifth Congress, First Session. This material has been largely used in Leo Huberman, *The Labor Spy Racket,* New York, 1937, and Clinch Calkins, *Spy Overhead,* New York, 1937.

The background of industrial unionism is treated in Walter Galenson, *Rival Unionism in the United States,* New York, 1940, but the controversy of the 1930's is found first-hand in the *Proceedings* of the American Federation of Labor and such a contemporary document as the C.I.O.'s *The Case for Industrial Unionism,* Washington, 1936. Subsequent developments are traced in Herbert Harris, *Labor's Civil War,* New York, 1940; Edward Levinson,

Labor on the March, New York, 1938; Bruce Minton and John Stuart, *Men Who Lead Labor,* New York, 1937; J. R. Walsh, *C.I.O., Industrial Unionism in Action,* New York, 1937; and Benjamin Stolberg, *Story of the C.I.O.,* New York, 1938. Three books by Robert R. R. Brooks are also very valuable; *When Labor Organizes,* 1937, *Unions of Their Own Choosing,* 1939, and *As Steel Goes,* 1940, all published by the Yale University Press.

Two biographies of John L. Lewis are Cecil Carnes, *John L. Lewis, Leader of Labor,* New York, 1936, and J. A. Wechsler, *Labor Baron, A Portrait of John L. Lewis,* New York, 1944. The latter is very much the better of the two. A useful autobiography of another labor leader is William Z. Foster, *From Bryan to Stalin,* New York, 1937.

The Second World War and Its Aftermath
Chapters XVIII–XX

The sources for recent labor history are even more voluminous than those for earlier periods. The mounting importance of the trade union movement is reflected in amplified studies of every phase of labor activity, new publications dealing with contemporary developments, and an ever wider range of articles in current periodicals.

The Monthly Labor Review, published by the Bureau of Labor Statistics, is especially valuable, as are also the *Labor Information Bulletin* of the Department of Labor, and the various publications of the Bureau of National Affairs, notably its *Labor Relations Reporter.* There is helpful material in the *Yearbook of American Labor—War Labor Policies,* New York, 1945; and *Labor in Postwar America,* New York, 1949; and in two volumes published by the Department of Labor under the title *Labor Yearbook: Mobilizing Labor for Defense,* Washington, 1951; and *The Worker's Story, 1913–1953,* Washington, 1953. While they must be used with care because of a Marxist approach, some useful information may also be found in the annual *Labor Fact Book,* issued by International Publishers. Invaluable are the annual *Proceedings* of the A.F. of L. and the C.I.O., and the *American Federationist* and the *C.I.O. News.*

Accounts of government labor policies are found in Harold W. Metz, *Labor Policy of the Federal Government,* Washington, 1945; Harold Metz and Meyer Jacobstein, *A National Labor Policy,* Washington, 1947; and E. C. Brown, *National Labor Policy,* Washington, 1950. An early but very good analysis of the Taft-Hartley Act is that published by the Bureau of National Affairs, *The New Labor Law,* Washington, 1947, but a more comprehensive background study is H. A. Millis and E. C. Brown, *From the Wagner Act to Taft-Hartley,* Chicago, 1950. Three important articles should also be noted: Sumner H. Slichter, "Taft-Hartley Act," *Quarterly Economic Journal,* LXIII (February, 1949); the same author's "Revision of the Taft-Hartley Act,"

Quarterly Economic Journal, LXVII (May, 1953); and Daniel Bell, "Taft-Hartley, Five Years Old," *Fortune,* vol. 46 (July, 1952).

On labor in politics see Joseph Gaer, *The First Round,* New York, 1944; and Fay Calkins, *C.I.O. and the Democratic Party,* Chicago, 1952. The role of union leaders is discussed in Eli Ginzberg, *The Labor Leader,* New York, 1948; Charles W. Mills, *The New Men of Power: American Labor Leaders,* New York, 1948; and Charles A. Madison, *America's Labor Leaders,* New York, 1950. Noteworthy individual biographies are Mathew Josephson, *Sidney Hillman, Statesman of American Labor,* New York, 1952; and Irving Howe and B. J. Widick, *The U.A.W. and Walter Reuther,* New York, 1949.

Among many other books dealing with more general aspects of the contemporary labor movement are Florence Peterson, *American Labor Unions,* New York, 1952; Jack Barbash, *Labor Unions in Action,* New York, 1948; Charles O. Gregory, *Labor and the Law,* New York, 1946; Malcolm A. Johnson, *Crime on the Labor Front,* New York, 1950; Charles E. Lindblom, *Unions and Capitalism,* New Haven, 1949; Frank Tannenbaum, *A Philosophy of Labor,* New York, 1951; Joel I. Seidman, *American Labor from Defense to Reconversion,* Chicago, 1953.

For a new general bibliography, see Ralph E. McCoy, *History of Labor and Unionism in the United States; A Selected Bibliography,* Champaign, Illinois, 1953.

INDEX

409